P9-APA-710

American Justice

Research of the National Institute of Justice

American Justice
Research of the National Institute of Justice

Edited by
Larry J. Siegel
University of Lowell, Massachusetts

West Publishing Company

St. Paul   New York   Los Angeles   San Francisco

Composition: *Parkwood Composition Service*

Copyediting: *Laura Beaudoin*

Cover Image: *"Parade Patrol" by David R. Becker*

Library of Congress Cataloging–in–Publication Data

Siegel, Larry J.

  American Justice: Research of the National Institute of
Justice / Larry J. Siegel, editor.

    p. cm.

  ISBN 0–314–56565–5

  1. Criminal justice, Administration of —United States.

I. Siegel, Larry J.   II. National Institute of Justice (U.S.)

HV9950.A49   1990

364.973—dc20   89—33583

                                              CIP

Contents

Preface

The study of crime and criminal justice is a dynamic, everchanging field of scientific inquiry undertaken on hundreds of college campuses around the nation. Change in the field has been fueled by a steady flow of research data, some of which has challenged long-cherished beliefs about the nature and extent of crime and the processes of justice. No source of this data has been more important than efforts funded and guided by the federal government's major research arm—the National Institute of Justice (NIJ). The NIJ publishes a variety of reports, manuals, bulletins, summaries, and guides that contain the most critical and essential findings from the hundreds of research projects it sponsors. These reports represent the cutting edge of knowledge about crime and justice and are essential additions to the literature of the field. They include "Research in Brief," "Research in Action," "CrimeFile" series, "Construction Bulletins," "Issues and Practices in Criminal Justice," and "Perspectives on Policing."

This text collects some of the most important and significant of these documents published in the past few years. It is the first systematic, comprehensive, and up-to-date collection of crime-related material published by NIJ.

Focus of the Text

This text is designed for use as a supplement in either criminology or criminal justice courses. Its content reflects the broad range of topics usually covered in the basic introductory course in these topic areas.

The book is divided into two basic parts: "Crime and Criminality" and "The Criminal Justice System." The first part contains selections from NIJ research reports dealing with the causes of crime and delinquency, victims and victimization, and drugs and crime. The second part is devoted to operations of the criminal justice system: the police and law enforcement, the judicatory system, probation and alternative sanctions, and correctional institutions and practices. While the selections here are by no means exhaustive, they provide a good overview of the direction NIJ research has taken and illustrate some of the more important research efforts it has funded.

Points of view or opinions expressed in the individual articles are those of the author(s) and do not necessarily represent the official position or policies of the U.S. Department of Justice or West Publishing Company.

This text could not have been produced without the close cooperation and encouragement of Paul Cascarano and Paul Estaver of the National Institute of Justice and Leslie Moore, Kristina Rose, Janet Rosenbaum, and the reference staff of the National Criminal Justice Reference Service.

The staff at West Publishing, Mary Schiller, the executive editor of this text, and I believe strongly that this material makes an important contribution to the understanding of crime and justice. It is this goal that motivates our work; therefore, all royalties accrued on this text are being donated to the National Center for Missing and Exploited Children, Arlington, Virginia.

1

Introduction

The problems of crime and justice are significant social concerns. There is unprecedented interest in identifying the root causes of crime and devising policies to deal effectively with criminal activity. Governmental interest in the crime problem is often prompted by the public's concern about violence and drug use and fear of victimization. Consequently, criminal justice agencies are continually seeking ways to improve law enforcement operations, reshape the court system, create more efficient correctional treatment, and devise effective crime prevention strategies.

Efforts to study crime and translate findings into research and action began early in the twentieth century. In 1919 the Chicago Crime Commission, a professional association funded by private contributions, was created. This organization acted as a citizens' advocate group and kept track of the ongoing activities of local justice agencies. The commission still carries out its work today.

The pioneering work of the Chicago group was soon copied in a number of other jurisdictions. In 1922, the Cleveland Crime Commission provided a detailed analysis of local criminal justice policy and uncovered the widespread use of discretion, plea bargaining, and other practices then unknown to the public. The Cleveland survey is sometimes viewed as the first to treat criminal justice as a "people processing system," a view still widely held today. Similar projects were conducted by the Missouri Crime Survey (1926) and the Illinois Crime Survey (1929).

In 1931 then President Herbert Hoover appointed the National Commission of Law Observance and Enforcement, which is commonly known today as the Wickersham Commission. This national study group made a detailed analysis of the American justice system and helped usher in the era of treatment and rehabilitation in the United States correctional system. The Wickersham Commission is credited with identifying the complex rules and procedures that characterize the criminal justice system.

The modern era of criminal justice study began in 1967 when the President's Commission on Law Enforcement and Administration of Justice (the "Crime Commission"), which had been appointed by Lyndon Johnson, published its final report entitled "The Challenge of Crime in a Free Society." This group of practitioners, educators, and attorneys had been charged with creating a comprehensive view of the criminal justice process and providing recommendations for its reform. Concomitantly, Congress passed the Omnibus

Crime Control and Safe Streets Act of 1968, providing for the expenditure of federal funds for state and local crime control efforts. This act helped launch a massive campaign to restructure the justice system by funding the Law Enforcement Assistance Administration (LEAA), an agency that provided hundreds of millions of dollars in aid to local and state justice agencies. Federal intervention through LEAA ushered in a new era in research and development in the criminal justice system.

The Federal Mission Today

Today the federal government is still at the forefront in providing resources and support for development and implementation of criminal justice research and action programs. Federal efforts fall under the Office of Justice Programs (OJP), a branch of the Department of Justice created on 12 October 1984 when then President Ronald Reagan signed into law the Justice Assistance Act of 1984 as part of the Comprehensive Crime Control Act of 1984. This act amended the Omnibus Crime Control and Safe Streets Act, recreated criminal justice research and statistics units in the Justice Department, and ordered that financial and technical assistance be granted to local and state governments. The act established five independent yet interrelated bureaus or offices with an administrative structure headed up by an assistant attorney general:

1. The **Bureau of Justice Assistance (BJA)** administers grant programs to improve local and state criminal justice systems. For example, it provides assistance, through Subtitle K of the Anti-Drug Abuse Act of 1986, to support programs that improve the apprehension, prosecution, adjudication, detention, and rehabilitation of drug offenders.
2. The **Bureau of Justice Statistics (BJS)** collects, analyzes, publishes, and disseminates statistical information on crime, victims of crime, criminal offenders, and the operations of the criminal justice system at all levels of government.
3. The **Office of Juvenile Justice and Delinquency Prevention (OJJDP)**, established by the Juvenile Justice and Delinquency Prevention Act of 1974, helps state and local government agencies improve their juvenile justice services. Today OJJDP also provides financial assistance for research and action on the problem of missing and exploited children.
4. The **Office for Victims of Crime (OVC)**, mandated by the Victims of Crime Act of 1984, awards grants to the states from the Crime Victims Fund to compensate crime victims and create programs to provide direct service to victims. The fund is financed by fines and penalty assessments on all convicted federal defendants.
5. The **National Institute of Justice (NIJ)** conducts research to increase knowledge about criminal behavior and criminal justice. It evaluates the effectiveness of various demonstration programs in operation around the United States.

These bureaus retain independent authority to conduct and sponsor programs, yet as integral parts of a singular agency they retain the same basic goal: to improve the operations of the nation's justice system. Consequently, the actions of one office influence the operations of the others: for example, data collected by BJS prompts research by NIJ, which leads to new program initiatives by BJA and OVC.

The National Institute of Justice

The National Institute of Justice (NIJ) is the major research arm of the United States Department of Justice. Its mission is to identify the strategies most effective in the fight against crime by emphasizing problem-oriented research and experimentation programs.

The NIJ's research agenda addresses long-term problems that overlap the institutional boundaries of police, court, and correctional agencies: drugs and crime, career criminals, crime prevention, victim compensation, and violent crime. It also targets newly emerging problems such as the effect of AIDS on the criminal justice system. The NIJ stimulates innovation in research and problem solving through cooperative working arrangements with state and local practitioners in governmental, private, and academic agencies.

Currently, the NIJ is most concerned about policy-oriented research in the following target areas:

the detection and tracking of drug use by criminal suspects;

improving the capacity to make more informed judgments about whether individual defendants or offenders represent an unacceptable danger to the community;

providing policy makers with information about the most cost-effective and equitable policy options;

reducing the chances for the recurrence of violence against victims of spouse assault;

reducing the number of crime victims through new strategies for deploying police and strengthening police-community ties;

increasing the use of alternative sanctions for offenders such as fines, house arrest, and electronic monitoring;

measuring the effect of various crime control strategies and determining their "true cost benefits" to the American public;

educating criminal justice professionals about AIDS and its implications for those whose duties may put them in contact with individuals at high risk for developing the disease.

Since its inception, NIJ has continually funded research and evaluation efforts reflecting these areas of national concern. The resulting body of literature is one of the most important sources of information on the nature of crime and the operations of the criminal justice system. It includes a variety of publications, the most important of which are described as follows:

"Research in Brief"—summaries of key findings from research projects funded by the NIJ.

"Research in Action"—brief discussions of emerging topics and practices targeted to criminal justice practitioners.

"CrimeFile"—background information and discussions about issues raised in the NIJ CrimeFile videotapes. This series is designed to stimulate discussion and raise awareness about recent research findings about crime and its control.

"Construction Bulletins"—a series designed to share information on innovative approaches to buildings and financing corrections construction.

"Issues and Practices in Criminal Justice"—presents the program options and management issues in a topic area, based on a review of research evaluation findings, operational experience, and expert opinion on the subject.

"Perspectives on Policing"—reports developed during meetings of police professionals and academic experts at the Kennedy School of Government at Harvard University. They inform Americans interested in policing of the development of information and perspectives formed at the Harvard meetings.

This text was motivated by the desire to make this information as accessible as possible to students of crime and criminal justice. The efforts of the National Institute of Justice to improve the operations of the justice system should always be kept in mind while reading the research reports contained in this volume.

2

Crime and Criminality

The Causes of Crime and Delinquency

Introduction

One of the most perplexing problems facing criminal justice practitioners and scholars is identification of the root causes of crime and delinquency. Without understanding why crime occurs it is difficult to plan effective strategies to control or eliminate its incidence.

Numerous theoretical models have been formulated that seek to explain why some individuals continually violate the law. Some view criminality as a matter of individual choice and decision making; others portray it as a consequence of biological and/or psychological traits; another view of crime focuses on environmental conditions; others consider socialization and the development of character as the key factor in criminality.

In the 1960s and into the 1970s it was generally agreed that crime was a social phenomenon. Most crime experts linked criminal activity to deteriorated

neighborhoods, families in turmoil, lack of jobs and economic opportunities, and other social factors. The prevailing view held that if environment and family life could be improved most criminals would forego law violations and become productive citizens. Federal and state governments funded numerous programs to improve conditions in the inner city and provide legitimate alternatives to crime.

While these views still hold sway today, there is no question that personal traits such as personality, diet, genetic makeup, mental state, and intelligence are now considered as variables associated with criminality.

One reason for broadening the focus of crime causation is the "discovery" of the chronic, or career, criminal by Marvin Wolfgang and his colleagues in a series of cohort studies conducted in Philadelphia. This term refers to a small group of offenders who are arrested five or more times as juveniles. While most offenders "age out" of crime, chronic offenders continue their criminal careers as adults.

The existence of a career offender presents a dilemma for the social view of crime. Since most criminals live in the same environment but only a small group are responsible for almost all serious crimes, it follows that there must be some personal characteristic that sets chronic offenders apart from both noncriminals and nonchronic offenders. This conclusion has inspired a number of criminologists to suggest that while some individuals may be inspired to commit an occasional crime because of economic or social conditions, the cause of serious, persistent criminality is a function of some individual trait, physical characteristic, or mental condition. For example, research on adopted youth seems to indicate that there may be a genetic basis for criminality and other antisocial behaviors such as alcoholism. Preliminary findings from a number of research projects indicate that adopted children behave more like their biological than their adoptive parents.

How might this changing concept of criminality influence the justice system? It certainly may have an effect on the sentencing and treatment of convicted offenders. Correctional treatment philosophy that favors helping offenders alter their behaviors by providing them with marketable job skills, upgrading their educational levels, and providing counseling may not be adequate to deal effectively with chronic offenders who do not respond to such efforts.

The reports in this section focus on areas of particular concern to the study of the nature and causes of criminality. The first two reports look at individual factors associated with criminality. The first report, by Lawrence Sherman, discusses the concept of the chronic offender and how the criminal justice system has responded to the problems they present. Then biological factors linked to crime causation are overviewed by Richard Herrnstein. The next three reports were selected because they present evidence on the relationship between criminality and three critical social phenomena. The first, "Families and Crime," by Rolf Loeber, provides an overview of the role early socialization plays in the crime process and how families can be trained to help youth resist antisocial activity.

The second, by J. Ronald Milavsky, focuses on the effects of viewing violent television shows on antisocial behavior. Richard McGahey then reviews the evidence linking unemployment to the crime rate. Finally, James B. Jacobs discusses the effect of alcohol abuse on crime and Franklin E. Zimring analyzes the relationship between gun control and the violent crime rate.

National Institute of Justice / CRIME FILE

Repeat Offenders

Lawrence Sherman, University of Maryland

1986

Who Are Repeat Offenders?

Repeat offenders are defined differently for different purposes. The law in many States, for example, prescribes stiffer penalties for people who have previously been convicted several times for specific offenses, such as drunk driving or burglary. Repeat offenders are defined more generally as people who commit serious criminal offenses at a high rate and over a long period.

Active repeat offenders tend not to specialize in one kind of crime but to take advantage of whatever opportunities arise. They are quite diverse in how much criminal activity they produce, with some far more active than others.

Even though repeat offenders are a small percentage of all criminals—about 15 to 20 percent, by one estimate—they commit the majority of serious, detected crimes. If these high-rate offenders could be identified and stopped from operating, the serious crime rate could be greatly reduced (assuming that other offenders would not take their places).

It has long been known that some people become habitual offenders, yet the proportion of crime committed by these people, and the policy implications of focusing criminal justice resources on them, have only recently been understood. Marvin Wolfgang and his colleagues at the University of Pennsylvania called attention to this issue in 1972 in a study of delinquency among boys born in Philadelphia in 1945. Of the boys ever arrested, 18 percent had five or more arrests and their arrests accounted for 52 percent of the arrests recorded for all boys studied.

Recent Rand Corporation studies further highlight the differences between ordinary offenders and high-rate offenders. In a survey of prison inmates, half of those who had been active robbers reported committing fewer than 5 robberies per year, but 10 percent of them

committed over 50 per year. Similarly, half of the inmates convicted for burglary had committed fewer than 5 burglaries per year, but 10 percent of them had committed more than 150 per year, with some reporting a rate in excess of 1,000 per year.

A number of attempts have been made to identify high-rate offenders at a point in their criminal careers when they are likely to continue committing crimes, but a number of difficulties must be resolved. First, there are ethical problems associated with focusing the attention of the criminal justice system—which is supposed to punish for past crimes—on individuals for the crimes they may commit in the future. Second, if these problems are resolved satisfactorily, there remain technical problems in distinguishing high-rate offenders from other offenders.

Should the Criminal Justice System Take Account of Future Crimes?

Since repeat offenders account for a disproportionate amount of crime, their identification and incarceration should prevent substantial numbers of crimes.

Many argue, however, that the criminal justice system exists to respond to crimes that have been committed by identifying offenders and imposing deserved punishments on them. This is the "retributive" purpose of the criminal justice system. From this perspective, the criminal justice system should not attempt to anticipate the offender's future criminality but should focus on his past culpability and blameworthiness. Proponents of such a view could allow some account to be taken of an offender's prior record because it may be more blameworthy to continue offending after previous convictions and punishments. They would not agree that those with longer prior records should be penalized because they are likely to commit more crimes in the future.

Most academics and virtually all practitioners reject this position. They endorse the "utilitarian" objectives of the criminal justice system as important additions to the retributive ones. They argue that the criminal justice system may, and should, respond differently to offenders who have committed the same crime if one is believed especially likely to be a serious offender in the future. This view is reflected in "habitual offender" laws which permit "three-time losers" to be sentenced to life imprisonment or unusually long terms.

Objections to "punishment for future crimes" surely preclude punitive measures against individuals never convicted of a crime. Individuals convicted of a crime, however, are vulnerable to removal from the community. When that happens, the nature of the removal, including its duration, becomes a matter of discretion subject to other limits. Officials exercising that discretion often take into account the risk of subsequent offending.

Some predictions of future crimes inevitably will be wrong. Some will incorrectly predict that an individual will commit crimes in the future (a "false-positive" error). Some will incorrectly predict an individual will *not* commit crimes in the future (a "false-negative" error). The degree of concern to be accorded these errors depends on what actions will result from the prediction, the seriousness of the crimes sought to be prevented, and the degree of departure from "normal" sentences. From a civil liberties perspective, concerned with limiting governmental intrusions on individual liberty, false-positive errors are highly objectionable. From a crime-control perspective, concerned with preventing future crimes, false-negative errors are deplorable. Both civil liberties and crime control are important goals of government and a careful balance must be struck between them.

Even when predictions are highly accurate, their use is subject to constraints. For example, there are limits to how much sentences can be extended without becoming unjust. A first-time robbery conviction may warrant a choice between 1 and 2 years, depending on the prediction, but not between 1 and 10 years.

The use of some personal characteristics may be inappropriate. Eye color, for example, even if it were correlated with future criminality, has no theoretical link to crime and so is objectionable. Similarly, race,

even though it might be correlated with future criminality, lacks a theoretical basis and its use in deciding punishment is broadly viewed as unacceptable. Thus, even those who approve of reliance on predictions accept limits on their use.

How Can Repeat Offenders Be Identified?

There have been many attempts to distinguish serious repeat offenders from others, with only limited degrees of success.

One persistent problem is that factors that correlate with criminality in one setting may operate differently in other settings. For example, involvement in crime is greatest in the late teenage years. Yet while older persons are much less likely to be involved in crime than teenagers, older persons who *are* actively involved in crime are likely to continue criminal activity, and so the age variable—being older—that ordinarily distinguishes nonoffenders from offenders operates differently in distinguishing among persistent offenders.

The longest tradition of use of predictions to distinguish between higher and lower rate offenders has been in parole. The U.S. Parole Commission, for example, uses a "Salient Factor Score" to assess prisoners' future likelihood of offending. The score is based on factors such as the number of prior convictions and prison commitments, the recency of criminal justice involvement, the prisoner's age, and the history of drug use. This score, along with information on the seriousness of the prisoner's offense, is used in deciding when a prisoner will be released.

There is much less experience with systematic police use of prediction devices as the basis for allocating police resources.

Police use a variety of methods to single out repeat offenders for special attention. Some methods are formal; they are based on an individual's number of convictions or arrests for violent crimes in the previous year. Other methods are much more informal. The Washington Repeat Offender Project (ROP), for example, relies heavily on criminal informants and other sources of information about people who are currently active in crime. A Minneapolis program, by contrast, uses a mixture of formal and informal methods, reviewing "nominations" from many sources and relying on extensive information and established criteria in order to focus on a small group of offenders.

None of these methods has ever been scientifically validated to see if it identifies the most active offenders currently on the streets, or even if all of the targets picked are currently active, serious offenders. However, a Police Foundation evaluation of the targets selected by Washington's ROP found that all of the targets had serious criminal histories and that the majority had been arrested within the previous year.

How Do Police Apprehend Repeat Offenders?

Most police programs deal with repeat offenders only after they have been caught. These "reactive" programs maintain a list of serious criminals. When anyone on the list is arrested, extra personnel are assigned to conduct an especially intensive investigation in order to increase the chances of a conviction and a prison sentence.

In contrast, "proactive" programs in Minneapolis and Washington are designed to catch repeat offenders who would otherwise not be arrested. Both cities originally emphasized surveillance but found that surreptitious "tailing" of a repeat offender 24 hours a day was boring and rarely produced an observable crime that could lead to an arrest.

Other methods include getting enoug information for a search warrant and then conducting raids on premises suspected to contain drugs and stolen property (as depicted in the program) and setting up opportunities for offenders to commit crimes in the presence of police (such as buying weapons or selling stolen goods).

What Rules Apply to These Methods?

The right to privacy is obviously jeopardized by ROP tactics. It is not clear what the U.S. Constitution intends with respect to putting people under surveillance in public places. Nor is existing case law clear on the degree to which the public should be protected from police acting as decoys or as seeming partners in criminal enterprises. These issues are much more ambiguous than, for example, our individual constitutional rights not to be searched or to have police enter our property, except under well-established rules and procedures. A zealous repeat offender program runs the risk that

individual officers will break the rules. Thus, careful supervision by police commanders and continued oversight by the courts are necessary both in making rules and in seeing that they are enforced.

One of the rules that may not be violated when following a repeat offender is "entrapment." Entrapment is not a crime in itself but is a legitimate defense to a criminal charge. A defendant who claims entrapment must generally show that he was "induced" by the police to commit the offense and would not otherwise have done so. It is not sufficient for the defendant to prove merely that the police provided the means and the opportunity to commit the offense, thereby creating a "trap"; this provides no legal defense.

The problem is in defining what constitutes inducement. Is merely planting or suggesting the idea of committing a specific offense an inducement? Or is it necessary for the police to persuade, pressure, coerce, or cajole the offender into committing the crime?

How Well Does Washington's ROP Work?

The Police Foundation's evaluation of the Repeat Offender Project in Washington, D.C., found that the targets of ROP attention were five times more likely to be arrested than were targets who were randomly assigned to a "control group" that ROP was barred from investigating. This means that, if the D.C. Police had no ROP, the offenders now targeted by ROP would be much less likely to be arrested, or to be arrested as often.

The Police Foundation evaluation also showed that ROP resulted in a decline in the number of arrests ROP officers made per year, compared with their productivity before they joined ROP. The benefit was that the officers in the program arrested people who, on average, had more serious criminal records and were probably more active offenders. Whether ROP actually reduced crime in Washington was impossible for the evaluation to determine.

Why don't more officers do ROP work? This question has an obvious answer to many critics of police crime control strategies. For a variety of historical and political reasons, police spend most of their resources answering emergency calls from citizens, or waiting to answer those calls. While there are many other things they could do which might reduce crime, police executives cannot risk diverting resources from reactive radio patrol work. The idea of policing criminals, or confronting problems, or focusing on targets other than citizen calls for service may seem sensible, but diverting resources from citizen calls can create a political hot potato for any police chief.

How Do Prosecutors Select Repeat Offenders?

Prosecutors' criteria are more formal than those used by police. The Charlotte system assigns mathematically precise weights to such factors as alcohol or drug use, age, and length of criminal career. Other prosecutors confine their criteria solely to characteristics of past offenses, such as the use of violence or a weapon. Some prosecutors believe in punishment only for past offenses and oppose using any "extralegal" considerations (such as drug use), even if they predict crime.

Virtually all urban courts have caseloads too large for all cases to be brought to trial. The normal procedure is to bargain with the defendant to plead guilty without trial in exchange for a reduction in charges or for a reduced punishment. Most cases must be handled this way to keep the system going, but prosecutors make exceptions for repeat offenders.

"Selective prosecution" of repeat offenders means that plea bargaining can be refused and that the prosecutor will press for conviction on the most serious charge possible with the longest sentence possible. Whether the prosecutor succeeds depends on how strong a case the police and prosecutor prepare, and how the judge reacts to the case.

Despite the priority both police and prosecutors give these cases, the arrested offender may be freed on bail or, upon conviction, may receive a short prison sentence or no prison sentence at all. The reason for both these outcomes is concern for fairness. Judges often do not believe it is fair to deny bail to people or to impose unusually high bail, even though police or prosecutors have labeled the people repeat offenders. For that matter, police and prosecutors often disagree about who is or is not a repeat offender.

Nor is it likely that a repeat offender convicted of selling stolen property in an ROP trap will receive a sentence substantially longer than would be received by a person not labeled a repeat offender who was charged with the same offense. The checks and balances of the criminal justice system limit the impact of repeat offender programs adopted by a single agency.

What Are the Prospects for Repeat Offender Programs?

Repeat offender programs seem likely to expand and proliferate. With the scarce resources of modern criminal justice confronted by growing demands, policymakers must increasingly establish priorities. The idea of focusing scarce resources on repeat offender programs—even with all the errors of prediction and ethical questions of such programs—provides an attractive basis for choosing which criminal justice course to take.

Discussion Questions

1. What does your community do about repeat offenders?

2. When is it legitimate to consider the likelihood of future crimes in deciding how to punish a past crime?

3. Does it make more sense for police to concentrate on repeat offenders or to maintain a rapid response time to citizen calls for assistance?

4. Should prosecutors establish a targeting committee with police so they can agree in advance about who will be treated as a repeat offender?

5. Should the juvenile justice system be altered to give special consideration to highly active repeat offenders? If so, how?

References

Blumstein, Alfred, Jacqueline Cohen, and Daniel Nagin, eds. 1978. *Deterrence and Incapacitation: Estimating the Effects of Sanctions on Crime Rates*. Washington, D.C.: National Research Council, National Academy of Sciences.

Chaiken, Jan M., and Marcia Chaiken. 1982. *Varieties of Criminal Behavior*. Report to the National Institute of Justice. Santa Monica, California: Rand Corporation.

Cohen, Jacqueline. 1983. "Incapacitation Research." In *Crime and Justice: An Annual Review of Research*, edited by Michael Tonry and Norval Morris. Chicago: University of Chicago Press.

Greenwood, Peter W., with Alan Abrahamse. 1982. *Selective Incapacitation*. Report to the National Institute of Justice. Santa Monica, California: Rand Corporation.

Martin, Susan, and Lawrence W. Sherman. 1985. *The Washington Repeat Offender Project*. Washington, D.C.: Police Foundation.

von Hirsch, Andrew. 1985. *Past or Future Crimes*. New Brunswick, New Jersey: Rutgers.

Wolfgang, Marvin E., Robert M. Figlio, and Thorsten Sellin. 1972. *Delinquency in a Birth Cohort*. Chicago: University of Chicago Press.

National Institute of Justice / CRIME FILE

Biology and Crime

Richard Herrnstein, Harvard University

1986

Background

From the earliest times, it has been believed that appearance reveals character. Over 2,000 years ago, the Greek philosopher, Socrates, was charged by his enemies with having a face that showed brutality. In his time, there were "physiognomists," readers of faces. Later on, there were also "phrenologists," readers of head shapes. Readers of palms can still be found in the Yellow Pages of many American cities. In William Shakespeare's "Julius Caesar," the sly conspirator, Cassius, "has a lean and hungry look ... such men are dangerous." In Robert Louis Stevenson's Victorian fantasy, Dr. Jekyll, a respectable, handsome doctor, destroyed himself by indulging too often in a chemical concoction that transformed him into diabolical, remorseless Mr. Hyde. Mr. Hyde was, and *looked*, evil—"pale and dwarfish ... hardly human ... troglodytic." The spirit of celebration—Santa Claus or Bacchus, the Roman god of wine—is pictured as rotund; the spirit of nationalism—our Uncle Sam or England's John Bull—as wiry or muscular. The word "character" almost tells its own story, meaning both a physical sign (as in the characters of an alphabet) and a psychological disposition.

It is not hard to see why, despite its ancient vintage, the belief in physical marks of character is rejected by most educated people. What hard scientific evidence there is of such visible signs suggests that they are too minor and unreliable to be useful. As a practical matter, it is sound not to judge a book by its cover and to recognize that beauty is only skin deep. Right or wrong, the belief in physical signs risks intolerance, superficiality, and quackery. Judging people by how they look is not only likely to be inaccurate, it is unfair.

So why begin this commentary with an idea whose time has evidently passed? The answer is that it is important for conceptual, if not practical, reasons. For criminal behavior, as for many other kinds of significant human behavior, it is likely that how people behave bears some relation to their biological constitutions.

Research on Body Types and Physique

In the 1930's, Earnest A. Hooton, an American anthropologist, compared standard physical measurements of over 10,000 male prisoners with those of noncriminals of corresponding ages and ethnic ancestries, and from corresponding regions of the country. Hooton discovered that criminals were, on the average, physically distinctive in small but statistically significant ways. In some samples, he also found small physical differences between groups of criminals convicted for different crimes. The physical correlates were things like particular ear shapes or eye colors or relative sizes of parts of the body or hair distributions—all in all, minor attributes that had no clear or obvious connection to crime besides the correlation itself.

What mattered to Hooton was not what the physical correlates of crime were so much as that there were correlates at all. From his evidence that criminals were physically distinctive, Hooton argued for a biological susceptibility to crime that also happened to show up in otherwise irrelevant physical characteristics, such as the shape of one's ear. The physical correlate was, then, a form of evidence, albeit indirect, of biological involvement in the tendency to break the law.

More such evidence began to accumulate in the 1940's, after William H. Sheldon, a physician, developed a new system for classifying human physique. A person's body build, in this system, is represented by three numbers for the three "dimensions" of physique—that is, endomorphy (soft, round), mesomorphy (large boned, muscular), and ectomorphy (linear, fragile). Each dimension is assigned a score on a 7-point scale (4 being the midpoint); the value for any individual is derived from objective measurements of the body, ideally after adjustments for age, health, and nutritional status. The average male's physique is approximately 4.0–4.0–3.5 (for endomorphy, mesomorphy, and ectomorphy, respectively); the average female's, approximately 5.0–3.0–3.5. Extreme values along any of the dimensions are relatively rare: for example, the 4–6–1 body type, which is highly mesomorphic and very weakly ectomorphic, is estimated to occur only twice per 1,000 males. This also happens to be one of the physiques disproportionately susceptible to criminal behavior.

Several studies, by Sheldon and by others, reported male and female offenders to be more mesomorphic and less ectomorphic, on the average, than nonoffenders who were matched for age, IQ, socioeconomic status, or ethnic ancestry. A small amount of evidence suggests that criminal recidivists have more atypical physiques (even more mesomorphy and less ectomorphy) than criminals in general. The third dimension, endomorphy, does not reliably correlate with criminal behavior. Not everyone who has high mesomorphy and low ectomorphy commits crimes, or vice versa. Indeed, it is likely that other pursuits besides crime attract the same sorts of body builds.

Physique, as measured in Sheldon's system, is a constitutional variable, not greatly affected by environment or experience, hence likely to be dependent on one's genes. Its correlation with criminal behavior implies that criminal tendencies involve genes to some extent. Sheldon and others have found that physique is correlated, although imperfectly, with personality and temperament. The mesomorphic component is typically associated with, among other traits, high activity levels, restlessness, a craving for adventure and danger, and aggressiveness; the ectomorphic component, with introspectiveness, self-consciousness, inhibition, rich inner psychic experience, and a capacity for delayed gratification. Mesomorphy unleavened by ectomorphy is therefore likely to be accompanied by a taste for uninhibited, aggressive excitement and by deficits in internal feelings and forbearance. As is described below, just such a combination of personality traits has been directly associated with criminal tendencies.

Research on Chromosomes

Modern biology provides more direct methods than the measurement of physiques or faces for deciding whether a psychological tendency has constitutional foundations. For example, a particular abnormality of the chromosomes has been disproportionately found among male criminals. Gender and gender characteristics are determined by 1 of the 23 pairs of chromosomes that contain the human genetic endowment. For genetically normal females, the sex-determining pair consists of two ordinary-sized chromosomes, called XX because of their microscopic appearance. Males normally have an XY pair instead, of which one of the chromosomes (the Y) is smaller. For less than 1/10 of 1 percent of the male population, however, there is an extra Y, so that instead of a sex-determining pair, there is a sex-determining triplet of chromosomes, XYY. The extra Y chromosome turns up unpredictably in any social class or ethnic group or family setting. Such men are taller than average and have other minor physical characteristics. They also have a 10 to 20 times greater tendency to break the law than do genetically normal men from comparable populations.

Even with their elevated criminal tendencies, there are too few XYY men to affect overall crime rates much. However, they again illustrate the power of genetic influences on offending, for any effect on behavior of the extra chromosomes is genetic by definition. Some, but evidently not all, of the elevated risk of criminal behavior among XYY males has been traced to the lower IQ scores they have been shown to have. The implication that IQ scores are to a degree controlled by genes and correlated with crime is briefly discussed below.

Research on Twins and Adoptions

Another approach to the biological basis of criminality is to compare identical and fraternal twins. Identical twins, arising as they do from a single fertilized ovum, share identical genes. Fraternal twins arise from two fertilized ova, and they have the same genetic overlap as ordinary sisters and brothers. Traits for which identical twins are more similar than fraternal twins are likely to involve genes. Familiar examples are height, weight, and general appearance, each of which is typically more similar for identical twins. From the results of about a dozen studies in Europe, Asia, and the United States, criminality can be added to the list. An identical, as contrasted with a fraternal, twin with a criminal record implies approximately twice the likelihood of a co-twin with a record, too. Identical twins are also more alike than fraternal twins in the frequency of criminal behavior they admit to in anonymous questionnaires. The differential resemblance of identical and fraternal twins is generally considered to be strong, though not by itself conclusive, evidence of genetic involvement in criminal behavior.

The main other source of evidence comes from studies of children adopted early in life and of their biological and adopting parents. For example, the criminal convictions among a sample of more than 4,000 Danish adopted boys were more dependent on their biological, as compared to their adoptive, parents' criminality. The more serious an offender a biological parent was, the greater the risk of criminality for his or her child, particularly for property crimes. Adopted boys who had a chronically criminal biological parent (three or more convictions) were three times more likely to become criminal than those whose biological parents were not criminal. The risk for the child depended neither on whether the child or the adopting parents knew about the biological parents' criminal records nor on whether the biological parents committed their crimes before or after the child was adopted. Swedish and American studies have confirmed the main conclusions and have extended them to female adopted children.

The bits of evidence may be individually disputed but, taken together, the case for some genetic involvement in criminal behavior cannot plausibly be rejected. On the average, offenders are distinctive in physical constitution, they are more likely to have chromosomal abnormality, and they tend to occur in families with other offenders whether or not they were raised by their criminal relatives. Unwholesome environments are surely among the significant predictors of crime; they are just not the only predictors. But genes do not cause crime as such. Rather, the evidence suggests a more complex chain of connections: genes affect psychological traits which in turn affect the likelihood of breaking the law. Intelligence and personality are the two traits most strongly implicated in this chain.

Research on IQ

Many studies have shown that the offender population has an average IQ of about 91–93, compared to the average IQ of 100 for the population at large. Since the general population includes an unknown fraction of offenders, the IQ gap between offenders and nonoffenders can only be estimated, but a conservative value is about 10 points. Different categories of offenders have different average IQ's, some even lower and some higher than 91–93. In general, however, the common offenses—the impulsive violent crimes and the opportunistic property crimes—are most often committed by people in the low normal and borderline retarded range.

Since test scores and crime rates are both correlated with socioeconomic status, it is sometimes suggested that status, rather than test score, is the critical variable in explaining criminal behavior. But the evidence says otherwise. At each socioeconomic level, offenders tend to have the lower IQ test scores; among people with the same scores, people from lower socioeconomic levels commit more crime. Thus, both cognitive ability (intelligence) and socioeconomic status (environment) contribute to the likelihood of criminal behavior, and there is some reason for concluding that ability contributes more.

IQ test items call on cognitive abilities of various sorts, each of which can be described as verbal or nonverbal. A vocabulary test is obviously verbal; a test of speed and accuracy in assembling the pieces of a jigsaw puzzle is nonverbal. Spatial reasoning is nonverbal; arithmetic reasoning is usually considered verbal. Tests are usually constructed so that the average person has equal verbal and nonverbal scores, but offenders average lower verbal than nonverbal scores. Even among groups of offenders and nonoffenders matched for age, overall IQ, ethnic background, and socioeconomic status, offenders have lower verbal scores than nonoffenders (and higher nonverbal scores, so as to equalize overall scores for the two groups). Low verbal scores may create a risk for criminal behavior because they impair a person's ability to formulate and follow internal standards of conduct, or because they lead to failure and frustration in school and on the job, or for all those reasons.

A large scientific literature indicates that the abilities measured by IQ tests are partly genetic. Verbal abilities are at least as heritable as nonverbal. The IQ's of children raised in foster homes correlate more closely with those of their biological parents than with their foster parents'. Identical twins have more similar IQ's than fraternal twins. In general, people who are more closely related by blood have more similar test scores. Estimates of the heritability of intelligence, by serious students of the subject, range from about 40 percent to 80 percent. This does not mean that intelligence is immune to influence by the environment, but it helps explain the evidence for an inherited biological factor in criminal behavior. Since crime correlates with IQ, and IQ is partly inherited, a heritable susceptibility to criminal behavior follows.

Research on Personality

Personality is a similar matter. Many studies have found that the average offender is distinctive, though not necessarily abnormal. He or she is likely to be impulsive, deficient in internal psychic experience and in emotional attachments to other people, mendacious, aggressive, unconventional, fatalistic—if not indifferent—about the future, drawn to adventure or danger, and emotionally disturbed or frankly psychotic. When these traits are sufficiently extreme, offenders are said to suffer from a psychiatric condition called "antisocial personality." Not every offender is atypical in personality, but in large samples, the signs of atypicality are undeniable.

Like intelligence, personality has a heritable component, although probably not to the same degree. The evidence on the heritability of personality is not as clearcut as that on intelligence, for several reasons. There has been less research on it. The measurement of personality has not been as well standardized. Personality is probably even more multifaceted than intelligence, and different aspects of it may have different heritabilities. Even so, we may conclude that the inheritance of personality traits is one of the ways in which the susceptibility to criminal behavior is transmitted by the genes.

Discussion Questions

1.   What public policy implications derive from the research findings concerning men with XYY chromosomes? Should all men be tested to find out which ones have the XYY chromosome? Should those who have it be locked up or in any other way be treated differently from other men?

2.   Does the research summarized in this commentary persuade you that biology plays a role in predisposing some people to crime? Why or why not?

3.   Assume that you are, or could be, convinced that biology influences criminality. Can you think of any practical uses to which such knowledge could be put?

4.   Should prospective adopting parents be provided information about the criminal records of available infants' parents? Why or why not?

References

Cattell, R.B. 1982. *The Inheritance of Personality and Ability: Research Methods and Findings*. New York: Academic Press.

Cortes, J.B., and F.M. Gatti. 1972. *Delinquency and Crime: A Biopsychological Approach*. New York: Seminar Press.

Glueck, S., and E.T. Glueck. 1956. *Physique and Delinquency*. New York: Harper.

Hartl, E.M., E.P. Monnelly, and R.D. Elderkin. 1982. *Physique and Delinquent Behavior: A Thirty-Year Follow-Up of William H. Sheldon's Varieties of Delinquent Youth*. New York: Academic Press.

Hooton, E.A. 1939. *Crime and the Man*. Cambridge, Mass.: Harvard University Press.

_____. 1939. *The American Criminal: An Anthropological Study*. Cambridge, Mass.: Harvard University Press.

Mednick, S.A., and K.O. Christiansen, eds. 1977. *Biological Bases of Criminal Behavior*. New York: Wiley.

Mednick, S.A., and J. Volavka. 1980. "Biology and Crime." In *Crime and Justice: An Annual Review of Research*, vol. 2, edited by Norval Morris and Michael Tonry. Chicago: University of Chicago Press.

Shah, S.A. 1970. *Report on the XYY Chromosomal Abnormality*. U.S. Public Health Service, publication no. 2130. Washington, D.C.: U.S. Government Printing Office.

Sheldon, W.H., with S.S. Stevens and W.B. Tucker. 1940. *The Varieties of Human Physique*. New York: Harper.

Sheldon, W.H., with S.S. Stevens. 1942. *The Varieties of Temperament*. New York: Harper.

Wilson, J.Q., and R.J. Herrnstein. 1985. *Crime and Human Nature*. New York: Simon and Schuster.

National Institute of Justice

CRIME FILE

Families and Crime

Rolf Loeber, University of Pittsburgh

1988

Which Family Factors Are Related to Crime?

Criminality runs in families. For many years, researchers have been trying to learn why that is so. Researchers have investigated how families with delinquent children differ from families in which children are not delinquent. They have found that parents of delinquent children often lack involvement with their children, provide poor supervision, and administer inadequate or erratic discipline. Some parents of delinquent youngsters are themselves not law abiding, thus providing examples of deviant behavior and values that their offspring may imitate.

Many delinquent youngsters grow up in families that experience adversities, such as marital conflict, divorce, parental illness, poverty, or low socioeconomic status. Few families face all these difficulties, but many confront one or more. It may be that different combinations of familial factors contribute to delinquency in offspring.

Being raised in poverty or being the child of criminal parents does not necessarily cause one to become a criminal. Nonetheless, there is substantial evidence that children raised in adversity are disproportionately likely to become delinquent. Although many individuals raised in adverse family circumstances are not criminals, overall, the chances for such children to become delinquent are greater than for children reared in happier settings.

Various indicators of family disruption or inadequacy are correlated with delinquent behavior. These same factors can also be used to predict the likelihood that a child will become delinquent.

Different explanations have been offered to account for the association between patterns of family life and patterns of delinquent behavior. Some analysts say the association results from social or economic conditions that influence the behavior of both children and parents. Other analysts blame poor parenting skills. Still others look to biological explanations. Research on the criminality of twins and adopted children, for example, suggests that genetic factors may predispose some children to become delinquents. Genetic factors, however, can be but part of the explanation. It is likely that all these explanations are relevant in particular cases and in varying combinations in different cases.

What Causes What in Families?

Explanations of delinquency that focus on the parents and their behavior as parents may appear one-sided. A complete explanation of delinquency no doubt must also incorporate biological, social, environmental, and other factors. Children inherit a proportion of their constitutional characteristics, such as intelligence, aggressive tendencies, and hyperactivity. Their social environment, first at home, and later at school, molds these characteristics over time. Nonetheless, there is substantial evidence that parents' approaches to raising and disciplining their children have a significant independent effect on the children's behavior.

Not all home environments are equally suited to dealing effectively with youngsters who exhibit problem behavior early in life. Parents differ greatly in their childrearing skills. Some parents are too harsh, irritable, and inconsistent. Others are too lenient, neglectful, or preoccupied with their own concerns. A number of studies have found that parents' childrearing practices, good or bad, are relatively stable and that early conduct problems, and later ones, are related to how youngsters are reared.

Increasingly, investigators, clinicians, and child-rearing experts are focusing their attention on early rather than later child problem behavior. A primary reason is that most children learn deviant and approved behavior in the family home long before they are exposed to deviant peers. If the conditions that predispose some children to become delinquents can be ameliorated or prevented, there is hope that later conduct problems can be reduced. Another reason for concentrating on early childhood is that the learning of deviant behavior is importantly shaped by the quality and quantity of parent-child interactions. Many forms of delinquency and serious misbehavior are more common among children raised in broken homes, or in conditions of poverty and material deprivation, than in families that do not suffer from these disadvantages. Nonetheless, for any specific category of family, the behavior problems are more pronounced in families characterized by poor parenting skills.

Accumulating evidence points to a relatively high degree of continuity between early conduct problems in youngsters and later delinquency. For example, early lying, disobedience, aggression, truancy, and drug use are known to be good predictors of various degrees of delinquency many years later. The evidence for this conclusion is based mainly on the experience of white males; most delinquency research that has focused on early childhood has not concentrated on white females or on minority children. There is, however, little reason to believe that these findings would not apply to white females and minority children. Many kinds of problem behavior appear to be more easily modifiable when the child is young and more difficult to change when the behavior has become entrenched over time.

Important changes can take place in the quality of interactions between family members when a child's misbehavior or delinquency increases over time. Many parents become very angry and short-tempered with a persistently troublesome child, or become disillusioned when they recognize that they cannot trust what the youngster tells them. Over time, parent-child conflicts may escalate, or both parties may become more distant and uninvolved.

One feature of youngsters' antisocial development is that they often direct antisocial behavior—particularly aggression and lying—against their parents. As a consequence, parents become less able to exercise their parental authority and may, in effect, especially with older children, abdicate their parental responsibilities.

Clinicians and researchers have long argued that parents' inadequate childrearing practices can be improved, regardless of whether the skills were inadequate to begin with or were undermined by youngsters' antisocial behavior. The basic idea is that improvements in childrearing practices can lead to improvements in the youngsters' problem behavior.

What Is the Evidence for Parent Training?

Systematic evaluation of parent training began only a few decades ago. Since then a number of studies have shown that well-planned training sessions can help parents improve their childrearing practices, which in turn can achieve improvements in children's behavior. Although parent training programs vary, most include the following features:

- Parents are taught to identify their children's problem behavior.
- Parents are taught to apply more appropriate consequences to misbehavior. They are encouraged to use less "nagging" and to increase the use of nonphysical punishment such as loss of privileges. At the same time, constructive behavior is rewarded.
- Parents are taught to negotiate the resolution of problems, especially with their older children.
- Parents are taught to supervise their children more closely and to monitor their comings and goings, their activities, and their choice of friends.

So far, these programs have been especially successful in dealing with aggression in children. Careful observations in family homes before, during, and after parent training have shown that the frequency of children's aggression was significantly reduced in the majority of the studies. This was confirmed by parental reports.

Most of the training programs that work with the natural parents have focused on preadolescent rather than on adolescent youngsters. It is likely that parent training is more effective when children are young; by middle adolescence behavior may be so entrenched or so subject to peer influences that changes can be made only with extraordinary efforts.

Another line of parent training has focused on foster parents who, for a period of time, work with problem youngsters whose own parents are unable to carry out their parental duties. These programs are often called "specialized child care," because the host parents are specifically trained for this task. Many of the principles listed above are used in their training; in addition, the parents are educated to develop positive relationships with the youngsters and, through the use of individualized written contracts between foster parent and child, to teach the children to become responsible individuals.

Parents in training programs are often assisted in their difficult tasks by a support network of other parents and supervisory staff. Both efforts—the training of natural parents and of specialized foster parents—appear to be more viable and humane approaches for dealing with problem children than institutionalization, which may be the only other option for some children.

What Are the Advantages and Limitations of Parent Training?

Although training of natural parents has been among the most promising approaches for dealing with the conduct of problem youngsters, a number of issues remain. For instance, we do not know enough about the effect of parent training on youngsters' concealment of their antisocial acts. And few studies have demonstrated that parent training prevents or reduces existing delinquency or drug use.

Although parent training programs show promise as an approach for dealing with conduct problems, especially in very young children, important issues must be resolved before we can say that parent training can play a major role in preventing delinquency. For example, existing programs are quite expensive. Many parents do not have insurance, cannot afford the cost of participating in these programs, and cannot afford to pay for their children's participation. It may not be realistic to expect that parent training can reach a significant fraction of parents of problem children. Moreover, it is not clear how long the beneficial effects of training last.

We need to learn much more about the effectiveness of parent training for minority families. Most of the training programs have been undertaken with white families; culturally appropriate programs for minorities

have not yet been developed. Finally, a proportion of parents are not immediately willing to participate. Some of them may join a training program if barriers such as access to day care or babysitting are overcome. Others may need to be sensitized through publicity campaigns on the benefits of parental training.

Another group of parents, however, are either unavailable or not quite capable of going through a parent training program. This heightens the importance of alternative procedures, such as a home visitor program for in-home training or specialized foster care. Although there have as yet been few evaluations of the effects of such foster care on children's behavior, the initial results are promising.

Turning to purely preventive approaches, it is quite possible that parents can be trained in skills that will help them curtail incipient problem behavior in their young children before the problems become difficult to manage. Unfortunately, such preventive approaches have not yet been investigated. The Perry Preschool Program (Berruetta-Clement, Schweinhart, Barnett, Epstein, and Weikart 1984), however, a program which was highly successful in preventing delinquency, contained a component that concentrated on parents in addition to the intensive preschool program.

What Is the Role of Government?

The role of government in parenting training and in the socialization of children is necessarily limited. Government cannot be expected to assume responsibility for raising children and teaching them to abstain from antisocial behavior or to adopt socially approved behavior. This is a task that requires patience and care over many years, a process which is unique to parents' bond with their children and is unlikely ever to be replicated in institutions outside the family.

Some commentators on the role of the family in American society have been apprehensive that some governmental interventions into family life may do more harm than good. They say, for instance, that some social service and social welfare programs may contribute to the breakup of families that otherwise would have remained together. It is possible, however, to conceive of governmental interventions that could help families function better and make childrearing more of a success.

Current governmental efforts have been aimed largely at improving the environment in which children grow up by bettering schools, housing, and nourishment. Major gains have been made in these respects (although not for all strata of the population); however, we have no way of determining if these interventions have kept some children from becoming delinquent or kept some families from breaking up.

Governmental efforts could more directly attempt to improve family functioning. For example, efforts could be made to help community organizations develop parent support groups, advice hotlines for parents, group training in parenting skills, and other low-cost programs directed to family stability. Parents-to-be, and particularly parents of high-risk groups of children, could be offered parent training programs. This would be particularly relevant for single parents or for parents of toddlers who show signs of hyperactive or other disruptive behavior. Pediatricians, general practitioners, and other service providers could be better trained to "flag" problem behaviors that warrant intervention and to counsel parents on how to obtain help.

More intensive programs could then be limited to families who need more intensive forms of intervention because their children exhibit unique or highly resistant problem behavior. Specialized professionals might give individualized training to the natural parents, or the children could be placed in specialized foster care families.

All these improvements could be accomplished on a voluntary basis, without affecting family autonomy. A portion of existing funds now used to deal with antisocial or delinquent youngsters in the courts, schools, and communities could be channeled toward the development of such preventive interventions.

In sum, both government and community organizations can help families to function better and to rear children in ways that lessen the chances that they will drift into serious forms of delinquency.

Discussion Questions

1. What rationales justify use of parent training as a tool to reduce delinquency?

2. Which forms of family malfunctioning are most susceptible to improvement as a result of parent training?

3. How can parents be helped to prevent delinquency in their offspring?

4. How can the government best support the viability of families and aid parents in dealing with children whose characteristics place them at high risk of becoming delinquents?

5. Should the government provide funds to support parent training and other programs aimed at improving family functioning?

References

Berrueta-Clement, J.R., L.J. Schweinhart, W.S. Barnett, A.S. Epstein, and D.P. Weikart. 1984. *Changed Lives: The Effects of the Perry Preschool Programs on Youths through Age 19.* Ypsilanti, Mississippi: High/Scope Press.

Hawkins, R.P., P. Meadowcroft, B.A. Trout, and C. Luster. 1985. "Foster Family Based Treatment." *Journal of Clinical Child Psychology* 14:220–28.

Loeber, R. 1987. "What Policy Makers and Practitioners Can Learn from Family Studies of Juvenile Conduct Problems and Delinquency." In *From Children to Citizens: Families, Schools, and Delinquency Prevention,* edited by J.Q. Wilson and G.C. Loury. New York: Springer-Verlag.

Loeber, R., and M. Stouthamer-Loeber. 1986. "Family Factors as Correlates and Predictors of Juvenile Conduct Problems and Delinquency." In *Crime and Justice: An Annual Review of Research,* vol. 7, edited by Michael Tonry and Norval Morris. Chicago: University of Chicago Press.

Patterson, G.R., and M.E. Gullion. 1968. *Living with Children.* Champaign, Illinois: Research Press.

Patterson, G.R., P. Chamberlain, and J.B. Reid. 1982. "A Comparative Evaluation of Parent Training Programs." *Behavior Therapy* 13:638–50.

Wilson, J.Q. 1983. "Raising Kids." *The Atlantic Monthly* 252:45–51.

National Institute of Justice   /   *CRIME FILE*

TV and Violence

J. Ronald Milavsky, National Broadcasting Company

1986

Introduction

There is no doubt that mass media have changed what people know and how they think and behave. Exactly how has been the subject of a great deal of speculative thought, imaginative writing, and even some scientific research. Much of this attention has focused on the influence of the mass media on violent behavior.

In the past, other media, such as comic books, radio, and newspapers, were thought to be possible causes of violence. For the past 30 years, however, television has received the most attention.

All media deal with violent subjects either in covering the news or in fictional stories and programs. According to public opinion surveys, a majority of people agree that there is too much violence on television. In 1982 the Gallup organization found that nearly two-thirds of the adult population thought that there was a relationship "between violence on television and the rising crime rate in the United States." Finally, people think that television has a strong influence on children. In one survey by Yankelovich, Skelly, and White, 76 percent of the people questioned agreed that "television has more influence on most children than the parents have." In effect, television's influence has become a socially accepted "fact."

However, the scientific evidence does not support such definite conclusions.

Research on Television and Violence

A considerable amount of research has been concerned with the impact of television on violence. Some of this has been conducted or sponsored by the Federal Government and some of it has been done by academic researchers.

1. *Government reports.* There have been two major Federal projects. The first, a report to the Surgeon General in 1972, commissioned new research. The second, sponsored by the National Institute of Mental Health (NIMH), reviewed studies done in the 10-year period following the publication of the Surgeon General's Report. The 1972 Report's conclusion was extremely tentative and found "a preliminary and tentative indication of a causal relationship." The 1982 NIMH report was more emphatic in its conclusion that television causes violence. However, this report was criticized severely in an evaluation commissioned by the National Academy of Sciences. The evaluation was undertaken at the behest of the U.S. Department of Justice, which wanted to know whether legislative regulation of television was warranted. The National Academy of Sciences' evaluation concluded that the evidence was insufficient to warrant regulatory or legislative action. The evaluators urged caution in drawing policy recommendations from the available research because it suffers from a number of scientific shortcomings and it deals almost entirely with mild forms of aggression among children, not with criminal behavior.

2. *Survey studies.* Survey studies examine correlations. From survey studies which measure both how aggressive people are and how much they watch violent programs, we know that people who are antisocially aggressive tend, more than most people, to watch television programs with violent content. It is hard to know what to make of that

correlation. It is not clear whether watching more violent programs *causes* people to be aggressive, or whether aggressive people choose to watch more violent programs.

This conundrum is an inherent weakness of survey research, which can indicate whether correlations exist, but not why. And that interpretive problem will become steadily more vexing. Because television is a mass medium, people can select what they want to watch from a wide variety of programs. Cable and satellite delivery systems have made 10 program services available to the average household, and this number will increase in the future.

3. *Experimental studies.* The basic limitation of surveys—that they reveal *when* two things are correlated but not whether one causes the other—can be avoided by undertaking a different level of research known as "experiments." Experiments are the most reliable kind of research for determining whether one thing causes another. In an experiment, subjects are randomly assigned to different treatments. In an experiment on television violence and violent behavior, some people would be randomly assigned to watch violent programs and others would be shown programs with no violence in them. People's aggressive behavior would be measured then or later, either by observation or through questionnaires. If the two groups truly are assigned randomly, differences between their aggression levels could be tested, using statistical formulas, to see if the differences were larger than would be expected by chance. If they were, an inference could be made that the presence or absence of exposure to material caused the difference.

Experimental studies far outnumber any other kind of study done on this subject. Most are conducted in laboratories where the researcher has a high degree of control over the experiment. A few experiments have also been done in real-life settings such as boys' homes or reform schools.

Laboratory experiments have been used to study whether children will imitate what they see. Most of the experiments deal with mild forms of aggressive behavior directed at toys, although in a few experiments more aggression was observed among children in recess or play situations. Serious interpersonal aggression was not studied because the constraints of research ethics do not allow placing people in real jeopardy.

Other kinds of laboratory experiments have been used to study whether seeing activities depicted in a dramatic story can lead people to act more aggressively. For example, these studies investigate whether people are more likely to imitate aggressive actions when these actions are shown to be justified in the dramatic presentation than when they were shown to be undeserved by the victim. One hypothesis is that watching aggression that is deserved by the character on whom it is inflicted in the film will lower the viewer's inhibitions against acting aggressively toward real people in similar circumstances. That hypothesis has been confirmed by the experimental studies.

The main problem with the experimental studies is that the very feature that gives them their power to detect effects, the degree of control over conditions, also makes one wonder whether they are too artificial to apply to real-life conditions. Just because children will imitate what they see on film or on television in a laboratory does not mean that they will do this in their homes. And even if children, in their play at home, seem to incorporate things they see on television, it does not mean that they will really try to hurt others using methods seen on television.

There are several reasons why one cannot be sure whether the findings of these kinds of studies can be applied to everyday situations. First, violence in real life is rare, is generally discouraged, and is punished, which helps explain why it rarely occurs. In order to encourage "real-life" aggressive behavior on the part of subjects, experimenters need to let the subjects know that they will not be punished. Further, for ethical reasons, experimenters cannot risk encouraging real, serious aggression. Therefore, experiments use substitutes for interpersonal aggression, such as punching a doll or pushing a "shock" button. Finally, the kind of visual violence used in the experiments is selected because it is thought to be the type that has the greatest chance of encouraging aggression. Clear and graphic acts, upon which the subject's attention is forced to focus, are often isolated from other events and are shown out of context. Acts of violence seen in normal television viewing, by contrast, are less graphic than those seen in experiments and are shown in context; moreover, the viewer's attention often is not fully focused on the screen. Thus the intensity of the experimental conditions may bear little resemblance to actual viewing conditions.

Some experimental studies have been done in realistic settings—with inconsistent results. One series of such experiments examined a real episode of a television dramatic program but showed two different endings. In one version, a charity collection box was broken into and the money stolen. This was the antisocial act to be imitated. In the other version, this did not happen, but everything else was the same. Although collection boxes strategically placed by the experimenters in natural surroundings, such as lunch counters, were broken into and the money stolen, those who saw the episode with the experimental ending did not break into the boxes any more often than those who did not. In another realistic experiment, in boys' homes, those who were shown only nonviolent television programs for a number of weeks turned out to be more aggressive than those who watched violent programs for the same period. The likeliest explanation is that the boys who watched only nonviolent programs felt deprived of some of their favorites and acted hostilely as a result. That is a very good example of why experiments in real-life situations may not turn out as neatly as they do in the laboratory.

Better Methods for Study of Television and Aggression

It is difficult to design convincing experimental studies of mass media effects in natural settings, so researchers have turned to other approaches.

1. *Longitudinal panel surveys.* Longitudinal panel surveys can measure interactions between television viewing and aggressive behavior among the same people over a period of time. For example, people might be questioned and tested concerning their viewing habits and their behavior once every 6 months for 3 years. Analysis of their answers over time can indicate if behavior changes are related to viewing.

The virtue of such an approach is that it allows the study of both viewing and behavior as they occur naturally. Other factors that might influence either viewing or behavior, or the relationship between them, may be studied at the same time by collecting extra information in the same surveys. For example, researchers can examine whether television violence has different effects on poor children, the friends of those who commit aggression, those who have emotional problems, or those whose parents don't get along.

However, no research design is perfect. The major problem with this kind of study is that it does not require random assignment of individuals to carefully controlled treatments; one cannot be as sure in an experiment that any one causal factor produced whatever change is observed. In order to rule out other things that might have influenced the outcome, the analyst has to see if changes in aggression vary when the other factors are also examined.

There are three major longitudinal panel studies of television and aggression. All of these studies have been either of children or of children and teens. One covers a 20-year time span, from the early 1960's to the early 1980's, while the other two followed children over a 3-year period, from 1970 to 1973 and from 1978 to 1981. Although the three studies differed in some details, they shared many features and reached similar results.

All three found a weak tendency for aggressive children to watch more violent television programs, a "correlation" which—as discussed above—could occur because aggressive children prefer violent programs.

The results from the three studies are ambiguous. In some cases, statistical tests showed small associations between viewing and later aggression, but in most cases they did not. In the two 3-year studies, when factors other than television were taken into account statistically, the relationships between television exposure and aggression either diminished or disappeared.

2. *"Time-series" studies.* Another kind of study, which examines television's effects as they occur in ordinary life, is called a "time-series analysis." These studies take advantage of the social statistics kept by various agencies, such as those on suicides, homicides, and automobile accidents. The study examines whether particular events on television are related to fluctuations within these series of social statistics.

David Phillips has studied what happens to suicide rates after the news media report the suicides of famous people like Marilyn Monroe. He has also attempted to study how suicide rates fluctuate after fictional suicides occur in television soap operas. Other studies have aimed at detecting fluctuations in homicide rates after the death penalty has been administered.

Phillips reported that homicides increase after professional boxing matches and decrease after executions, and that suicides increase after reported suicides of famous people and after fictional suicides have occurred in daytime television soap operas. In several studies, the changes in the social statistics are reported as occurring after a specific short length of time—for instance, exactly 3 days.

The virtue of these sorts of studies is that they involve serious acts of violence and not the playful aggression or other kinds of mild aggression that are usually studied. However, they also have serious drawbacks. First, boxing matches, executions, and suicides in soap operas are rare events, and any mistake can strongly affect one's results. For example, one researcher found two errors in Phillips' study of 22 executions—and these errors reversed the result. Second, other things can happen at about the same time as the events being studied and they can affect the result without being detected. Although the researcher can take as many things as possible into account, it is not possible to take everything into account that may have influenced the statistics.

The topics of Phillips' studies are extremely important. As a result, a number of researchers have attempted to determine if they can reproduce his results, and they have reached different conclusions. It is therefore prudent to wait until other attempts at reproducing Phillips' findings are completed before accepting the remaining studies as conclusive.

No definitive answers have come from other attempts to document the existence of acts in real life that seem to imitate acts depicted on television. One study of 58 incidents of alleged movie-inspired violence, including a number of incidents involving imitation of the Russian roulette scenes in "The Deer Hunter," concluded that no clear evidence of causal links could be found.

Even though most people believe that television influences violent behavior, the scientific evidence is not conclusive. As J.L. Freedman has put it,

> ... the available literature does not support the hypothesis that viewing violence on television

causes an increase in subsequent aggression in the real world. It remains a plausible hypothesis, but one for which there is, as yet, little supporting evidence.

This carefully worded conclusion does not say that television has no effect on violent behavior; it says that we do not yet really know whether it does.

We are dealing with what is at most a small influence of television on behavior that is currently more strongly influenced by a host of other factors. It is not surprising that attempts to isolate television's effects in natural settings do not provide conclusive results.

We cannot be sure that our common belief in television's impact on violence is correct. However, since an effect cannot entirely be ruled out, both those who produce television programs, and those who watch them, must be alert to the possibility of a causal link between violent television and violent behavior.

Discussion Questions

1. Do you think violent television shows cause aggression in young children?
2. If the evidence of a linkage between mass media and violent behavior is inconclusive, why should we worry about the problem?
3. Some people argue that the content of television programs should not be the concern of government, no matter what research shows about its impact on viewers. Do you agree?
4. What is the responsibility of parents in controlling what a child watches on television?
5. Would you favor the establishment of government censorship of violence on television?

References

Comstock, G.A., and E.A. Rubinstein, eds. 1972. *Television and Social Behavior*. Washington, D.C.: U.S. Government Printing Office.

National Institute of Mental Health. 1982. *Television and Behavior: Ten Years of Scientific Progress and Implications for the Eighties*. Washington, D.C.: U.S. Government Printing Office.

Cook, T.R., D.A. Kendzierski, and S.V. Thomas. 1983. "The Implicit Assumptions of Television Research: An Analysis of the 1982 NIMH Report on Television and Behavior." *Public Opinion Quarterly* 47:161–201.

Freedman, J.L. 1984. "Effect of Television Violence on Aggressiveness." *Psychological Bulletin* 96(2):227–346.

Milavsky, J.R., R.C. Kessler, H. Stipp, and W.S. Rubens. 1982. *Television and Aggression: A Panel Study*. New York: Academic Press.

National Institute of Justice   *CRIME FILE*

Jobs and Crime

Richard McGahey, New York University

1988

Paradoxes About Crime and Economic Distress

Many people who are arrested for common street crimes are poor and unemployed, as are most prison inmates. Offenders and prisoners are much more likely to be poor and unemployed than the general population. Poor neighborhoods in American cities have much higher crime rates than wealthier neighborhoods. It may seem logical to conclude that unemployment and poverty are major causes of crime and that crime could be reduced substantially by employment programs.

Are ivory-tower academics debating an issue that everyone else understands? Isn't it obvious that crime is caused by poverty and unemployment? Research and innovative programs during the past 20 years have provided conflicting and disappointing evidence for those who believe in a simple, causal relationship between unemployment and crime.

Consider these paradoxes. During the 1970's, Sun Belt cities had faster rates of economic growth than older cities in the Northwest, but the Sun Belt cities also had higher crime rates. Extremely poor rural areas traditionally have low crime rates. Towns with rapid economic booms, like oil pipeline towns in Alaska or mining towns in Colorado, had rapid increases in crime as their economies grew.

Although unemployment and poverty do not automatically cause crime, it does not necessarily follow that there is no relationship between unemployment and crime. And there are complex reasons why job programs aimed at reducing crime have not had clear crime reduction effects. Much recent research and policy analysis has been devoted to untangling the complexities. Many of these issues are still unresolved, especially those concerning the use of antipoverty and employment programs in a crime fighting strategy.

Reviewing the Evidence and Specifying Relationships

In discussing the relationships between crime and economic distress, it is important to be specific about the type of crime, the type of potential crime, and the specifics of any policy aimed at reducing crime. There has been a substantial amount of research on the relation between unemployment and crime. Some of it analyzes statistics on national crime rates and the business cycle. Some of it focuses on the effects of experiments in which employment opportunities are made available to offenders or ex-prisoners. All of this research provides important sources of information about the relationship between economic conditions and crime; none of it is definitive.

1. *Aggregate studies.* Many studies on crime and the economy have examined aggregate national crime rates and economic indicators such as the unemployment rate. Scholars looking for consistent and reliable connections or correlations between such rates use a variety of complex statistical techniques. Unfortunately, the results are ambiguous. Some researchers find consistent relations between economic distress and crime, but many others have been unable to confirm such findings. Studies vary in the type of data they use, the time periods and geographic areas studied, and the statistical techniques they employ, which makes it hard to compare their findings. But the lack of consistent confirmation of even general trends has caused many

scholars to be skeptical about an automatic relationship between economic distress and criminality.

2. ***Experimental programs.*** A second source of information comes from evaluations of programs that have been organized primarily for the purpose of studying the relations between crime and unemployment. In such programs various target groups, such as ex-offenders, unemployed youth, single parents on welfare, and ex-addicts, are given job experience, training, and support services such as counseling. To make the findings of the studies more reliable, some people are assigned randomly to the program, while others continue their regular street life. The experiences of the two groups are then compared to see if the program has had any discernible effect.

One major Federal program, the "supported work" program of the Manpower Development Research Corporation, had disappointing results in terms of reducing crime for ex-offenders and unemployed youth, and some success with the ex-addict group. Other programs have had similar disappointing results, with the exception of the Job Corps, a program for disadvantaged youth that seems to have reduced crime among its participants. But, as with the aggregate studies, the overall research results have been inconsistent and hard to interpret.

3. ***Studies of individuals.*** These studies are another source of information and have been of two types: statistical studies of ex-offenders, arrestees, and inner city youth; and "ethnographic" field studies, conducted by urban anthropologists, of small groups of "high risk" youth.

The statistical studies do not point to any consistent relationship between unemployment and crime. For certain types of offenders, especially older ones, there may be a direct relationship between crime and unemployment. Inner city youth who have high expectations about potential income from crime report more criminality than those who do not. The ethnographic studies, while not statistical in nature, provide rich detail about the lives of young people in urban areas, and they show a variety of relationships between unemployment and crime.

Part of the problem in trying to link crime and unemployment is that each is a very complicated

subject. Many factors besides the economy can influence crime. Crime patterns may be tied to deterrence from police, courts, and prisons; to differences in families and neighborhoods; and to other unobserved factors. Economic conditions, in turn, are influenced by relationships among international competition, government policy, and personal and structural factors. Sorting out the effects of these many factors is extremely difficult.

4. ***Research: a summary.*** Any broad assertion about *the* relationship between economic distress and crime is likely to be misleading. A critical observer asks which types of crime are at issue. What are the specific effects being proposed and how would they work? What other unobserved factors might cause the same effects? Does the alleged relationship make sense in light of other information that is available?

This may help clarify [Professor] Philip Cook's answer to the question, "Is there any connection between general economic conditions and the crime rate?" His response, "It depends." Some analysts claim that the economy has a consistent, measurable impact on crime; for every percentage point rise in unemployment, crime goes up by some stated percentage.

Such broad claims are not well supported by the findings of empirical research. However, even Professor Cook, who has criticized the broad claims, has found evidence that certain types of crime, notably robbery and burglary, appear to increase during recessions and economic slumps. Cook's work suggests that while economic downturns may have no impact on many crimes—murder, for instance—they may have an influence on the number of burglaries and robberies. Although these findings are tentative, they are based on research that specifies the type of crime in question and provides a focused explanation. Since robbery and burglary are income-oriented crimes, it is plausible that such crimes would be influenced by economic conditions.

Specifying the Questions

A consistent theme emerging from the recent research is the need to narrow the questions being asked and to be specific about the groups being examined. For example, ex-convicts released from prison, often after several years of incarceration, may face a unique set of problems. They may have little job experience, few skills, no money, and weak networks for finding new jobs. (This last factor is important, because most people find jobs through personal contacts, such as relatives or neighbors.) Focused attention might be given to school-age teenagers who are at risk of dropping out of school and often engage in crime.

Since these groups may have different needs, a single program may not work for both. For example, men in their early 20's generally try to establish careers and form families, while teenagers are less likely to be doing so. A full-time employment program that is appropriate for a man in his 20's is likely to have limited impact on a teenager. Since continued schooling may be more helpful for teenagers, some programs concentrate on keeping teenagers in school by linking part-time or vocational employment to continued school attendance.

Programs for teenagers face another problem. Many young people engage in some crime well before they are in the legitimate job market. In 1983, 30.4 percent of persons arrested for major street crimes were under 18 years of age, several years before they would likely enter the legitimate job market in any serious fashion. Economist Paul Osterman of Boston University, an expert on youth unemployment, calls the teenage years an "exploratory" period where labor market behavior is erratic. Youth from poor families, however, still need income, and many seem to get it from crime. Yet it is unlikely that a career-oriented, full-time employment program would have much impact on teenagers under 18 years old.

Learning From Experience— Program Options

All this evidence is being considered by people responsible for public policy, both for the design of anticrime programs and for general debates over economic issues. The question posed by Professor James Q. Wilson— why do employment programs produce such disappointing anticrime results—deserves some consideration. Thinking about the possible reasons can help us reach judgments about what new programs, if any, might help to reduce crime.

The rationale behind most anticrime employment programs is that the programs will improve job prospects for people who will then have less need to resort to crime for income. But if the first step does not occur—if the programs do not reduce unemployment— then we have not really tested the impact of improved jobs on crime. A variety of sometimes conflicting explanations are offered for why most public employment programs have not achieved permanent labor market improvements for many of the poor. Among the reasons: participants' lack of skills and education, scarcity of jobs in inner city neighborhoods, participants' poor work attitudes, racial discrimination, and weak job-finding networks among the poor.

Many analysts agree that previous employment programs may have misjudged the depth of the problems faced by the urban poor. Employment programs that concentrate on the hardest to employ are likely to be very expensive and not very successful. Conversely, those that concentrate on the unemployed who are not "hard core" may cost less and yield greater success but not employ those at greatest risk of crime. Ideally there should be programs for each category of unemployed, but sufficient funds are seldom available for everything that needs doing. Thus programs to combat crime and unemployment face a persistent policy problem—where to concentrate limited public resources.

A related problem has to do with "targeting"— aiming programs at specific groups of people, such as ex-convicts. Targeting can raise equity concerns: why should ex-offenders be given special opportunities that are not available to unemployed people who have not committed crimes? Some policy analysts think that employment programs should not concentrate explicitly on groups like ex-offenders, because the programs would stigmatize the very people they are trying to help. The question here is whether the labor market problems of ex-offenders (or any other target group) are specific enough to justify targeted programs, or whether they are largely due to the same factors that affect most of the urban poor.

Of course, there are more extreme positions. Some argue against all such employment programs, feeling that they undercut initiative. They believe that the work attitudes and values of some of the urban poor are so out of line with mainstream values that any special program is doomed to failure. Such analysts sometimes refer to an urban "underclass" that has different norms and values from the rest of the population. In contrast, others argue that the government has a responsibility to ensure that jobs are available for all who want them. They believe the government should spend more on creating large-scale public jobs, either by diverting funds from other activities or by raising taxes. These positions clearly go well beyond the crime question to matters of basic social policy.

This discussion has not settled, and cannot settle, the broad questions about the relationships between crime and unemployment. Many researchers and policymakers are skeptical about finding any consistent or simple relationship that can guide policy. But we should not forget that many ex-offenders and program administrators believe that employment programs have made a difference.

Earlier efforts to reduce crime through employment programs have had disappointing and partial results. One of the consequences is that proposed policies now cover a wide range of options, including massive public employment, more carefully targeted programs for different groups, and elimination of most, if not all, employment programs with specific anticrime goals. As in many other areas of public debate, research and policy expertise on crime and unemployment can help us clarify the questions but are unlikely to provide the answers.

Discussion Questions

1. Why should there be programs designed to help criminal offenders?

2. Do you think the government should withdraw from job programs and depend on private enterprise to meet the needs of the jobless?

3. Should we pay more attention to the research results which suggest that job programs make little or no difference in the lives of criminals or should we listen instead to people like social workers and former criminals who believe that job programs do make a difference?

4. What are the pros and cons for "targeting" job programs at specific groups of people such as ex-convicts or teenagers?

5. A number of different proposals have been made for reducing teenage unemployment—lowering the minimum wage, providing more part-time work, working through the Job Corps or through mandatory National Service. Do you believe any of these approaches would be likely to reduce crime?

References

Curtis, Lynn A. 1985. "Neighborhood, Family, and Employment: Toward a New Public Policy Against Violence." In *American Violence and Public Policy*, edited by Lynn A. Curtis. New Haven, Conn.: Yale University Press.

Freeman, Richard B. 1983. "Crime and Unemployment." In *Crime and Public Policy*, edited by James Q. Wilson. San Francisco: Institute of Contemporary Studies.

Murray, Charles. 1984. *Losing Ground: American Social Policy, 1950–1980*. New York: Basic Books.

Silberman, Charles. 1978. *Criminal Violence, Criminal Justice*. New York: Random House.

Thompson, James W., et al. 1982. *Employment and Crime: A Review of Theories and Research*. Washington, D.C.: The National Institute of Justice.

Wilson, James Q., and Philip J. Cook. 1985. "Unemployment and Crime—What is the Connection?" *The Public Interest*, Spring (79):3–8.

National Institute of Justice   **CRIME FILE**

Drinking and Crime

Professor James B. Jacobs, New York University

1986

Alcohol Consumption

Alcohol abuse is one of the Nation's gravest health and social problems. It is also one of its most serious crime problems. According to Harvard psychiatrist Dr. George Vaillant, 10 to 15 percent of the male population at some point in their lives consume eight or more alcoholic drinks daily. A small percentage of this group continue at this level for a lifetime; about half revert to controlled drinking or achieve stable abstinence; a quarter deteriorate to chronic alcohol dependence, unable to quit drinking without suffering withdrawal symptoms and eventually needing detoxification. This last stage is reached by 3 to 5 percent of American adults, with men outnumbering women by three or four to one.

Alcoholics are not the whole problem. Even if all alcoholics were suddenly cured, there would still be a serious alcohol problem in the United States. Many "social drinkers" cause accidents, lose time from work, cause problems for their families and friends, and commit crimes while intoxicated. Binge drinkers may be abstinent or drink moderately for long periods and then drink excessively for short periods, during which they may be extremely dangerous to themselves and others.

The consumption of alcoholic beverages is a major part of our culture. Drinking is a social custom in contexts as diverse as christenings and wakes, business lunches and fraternity parties, ball games and New Year's parties, teenage dating and fine dining. The powerful alcoholic beverage industry aggressively markets its products. Television and movie heroes and heroines continually reinforce the impression that hard drinking is associated with glamour, romance, excitement, and success. (The next time you watch television, count the number of drinking episodes in an hour of programs and observe the kinds of images that are associated with drinking.)

While statistical data on changes in alcohol consumption over time are of questionable reliability, it appears that since World War II more Americans drink and more drink excessively. (However, approximately 30 percent of the population are abstainers.) Alarmingly, there are strong signs of a growing alcohol problem among our Nation's youth, even among adolescents. A 1981 survey revealed that 93 percent of high school seniors had at least tried alcoholic beverages, 71 percent reported use within the past month, and 41 percent reported binge drinking (five or more drinks on a single occasion) within the past 14 days. It has been estimated that between one-third and one-half of the young people in the United States become intoxicated once every 14 days.

Drinking and Crime

There is a close relationship between alcohol and crime, and there is good reason to believe that consumption of alcohol causes crime. The most obvious crimes in which alcohol plays a role are drunk driving and public drunkenness, but alcohol is also a factor in large percentages of violent crime and intrafamily crime.

1. *Drunk driving.* On late weekend nights, perhaps 5 to 10 percent of drivers are under the influence of alcohol; many are also under the influence of other drugs. A driver with a blood alcohol level of .15 (approximately 8–10 drinks) is 18 times more likely to have a traffic accident than is a sober driver. It is estimated that drunk drivers are responsible for approximately half of the 45,000 traffic deaths each year. About 60 percent of those killed are the drunk drivers themselves. They also kill approximately 9,000 pedestrians, bicyclists, motorcyclists, vehicle drivers, and passengers each

year. There are in addition hundreds of thousands of serious injuries annually. These statistics should place drunk driving at the top of the list of serious crimes.

In the last decade the Nation has seemingly awakened to the enormous destruction that drunk drivers wreak on us, due in large part to the extraordinary efforts of anti-drunk-driving pressure groups like Mothers Against Drunk Drivers (MADD) and Remove Intoxicated Drivers (RID). State legislatures have enacted hundreds of new laws making prosecution easier, limiting plea bargaining, increasing fines, expediting license revocations, and mandating short jail terms. In most States it is now a crime to drive with a blood alcohol concentration of .10 percent or greater. (In many European countries the limit is .05 percent.) The police have greatly increased their enforcement efforts; many departments have set up drunk driving roadblocks, "sobriety checkpoints," where every driver is stopped for a cursory inspection for signs of intoxication. Some new programs encourage citizens to phone in sightings of drunk drivers to special anti-drunk-driving task force operators.

The magnitude of drunk driving offending and enforcement is staggering. There are approximately 2 million drunk driving arrests annually, more arrests than for any other offense for which national data are compiled. Drunk driving is the most common crime prosecuted in many of our criminal courts, and drunk drivers are the largest category of probationers. Millions of drunk drivers have passed through special "DWI schools" in the last decade. Drunk drivers constitute an increasing percentage of the jail population, and some local communities have had to build, purchase, or lease special jails just for drunk drivers. Many States have anti-drunk-driving programs to coordinate all enforcement, treatment, and public education efforts. It is too soon to tell whether all of these initiatives can significantly reduce the amount of offending.

2. *Public drunkenness.* Public drunkenness is another drinking offense. In the late 1960's and early 1970's there was a major movement to decriminalize public drunkenness and to deal with public drunks as a public health problem. In many areas, this meant not dealing with them at all. The nationwide number of arrests for public drunkenness has dramatically decreased. Of course, the police still retain the option, in certain cases, of arresting public drunks for disturbing the peace or for disorderly conduct.

Since the mid-1970's the move to decriminalize public drunkenness has slowed down. Some criminologists have begun to rethink the wisdom of decriminalization, pointing to its negative effects on the quality of community life. The presence on the streets of boisterous, obstreperous, and sometimes belligerent drunks contributes to a sense of social disorder. The question is whether treating public drunkenness as a crime has any significant effect other than to clog our courts and crowd our jails. Decriminalization was probably motivated as much by the desire to save money and allocate police resources to higher priority activities as by any concern for the rights of drunks.

3. *Violent crimes.* Alcohol also plays a major role in violent crime. In Marvin Wolfgang's classic study of homicide in Philadelphia, he found that the killer, the victim, or both were drunk in more than half the cases. That finding seems also to apply to rapes. Needless to say, many aggravated assaults involve alcohol; indeed, a large number occur in taverns or among drinking companions. Alcohol also plays a prominent role in crimes within the family. A high percentage of wife beatings, child abuse, and child sexual abuse are committed by men who are drunk. Recent research sponsored by the National Institute of Justice found that a majority of new prison inmates had severe alcohol problems.

Alcohol as a Cause of Crime

That so large a percentage of perpetrators of serious crimes drink heavily beforehand does not prove that alcohol causes crime. People may first decide to commit their crimes and then get drunk to muster courage or allay fears. For some violent offenders heavy drinking *and* savage behavior are both symptoms of deep psychological problems. Still, the relationship between drinking and violence is not subtle or difficult to understand. It is common knowledge and scientifically demonstrable that alcohol releases inhibitions and distorts judgment. The "fighting drunk" is a regular member of tavern culture and can easily be recognized at fraternity parties. Even sedate cocktail parties produce a few belligerent if not violent drinkers.

Our criminal jurisprudence has difficulty dealing with intoxication. The fundamental problem is in deciding whether intoxication should aggravate, mitigate, or have no effect on guilt, blameworthiness, and punishment. It is a foundation of our criminal jurisprudence that for a person to be guilty of a crime he must have a *mens rea*, a guilty mind. This means that for most serious crimes the prosecutor must prove that the defendant acted intentionally, knowingly, or recklessly. How does the defendant's drunkenness bear upon his guilt? The answer supplied by the *Model Penal Code*, and the many State criminal codes patterned after it, is that voluntary intoxication is admissible to rebut criminal intent or knowledge but not recklessness. This means that extreme drunkenness can mitigate the degree of the offense, but it cannot eliminate all criminal responsibility. At the sentencing stage of a criminal case, a judge may well regard drunkenness at the time of the crime as a mitigating factor, despite the empirical reality that alcohol is associated with so much violent behavior.

What Can Be Done?

Despite massive efforts by the medical and mental health communities led by the National Institute on Alcohol Abuse and Alcoholism, there are no certain cures for alcoholism. The rate of cure from inpatient programs seems no better than from less expensive outpatient programs. A great percentage of alcoholics who are cured are aided by Alcoholics Anonymous. Some psychiatrists disdain the effort of curing alcoholism in favor of dealing with "underlying pathologies." Other doctors regard alcoholism as a disease—possibly one with an element of genetic predisposition—which causes myriad health, psychological, and interpersonal problems. There is less attention and there are few programs to deal with binge drinking and alcohol abuse and dependencies short of alcoholism. The need for alcohol abuse treatment and counseling is not being met, especially in jails and prisons.

Americans have been exhorted to drink moderately since the beginning of the Republic, and such exhortations are common today. The media are filled with warnings against excessive drinking, especially drinking and driving. Still, human nature and a cultural and social system that promotes alcohol consumption make it unlikely that, in the short run, public education can reduce the amount of excessive and pathological drinking. If, as a society, we want the pleasures and benefits of abundant alcoholic beverages, it seems we must also absorb a very heavy cost.

What is the alternative? The Nation's experience with prohibition was not happy and left us with a strong belief that prohibition cannot work. The validity of this belief appears to be borne out by our lack of success in preventing people from purchasing illicit drugs such as marijuana and cocaine, which are far less established than alcohol. Perhaps there are public policies short of prohibition that could reduce alcohol abuse either through prevention or treatment. For example, spurred by the movement against drunk driving, Congress recently passed a law that encourages States to raise their minimum drinking age to 21 or face the loss of Federal highway funds. Many States have rapidly fallen into line. The evidence suggests that a higher minimum age will reduce teenage alcohol consumption and highway fatalities.

Some people believe that alcohol advertising should be removed from television. Others advocate increasing the tax on alcoholic beverages to decrease consumption. Still others would establish earlier closing hours for taverns, ban "happy hours," and impose civil liability on tavern owners when their drunk customers injure themselves or innocent third parties. Naturally, these proposals are strongly resisted by the alcoholic beverage industry, by tavern associations, and probably by a majority of the public, which consists of tens of millions of people who find alcohol consumption a major pleasure in life and who themselves drink responsibly.

Discussion Questions

1. Should people who commit crimes while intoxicated be dealt with more or less harshly than people who commit crimes while sober?

2. Does a solution for drunk driving depend upon a solution for alcohol abuse?

3. What should be done with a social drinker—who is not an alcoholic and who is ordinarily careful not to drink and drive—who does drive after drinking and kills a pedestrian?

4. How should public drunkenness be handled?

5. Should laws be passed—such as increases in the drinking age, increases in taxes on alcohol, or bans on "happy hours"—with the aim of discouraging alcohol consumption?

6. Should drunk drivers be jailed? If so, for how long?

References

Beauchamp, D.E. 1980. Beyond Alcoholism: Alcohol and Public Health Policy. Philadelphia: Temple University Press.

Bureau of Justice Statistics. 1983. Prisoners and Alcohol. Washington, D.C.: National Institute of Justice.

Gusfield, Joseph. 1963. Symbolic Crusade: Status Politics and the American Temperance Movement. Urbana: University of Illinois Press.

Moore, Mark, and Dean Gerstein. 1983. Alcohol and Public Policy: Beyond the Shadow of Prohibition. Washington, D.C.: National Academy Press.

President's Commission on Law Enforcement and Administration of Justice. 1967. Task Force Report: Drunkenness. Washington, D.C.: U.S. Government Printing Office.

President's Commission on Drunk Driving. 1983. Final Report. Washington, D.C.: U.S. Government Printing Office.

Ross, H. Laurence. 1982. Deterring the Drinking Driver: Legal Policy and Social Control. Lexington, Massachusetts: Lexington Books.

Vaillant, George. 1983. The Natural History of Alcoholism. Cambridge: Harvard University Press.

National Institute of Justice

CRIME FILE

Gun Control

Franklin E. Zimring, University of California at Berkeley

1986

Firearms and Violence

Americans own a greater number and variety of firearms than do the citizens of any other Western democracy, and they also use their guns against one another much more often. This special significance of firearms in American life has led to a protracted and acrimonious conflict about gun control. Gun control laws in the United States have not achieved the levels of public safety that their supporters had hoped for. Firearms continue to multiply, and deaths from guns have increased since the early 1960's to roughly 30,000 per year. From the failure of existing gun control laws, opponents conclude that controls cannot work, while proponents declare that existing laws must be better enforced or different kinds of controls tried.

The central task of firearms controls through public law is to reduce the hundreds of thousands of occasions each year when guns are used illegitimately without unduly disrupting the millions of occasions when guns are used legitimately—including hunting, target sports, self-defense, and collecting. A perfect gun control law would eliminate the unlawful use of guns and leave all legitimate users undisturbed. Real world choices involve harder tradeoffs.

What exactly is the "gun problem"? Advocates of control begin by pointing out that more than 20 percent of all robberies and about 60 percent of all homicides are committed with firearms. Their opponents reply that the vast majority of the country's 130 million firearms are not involved in violence, and that crime rather than firearms is the real problem. "Guns don't kill people," they assert, "people kill people."

Serious assault with a gun is, according to the best estimates, three to five times as likely to cause death as a similar attack with a knife, the next most dangerous weapon. And gun robberies are three to four times as likely to result in the death of a victim as are other kinds of robbery.

Firearms are often discussed as a general category, without distinguishing among handguns, rifles, and shotguns. In some respects that approach is appropriate because a rifle or a shotgun, if used in an attack, is at least as dangerous as a handgun. Even a superficial study of statistics on firearms and violence, however, suggests that the handgun presents special problems. The handgun—small, easy to conceal, and relatively unimportant in hunting—accounts for about one-fourth of the privately owned firearms in the country, but it is involved in three-fourths of all gun killings. In the big cities, handguns account for more than 80 percent of gun killings and virtually all gun robberies.

Even though the most common reason for owning a handgun is for household self-defense, studies suggest that loaded household handguns are more likely to kill family members than to save their lives. A Detroit study found that more people died in 1 year from handgun accidents alone than were killed by home-invading robbers or burglars in 4 1/2 years. The discovery that self-defense handguns are from this standpoint a poor investment suggests that rejecting handgun ownership makes sense from a safety perspective, even if other families retain their guns. But if unilateral disarmament is rational, why do people not give up their guns voluntarily, and why do handguns continue to proliferate in the cities?

To some extent, urban gun ownership for self-defense results from misinformation about the risk of accidental death and the usefulness of guns in defense of the home. However, it is foolish to think that millions of American families keep handguns merely because they have not read the statistics, or to suppose that showing them data will change their minds. The risk of accidental or homicidal death from a loaded gun in the home—although greater than the chance that the gun will save lives—is nevertheless small. In the majority of homes with handguns, the only real use of the gun may be to make its owner feel safer. People will reject statistics that show otherwise because, even if their guns do not give them any real measure of protection, they have no other way to deal with their fears.

Gun Control Strategies

Simply because the problems are real does not mean that the solutions are easy. Indeed, the extent of the gun problem in the United States should be a warning that reducing gun violence will be difficult and expensive. There are already more than 20,000 gun laws in the Nation to match the thousands of gun killings. Why should gun laws decrease the rate of criminal killings when criminals, by definition, do not obey laws?

A number of different types of gun control strategies have been attempted and proposed. How are these various laws supposed to work, and is it likely that they will?

1. *Place and manner restrictions.* Most of the gun laws in the United States attempt to separate illegitimate from legitimate gun use by regulating the "place and manner" in which firearms may be used. They prohibit the carrying of firearms within city limits or in a motor vehicle, the carrying of concealed weapons on one's person, or the discharging of a firearm in a populated area. Such laws attempt to reduce firearm violence by authorizing the police to intervene before violence or crime actually takes place. Since there are obvious limits to the ability of police to prevent firearm violence and to discover persons who violate place and manner laws, these laws may deter at most a limited amount of gun violence.

2. *Stiffer penalties for firearm violence.* Members of the National Rifle Association have been among the most vocal supporters of laws that increase prison sentences, or make them mandatory, for persons committing crimes with guns. Such laws do not make it harder for potential criminals, or anyone else, to obtain guns, but they are intended to reduce gun crime by making punishments for crimes with guns so severe that potential criminals either will commit the crime without a gun or will not commit the crime at all. More than half of the States

have laws providing for longer sentences for criminals who carry or use a gun while committing a felony.

In order to reduce the number of gun crimes, such laws would have to deter persons who would not be deterred by the already stiff penalties for gun crimes. Can the threat of additional punishment succeed? Perhaps the robber could be deterred from using a gun if the punishment for gun robbery were several times greater than that for nongun robbery.

The issue is especially complicated for the crime of gun assault, that is, actual shootings; he who attacks with a gun is already risking the law's maximum punishment if his victim dies. How much additional deterrence can come from lesser mandatory penalties for nonfatal attacks? Proponents of this approach suggest that the apparently severe penalties for crime are misleading; in reality light punishments are often given. Of course, the same thing can happen with mandatory sentences; one way or another they may not be imposed.

There may be some hope of reducing gun crime by increasing the gap between the penalty for that crime and the penalty for other crimes. At the same time, there is reason to doubt that such a program will have a major effect on the rates of gun killings and assaults.

3. *Prohibiting high-risk groups from owning guns.* Another strategy is to forbid certain high-risk groups from owning firearms. The groups usually covered include those with serious criminal records, the very young, alcoholics, drug addicts, and mental patients. Nearly every State and the Federal Government prohibit some type of high-risk ownership. However, many of these laws do not require proof of eligibility to own a gun before purchase. Instead, the ineligible person will be subject to criminal penalties if caught possessing a firearm. If such laws could reduce the number of guns owned by people subject to the prohibition, they would indeed reduce gun violence. But enforcing such laws is neither easy nor effective. It is not *easy* because, by not requiring purchasers to prove that they are not in the prohibited class, the law is still trying to use the threat of future punishment as a substitute for making it more difficult for high-risk groups to obtain guns. It is not *effective* since most homicides are committed by persons who would qualify for ownership under any pro-

hibition that operated on only a minority of the population.

4. **Permissive licensing.** Many States try to enforce the ban on gun ownership by high-risk groups by requiring people to qualify themselves before they can buy guns. This type of restriction takes one of two forms: a license to buy a gun, or an application to purchase coupled with a waiting period. Permissive licensing is thought to be an advantage over a simple ban on ownership because it makes persons prove that they are eligible to own a gun before they can obtain a license. Such a system does not depend solely on the prudence of the people barred from ownership because they are not thought to be good risks. However, adoption of such a system is also precisely where opponents of gun control draw the line because licensing imposes costs and inconveniences on all gun owners.

Finding appropriate gun control strategies also involves constitutional considerations and the balance between Federal and State responsibility for crime control. The second amendment to the United States Constitution provides for a right of the people to bear arms, and many State constitutions contain similar provisions. While there is dispute as to what that provision of the second amendment means, it has never been held to invalidate Federal or State gun control legislation. Nonetheless, the "right to bear arms" is frequently invoked as a reason to avoid restrictions on legitimate gun ownership and use.

Would licensing work, assuming that the opponents could be outvoted? Like ownership prohibitions, it would not prevent the majority of gun killings, which are committed by persons who would qualify for ownership. But would it at least keep guns from high-risk groups?

The problem with permissive licensing is that it leaves some 35 million handguns in circulation. Half of all the handguns in the United States are acquired secondhand, and most of these are purchased from private parties, who may not ask to see licenses. Moreover, there are 35 million handguns available to steal. In short, it is extraordinarily difficult to let the "good guys" have all the firearms they want and at the same time to keep the "bad guys" unarmed. It does not appear that States with permissive licensing systems made much progress in reducing gun violence during the years when the Federal Government failed to control interstate

traffic in most firearms. With stronger Federal aid, the potential of such laws is still limited, but it is not known how limited.

5. **Registration.** Under registration laws, every gun is registered as the property of a particular licensed owner. Several States and cities have such laws, often coupled with other types of gun controls. Gun registration thus usually requires owners to provide information about the guns they own, in addition to the information about themselves that is required to obtain a license. An analogy to the registration system for automobiles is often drawn by supporters of such controls.

The best argument against registration is clearly its cost, but the debate centers on the purpose of registration. If criminals—who, it must be remembered, do not obey the law—fail to register their guns, how can registration possibly reduce gun crime? The answer usually offered is that registration is designed only as a support to any system that seeks to allow some people, but not others, to own guns. If such a system is to prove workable, then some method must be found to keep guns where they are permitted by making each legitimate gun owner responsible for each gun he owns. After all, some of the "good guys" would otherwise transfer guns through the second-hand market to "bad guys" and thus frustrate permissive licensing systems. If registration helped to keep the "good guys" good, it could help prevent gun violence, even if not a single criminal were polite enough to register his gun.

It is also possible that gun registration will deter the qualified owner from misusing his gun since it can be traced to him; yet no one is quite sure how much deterrence would result. All in all, it is difficult to estimate how much additional prevention a licensing system obtains by requiring registration, but it seems self-defeating not to require registration of some kind in any system that seeks to bar certain groups from gun ownership.

6. **Cutting down on the handgun.** The most extreme solution to firearms violence is to reduce substantially the number of handguns owned by civilians. Under this proposal, no one would be permitted to own a handgun unless he had a special need for it. Two approaches have been enacted: restrictive licensing and handgun bans. Under restrictive licensing, persons who want to own a gun must establish their need for one before they can receive

a license. Under a handgun ban, certain classes of persons (for example, police officers and members of gun clubs) are exempted from the operation of the law. Thus, a handgun ban is not necessarily a more restrictive control than restrictive licensing: whether it is depends on the classes allowed to possess guns. Moreover, handgun bans usually exert no direct control over those who are exempt from its coverage, whereas a restrictive licensing system licenses those who would probably be exempted under a ban. A significant minority of American cities have experimented with either restrictive licensing or handgun bans.

Many gun owners doubt that such plans will work because "when guns are criminal, only criminals will have guns." Moreover, they argue, if handguns are illegal, criminals will switch to other kinds of guns, a development that will not reduce gun crime but will spur efforts to confiscate all kinds of civilian firearms.

Both of these arguments have some force, but they must be balanced against important facts about the relationship between guns and violence in the United States. First, guns are more lethal than other weapons. Thus, substantially reducing the number of handguns should reduce the number of homicides resulting from accidental weapon use and the use of a weapon to settle an argument, even though some criminals will undoubtedly continue to use handguns. Second, it appears to be harder than one might suspect for the handgun robber or attacker to switch to a rifle or other "long" gun. For this reason, the average handgun is many times more likely to kill than the average long gun. States that try to restrict handguns find that their major problem becomes not the long gun but the illegal handgun.

The real difficulty in restricting the handgun is how to reduce the number of such guns in circulation enough to make headway against gun violence, and, if it can be done, how long this will take and what its cost will be. It is possible, by law, to put a stop to the manufacture of handguns at any time, but even if this were done, some of the 35 million handguns in the civilian inventory would still be killing people in the 21st century. Under the best conditions, collecting the vast arsenal of civilian handguns would be neither easy nor swift. Americans do not live under the best of conditions—the very crime rate that makes many people want gun control also makes gun control extremely difficult

to achieve. How many citizens would turn in their guns when the law took effect? How long would it take to remove the guns from the streets, where they do the most harm? Should urban households be left fearfully defenseless? Is it desirable to add yet another victimless and unenforceable crime— possession of a handgun—to the depressingly long list of such crimes that have already accumulated? These are not easy questions to answer.

Finding appropriate gun control strategies also involves constitutional considerations and the balance between Federal and State responsibility for crime control. The second amendment to the United States Constitution provides for a right of the people to bear arms, and many State constitutions contain similar provisions. While there is dispute as to what that provision of the second amendment means, it has never been held to invalidate Federal or State gun control legislation. Nonetheless, the "right to bear arms" is frequently invoked as a reason to avoid restrictions on legitimate gun ownership and use.

The traditional division of authority for crime control between the Federal Government and the States also limits the extent of Federal involvement in gun control. Street police work is the province of local government in the United States. Gun control laws that require police enforcement must be carried out by municipal police.

But whatever gun control strategies are tried, it seems that local initiatives must have State and national support if they hope to achieve their goals. When jurisdictions pass strict laws against certain kinds of gun sales and resales, guns leak in from other jurisdictions that do not have the same controls. Moreover, the existing Federal law designed to assist States and localities has not been adequately enforced. Any gun control policy will be something of an experiment in the coming years. It is not known how effective any law can be when there are so many guns in circulation and so much pressure to keep them there.

Discussion Questions

1. Why are rates of gun ownership and criminal use of guns higher in the United States than in other Western countries?

2. If handguns were outlawed, would firearm violence decrease?

3. Which would be the most effective way to control the illegal use of guns:

a. by imposing stiffer penalties for firearm violence;

b. by denying guns to high risk groups; or

c. by increasing control of ownership by licensing or registration?

4. Would you support a ban on handguns? Why? Why not?

References

Cook, Philip. 1983. "The Influence of Gun Availability on Violent Crime Patterns." In *Crime and Justice: An Annual Review of Research,* vol. 4, edited by Michael Tonry and Norval Morris. Chicago, Illinois: The University of Chicago Press.

Newton, George D., Jr., and Franklin E. Zimring. 1969. *Firearms and Violence in American Life: A Staff Report Submitted to the National Commission on the Causes and Prevention of Violence.* Washington, D.C.: National Commission on the Causes and Prevention of Violence.

Wright, James D., Peter H. Rossi, and Kathleen Daly. 1983. *Under the Gun: Weapons, Crime, and Violence in America.* New York: Aldine Publishing Company.

Victims and Victimization

Introduction

One of the most significant recent developments in the criminal justice system is concern for the victims of crime. Within the past two decades, a great deal of interest has been devoted to the financial problems, mental stress, and physical hardship suffered by crime victims. Assisting the victim in dealing with these problems has become the responsibility of society and, specifically, the criminal justice system. Law enforcement agencies, courts, and correctional systems have come to realize that due process and human rights exist both for the defendant and for the victim of criminal behavior.

Beginning in the mid-1960s the Department of Justice conducted crime victim surveys that found that more crime existed than was originally thought because many victims were reluctant to report crime to the police. In addition, these surveys found that victims of crime had negative attitudes as a result of insensitive treatment received in the criminal justice process. Consequently, the Department of Justice provided research funds for victim-witness programs, which identified the needs of victims and witnesses who were involved in a criminal incident.

Because of public concern over violent personal crime, then President Ronald Reagan created a Task Force on Victims of Crime in 1982. This group was to undertake an extensive study on crime victimization in America and determine how victims of crime could be given assistance. It found that crime victims had been burdened by a justice system that had been originally designed for their protection. While their roles as victims and/or witnesses were often overlooked, the criminal defendant's rights and needs were a focal point of legal attention. The task force suggested that a balance be achieved between recognition of the rights of the victim and provision for due process for the defendant. Its most significant recommendation was that the Sixth Amendment to the Constitution be augmented by this statement: "In every criminal prosecution, the victim shall have the right to be present and to be heard at all critical stages of the judicial proceedings." Other recommendations included providing for protection of witnesses and victims from intimidation, requiring restitution in criminal cases, developing guidelines for fair treatment of crime victims and witnesses, and expanding programs of victim compensation.

One of the primary concerns of victim advocates has been for victim compensation programs created by state legislation; forty-four states, the District of Columbia, and the Virgin Islands have enacted victim compensation programs. The 1984 Federal Victims of Crime Act provides federal grants to assist states that have developed compensation programs. As a result of such legislation, the victim ordinarily receives compensation from the state to pay for damages, medical treatment, and social services associated with the crime. Rarely are two compensation schemes alike, however, and many state programs suffer from lack of adequate funding and proper organization within the criminal justice system. The victim assistance projects that have been developed, however, also seek to help the victim learn about victim compensation services and related programs.

In addition to victim compensation and victim service programs, some states have passed laws that assure victims basic services within the criminal justice system. Just as the offender has the right to counsel and a fair trial, so society also has the obligation to ensure basic rights for law-abiding citizens. These rights range from adequate protection under the law from violent crimes to victim compensation and notice so that victims can participate in various stages in the case against the accused offender.

The research reports in this section reflect some of the most important current efforts to help the victims of crime. First, papers by Peter Finn and Robert C. Davis discuss the general problem of crime victimization and how the criminal justice system is attempting to provide victims with aid and assistance. Then Peter Finn and Beverly N.W. Lee report on the current state of victim assistance programs and how their capacity is being strained by the need to help the victims of domestic violence and sexual assault. James Garofalo and Maureen McLeod discuss how Neighborhood Watch programs have been organized to reduce the probability of victimization, and Peter Finn reports on the success of a block watch program initiated in Philadelphia. Finally, Kenneth R. Freeman and Terry Estrada-Mullaney report on their research on one of the most disturbing aspects of victimization, child sexual abuse, and how attorneys are using anatomically correct dolls to obtain evidence in court.

National Institute of Justice / CRIME FILE

Victims

Peter Finn, Abt Associates, Inc.

1986

Being a Crime Victim

There were an estimated 40 million victimizations in 1983, ranging from stolen cars to murder. In 1982, an estimated 3.2 percent of the Nation's population were victims of rape, robbery, or assault—the equivalent of about 6 million Americans. Nearly 1 of every 12 males aged 16 to 19 is the victim of a violent crime each year.

Most crime victims experience physical suffering, financial loss, or emotional distress. Physical injuries occur in nearly one-third of all violent crimes. Financial losses include destruction of property, loss of money and other valuables, loss of income, medical expenses, and rehabilitation costs. Victims may also feel obliged to incur substantial expenses in self-defense—as by installing burglar alarm systems.

Emotional distress, often the most important consequence of victimization, can include feelings of fear, anger, shame, self-blame, helplessness, and depression. Sometimes long-term emotional disabilities also result—including sleeplessness, loss of concentration, and fear of being left alone.

Crime victims often receive insensitive or callous treatment from the criminal justice system:

- There may be insensitive questioning.
- There may be innuendos that the victim was somehow at fault. (There is a dilemma here—often the police do not know who was at fault and whether the apparent victim was the aggressor or somehow provoked the offender; aggressive questioning may be a necessary investigative technique.)
- The victim may have difficulty learning what is happening with the case.
- Property may be kept as evidence for a long time or may never be returned.
- Wages may be lost for time spent testifying in court.

- Time may be wasted as victims appear for court proceedings only to have the case postponed or dismissed.
- Victims may experience indifference to their fear of retaliation if they cooperate with the authorities.
- Victims may be anxious about testifying in open court and fearful of being questioned by defense attorneys.

Rising Concern for Victims and Witnesses of Crime

Concern for victims and witnesses has been increasingly expressed within the criminal justice system and by various advocacy groups.

A large proportion of crimes are never reported, and this may result partly from victims' dread of "getting involved." Many victims and witnesses refuse to testify because of the inconvenience or distress they may experience or because they are afraid they will suffer reprisals from the defendant. As a result, cases are dismissed for lack of "prosecutability." Yet the probability of conviction increases markedly with the number of available witnesses. Failure to address a victim's personal problems stemming from the crime may reduce the quality of the evidence the victim provides to investigating officers—an alarming consideration when the single most important determinant of whether a case will be solved may be information supplied by the victim.

Thus, it is not without reason that "the most important person in the criminal justice system may not be the judge, police officer, or prosecutor—it may be the victim."

Several special interest groups have become troubled by the psychological and financial burdens that crime imposes on its victims. Women's groups particularly are concerned about the double trauma of rape victims, who are first assaulted by the rapist and then are often handled insensitively by the criminal justice system. In 1975 and 1976, social service providers and criminal justice personnel organized a National Organization for Victims Assistance (NOVA) to promote a victim-oriented perspective in the administration of criminal justice.

Advocacy groups do not seek to reduce the protection afforded the defendant by the courts, nor do they attempt to pressure law enforcement officers, prosecutors, and judges to "bend the rules." Rather, they work to improve the treatment of victims and witnesses in order to create a balance between the consideration shown to them and the attention paid to defendants.

Government Efforts To Improve Treatment of Victims

The need to improve how victims are treated has led to a number of significant actions on the part of both the Federal Government and most State legislatures.

Two pieces of Federal legislation and a presidential task force have played major roles in drawing attention to the suffering of victims and witnesses and the need to alleviate their stress. The Federal Victim and Witness Protection Act of 1982 is designed to protect and assist victims and witnesses of *Federal* offenses by (1) making it a felony to threaten or intimidate a victim or witness, (2) providing for inclusion of a victim impact statement in presentence reports, (3) furnishing explicit authority for Federal trial courts to order offenders to make restitution to victims, and (4) requiring judges to state on the record the reasons for not ordering restitution. The legislation directs the Federal Government to exercise a leadership role in the victim-witness movement and to provide a model for legislation for State and local governments.

The Attorney General has required all U.S. Attorneys' offices and investigative agencies (like the FBI) to designate or employ a victim-witness coordinator to ensure that victims and witnesses are furnished a list of specific services, ranging from providing victims the opportunity to address the court at the time of sentencing to providing a waiting area separate from that of the defendant and defense witnesses.

In 1982, the President appointed a special Task Force on Victims of Crime. After hearing testimony from almost 200 witnesses, including some 60 victims, the Task Force proposed the most comprehensive and detailed recommendations yet issued for action at the Federal, State, local, and private levels to assist victims and witnesses of crime. By taking a leadership role and increasing public awareness of the problem, the Task Force added to the gathering momentum of the victims' movement.

A second piece of Federal legislation, the Victims of Crime Act of 1984, established a Crime Victims Fund of up to $100 million a year, consisting of fines collected from persons convicted of Federal offenses. The Act directs the Attorney General to make grants to States for victim compensation programs and authorizes funding to States for service programs to assist crime victims.

States, too, through a wide variety of statutes, have increasingly taken an active role in furthering the interests and rights of victims. State activity is likely to continue to expand rapidly.

Thus far, the most commonly enacted form of State legislation—passed in at least 38 States—has established programs of compensation to victims of violent crime. To be eligible, victims must have reported the crime and have cooperated with the investigation and prosecution. However, the victim is eligible for compensation whether or not there has been an arrest. Criteria for eligibility commonly include:
■ Residence in the State.
■ Demonstration of financial hardship.
■ Use of a deductible (like private insurance).
■ Minimum financial loss.
■ Not being related to or living with the offender.

Victim compensation programs have not accomplished all that their proponents hoped. There may be long delays in receiving compensation awards, and a great deal of paperwork and red tape are typically involved.

Compensation is generally provided for unreimbursed medical expenses, funeral expenses, loss of earnings, and support of dependents of deceased victims. Property loss is not reimbursed. Only a few States provide compensation for psychotherapy. Most laws set a ceiling on the amount a victim can recover, generally in the range of $10,000 to $15,000.

Legislation in some States also provides for one or more of the following additional services:
■ *Victim notification*—notifying victims of the status of court proceedings such as plea negotiations, sentencing, and parole decisions.

- **Victim impact statements**—informing the sentencing judge of the physical, financial, and emotional impact of the crime on the victim or the victim's survivors.
- **Restitution**—providing for restitution as a court-imposed sanction on convicted offenders. As a condition of probation or in addition to jail, the offender can be ordered to compensate the victim for injury or loss caused by the offense. While most State laws explicitly authorize restitution at the judge's discretion, a few laws make restitution mandatory in certain cases or require a judge to state the reasons for not ordering restitution. Enforcing restitution orders is often difficult when the defendant is poor or defies court-ordered restitution.
- **Protection against intimidation**—protecting victims and witnesses from intimidation. Intimidation of victims and witnesses has long been a widespread problem. This legislation makes it a crime to engage in intimidation and also authorizes criminal courts to issue protective orders forbidding defendants from communicating with or even coming near witnesses.

Other State laws designed to recognize victims' needs include provision for the expeditious return of victims' property seized as evidence, the protection of victims' and witnesses' jobs while they are participating in criminal proceedings, increased witness fees, and passage of criminal laws that authorize enhanced penalties for crimes against victims who are felt to be especially vulnerable—such as the elderly, spouses, children, victims of sexual assault, the handicapped, and even law enforcement officers.

While laudable on paper and a major sign of progress, many of these laws require the full cooperation of the criminal justice system and close monitoring by advocacy groups and individual victims and witnesses if they are to be properly carried out.

Victim-Witness Assistance Programs

In 1974, the Law Enforcement Assistance Administration (LEAA) funded eight victim-witness assistance programs through the National District Attorneys Association. Eventually, LEAA contributed $50 million to victim-witness programs nationwide. Since then, victim assistance programs have proliferated. Today there

are an estimated 1,000 to 2,000 programs. The National District Attorneys Association, the American Bar Association, and the National Judicial College have gone on record supporting the development of such programs. The Presidential Task Force concluded that "the only way of ensuring that the needs of victims and witnesses are met is to have a separate unit dedicated to their assistance." The Task Force recommended that each prosecutor's office establish and maintain direct liaison with victim-witness units and other victim service agencies, noting that prosecutors "will profit from better cooperation of a victim who feels he has been protected and assisted."

Within the criminal justice system, prosecutors' offices are the most common sponsors of victim-witness programs, though a number of law enforcement agencies and community-based organizations have also established programs that provide many of the same services. Of 25 programs contacted in one study, more than 80 percent provided the following services:

- **Personal advocacy**—acting on behalf of victims or witnesses to ensure that they receive appropriate handling by social service agencies and the criminal justice system.
- **Referral**—recommending or obtaining other sources of assistance not provided directly by the program.
- **Restitution**—working with prosecutors to urge judges to order or probation authorities to collect restitution; helping fill out application forms for victims of violent crime to receive compensation in States that have this program.
- **Court orientation**—providing information on the criminal justice system and the victim's or witness' responsibilities in court.
- **Transportation**—transporting witnesses to and from court and, less often, to shelters or social service agencies.
- **Escorting**—accompanying witnesses to the courtroom and sitting with them during the proceedings.

Perhaps the single most common and important function victim programs provide is counseling—lending a sympathetic and trained ear to help victims "ventilate" fear and anger, rebuild self-esteem, cope with their sense of vulnerability, avoid self-blame and self-recrimination, reduce feelings of shame, and relieve uncertainty.

Furthermore, unless their emotional needs are met, many victims will either not testify—and thereby force the prosecutor to drop the case—or they will testify so poorly that the prosecutor loses the case. Thus, many prosecutors have come to value these programs' ability to prepare victims and witnesses.

Programs help ensure that victims and witnesses will appear in court by assisting them in dealing with the inconvenience and frustration of repeated appearances as well as with feared or actual intimidation by defendants and defense attorneys. In addition, since many witnesses fail to appear in court because they don't realize they are supposed to testify, or don't remember the date or where to go, many programs benefit prosecutors and judges by reminding witnesses of upcoming court dates.

Thus, victim assistance programs generally perform a dual function—providing badly needed services to victims and witnesses and helping the criminal justice system accomplish its mission to see that justice is done.

Obtaining funds for victims programs is not always easy. Originally, most victims programs secured all or most of their initial funding from the Federal Government. By 1982, however, over three-quarters of 25 programs contacted in one study received more than half their funds from State and local governments, with almost half the programs using combined funding from two or more sources.

With the passage of the Victims of Crime Act of 1984, however, Federal funding for existing programs can be expected to increase, even though 50 percent of the money may go to fund victim compensation programs.

While funding often comes from general revenues, the trend has been to fund victim services through penalty assessments or fines on all convicted offenders. In 1982, for example, California levied penalties at a rate of $4 for every $10 in fines; this levy raised $24 million annually, with $5.2 million going to the State's 35 victim-witness assistance programs. Every program received $37,000, with the remaining funds allocated according to population and crime levels.

Programs have used a variety of innovative approaches to fundraising. The Greenville Victim Assistance Unit requests small contributions from local businesses, foundations, and volunteer organizations. Grants have been secured from J.P. Stevens, the U.S. Jaycees, General Electric, and the Women's Legal Auxiliary. The Victim/Witness Liaison Office in Broward County, Florida, raises money from condominium associations and recreation centers. Las Vegas' Victim Witness Assistance Center was awarded $25,000 in

fines assessed on a popular singer for violating customs regulations.

Many programs are resourceful in the ways they reduce or eliminate service and equipment costs. The Greenville staff persuaded a lock repair service to provide locks at cost for indigent victims of break-ins. By assisting prosecutors with their paperwork in the complaint room and at arraignment, New York City's Victim Service Agency obtained free use of a telephone, reproduction equipment, and work space. Programs can realize substantial savings by using volunteers to provide victim services. Indeed, the Victims of Crime Act requires as a condition of funding that organizations must promote the use of volunteers to the extent practicable.

The criminal justice system is ultimately responsible for ensuring that the needs of victims and witnesses are met. Initially, the response to the needs of victims and witnesses took the form of separate programs specializing in victim-witness treatment. However, as the victims' rights movement has gained momentum, law enforcement agencies, prosecutor's offices, and the judiciary in many jurisdictions have recognized that their obligation for meeting victim needs extends *beyond* working with or even implementing a program. Rather, each agency in the system is learning to be more responsive in its own daily contacts with victims and witnesses, incorporating services as part of its normal operating procedures rather than delegating them to a separate program. For example, the Middlesex County, Massachusetts, District Attorney's Office has instructed its assistants that "it is the professional responsibility of every attorney in this office to be accessible, informative, and helpful to victims and witnesses. Such responsibility is not intended to be delegated to the Victim Witness Services Bureau."

Nevertheless, many needed services require the undivided attention of a separate program. Counseling, in particular, is beyond the resources and expertise of criminal justice agencies. Thus, the ideal combination is for law enforcement officers, prosecutors, and judges to perform those victim-witness services they have the training and time to provide, and to work with a victim program for those services that an independent organization can best provide. In this manner, the rights of the victim will truly be balanced with the rights of the defendant. And these victim and witness rights must be provided—because it is right, and because it is the only way to ensure that justice is attained.

Discussion Questions

1. Is it fair to collect fines or order restitution from convicted offenders in order to compensate victims? If so, how should the amount of the fine, or the nature of the restitution, be determined?

2. If compensation to victims is provided in some States for such things as medical expenses and loss of earnings, should compensation also be provided for psychological counseling? Should it be provided for "pain and suffering"?

3. Many observers believe that the victim is a very important person in the criminal justice system. Are we apt now to go too far in protecting the rights of the victim at the expense of the rights of the defendant?

4. In deciding sentences, judges sometimes consult statements or listen to presentations concerning the impact of the crime on the victims—or their suffering, their financial hardships, and their inability to carry on a normal life. What influence, if any, should this information have on the sentences imposed?

5. If the criminal justice system should pay increased attention to the needs and rights of victims and witnesses, how can law enforcement officers, prosecutors, and judges be motivated and assisted to do so?

References

Bureau of Justice Statistics. 1984. *Victim/Witness Legislation: An Overview.* Washington, D.C.: U.S. Department of Justice.

Finn, Peter, and Beverly Lee. 1985. *Serving Crime Victims and Witnesses.* Washington, D.C.: U.S. Department of Justice.

Galaway, Burt, and Joe Hudson, eds. 1981. *Perspectives of Crime Victims.* St. Louis: C.V. Mosby.

President's Task Force on Victims of Crime: Final Report. 1982. Washington, D.C.: U.S. Government Printing Office.

Young, Marlene A. 1983. *The Victim Service System: A Guide to Action.* Washington, D.C.: The National Organization for Victim Assistance.

Statutes

The Federal Victim and Protection Act of 1982, Public Law 97-291.

The Victims of Crime Act of 1984, Public Law 98-473.

National Institute of Justice

*Research
in Action*

Crime Victims:
Learning How to Help Them

Robert C. Davis, Victim Services Agency

May/June 1987

Future legal historians may well call the 1980's the decade in which a start was finally made toward recognizing victims of crime as central characters in the criminal event, worthy of concern, respect, and compassion. Since 1981, President Reagan has proclaimed National Victims of Crime Week annually to focus attention on victim problems. In April 1982, he established the President's Task Force on Victims of Crime, which made 68 recommendations for addressing the problems of victims. Then in 1984 the Attorney General's Task Force on Family Violence presented 63 recommendations for combating violence within the family and aiding its victims.

Crime victims have also been the subject of a good deal of legislation. The 1982 Omnibus Victim and Witness Protection Act requires use of victim impact statements at sentencing in Federal criminal cases, greater protection of Federal victims and witnesses from intimidation by defendants or their associates, restitution by offenders to victims of Federal crimes, guidelines for fair treatment of victims and witnesses in Federal criminal cases, and more stringent bail laws. The Comprehensive Crime Control Act and the Victims of Crime Act of 1984 authorize Federal funds for State victim compensation and victim assistance programs. These funds are distributed by the Office of Justice Programs, through its Office for Victims of Crime and Bureau of Justice Assistance.

More than 35 States have enacted comprehensive legislation protecting the interests of the victim, compared with 4 before 1982. State victim compensation programs have continued to expand (43 States and the District of Columbia now have such programs), as have victim assistance services in the community.

Research has played an important role in the rethinking of public policies about crime victims. Much of that research has been sponsored by the National Institute of Justice. Institute-supported projects have provided legislators, criminal justice planners, and practitioners with new information on the effects of crime on victims, on the success of programs to help victims recover psychologically and financially, and on ways of helping victims through the criminal justice process.

This article reviews some of the significant findings of NIJ research on victims. It also reports on studies now in progress and on questions that still need to be answered. (Most of the research reports discussed are listed in references at the end of the article.)

Crime Takes Psychological Toll

Only recently have people come to realize that victims of crime experience crisis reactions similar to those experienced by victims of war, natural disasters, and catastrophic illness.

Research in 1975 focused on victim experiences both with crime and with the criminal justice system. The findings had a significant impact on the thinking of criminal justice planners and the development of programs for victims and witnesses. Researchers at Marquette University[1] interviewed 3,000 victims and witnesses from cases active in Milwaukee County's court system and 1,600 persons identified as victims of serious personal crimes by a previous National Crime Survey.

They found mental or emotional suffering to be the most frequent problem expressed by victims in general, while time and income loss posed the greatest difficulties for victims involved in the court process. The fear and emotional distress experienced by victims often extended as well to the victims' families and friends.

The study produced a wealth of policy recommendations to improve the treatment of victims and witnesses in the courts. Many have since been widely adopted.

The Milwaukee study introduced the term "secondary victimization" to characterize the distress experienced by the family and friends of crime victims. In 1982, a research team from the New York Victim Services Agency,[2] pursuing this theme, questioned 240 New York City victims of robbery, nonsexual assault, and burglary. They asked about problems and needs stemming from the crime and about organizations and individuals to whom victims turned for assistance.

While few victims had sought assistance from organizations, virtually all had received help from friends, neighbors, or relatives. The help ranged from listening while victims "ventilated," to aiding in apprehending the criminal, to lending money, to helping with replacement of doors, windows, and locks.

The New York researchers then contacted supporters named by the victims and interviewed them about the costs (and benefits) incurred in helping the victims. Most supporters reported being glad to help, but many said that their own fears about crime had been heightened because of the victim's experience. Such reactions were most prevalent among family members and neighbors of victims.

The study showed that the effects of crime hit hardest among the poor. Psychological distress and crime-related problems were more common among the less affluent and less educated, and these differences persisted at least up to 4 months after the crime. Similarly, poorer, less educated supporters were more likely than affluent supporters to report that providing assistance had placed a burden on them.

In a surprising finding, an earlier study revealed that nearly as many burglary as robbery victims underwent a "crisis reaction" during the weeks following victimization. In fact, according to researchers at the American Institutes for Research,[3] the impact of crime on victims' emotions and everyday behaviors was actually greater for burglary than for robbery victims.

Psychological reactions of victims were examined in depth under a 1984 NIJ study funded in response to a Victims Task Force recommendation. Researchers at the Medical University of South Carolina[4] interviewed female victims of sexual assault, robbery, aggravated assault, and home burglary, identified through a random victimization study.

Psychological adjustment of victims was measured against that of a sample of nonvictims. Details were gathered about current psychological status, previous mental health history, treatment history, and about the crime itself. This research provides the first reliable information about the proportion of victims in various crime categories who experience serious adjustment problems. Results indicate that victims of sexual assault suffer more adverse psychological reactions and adjustment problems than victims of robbery and burglary.

Helping Crime Victims Cope

Research detailing crime's impact on victims helped build support for creation of special service programs to help them cope. As victim witness programs proliferated during the 1970's, so did evaluations of these programs. Most evaluation efforts, however, were limited in scope, often confined to questioning victims about how they felt about services they used.

In fact, little was known about the effect of one of the key services offered: crisis intervention. An NIJ-funded assessment by the American Institutes for Research[5] in 1981 found that no studies had "examined whether the project clients suffer less trauma, either in the short or long run, than victims who go without help."

Crisis Intervention Program Research

To rectify this lack, researchers at the Institute for Social Analysis[6] evaluated the effectiveness of a program in which victim counselors called in by the police aided victims at the crime scene. The researchers interviewed victims twice within 6 months of the crime.

The study found that victims of robbery, burglary, and nonsexual assault were traumatized by crime, although not to as great an extent as rape victims. Prior life stress contributed significantly to the "initial, most troubling stages" of victims' psychological distress and, in fact, was the strongest single determinant of victim distress.

However, the authors noted that victims who received project services differed markedly from those who did not: the police summoned counselors only for the most traumatized victims. It was therefore not surprising that the measures of emotional trauma did not indicate any substantial effects for those who received services.

To learn more about crisis intervention services, the New York Victim Services Agency[7] studied victims of robbery, burglary, assault, and rape. The victims were randomly assigned to one of four experimental groups: (a) crisis intervention with supportive counseling, (b) crisis intervention using a form of cognitive/behavioral therapy, (c) material assistance only, or (d) a control group receiving no services.

Three months later no differences were apparent between the experimental groups on measures of psychological or material recovery from the effects of crime. However, the vast majority of victims chose to attend only one session of counseling. Research now in progress in New York is examining how counseling can be more helpful to victims. Specifically, the study is finding out if giving victims information on how to protect themselves from future crime can lead to speedier psychological recovery.

Victim Compensation Program Research

In 1981, the U.S. Attorney General's Task Force on Violent Crime observed that there was a need for study of "the various crime victim compensation programs and their results." The National Institute then funded a survey of how victim compensation programs were structured and run. The survey[8] reported that only a small fraction of victims at that time were aware assistance was available and applied for it. The authors also found that compensation programs had generally served increasing numbers of victims while maintaining low administrative costs relative to other kinds of benefit programs.

The Victim in the Criminal Justice System

In the 1970's and early 1980's, the criminal justice community began to realize that victims play a key role in the ability of the police and courts to bring criminals to justice.

For many years studies have continued to show that the victim is crucial in helping police apprehend criminals. Research by the Rand Corporation[9] in 1975 reported that information supplied by the victim to the first police officer responding to a crime is more important than any followup investigative work.

A 1984 study by the Police Executive Research Forum[10] underscored the importance of the victim's actions. The research found that the time it took *citizens to call the police* affected the probability of on-scene arrests to a greater extent than the time it took *police to respond to the call.* And earlier research by the Institute for Law and Social Research[11] reported that a larger number of citizen witnesses in a case, as distinguished from police or professional witnesses, increased the chances of conviction.

Based on research findings in this area, the National Institute produced public service announcements that dramatize how citizen action—or inaction—can affect criminal justice outcomes.

The System's Response to Victims

Victims are more likely to report a crime if they think the police will respond effectively. And victim satisfaction with police response seems to be determined primarily by the predictability rather than the speed of the police response. Victims will accept a delayed response in nonemergency cases if they are told in advance when to expect police.[12]

The earlier research in Milwaukee, examining the impact of crime on victims, also measured victim reactions to the criminal justice system. One significant finding was that a positive experience with the criminal justice system led victims to be more willing to cooperate with officials in the future.

The study recommended several ways to make involvement in prosecution more attractive to victims, including the use of equitable witness fees and establishing an Office of Justice Advocates to represent the needs of victims, witnesses, and jurors within the criminal justice system. Other recommendations stressed the importance of modifying criminal justice policies and procedures to make them more responsive to victims and to keep both victims and witnesses better informed throughout the adjudication process.

Other research[13] showed that some victims and witnesses fail to cooperate with prosecutors because officials do not communicate important information to them: prosecutors or police may fail to inform people that they are needed as witnesses or to tell them when they should appear in court.

Rape Victims

How the criminal justice system deals with particularly traumatized groups of victims—rape victims—was the focus of a 1976 study by the Battelle Memorial Institute Law and Justice Study Center.[14] The research surveyed police and prosecution agencies nationwide and looked at practices in several jurisdictions.

Police officers and prosecutors at that time lacked training in putting together the essential ingredients for successful prosecution of rape cases, Battelle concluded. Reports were distributed to help patrol officers, prosecutors, police and prosecutor administrators, and legislators improve the chances for successful prosecution of rape cases and to make criminal justice more responsive to the needs of rape victims.

Domestic Violence Victims

Are nonstranger violence cases treated less severely by the courts than stranger-to-stranger cases? If so, is this because that is what the victims want?

Research by the Institute for Social Analysis in 1983[15] sought answers to these questions in a study of four jurisdictions. In the four sites, the dismissal rate for nonstranger violence cases was three times higher than for stranger-to-stranger cases, the researchers found. Nevertheless, nonstranger victims were more satisfied with case outcomes than stranger-to-stranger victims. The reason: they were likely to believe that the defendant's behavior would change as a result of punishment imposed by the court or simply as a result of arrest and prosecution.

Many police forces are changing the way they respond to family violence, especially spouse abuse, at least in part because of findings from an Institute-sponsored experiment published in 1984.[16] Police policy in responding to domestic disturbances generally was to counsel the parties or to order the aggressor party to leave the premises for 8 hours or more.

The Institute experiment, however, found that arresting the aggressor leads to fewer repeat offenses. Conducted by the Minneapolis Police Department, the controlled experiment randomly assigned officers to provide one of three responses to violent domestic disputes. The research showed that only 10 percent of aggressors who were arrested repeated their violence within 6 months compared to 19 percent of those

involved in mediation and 24 percent of those who were ordered to leave the home.

The study is currently being replicated in six more cities, to refine understanding of the most appropriate police response to domestic violence situations.

Child Victims

How the courts deal with child victims is the subject of research conducted by the American Bar Association.[17] This study examined data in three counties (Fairfax, Virginia; Mercer, New Jersey; Santa Cruz, California) to see if the courts are too lenient in sentencing child sexual abusers. It also examined the practices of criminal justice and child welfare agencies in processing child sexual abuse cases over a several-year period.

While the study's statutory review found little difference between sentencing provisions for offenses involving child versus adult victims, analysis of case files revealed a pattern of more severe sentences in adult victim cases. In cases involving child victims, a higher proportion of abusers knew or were related to their victims, which may help explain the greater leniency observed. Almost half of the confirmed child victim cases did not result in an arrest, and only 63 percent of those arrested were prosecuted, with the offenders often being allowed to plead guilty to a misdemeanor. The study pointed out the need for better interagency coordination in such cases, and for greater community consensus on what sanctions are appropriate.

The Institute has also examined both research and experience in the use of child victims as witnesses. A report by Abt Associates, Inc.,[18] describes new techniques and legal theories for obtaining a child victim's testimony with a minimum of trauma for the child. Two research efforts now being conducted in Colorado[19] and North Carolina[20] are examining the effects of criminal justice system participation on child victims of sexual assault.

Consideration of Victim Impact

Several major research projects have focused on the idea that a crime's effect on the victim ought to play a larger role in sentencing decisions.

A 1984 study by the Institute for Law and Social Research[21] sought to understand how criminal justice officials learn about victim harm, how victim harm affects their decisions about cases, and how victims respond to their experiences with the criminal justice system. The researchers interviewed police, prosecutors, judges, and victims at eight sites chosen to include providers of both extensive and limited services for victims.

The study found that of three variables examined (injury, psychological harm, and property stolen), only victim injury appeared to be important in prosecutors' screening decisions. None of the three factors was important in sentencing decisions.

The study also found that the majority of police officers, prosecutors, and judges felt that current levels of victim involvement were about right. Yet victims felt that being better informed, punishing the defendant more harshly, and providing more social services were important to increasing their satisfaction. Moreover, sites with full-service victim programs (where officials were more influenced by victim-related factors than practitioners elsewhere) were found to have the highest levels of victim satisfaction.

The first systematic effort to allow victims a chance to participate directly in case decisions was described in a 1979 report by the University of Chicago Law School.[22] Researchers evaluated an experiment in Dade County, Florida, in which victims participated in pretrial settlement conferences for certain criminal cases selected on a random assignment basis. At the conferences, judges, attorneys, the arresting officer, defendants, and victims discussed the incident and tried to fashion an appropriate decision.

The results were mixed. Only a third of the victims attended the conferences; many victims, however, told researchers they had not been notified that a conference was scheduled. Most victims who did come said little and did not demand unreasonable punishment, the authors noted.

The authors found some evidence that victims whose cases went to conference were more satisfied with the way their cases were processed than other victims were. However, no differences were found between victims who did attend and those who did not with regard to their satisfaction with case outcomes or with the criminal justice system.

Several years later, NIJ awarded a grant to the Institute for Law and Social Research (INSLAW)[23] to replicate the Dade experiment in three additional sites. INSLAW found that victims who attended settlement conferences were more satisfied with case outcomes

and with the idea of plea bargaining than victims who did not attend. The level of victim participation was similar to that in earlier results. About half of invited victims attended, and victims who did come usually only described the facts of the case.

Another study has provided some of the first empirical data on a procedure which is gaining acceptance across the country. In California, a 1982 Victim's Bill of Rights included a provision that victims had the right to appear and be heard at adult felony sentencing proceedings and at parole eligibility proceedings for adults and juveniles. The effects of the provision on victims and on criminal justice personnel—judges, clerks, prosecutors, parole officers, and probation officers—were examined in a 1983 Institute grant to the University of the Pacific's McGeorge Law School.[24]

The study found that inadequate notification procedures were a major problem: less than half the victims sampled were aware that they had the right to appear and speak at sentencing. Less than 3 percent of the eligible victims actually did appear.

Most victims interviewed said the right to speak at hearings was important, but most also indicated that they would need more information, more support, and some legal assistance to be able to exercise this right effectively. Victims also wanted information about the status of the case against the defendant as much as they desired the legal right to participate in the case.

Research is now giving special attention to the impact and effectiveness of various reforms designed to make the criminal justice system more responsive to victims. For example, the Institute is currently funding a nationwide examination[25] of States with legislation allowing victim impact statements, to determine how the legislative intent has been implemented through administrative regulations and through actual practices of criminal justice and victim services personnel.

Similarly, the Institute has helped promote the view of the victim as a vital participant and witness by supporting research on how victims are treated by the system; on innovative programs and legislation to expand the victim's role; and on the victim's historical status in the criminal justice system and rights under the law.

Currently under way is a nationwide study of the more than 30 States with victim bill of rights legislation.[26] The research will determine how legislative intent is being carried out, identify successful approaches to meeting the needs of crime victims, and pinpoint victim concerns requiring additional attention.

Unresolved Issues

The availability of services for victims and a larger role for victims are becoming part of the American criminal justice system. Research has provided the underpinning to many of today's innovations in the treatment of victims. But there remains much to be learned about ways to make these reforms as effective and as efficient as possible. The following highlights only a few of the issues research might address.

More information is needed on the effects of service programs for victims. These are some specific questions that might be addressed:

■ Which counseling techniques work best for which victims?

■ Can we learn something about which techniques might be most effective by studying differences in coping styles between victims who do and those who do not recover quickly after the crime?

■ Can police officers, whose behavior seems to significantly shape how victims react to their experience, be trained successfully in techniques to alleviate victims' trauma?

■ Do programs designed to aid victims in the court process promote greater willingness of victims to cooperate with officials?

■ Are compensation programs aiding those victims with the greatest needs or are such victims often excluded due to lack of information or overly complex application procedures?

Secondly, more research is needed about the role of the victim in the criminal justice system. Current research on victim impact statements will yield important information on the administrative effects of such statements. But we still need to learn about other basic issues involving the use of impact statements:

■ How many victims actually want the opportunity to make a statement?

■ Does the opportunity to make a statement promote the healing of psychological wounds?

■ Do victims view the opportunity to make impact statements as meaningful involvement in the criminal justice process? If so, do impact statement opportunities increase satisfaction with the criminal justice system? What new incentives can be developed to increase victim participation?

Research might provide useful answers to questions on other victim-related issues as well. For instance:

■ Do elderly and child victims have special psychological or material needs that are currently not being addressed?

■ What are the benefits and impediments to having the private sector ease victims' financial burden through employee counseling and referrals and provision of paid leave for medical treatment or court appearances?

Unquestionably, the attention given to victim issues over the past two decades has changed police, prosecutor, and court procedures throughout the United States. In many jurisdictions programs now exist to help reduce the trauma of victimization and to ease the victim's way through the criminal court process.

Research projects funded by the National Institute of Justice and others have provided the impetus and rationale for many reforms in the treatment of victims. Continued collaboration by researchers and practitioners can help sustain these advances and lead to new ways of helping victims of crime.

Discussion Questions

1. Should police officers be required to receive training to deal with the problems encountered by the victims of crime?

2. Should every state adopt a Victim's Bill of Rights? How could these rights interfere with those of criminal defendants?

3. What factors do you think motivate victims to report crime to police? What conditions might encourage crime reporting?

4. Why are aggressors in domestic violence cases less likely to repeat their attacks if they are formally arrested by police rather than asked to leave their homes or referred to mediation? Should all domestic violence disputes lead to an arrest?

Notes

Reports are available for some but not all of the studies discussed in the article.

1. R. Knudten and associates, 1975.

2. R.C. Davis, 1982.

3. B. Bourque and associates, 1978.

4. D. Kilpatrick, 1984.

5. R. Cronin and B. Bourque, 1981.

6. B. Smith, R. Cook, and A. Harrow, 1982.
7. R.C. Davis and P. Fisher.
8. D. McGillis and P. Smith, 1981.
9. P. Greenwood and J. Petersilia, 1975.
10. W. Spelman and D. Brown, 1984.
11. B. Forst and associates, 1978.
12. T. Pate et al., 1976.
13. F. Cannavale and W. Falcon, 1976.
14. D. Chappell, 1976.
15. B. Smith.
16. L.W. Sherman and R.A. Berk, 1984.
17. J. Chapman.
18. D. Whitcomb, E.R. Shapiro, and L. Stellwagen, 1981.
19. B. Goodman, University of Denver.
20. D. Runyan, University of North Carolina.
21. J. Hernon and B. Forst, 1984.
22. W. Kerstetter and A. Heinz, 1979.
23. D. Buchner et al., 1984.
24. E. Villmoare, 1983.
25. M. McLeod, State University of New York.
26. S. Hillenbrand, American Bar Association.

National Institute of Justice

Research in Action

Establishing and Expanding Victim-Witness Assistance Programs

Peter Finn, Abt Associates and Beverly N.W. Lee, The Berwick Group

August 1988

Experience has shown that the only way of ensuring that the needs of victims and witnesses are met is to have a separate unit solely dedicated to their assistance. The efforts of those [existing] units ... shine brightly in the otherwise dim landscape of general institutional neglect of those on whom the criminal justice system relies.

—*President's Task Force on Victims of Crime (1982)*

Since the early 1970's, attention to the needs of crime victims and witnesses has grown steadily, propelled by a combination of grassroots and government concern. The movement was given strong visibility by the President's 1982 Task Force on Victims of Crime, which urged widespread expansion of victim assistance programs that were already proliferating. Today, as many as 4,000 programs are helping crime victims to cope with the hardships of victimization and to deal with the often troublesome demands of the criminal justice system.

A recent National Institute of Justice sponsored study—Serving Crime Victims and Witnesses[1]—examined the organization and operation of 25 programs nationwide, giving particular attention to programs in 6 jurisdictions (Figure 2). The study found that programs can vary widely in structure, in the number and type of services they provide, and in the groups they help—yet they can still effectively meet the needs of victims and the criminal justice system.

Despite these variations in program organization and operations, the study results suggest broadly applicable recommendations both for starting and improving a program.

Choosing Services

The first and toughest planning decision is selecting or reevaluating the combination of services to offer—there is always more to do than any program has time to accomplish. In selecting services to provide, program staff have to balance the sometimes conflicting considerations of:

■ meeting the most urgent needs of victims and witnesses in the jurisdiction;

■ providing the maximum possible benefit to the criminal justice system as well as to victims and witnesses; and

■ staying within the program's budget.

Table 1 shows the range of services a program can provide, along with the percentage of 25 programs contacted in 1986 that furnish each service.

Most programs give highest priority to crisis intervention,[2] followup counseling, helping victims secure their rights, and court-related services. Beyond this core of essential services, planners and administrators must decide for themselves which additional services are most needed.

For example, the Alameda County (California) Victim/Witness Assistance Program learned that victims were having difficulty getting back property kept as evidence, and finding out the status and outcome of their cases. The program therefore established property return and informing victims and witnesses about their cases as two of its major services.

Planners for the Minneapolis-St. Paul Crime Victim Centers telephoned 451 victims and witnesses during a 3-month period before the program began and again 9 months after the centers opened. The initial

Table 1   Percentage of 25 programs providing
specific victim-witness services

Services	Programs contacted in 1986 (N =25)
Emergency services	
Medical care	8%
Shelter or food	32%
Security repair	40%
Financial assistance	44%
On-scene comfort	52%
Counseling	
24-hour hotline	28%
Crisis intervention	76%
Followup counseling	80%
Mediation	44%
Advocacy and support services	
Personal advocacy	92%
Employer intervention	96%
Landlord intervention	88%
Property return	96%
Intimidation protection	76%
Legal/paralegal counsel	44%
Referral	100%
Claims assistance	
Insurance claims aid	48%
Restitution assistance	88%
Compensation assistance	96%
Witness fee assistance	80%
Court-related services	
Witness reception	76%
Court orientation	92%
Notification	84%
Witness alert	68%
Transportation	84%
Child care	68%
Escort to court	100%
Victim impact reports	72%
Systemwide services	
Public education	92%
Legislative advocacy	84%
Training	92%

responses showed what kinds of assistance were needed while the followup findings indicated what improvements in service mix should be made.

While some services—such as counseling—are best provided by the staff of victim-witness programs, there are other services that the program should encourage and assist police, prosecutors, and judges to furnish as a routine part of their jobs. For example, police are best equipped to provide physical protection to threatened victims and witnesses; prosecutors can obtain victim impact statements and present them to judges as part of sentencing recommendations; and judges can help reduce intimidation by providing separate waiting areas for witnesses.

Fortunately, criminal justice professionals across the country are recognizing more and more that their obligation to meet the needs of victims and witnesses extends beyond working with or sponsoring programs. It includes being responsive to these needs in their own daily contacts with victims and witnesses and incorporating services as part of their normal operating procedures.

Limited resources may require program planners and administrators to establish priorities for assisting different types of clients and then periodically reassess these priorities. For example, most programs consider rape victims a top priority, while others make sure that spouses and children of homicide victims receive careful attention. The Victim Service Council in St. Louis County gives priority to indigent clients.

Staff can also choose to serve only victims who report the crime, only victims whose case is prosecuted, or all victims regardless of case status. However, the choice of clients to serve may dictate—or be limited by—a program's physical location. For example, Crime Victim Centers in Minneapolis-St. Paul can assist victims regardless of whether they have reported the crime, because the program has four storefront offices where victims can walk in off the street.

The type of clients served may be influenced by program sponsors. For example, programs sponsored by prosecutor offices generally restrict services to victims whose cases are brought to trial; these programs also offer limited on-scene crisis intervention and early contact with victims. On the other hand, prosecutor-sponsored programs find it easier to provide extensive court-related services to victims than do programs run by police, community-based organizations, and other groups.

Sponsorship can also influence how effectively staff can advocate for victims vis-a-vis the criminal justice system. In identifying services to provide and types of victims to assist, it is best to start with a fairly narrow mission and, if appropriate, expand later.

Starting with a highly targeted effort avoids the risk of doing many things poorly instead of doing a few things well. It also prevents raising unrealistic expectations—leading to disappointment—among funding sources, the criminal justice system, and program staff.

Selecting Staff

Figure 1 summarizes the principal considerations in identifying and recruiting staff. Of course, the staff skills that are needed depend to some extent on the services to be performed—for example, if counseling will be provided immediately after the crime, individuals with experience in crisis intervention will be necessary. However, strict staff requirements concerning education or previous work experience are not usually necessary. Program planners instead need to identify potential staff who:

- have positive feelings toward the criminal justice system;
- can relate to victims in situations of stress without making judgments;
- have the resilience and flexibility to work overtime and to deal with a variety of problems on short notice.

A first-rate director is especially vital to program success. In addition to management and supervisory ability, a program director must also have skills in direct service delivery, public relations, and entrepreneurship.

Volunteers can save programs money and expand service delivery. By training volunteers to respond to victims of sexual assault, Portland's Victim Assistance Program can provide 24-hour crisis intervention to rape victims. Volunteers handle clerical assignments, court escort, witness notification, and witness orientation. With appropriate personal qualities, and adequate training and supervision, volunteers can also provide crisis intervention (as in Portland) and followup counseling.

Finding appropriate volunteers can be time consuming, and volunteers need considerable training to be effective in anything beyond simple clerical tasks. Some volunteers can be undependable or can lose interest quickly. Planners can minimize these drawbacks with careful screening, thorough training, and close supervision.

Timing is also important. It may be advisable not to involve volunteers until the program is well underway and paid staff have enough free time to recruit, screen, train, and supervise them properly. Staff may be recruited through newspaper advertisements and posting notices in college placement offices. Many programs hire former volunteers who have proven their worth.

The Alameda County program usually hires well-known staff from the agencies with which it has been working. As in many occupations, the single most common recruitment method is word of mouth.

Only on-the-job training can provide new paid staff and volunteers with first-hand experience in dealing with victims and witnesses. However, preservice training is just as important. Depending on staff assignments, the training should impart counseling and interviewing techniques, crisis intervention skills, knowledge of how to tap community resources to secure additional assistance for victims, and—for all staff—a thorough understanding of how the criminal justice system operates.

The most effective training includes role play that simulates actual cases. Observing staff during working hours ("shadowing") and assigning newcomers to one staff member as a "buddy" are also valuable. Figure 2 summarizes the principal features of the preservice and inservice training programs of six victim-witness programs.

Networks

Planners need to develop close ties with criminal justice personnel and other human service providers to obtain help in serving victims and witnesses and to avoid duplication of services.

Developing networks also enables program staff to contact victims and witnesses in a systematic manner. The Alameda County program identifies more than 80 percent of its clients from charging sheets that the District Attorney's Office agreed to deliver routinely to the staff. In Greenville, South Carolina, the Law Enforcement Center forwards a daily offense bulletin to the Victim Witness Assistance Unit, listing all the previous day's criminal incidents by victim, location, and police officer involved. The Woman's Crisis Line in Portland, Oregon, refers rape victims to the Victim Assistance Program whenever court orientation will be helpful for the women.

Planners should expect to devote significant time and effort to establishing effective cooperation with other groups. Demonstrating ways in which the program can benefit police is effective in gaining police cooperation. For example, by calming people and addressing their emotional and financial needs, program staff enable victims to concentrate on giving

Figure 1   Summary of considerations in identifying and recruiting staff

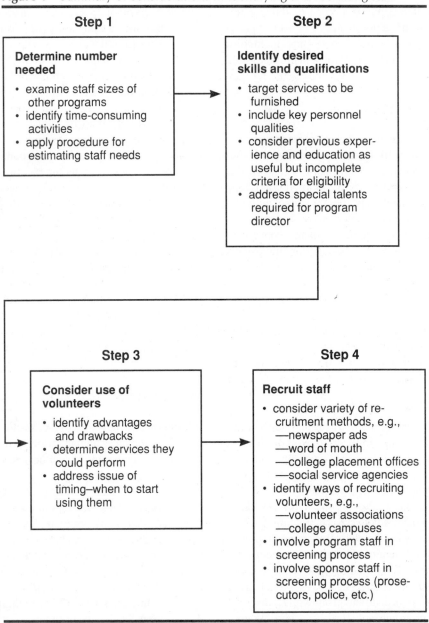

Step 1

Determine number needed

- examine staff sizes of other programs
- identify time-consuming activities
- apply procedure for estimating staff needs

Step 2

Identify desired skills and qualifications

- target services to be furnished
- include key personnel qualities
- consider previous experience and education as useful but incomplete criteria for eligibility
- address special talents required for program director

Step 3

Consider use of volunteers

- identify advantages and drawbacks
- determine services they could perform
- address issue of timing—when to start using them

Step 4

Recruit staff

- consider variety of recruitment methods, e.g.,
  —newspaper ads
  —word of mouth
  —college placement offices
  —social service agencies
- identify ways of recruiting volunteers, e.g.,
  —volunteer associations
  —college campuses
- involve program staff in screening process
- involve sponsor staff in screening process (prosecutors, police, etc.)

accurate information to police officers and deputy sheriffs. Program staff can offer to save police time by taking responsibility for distraught victims at the scene after the officers have completed their investigation, by locating hard-to-reach witnesses, and by establishing a standby system for notifying police when they need to testify in court.

An important strategy for developing a relationship with police is to identify one or two key individuals in the department who are respected by their colleagues. Gaining their support can mean they will recommend the program to other personnel in the department. When possible, planners should involve these individuals in setting up the program.

Many programs also start out by honoring police requests for assistance with nonvictims to build a working relationship. Only later do they restrict their services to bona fide crime victims.

It is often easier to gain the cooperation of *prosecutors* because they benefit more obviously and immediately by working with a program. For example, prosecutors can devote increased time to strictly prosecutorial functions if program staff agree to take on responsibility for explaining court procedures to victims and witnesses, allaying their fears about testifying, and persuading them to see the case through.

Planners can also offer to contact witnesses to ensure that they appear in court—and on time—in order to reduce the burden on prosecutors for conducting this essentially clerical task.

Program staff need to arrange for *judicial* involvement in order to get permission to sit with troubled victims during court proceedings. Judges can also permit program staff to be present during sentencing to

Choosing Services and Client Groups

The **Alameda County** District Attorney Victim/Witness Assistance Program in Oakland, California, serves a population of slightly over 1 million, 18 police departments, and 8 courts. With an annual budget of nearly $331,000, offices in 2 locations, and 10 full-time staff members, the program focuses exclusively on victims, even though it is administered by the district attorney.

Program staff identify more than 80 percent of their clients from prosecutor charging sheets that are routinely delivered to the program. Police reports on all incidents involving sexual assault, child molestation, homicide, and domestic violence are automatically forwarded to the program.

Police and prosecutors also call the program directly with requests for assistance. Staff is available during working hours for telephone or walk-in consultation whenever victims require emotional support. Staff members also visit the homes of elderly victims and children.

Victim notification and orientation consists of explaining, by letter and telephone, each stage of the litigation process. Staff members may also meet with victims before a court session, show them the physical layout of the courtroom, explain the upcoming proceedings, and escort the victim during hearings and trials.

The Police Crisis Intervention Unit in **Scottsdale**, Arizona, is a police-based program operating in a city of 112,000. The city funds the program as part of the Scottsdale police budget. Funding in 1985 was $188,000, which supports a full-time staff of four. The program serves no witnesses, but in addition to helping victims, the staff also assists many people who are not victims of crime, including accident victims, families of runaways, and disoriented individuals.

Police referrals account for 80 percent of the unit's caseload. Officers drop off police reports with a request for assis-

tance, and they bring victims to see the program specialists at the station. After working hours, police can still refer victims by telephoning the specialists at home or paging them on beepers. Most of the remaining caseload is the result of direct calls from victims and walk-ins.

The program's principal services are 24-hour crisis intervention, referrals, orientation to court procedures, and transportation. The staff also provides emotional support to many victims during municipal court proceedings, and city judges often call the unit when victims become upset in court.

The **Greenville County**, South Carolina, Victim/Witness Assistance Unit is a small program run by the District Attorney. The program has two full-time and five part-time paid staff, and a budget of $101,000. The program serves a 2-county area of almost 300,000 people.

The program identifies 90 percent of the unit's caseload from a daily offense bulletin forwarded by the city and county police departments. Police also call the program two or three times a day for help in calming a disturbed victim, interviewing a child, locating a missing witness, or answering questions from victims and families of homicide victims.

The program's major services are witness notification, short-term counseling, victim advocacy, and orientation to the criminal justice system. The unit often helps prosecutors in witness management, such as securing the addresses and phone numbers of key witnesses, handling arrangements for out-of-State witnesses, and coordinating witness and victim arrival, transportation, and escort.

Finally, the unit acts as a buffer between prosecutors and victims who have questions or complaints about a case.

Figure 2   Summary of training programs in six programs visited for onsite study

Program	Preservice		Inservice	
	Volunteers	*Paid staff*	*Volunteers*	*Paid staff*
Alameda County, California Victim/Witness Assistance Program	(already have the requisite counseling skills)	• overview of criminal justice system • introduction to key actors, including those in other agencies of the program's referral network • observation and work with "buddy"	• on-the-job on the program's procedures	• workshops and conferences (at least 3 per year per staff member)
Greenville, South Carolina Victim/Witness Assistance Unit	• orientation as part of screening		• workshops • on-the-job supervision • annual regional victim assistance conference	• on-the-job supervision • annual conference
Portland, Oregon Victim Assistance Program	• job definition • orientation from police, prosecutors, hospital staff • instruction on making referrals • assignment to "buddy" to observe, work side by side with	None (may consult with more experienced staff or director as needed)	• seminars • continuing legal education (for update on laws)	
Minneapolis-St. Paul, Minnesota Crime Victim Centers	given over six weeks	given over two weeks	• monthly lectures by representatives of other agencies updating staff on changes in case processing, client eligibility, or latest developments in the field to maintain and expand referral network	
	• reading assignments, including procedure manual • films • briefings on cases likely to be encountered • observation of staff in action • visit to shelters and hospitals • participation in police ride-alongs • role play			

provide victim impact statements and recommendations for restitution.

The most valuable *human service providers* to work with are counseling groups, government social service agencies, legal aid services, and shelters.

Usually a quid pro quo can be arranged. A shelter in St. Paul is always ready to provide bed space for referrals from Crime Victim Centers. This is because women whom the shelter sends to the Centers for assistance always receive court followup, transporta-

Figure 2 Continued

Program	Preservice		Inservice	
	Volunteers	*Paid staff*	*Volunteers*	*Paid staff*
St. Louis County, Missouri Victim Service Council	• reading materials • seminar on job definition (exercises, role play) • communications skills • criminal justice system orientation • office procedures forms • community resources • referrals • one-to-one training	N/A	• sessions on special topics (e.g., domestic violence or physical assault) or discussion of cases three times a year	
Scottsdale, Arizona Police Crisis Intervention Unit	N/A (no volunteers)	• orientation to criminal justice system and to agencies in the program's referral network • participation in ride-alongs • work with more experienced staff; accompany them on call	N/A	• seminars and workshops

Source: Interviews with directors and staff of the above programs conducted by Abt Associates, Spring 1982 and 1986.

tion, and assistance in moving their possessions into the shelter at any hour of the day or night.

Building a network of community agencies may also furnish opportunities to train other local human service providers to treat victims with sensitivity, generating referrals for the victim witness program.

Funding

Several guidelines are available for estimating program costs—or the costs of program expansion. First, planners can expect that the most costly services will be 24-hour availability, crisis intervention at the crime scene, multiple contacts with a client (rather than one-time only intervention), emphasis on direct service

delivery rather than referral, and the allocation of significant resources to nonclient services such as research, training, public relations, and lobbying for statutory change.

Budget figures from existing programs provide another guideline for anticipating program costs. Most programs are willing to share this information. Table 2 provides the 1985 budget, staffing pattern, and services offered by the six programs visited for the National Institute of Justice study. As the table shows, programs have operated with vastly different budgets.

Budget figures are high for the Alameda County and Portland programs in part because of their extensive systems of victim notification conducted for the district attorney. Although it uses many volunteers, the Minneapolis-St. Paul program has a relatively large

Table 2 Staff size in relation to selected program characteristics in six site programs[1]

Program	Staff size			1985 Budget	Cost per person year[a]	Major Services	Annual caseload[b]	Population served	Cost per resident
	Paid full-time	Paid part-time	Volunteers (full & part-time)						
Alameda County Victim/Witness Assistance Program	10	-	1	$331,000	$33K	• counseling • victim notification • court orientation • victim compensation assistance • referrals	2,600[c]	1,100,000	$ .30
Greenville Victim/Witness Assistance Unit	2	5	25	$101,000	$28K	• counseling • victim orientation • victim advocacy • victim orientation • public education	2,000	300,000	$ .34
Minneapolis-St. Paul Crime Victim Centers	4	1	30	$261,000	$60K	• onscene crisis intervention • victim advocacy • victim orientation • public education	3,000[d]	2,086,000	$ .13
Portland Victim Assistance Program	9	3	38	$325,000	$33K	• onscene crisis intervention (rape victims only) • court orientation • victim notification • counseling • restitution assistance • referrals • public education	13,616[e]	570,000	$ .57

Table 2 Continued

| Program | Staff size | | | 1985 Budget | Cost per person year[a] | Major Services | Annual caseload[b] | Population served | Cost per resident |
	Paid full-time	Paid part-time	Volunteers (full & part-time)						
St. Louis Victim Service Council	4	1	21	$105,000	$24K	• crisis intervention • victim advocacy • witness orientation • system advocacy • public awareness • court orientation	2,037	1,918,000	$ .05
Scottsdale Police Crisis Intervention Unit	4	-	-	$188,000	$47K	• onscene crisis intervention • referrals • victim advocacy	2,000	112,000	$1.67

[In examining this table, the reader should consider that no attempt has been made to judge the quality of services the programs provide. In addition, the programs are not strictly comparable, since programs do not keep similar data or assign their staff identical responsibilities. The data are intended to suggest the range of costs, caseloads, and services associated with various staffing patterns.

[a] Assumes each paid part-time staff person works one-third time. Does not include volunteers.

[b] Number of victims and witnesses to whom program provided some sort of assistance in 1985 beyond telephoning or writing to see if they needed assistance.

[c] Also provided verbal or written information to victims and witnesses on over 11,000 occasions.

[d] Involved spending at least 15 minutes of assistance.

[e] Involved spending at least 10 minutes of assistance.

budget because staff serves two major cities with a combined population of more than 2 million. The program has the added expense of renting four storefront offices.

St. Louis has a smaller budget because its volunteers work long hours and perform many of the tasks paid professionals would otherwise have to do. Per-resident costs are relatively high for Scottsdale because the program provides services almost exclusively to victims, and victim services tend to cost more per client than do services to witnesses.

Programs can secure funds from a wide range of sources. In fact, over half the 25 programs contacted for this study combine funding from two or more sources. The most frequently used sources are State and local government.

Twenty-one States provide direct funding for victim services. The best source of information on public money is elected officials, who can provide contacts with appropriate public agencies. An effective selling point with some potential funding sources is a plan to use or to expand the use of volunteers.

St. Louis' Victim Service Council persuaded the city council to provide funds partly by demonstrating that the public would get one free dollar of volunteer time for every tax dollar provided.

Federal Support

Through the 1984 Federal Victims of Crime Act (VOCA), the Federal government is another significant source of public funding. The act established a Crime Victims Fund of up to $100 million annually, with the money coming from fines and new penalty assessment fees on Federal offenders.

While up to half the money in the fund may be used to supplement State victim compensation programs, most of the remaining money is earmarked for victim programs. As of early 1987, 1,364 programs had already received some VOCA funds.

VOCA funds are distributed by the States based on Federal guidelines and additional criteria each State chooses to establish. For example, the Federal Government requires new programs to demonstrate that at least half their budget will come from other sources besides the VOCA grant. Existing programs must have one-quarter of their funding from other sources.

Supplemental Funding

Even with government funding, most programs will have to supplement their budgets. Two potential funding sources worth exploring are the private sector and the courts.

■ The Greenville Victim/Witness Assistance Unit sends letters to local businesses and to foundations and volunteer organizations requesting contributions. Grants have been secured from J.P. Stevens, the U.S. Jaycees, General Electric, and the Women's Legal Auxiliary.

■ Las Vegas' Victim Witness Assistance Center arranged to receive $25,000 in fines assessed on a popular singer for violating customs regulations. Other creative funding ideas are provided in *Fundraising and Victim Services*, published by the National Organization for Victim Assistance, Washington, D.C.

Planners can also explore innovative ways to reduce the costs of services and equipment, or obtain their use without charge. The Greenville staff persuaded a lock repair service to provide locks at cost for indigent victims of break-ins. By assisting prosecutors with their paperwork in the complaint room and at arraignments, New York City's Victim Services Agency obtained access to a telephone, reproduction equipment, and work space at no cost.

As noted, using volunteers can lead to substantial savings in service delivery. Finally, by transferring some services to criminal justice agencies, programs can devote their resources to those activities that they alone can effectively provide.

Other Sources of Information

In starting or improving a program, program planners and administrators should turn first to other programs. To obtain ideas for setting up its own operation, the initiator of the Greenville program examined 70 requests for Federal funding of victim witness programs.

Other planners have telephoned the directors of successful existing programs for advice. The needs of victims themselves play an indispensable role in guiding program operations; victims' concerns can be identified through initial needs assessment and periodic followup surveys.

Advisory committees can provide expert information on starting or improving a program, and they can help identify resources in the local community and gain community support. Advisory bodies can often secure leads to funding sources, as well.

Discussion Questions

1. What are the most urgent needs of victims and witnesses?
2. How does networking help the development of victim–witness programs, and what types of agencies should be part of the network?
3. What is the role of volunteers in helping victims, and what kind of training should they undergo?

References

Cronin, Roberta C., and Blair B. Bourque. National Evaluation Program Phase I Report: *Assessment of Victim/Witness Assistance Projects*. Washington, D.C., National Institute of Justice, 1981.

National Organization for Victim Assistance (NOVA). *Newsletter*. Washington, D.C.

President's Task Force on Victims of Crime. *Final Report*. Washington, D.C., U.S. Government Printing Office, 1982.

Susman, Marjorie, and Carol Holt Vittert. "Building a solution: A practical guide for establishing crime victim service agencies." St. Louis, National Council of Jewish Women, St. Louis Section, 1980.

Young, Marlene A. The Victim Service System: A Guide to Action. Washington, D.C., National Organization for Victim Assistance, 1983.

Notes

1. Peter Finn and Beverly N.W. Lee, *Serving Crime Victims and Witnesses*, National Institute of Justice, Washington, D.C., June 1987.

2. A recent study by the New York City Victim Services Agency fails to demonstrate that victims who receive crisis intervention or material assistance show any more psychological improvement or practical adjustment than do victims who do not receive such services. However, the study notes that the assistance may have benefited victims in ways that the evaluation did not measure. Furthermore, most victims who received an hour's counseling or material aid believed the assistance was helpful. See Robert C. Davis, "Studying the Effects of Preliminary Services for Victims in Crisis," *Crime and Delinquency* 33, 4 (1987): 520–531. Preliminary findings from another study suggest that many victims do not want counseling but do request material assistance.

National Institute of Justice / *Research in Action*

Improving the Use and Effectiveness of Neighborhood Watch Programs

James Garofalo, SUNY Albany and Maureen McLeod, SUNY Albany

April 1988

Citizen involvement in crime prevention has grown considerably during the last 10 years, resulting in programs that promote home security, area surveillance, and citizen reporting of crimes to the police. The Bureau of Justice Statistics reported in 1986 that about one family in five lives in a neighborhood with such a program. In those areas, a substantial proportion—38 percent—participate.

These programs have different names in various parts of the country: Crime Watch, Block Watch, or Community Alert, for example. The most commonly used label is Neighborhood Watch. Thousands of Neighborhood Watch programs exist in the United States, and it is fair to describe them as the backbone of the Nation's community crime prevention effort.

Neighborhood Watch asks residents of an area to get to know each other, watch out for each other, be alert, and be willing to call the police when something is amiss. Thus, it can be a vehicle toward a number of community crime prevention goals: decreasing opportunities for offenders to act undetected, improving citizen-police relationships, overcoming people's feelings of powerlessness about crime, enhancing a "sense of community" among neighbors, and raising the level of informal social control that people exercise over their environments.

This report outlines the results of a national study of Neighborhood Watch carried out in 1985. The study assessed what is happening in Neighborhood Watch programs (including their strengths and weaknesses) and identified ways to improve existing programs and facilitate the development of new programs. Examination of local evaluation reports on Neighborhood Watch programs shows:

■ Neighborhood Watch can produce at least short-term reductions in certain types of crime, particu-

larly residential burglary, though the amount of crime reduction in some Neighborhood Watch programs may be difficult to ascertain because of weaknesses in the local evaluation.

■ Neighborhood Watch programs are more likely to be effective when they are part of general-purpose or multi-issue community groups, rather than when they address crime problems in isolation.

■ Participation in Neighborhood Watch tends to increase *awareness* of crime as a problem, but effects on the *fear* of crime are uncertain.

■ The ability of Neighborhood Watch to produce greater community attachment is uncertain.

Research Method

The research had three primary components. First, questionnaires were sent to 2,300 Neighborhood Watch leaders nationwide. Given the response rate of 26 percent, the survey results must be interpreted cautiously. Researchers then visited 10 communities to observe programs in operation and interview program managers and participants. The researchers also reviewed evaluation reports, handbooks, newsletters, and training manuals. Other documents, including funding proposals submitted by local crime prevention groups to a State agency and the results of a survey of 500 block captains in one city, were examined.

National Overview

The Neighborhood Watch programs that responded to our survey were relatively new ones. The formation of programs peaked in the late 1970's and early 1980's, a time when several national projects emphasized Neighborhood Watch. Few programs were established before the mid-1970's, and there appears to be a decline in program initiation during recent years.

The survey responses paint a picture of voluntary citizen activity in close association with law enforcement. Virtually all the programs received startup and ongoing advice from local police or sheriff's departments. However, fewer than half reported receiving financial assistance during startup. For them, the primary source of funds was voluntary contributions. More than 70 percent indicated that they have no formal operating budget. Approximately 80 percent of the administrative staffs of the programs are volunteers.

The neighborhoods in which programs exist are predominantly middle-income, racially homogenous areas with no commercial establishments. In most cases, the population consists primarily of long-term residents living in single-family, owner-occupied homes. Residential burglary seems to be the focal concern of the program. Neighborhood Watch was much more likely to be instituted to prevent development of a crime problem than to deal with an existing crime problem.

Newsletters and regularly scheduled meetings are used extensively to disseminate information to participants. Approximately 60 percent of the responding programs report using at least one of these and 40 percent use both.

Neighborhood Watch groups engage in a wide range of specific crime prevention activities as well as crime-related and community-oriented activities.

Engraving property with identification numbers and conducting home security surveys are especially common. There is also a focus on physical environmental concerns, crime reporting mechanisms, and assisting crime victims.

All the surveyed programs use informal surveillance, but less than 10 percent restrict themselves to that activity, as Table 1 shows.

The 66 programs engaging in "organized surveillance" use citizen patrols in addition to informal surveillance. The popularity of efforts to resolve environmental concerns (graffiti, trash collection, etc.), and to improve street lighting, as well as crime-tip hotlines and block parenting, were confirmed in site visits and through other contacts with Neighborhood Watch programs. However, these sources suggest that the survey underestimates the extent to which telephone chains are used in Neighborhood Watch and overestimates the proportion of programs engaging in victim/witness assistance.

Organization and Sponsorship

There is a typical Neighborhood Watch structure in the United States. A single agency, usually a police department, sponsors programs throughout the jurisdiction. The basic organizational unit is a single block, whose participants choose a block captain. Groups of blocks are generally headed by a neighborhood coordinator.

In some places, an additional organizational level exists between neighborhoods and the jurisdiction-wide sponsor. This model is found most often in small- to medium-sized cities, towns, and suburbs. Variations exist primarily in larger cities where major subsections of a city have well-established identities not easily amalgamated into a unified structure.

Another important variation on the structure is the use of some organization or agency other than the police as the jurisdiction-wide sponsor. While non-police sponsors may exhibit a more single-minded concentration on community crime prevention than do most police departments, they often lack the authority that many Neighborhood Watch participants seek.

However, there are benefits to sponsorship by organizations that address a variety of issues, including those not directly crime-related. Neighborhood improvement groups, homeowners' associations, block clubs, and so forth have established organizational structures, and their memberships consist of the people who are most active in dealing with community issues. These groups can integrate crime prevention with other local concerns because of the range of interests among their members and their links with other organizations, institutions, and public agencies.

Issues in Neighborhood Watch Operations

Information from site visits identified a variety of issues that commonly confront Neighborhood Watch programs.

1. **Role of the Police**
   Police departments are heavily involved in starting and managing Neighborhood Watch Programs.

Table 1   Activities engaged in by Neighborhood Watch Programs (based on program survey responses)

Activity	Number	Percent
Neighborhood Watch only	49	8.9
Crime prevention specific		
Project Operation Identification	425	80.6
Home security surveys	357	67.9
Street lighting improvement	183	34.7
Block parenting	144	27.3
Organized surveillance	66	12.0
Traffic alteration	37	7.0
Emergency telephones	24	4.6
Project Whistle Stop	18	3.4
Specialized informal surveillance	18	3.4
Escort service	12	2.3
Hired guards	11	2.1
Environmental design	7	1.3
Lock provision/installation	4	0.7
Self defense/rape prevention	3	0.5
Crime related		
Crime tip hotline	197	37.5
Victim witness assistance	101	19.2
Court watch	17	3.2
Telephone chain	7	1.3
Child fingerprinting	2	0.4
Community oriented		
Physical environmental concerns	201	38.1
Insurance premium deduction survey	20	3.6
Quality of life	9	1.6
Medical emergency	4	0.7

Most citizen groups appear to want the legitimacy that police sponsorship confers. Current evaluations indicate that successful programs are more likely to involve some form of citizen and police collaboration (Rosenbaum et al. 1987).

Deteriorated, low-income, heterogenous neighborhoods with a high crime rate are more resistant to Neighborhood Watch organizing efforts than stable, homogeneous middle-class neighborhoods populated by homeowners. Intergroup conflicts and distrust of the police make it more difficult for Neighborhood Watch to succeed under police sponsorship in such neighborhoods.

The police role in program initiation can be characterized by whether police crime prevention officers actively try to organize citizen involvement or respond to citizen requests for their assistance.

After the program is established, police departments rely primarily on formal links to maintain contact with programs: Newsletters, meetings, organizational structures, and criteria that groups must satisfy periodically in order to retain official certification as Neighborhood Watch programs.

Police departments face certain problems sponsoring Neighborhood Watch programs. These include: (1) providing leadership and setting goals while fostering self-sufficiency and experimentation among citizen groups; (2) integrating of crime prevention with more traditional police functions without allowing crime prevention resources to be absorbed by those functions; (3) generating citizen interest without using scare tactics or promising more than can be delivered; and (4) selecting police officers with the interest and aptitude for working with citizens and providing adequate reward structures for such officers.

2. **Participation and Survival of Programs**

Continuing participation by residents is critical to a program's survival and effectiveness. Programs in stable, low-crime neighborhoods do not give participants enough to do; motivating people to remain alert is difficult when the situations for which they are to remain alert rarely occur. In contrast, crime in other neighborhoods may be so frequent and deep-rooted that the relatively mild intervention represented by Neighborhood Watch may be seen as insufficient to deal with the problem.

For both kinds of neighborhoods, the solution seems to lie in linking Neighborhood Watch with more general community problem-solving efforts, placing Neighborhood Watch within multi-issue local associations, and addressing local concerns that arouse and enlist the energies and interest of the residents, whether these be jobs for youth, deteriorating housing, drug dealing, trash pickups, or barking dogs.

3. **Program Operations**

A variety of techniques have been developed by Neighborhood Watch programs. Among these are:

■ *Internal communications.* Approaches used include a hierarchical organizational structure (in which each participant is only responsible for contacting a small number of others), telephone chains, computer-assisted telephoning, periodic meetings, and newsletters.

■ *Neighborhood Watch signs.* The design and size of Neighborhood Watch signs vary little throughout the Nation. However, communities follow different procedures for deciding where to place signs and how to pay for them.

■ *Enhancing surveillance.* Improving street lighting and removing visual impediments are the primary physical means of enhancing surveillance. A number of jurisdictions also are involving mail carriers and utility workers as a way of increasing the numbers of persons "watching out" on a more routine basis.

■ *Beyond watching and reporting.* The basic instruction to Neighborhood Watch participants is to watch and report to the police. Some Neighborhood Watch groups take more active steps, and

participants may be encouraged to go outside when something suspicious is observed, demonstrating their collective presence. In some programs participants leave their homes to photograph suspicious persons or vehicles.

■ *Police innovations.* Several police departments give their crime prevention officers sufficient latitude and resources to engage in community organizing and problem-solving efforts that go well beyond the traditional police role. These officers become key resources in the neighborhoods where they operate, helping residents to deal with other public agencies, to resolve disputes, and to address quality-of-life issues not normally considered within the police purview.

Conclusions and Recommendations

Neighborhood Watch has the potential for reducing property crimes, particularly residential burglary. The extent of crime reduction that has actually occurred is difficult to ascertain, however, because of weaknesses in some evaluation designs. There is little evidence that Neighborhood Watch, by itself, produces increased neighborhood attachment or sense of community.

The primary issues facing Neighborhood Watch today are how to maintain citizen participation in existing programs and how to make Neighborhood Watch attractive and effective for heterogenous, low-income, unstable, high-crime neighborhoods.

There are costs and benefits associated with police or civilian sponsorship of Neighborhood Watch. The police provide expert information and a stamp of legitimacy that most Neighborhood Watch participants want, but community crime prevention functions are often secondary to the other duties police departments perform.

Civilian organizations do not possess the aura of authority, but they are often more capable of giving crime prevention their undivided attention. Some form of partnership or collaboration between citizens and police in Neighborhood Watch can achieve the best of both worlds.

The following recommendations can help improve Neighborhood Watch programs:

■ The people who organize, lead, and participate in Neighborhood Watch should be encouraged to develop innovative practices and link Neighborhood Watch to other local concerns. Less emphasis should be placed on formal standards for Neighborhood Watch programs, primarily certification and recertification criteria. Alternative ways of operating Neighborhood Watch should not be precluded by jurisdiction-wide, predetermined criteria.

■ Neighborhood Watch organizers and managers should make greater efforts to consider the characteristics and needs of specific neighborhoods and to tailor Neighborhood Watch efforts to them. Neighborhood Watch functions should be lodged within existing neighborhood or block associations when possible. Where a local association does not exist, organizers should be open to Neighborhood Watch as a possible starting point for one.

■ Police departments, as the primary sponsors of Neighborhood Watch, need to strengthen crime prevention units by enhancing their organizational status, giving them sufficient resources, selecting personnel likely to work well with community groups, and providing appropriate rewards and a career path for such personnel.

■ When citizen interest wanes, Neighborhood Watch sponsors should innovate rather than merely exhort. Flexibility and innovation in the basic Neighborhood Watch model can be enhanced by building on such existing tools as meetings and newsletters to create networks for exchanging promising ideas and information among jurisdictions.

Discussion Questions

1. What is a Neighborhood Watch program, and what are its main objectives?

2. What is the role of police agencies in supporting Neighborhood Watch programs, and how could that role be expanded?

3. Discuss the major techniques used in developing Neighborhood Watch programs. Do you have any ideas for future efforts?

4. What are the major roadblocks to citizen involvement in crime prevention at the neighborhood level?

National Institute of Justice

Research in Action

Block Watches Help Crime Victims in Philadelphia

Peter Finn, Abt Associates, Inc.

November/December 1986

An emergency call sends police officers rushing to the scene of an assault, where they find a young man who has been savagely beaten by a gang of thugs. They rush him to the hospital, talk to witnesses, and set off to catch the criminals who did it.

The criminal justice system knows its job: find the suspects, charge them, prosecute them, punish them if convicted. A corps of highly trained professionals—police officers, attorneys, judges, probation officers, corrections officials—stands ready to do its part.

But the victim and his family need help, and they need more than medical attention and a sympathetic interview. Police and prosecutors have come to recognize this need in recent years, but often their agencies are not equipped to do much about it.

When a crime like this occurred in Philadelphia recently, the victim's family received a telephone call from someone in the neighborhood offering to help. The caller was a member of the block watch (sometimes called town watch, block club, or neighborhood watch) in which local residents band together to keep an eye on their neighborhood and to alert police whenever they see something suspicious. In most communities, block watch members play no role after a crime has been committed, but in Philadelphia many members have been trained to provide crucial assistance to victims.

The call from the block watch neighbor was simple: "How are you getting along? Is there anything I can do to help?" When the neighbor found that the victim's mother was distraught, she comforted her and helped her get information about her son.

Eventually, the young victim began to express a commonly held fear—that his attackers would assault him again if he pressed charges. The block watch

neighbor reassured him. When it came time to go to court, the neighbor escorted the victim and sat through the proceedings.

Such neighbor-to-neighbor involvement is common in northwest Philadelphia. It is the result of a pioneering partnership among police, a victim assistance program, and neighborhood block watch organizations. Together, they help victims with short-term, immediate needs and with the long-term goal of making the neighborhood safer.

The effort blends several themes that have run through recent efforts to improve the criminal justice system's responsiveness to crime: attention to the needs of victims, the use of volunteers to make communities safer, and the need to go forward despite the shortage of funds for major expansion of government services.

In most places, block watch programs limit themselves to surveillance, and victims' programs often have inadequate resources to provide all the help that victims need. The Philadelphia program is unusual: it enables block watch volunteers to expand their traditional role by assisting victims after a crime has occurred.

In Philadelphia, neighborhood block watch programs continue to patrol local communities looking for potential crimes. But many participants have been trained to provide specific services to the victims: reassurance, referral, practical assistance, explanations of procedures, and followup.

Why turn to block watches for helping victims? First, block watch members have already demonstrated their concern about local community problems. They are organized and committed to take action. Savvy block watches also know that they must diversify to keep members motivated. Furthermore, thousands of block watch members across the country already informally help neighbors victimized by crime. In short, many people who are aroused enough to stop crime are also predisposed to help its victims.

Beginnings

The catalyst for the Philadelphia program was Catherine Bachrach, a former Peace Corps worker who was district supervisor of a citywide crime prevention organization and eventually director of a victim assistance effort, the Community Safety Program.[1] Begun in 1981 by the Northwest Interfaith Movement, the program serves the 375,000 residents of the northwest part of the city, which has one-quarter of Philadelphia's area and one-fifth of its crime.

Working with the crime prevention organization, Bachrach discovered that a number of block watch volunteers were interested in helping victims—not so much because they saw the victim's need for emotional support, but more because they wanted frightened victims to show up in court. Residents knew that many cases were dismissed at the preliminary hearing—the first stage of the court process—simply because victims failed to testify. Often victims lacked transportation, feared getting involved in the criminal justice system, or were afraid of retaliation by the defendant. If neighbors offered to accompany them to the preliminary hearings, victims might be more willing to testify and more cases might be prosecuted. To help, some block watch members volunteered to escort victims personally to court.

At the same time, some victims were contacting the crime prevention organization for help in coping with anxiety caused by the crime. Bachrach decided to link the unmet needs of victims with block watches' concern with crime prevention. She gave victims and block watches the same message: "If you and your neighbors show up in court, the system will take notice. Then, with appropriate sentences, you'll be safer

in your neighborhood as criminals spread the word that your part of town is not a 'safe' place in which to rob and steal."

Bachrach tested the collaboration several times. The results suggested that the criminal justice system treated cases more seriously when block watchers were involved in the proceedings. Fewer cases were dropped, cases were assigned to more experienced prosecutors and were more thoroughly prepared, and sentences were more severe.

Shaping a Formal Partnership

When Bachrach became head of the Community Safety Program in early 1981, she knew the small program could never by itself meet the needs of the 15,000 yearly victims of serious crimes in northwest Philadelphia. If block watch members could perform even a few simple victim assistance services, the Community Safety Program would be free to concentrate on professional or complicated victim services, such as counseling in serious cases and showing victims how to file crime compensation applications.

Block watches could also help refer victims to the new program. In Philadelphia, the Community Safety Program could not routinely obtain names of victims from police, but block watches, working closely with police, could. In addition, some victims ordinarily would avoid the service because they saw it as an intimidating, impersonal bureaucracy. But they might contact it on the recommendation of their own neighbors. Finally, block watches could extend the reach of the Community Safety Program by providing information to the wider community about victim needs and the victim compensation programs.

Bachrach made working with block watches a major focus of the new program. She started encouraging victims to ask neighbors to accompany them to the preliminary hearing, the trial, and sentencing. At the same time, she began on a case-by-case basis to contact block watches—with the victim's permission—to urge them to escort the victim to court.

It was clear, however, that block watch members would need training if they were to be more than escorts. Within a few months, Bachrach conducted the first of many training sessions for active block watch members to explain how a sensitive and concerned neighbor could provide emotional support to victims and furnish

---

1. Since the completion of this article, the Community Safety Program has separated from the Northwest Interfaith Movement and become an independent, nonprofit organization. The program's new name is Northwest Victim Services.

accurate information about the criminal justice system. The training was intended to develop a core of reliable volunteers.

Preliminary Hearing Services

In March 1982, the Community Safety Program decided to focus on the preliminary hearing—the first formal step leading to a trial. The site was the 14th Police District station—one of four police districts in northwest Philadelphia and one of 10 stations in the city where preliminary hearings are held. The district covers 10 square miles and has 115,000 residents. The district ranked sixth among the city's 23 police districts in 1984 in major crimes.

The preliminary hearing is a critical point in the prosecution as well as a stressful event for victims. The hearing is held in local police stations 3 to 10 days after arrest. Victims are suddenly introduced to the confusion of the criminal justice system. Often they are startled to find themselves sitting or standing almost next to the defendant.

Program leaders turned to block watch members active in aiding victims to help program staff furnish information and accompany victims to the court.

Bachrach worked closely with the Community Safety Program's advisory board—in particular, a defense attorney, a detective, and an assistant district attorney—to design the service, to prepare informational handouts, and to write a formal proposal to the commissioner. The district attorney and the presiding judge of the Municipal Court were enthusiastic about the proposed arrangement. The district attorney assigned a special assistant to smooth the way, and the judge cleared the project on a trial basis with the police commissioner. The project was named the Information and Support Service.

As the final step, trained block watch volunteers participated in an orientation session that would equip them to help the staff implement the project.

There were a few problems. Police officers were irate on one occasion when a block watch volunteer told the wrong victim that her case had been postponed and she could go home; the judge almost dismissed the case. While mistakes like this one are rare, they underscore the importance of comprehensive training. Overall, however, observers concluded that volunteer block watch members can effectively orient victims to the

proceedings and can make them feel less anxious about testifying in court.

The Vital Role of Law Enforcement

From the beginning, it was obvious that any community program needed the police to work with it as full partners in helping victims. Bachrach knew that the program had to demonstrate its effectiveness and staying power before police administrators would agree to promote it.

The program also had to prove that it could be trusted—that a block watch member would not ruin a case by giving bad advice to a victim or by tampering with evidence; that victims' privacy would be respected; and that the program and a block watch would not join forces to protest the way police handled a victim. Some officers were especially concerned that encouraging block watches to assist victims might stimulate unreasonable citizen demands for additional police services.

Program staff members began by working informally with individual officers on specific cases as the need arose. But once the Information and Support Service had been set up, a few detectives began to approach the program for help in getting frightened or apathetic victims to show up in court.

The program also let commanding officers know when block watch members were especially disturbed about a specific crime so that special police attention could be devoted to the case, thus averting community accusations of police inaction. A case involving a stabbing, for example, aroused considerable community concern. The program kept the detective assigned to the case informed of the availability of block watch members to accompany the victim to the lineup and the preliminary hearing.

The Community Safety Program and police also began to work together in training block watch members and volunteers. Police had participated in the program's first training sessions in May 1982. Subsequently, the program and police cosponsored a series of workshops for block watches. By October, the Community Safety Program was using the police department's monthly district community workshops to run a mock trial for prospective Information and Support Service volunteers, most of whom were block watch members, to show them how the criminal justice system worked and how they could help.

Eventually, the police also helped the program to expand its contacts with block watches. Some officers identified active block watches that seemed like good candidates for providing victim services, encouraged block watch members to volunteer, and told victims they could get help from their block watch and from the Community Safety Program.

Although she did not formally approach the police command, Bachrach carefully kept each successive police captain in the 14th district informed of her

---

Block Watches Help Crime Victims in Various Ways

Most of the services that block watch volunteers offer to victims can be provided by any properly motivated volunteer; other services require training. No block watch can provide all types of help. Figure 1 lists many of the types of assistance block watch members in Philadelphia have provided to victims.

Here are some examples of block watch activities:

■ *Reassuring the victim.* Let victims know that neighbors are concerned and ready to help. This may involve nothing more than saying, " How are you getting along?" "I just wanted to say we're around the corner if you need some help." "Call me if you get scared."

■ *Staying with victims for an hour or two after a crime.* Many people are afraid to be alone after a traumatic event. Having someone there is particularly helpful with elderly men and women, who sometimes become virtual recluses after being victimized.

■ *Listening.* Let victims express their fears, retell what happened, and reveal their worries about the future. Often, neighbors are better listeners than friends and family who may be impatient with the victim's anxieties or contribute to the victim's feeling at fault for letting the crime occur. Neighbors may even be more effective than trained counselors because some victims trust only people they know and are intimidated by "professionals."

■ *Providing practical assistance.* When a neighbor came home one night to find that burglars had ransacked her house after pushing in the skylight, a couple of agile block watch members temporarily boarded up the roof to prevent anyone from returning. When another family had all their money, major appliances, and food stolen, the block watch lent them money from its treasury and collected food from the neighborhood. Block watch members sometimes babysit when victims make trips to the doctor or court.

■ *Accompanying victims to court or to local services.* A mugging victim who ignored two court summonses to appear at a lineup agreed to go only when a block watch captain arranged for three neighbors to accompany her. One block watch captain pleaded to get permission from a badly bleeding—but uninsured—victim to call an ambulance but

ended up driving the injured man to the hospital to spare him the $100 ambulance fee.

■ *Helping victims obtain other help.* This might include filing with the crime victims compensation program or requesting financial assistance from a community safety program, or seeking local professional counseling.

■ *Helping victims make informed decisions.* One block watch captain strongly encouraged a mugging victim who was reluctant to report the crime to telephone the police. The volunteer had learned in training that reporting helps victims regain a feeling of control over their lives. He also explained to the victim that insurance compensation often depends on reporting the crime to the police within 48 to 72 hours.

■ *Explaining the criminal justice system.* Let victims know what to expect when police arrive and what will happen in court.

■ *Providing liaison with police and prosecutor.* When victims are afraid to leave their homes, a block watch can persuade the police to increase local street patrol or persuade the prosecutor to ask the court's warrant unit to make an extra effort to locate a defendant who may have jumped bail.

There are some caveats to consider, however. Some social service professionals warn that block watch members who are ineffective may cause damage if they try to help victims who feel suicidal, cannot meet the ordinary demands of their daily routines, express unrelenting anger and guilt at having been victimized, or are unable to put the experience behind them. These victims need professional counseling. As a result, block watch members should rarely become involved with victims of sexual assault, families of murder victims, and battered spouses, leaving such cases to professionals.

Bachrach nonetheless believes that one should not underestimate what a sensitive, trained volunteer can do for even seriously troubled victims. Moreover, in many communities, professional counseling services are either unavailable or prohibitively expensive, so the block watch members are a viable alternative to no assistance at all.

activities. Because of her low-key but determined leadership, commanding and line officers alike learned that Bachrach fully understood and respected police work. Credit for building police support also goes to an especially committed community relations officer whose strong belief that block watch members could help victims led him to share neighborhood contacts and help set up and run the training workshops.

Another important factor that stimulated police involvement was the city government's high priority on promoting good police-community relations. Detectives and community relations officers increasingly felt they had support from their commanders for working with the program. At the same time, police administrators' support was strengthened as they received positive reports about the program from their staff. Bachrach knew that the police were truly committed when she went to explain the program to new captains in the district and found that they had already been briefed about the program from their predecessors—and were ready to support it.

Expanding the Program

While the initial program began as a grassroots affair, the program was introduced into the 35th police district—in the largest and busiest section of the city—largely from the top down. Some months after the Information and Support Service had been set up in the 14th district, a court officer invited the captain of the 35th Police District's Division to attend a mock trial training session for volunteers at the 14th district's monthly police community workshop. Impressed by what he heard and saw, the captain asked the Community Safety Program to set up a similar service in his district.

With 152,000 people, the 35th district is the city's most populous and currently has the highest major crime rate in the city.

Expansion of the program had to wait nearly 6 months until Bachrach was able to amass the required funds, staff, and trained volunteers. However, because some block watches from the 35th district had participated in its training sessions, the program had a head start in recruiting volunteers and promoting victim assistance in the new district. The partnership also flourished quickly because of favorable reports from officers recently transferred from the 14th district. Once again, a well-established community relations officer, along with a highly regarded detective, provided critical

support. They actively promoted the partnership among local block watches and cosponsored training of program volunteers.

Building and Maintaining Comprehensive Police Support

In both districts, captains and lieutenants worked out some concerns about how the arrangement might affect patrol or investigative operations.

The program, in turn, made every effort to accommodate the needs of the police department. Staff members took care to follow through on every police request, at any hour, whether or not it related to victim assistance. One Sunday evening, for instance, a police official telephoned Bachrach at home for help with an officer who was having a serious family problem. The next morning Bachrach appeared in the captain's office with a detailed list of sources of assistance. Bachrach also sent letters of commendation to the captains when an officer used the program effectively; the letters went into the officers' personnel files. These and other seemingly small actions were noted and appreciated by police.

The program advisory board also helped in working with the police. A detective and retired police community relations officer on the board promoted the effort among other officers, and they conveyed police concerns about the partnership to the board for action. The board helped design volunteer training workshops and develop the Information and Support Service.

The program proved useful in mediating occasional conflicts that arose between block watches and police over how victims were treated. One such case involved a victim who complained that she was being repeatedly harassed by burglars and was not getting adequate attention from the police. Concerns were raised about apparent inaction by the police department.

Bachrach met with the victim, her block watch, and the police to try to resolve the issue. She encouraged the block watch to increase its patrols of the woman's street and home, and she helped to explain to the victim, the block watch, and the press the detectives' strenuous efforts to apprehend the burglars and their limitations in doing more.

For the most part, block watches themselves tried to steer clear of problems with the police by avoiding any activities that might encroach on law enforcement, such as directly trying to protect victims against intimi-

Figure 1. Assistance block watches provide victims

Type of assistance	Training importance
Reassurance	
Express concern	desirable
Offer to help	desirable
Stay with the victim	desirable
Lend sympathetic ear	desirable
Practical assistance	
Babysit	not necessary
Keep watch over house	not necessary
Make security repairs	not necessary
Provide transportation	not necessary
Lend emergency pocket money or food	not necessary
Help complete crime victim compensation forms	necessary
Criminal justice system orientation	
Encourage reporting of the crime	desirable
Explain the criminal justice system	necessary
Reduce fear of criminal justice system	necessary
Escort	
Accompany to lineup	necessary
Accompany to court	necessary
Intermediary with law enforcement agency or prosecutor	
Obtain quick law enforcement assistance	necessary
Inform victim of case status	necessary
Inform prosecutor of special victim needs	necessary
Referral	necessary

dation or to collect or touch evidence. In fact, block watch members often assisted investigating officers by warning the victim not to touch anything that might be used as evidence and by calming the victim so the police interview could begin promptly.

As the partnership expanded in each district, officers noticed increased community understanding and support. By assisting victims, the police demonstrated sensitivity to community needs. Police were invited more frequently to block watch and community meetings, and cooperation between community groups and the police grew. Despite their understandable reluctance to describe their operations to the public, police found that explaining how the department assigned priorities to calls for assistance helped residents become more tolerant of the time it took to answer complaints about disorderly behavior.

The community began to understand how difficult it is for police to provide everything the public expects of them. In fact, some block watch members began to

explain and defend police priorities to their neighbors. While at first there were more requests for police services, as some officers originally feared, soon there were fewer and more reasonable requests.

By the end of 1983, the partnership had grown into a formally approved and fully operating arrangement throughout northwest Philadelphia.[2]

Currently, the Community Safety Program links block watch members with victims in need. Training has taken place both informally at block watch meetings and formally in the 12 volunteer training sessions conducted to date.

---

2. The program also worked with two other northwest Philadelphia police districts because the detective division headquartered in the 35th district serves all four of northwest Philadelphia's districts and because preliminary hearings for crimes committed in the other two districts were held at either the 35th or 14th district stationhouses. However, collaboration with these other two districts was modest because of their small population and relative lack of crime.

The program coordinates the entire effort and mediates misunderstandings and disagreements. The police refer victims both to the program and to block watches, identify potential program volunteers, join in training, and cooperate with the Information and Support Service at the preliminary hearing. Block watch members provide most of the 75 trained volunteers who staff the preliminary hearing information desk. They also help victims in a variety of other ways.

Dealing with Liability Issues

From the beginning, program staff members were concerned about the Community Safety Program's liability if volunteers had an accident while transporting a victim to court or if they gave a victim misinformation (or even accurate information) that caused emotional distress. In such cases, victims might sue the program. In addition, volunteers might sue the program if the victim, or the defendant, assaulted them.

The Northwest Interfaith Movement's attorney examined the organization's liability policy and determined that only if staff were negligent in using volunteers could a victim or volunteer successfully sue the program—for example, if staff failed to screen volunteers for mental stability, or if they placed a volunteer in a risky situation without warning. The liability policy protects the program if staff are found negligent.

To avoid lawsuits, staff screen volunteers carefully. They rigorously train volunteers in what to say—and not say—to victims. They explain the legal position as well. (They can be successfully sued by a victim if they are negligent, and they cannot sue the program unless the staff are negligent.) Some volunteers have begun to be more cautious about transporting victims to court themselves; instead, they arrange for the police department or district attorney's office to provide transportation for both them and victims. Block watches elsewhere have taken out insurance policies.

Training Volunteers

Bachrach knew from the start that neighbors who tried to help victims could sometimes make things worse rather than better. Even providing reassurance can be damaging if the block watch member implies, even inadvertently, that the victim was to blame for the crime, or scolds the victim for losing control. Neighbors could also take complete charge of the victim's welfare and encourage an unhealthy dependency. In addition, block watch members could misinform victims about the criminal justice process or prejudice them against the system.

To prevent these problems, the Community Safety Program provides four 2-hour weekly training sessions for all block watch members who become program volunteers. The sessions instruct volunteers in:

- What the victimization experience is like and how to understand it, typically by having victims describe what they experienced and the type of help they wanted.
- What victims need immediately after the crime and over the long term.
- How to respond to victims—for example, how to listen, how not to blame.
- When to recommend that victims seek professional help.
- How the criminal justice system works.

In addition, to orient block watch members who are not formally involved in the program, Community Safety Program staff attend block watch meetings where they promote awareness of victim needs and suggest how members can help victims even without formal training. The program provides continuing education to block watches by issuing a quarterly newsletter, making periodic announcements of new referral sources, and offering relevant lectures.

Problems Experienced

To protect confidentiality, police and the Community Safety Program only provide block watches with victims' names and telephone numbers if the victims give permission. Occasionally, this causes a delay. Block watch volunteers may not know a neighbor has been victimized for some time after the incident has occurred. Block watches often try to minimize this delay by publicizing their victim services. They tell neighbors about them and talk to community and church groups. Many victims, of course, contact their block watch on the advice of the police or the Community Safety Program.

Bachrach found that some block watch members ignore victims because the help they can give seems so trivial. Training explains the importance of simple acts of neighborliness, such as expressing concern over the incident or staying with the victim for a half-hour after the crime. In some block watches, members who have themselves been crime victims also help counteract apathy by providing first-hand descriptions of a victim's problems and needs.

Effective victim services also have difficulty taking root in neighborhoods with many transient residents, or in block watch programs that lack the structure and organization required to go beyond crime prevention activities.

Keeping up Interest

To foster interest, program staff members often encourage victims to join the block watch, since past victims can be a potential source of new members. Once they have joined, victims can explain to the members how important and easy it would be to help other victims. When giving presentations to block watches, staff members often bring one or two victims to describe how reassuring it was when a neighbor took a few minutes to offer assistance.

Apathy is also overcome as members realize that they, too, benefit from helping victims. Block watches have learned from experience that to remain in existence they must engage in more activities than simply patrolling the neighborhood. Program staff and police can often show block watches how adding victim services can help maintain members' interest in the group.

On a more personal level, some retired or semiretired block watch members discover that helping victims is a stimulating way to remain active. Others simply find it satisfying to help people in need. Assisting victims also affords members a chance to get to know their neighbors. A few block watch captains enjoy developing a special relationship with patrol officers and detectives. Local residents who assist victims receive public recognition and awards at annual receptions attended by high-ranking law enforcement and city officials.

Spreading the Partnership to Other Communities

The Philadelphia partnership shows that not just victims—but also the police, block watches, and the entire criminal justice system—can benefit from a coordinated effort. The specific manner in which the three

groups collaborate in Philadelphia reflects local conditions—for example, the convenient location of the preliminary hearings in police stations and the strong pressure from the mayor's office to improve police-community relations.

Other jurisdictions that plan block watches will need to tailor their approach to the opportunities and constraints their own communities present. For example, if existing services are capable of transporting and escorting victims to court, the partnership might focus instead on training block watch members to provide crisis intervention to victims immediately after the crime and on arranging for block watches to find out quickly when someone has been victimized.

Other groups besides a victim assistance program can initiate the partnership. Police and sheriff's departments may be in a good position to introduce collaboration in many communities, because law enforcement officers are often the first to come into contact with victims and already understand many of their needs for immediate assistance.

When a law enforcement agency with an established relationship with block watches takes the initiative, developing the partnership can be much easier. Even without such a formal link, block watches almost always look to law enforcement for leadership, because their principal concern is crime prevention.

Although busy police administrators and sheriffs traditionally have not regarded helping victims as a part of their official responsibility or may have a reluctance to work closely with outside organizations, the Philadelphia experience shows that law enforcement stands to gain a great deal from becoming a full partner in a well-organized arrangement to help victims. In many departments there is a new breed of police community relations officer and police commander looking for ways to reach out to the community. Even one or two dynamic officers can be enough to start a strong program.

Why Philadelphia Succeeded

Three key ingredients contributed to northwest Philadelphia's success. The first was the leadership of a self-motivated, energetic, and far-sighted program director and the assistance of a highly supportive advisory committee. These individuals saw the partnership as a cost-effective way to assist victims of crime. Furthermore, by not being formally affiliated with a large bureaucracy, they could act boldly and quickly. The program also had in Bachrach a full-time staff person who could start a major new effort (although not without considerable unpaid overtime).

The second ingredient, which enabled the partnership to take root, was the existence of a few line officers in each police district who believed in the arrangement, and their police commanders who eventually lent their support.

The third indispensable ingredient was the willingness of block watch captains and members to experiment with a new neighborhood service.

Hundreds of communities have these ingredients— a dedicated victim assistance program director, a core of innovative law enforcement officers, and at least a few adventuresome block watches. Some jurisdictions will be eager to initiate this kind of arrangement because the partnership aids all three parties. These organizational benefits can be achieved without losing sight of the goal: to expand services to crime victims at a time when no single agency or organization can shoulder the entire burden for meeting the needs of this neglected group.

Discussion Questions

1. What was the catalyst that encouraged creation of the Philadelphia block watch program, and how could the Philadelphia model be applied to other areas?

2. What was the role of law enforcement agencies in the Philadelphia project? How can such programs encourage police support?

3 Discuss the ways block watch programs can help the victims of crime.

4. What were some of the major difficulties encountered by the Philadelphia program, and what actions were taken to counteract the problems?

National Institute of Justice

Research
in Action

Using Dolls to Interview Child Victims:
Legal Concerns and Interview Procedures

Kenneth R. Freeman, Los Angeles County Deputy District Attorney
and Terry Estrada-Mullaney, San Luis Obispo County Deputy District Attorney

January/February 1988

Prosecutors everywhere were stunned. The court affirmed a civil rights lawsuit judgment of $200,000 in punitive damages assessed personally against two deputy district attorneys. Did the Colorado Supreme Court case foreshadow things to come?

The case was *Higgs* v. *District Court (Douglas County)* 713 P.2d 840 (Colo. 1985). In its opinion, the court warned prosecutors that if they perform functions normally done by police officers (such as witness interviews), those functions must be done correctly, or prosecutors could face financial consequences.

In Fairfax County, Virginia, a father who previously had been arrested and accused of abuse was awarded $55,000 in a lawsuit against the Fairfax police officer who arrested him and interviewed his 10-year-old daughter. The daughter claimed that the police officer coerced her into saying that her father had photographed and molested her.

Both the *Higgs* case and the Fairfax, Virginia, case underscore the fact that even if you are the most conscientious front line law enforcement officer or prosecutor, you must be aware of the trial consequences of your investigative activities.

In child abuse cases, the victim interview is a particularly important area. When you use anatomical dolls, additional sensitive areas arise. Both prosecutors and police have been the subject of civil rights lawsuits that claimed in part that anatomical dolls were misused during victim interviews and, that as a result of this misuse, criminal charges were improperly initiated.

This article examines the possible advantages and disadvantages of using anatomical dolls, discusses when and where they may best be used, and looks at tech-niques to help you avoid the charge that dolls were misused during your interview.

The article is for those who work in law enforcement and prosecution, not therapy. It examines victim interviews as they will be seen at the trial under the scrutiny of defense attorneys and defense experts.

Court Rulings Send a Warning

In the *Higgs* case, the court held that prosecutors have absolute immunity from civil damages *only* when performing an "advocatory" function. When they perform an "investigative" function or an "administrative" function, they are only qualifiedly immune and could thus be *successfully sued* for damages.

Before *Higgs*, prosecutors argued that they have the duty to investigate and to discover new material the police may have missed. *Higgs*, however, said that if an activity is normally performed by police, it is investigative, and prosecutors can lose immunity if they do a police officer's job. Unfortunately, the court did not decide the issue of where to draw the line between investigation and prosecution.

Dolls are one of the many tools law enforcement teams can use to investigate an allegation of child sexual abuse. Obviously, you must use the dolls carefully and conduct the interview properly.

Defining Anatomical Dolls

Anatomical dolls differ from ordinary dolls; they have certain parts that are supposed to represent genitalia and resemble some orifices of the human body. Mental health professionals have referred to anatomical dolls in various ways—anatomically correct dolls, sexually anatomically correct dolls, or simply SAC dolls.

These past definitions have now been discarded, and professionals currently refer to the dolls as anatomically detailed or simply anatomical dolls. It is best not to call the dolls anatomically correct dolls because they are *not* anatomically complete and are *not* anatomical to scale.

For years, police and mental health and other professionals have used dolls in dealing with child abuse. Before the advent of anatomical dolls, they used ordinary dolls such as Ken and Barbie. Today, anatomical doll manufacturing has become a thriving industry, and many books and articles have been published on how best to use the dolls. Available as male, female, adult, and child, dolls come in various skin tones.

Using Dolls in Interviews

Increasingly, police and prosecutors are using dolls as an aid to interviewing children. You can use dolls at investigative interviews, case evaluation interviews, and during courtroom testimony. Indeed, some States have statutes that give a prosecutor the right to allow child witnesses to use the dolls in court to show what happened to them.

Anatomical dolls are not a crutch. They cannot be substituted for sound interviewing techniques. Indeed, trial attorneys have found that using dolls during interviews creates new issues not contemplated by those outside the criminal justice system.

Both research and the experience of criminal justice practitioners suggest that proper use of anatomical dolls can help you achieve several goals:

Establishing Rapport and Reducing Stress

The more stressed and nervous a child is during an interview, the more difficult the interview becomes, and the higher the anxiety level. Most children relate well to dolls, which can have a calming effect on them. Dolls can help the atmosphere become more relaxed for everyone. Also, because it is easier for the child to use dolls to show what happened than to tell what happened, dolls help you gather more information in less time and with fewer tears. This reduces the pressure on you, the interviewer, to ask the right questions. If dolls are visible as the child enters the room, they can create a softening effect, giving the area a child-oriented appearance.

Establishing Competency

During the get-acquainted period, you can show the dolls and ask the child about his or her dolls at home. Ask questions regarding colors, nonsexual body parts, and so forth. In this way, the dolls function as a bridge, permitting you to ask questions about something the child feels comfortable with as opposed to something as dry and routine as the standard competency questions. This introduction to the dolls has the further advantage of appearing more natural to both the child and to anyone who later scrutinizes the interview by cross-examination. Competency is thus integrated into the entire interview and is a less fruitful subject for cross-examination.

Reducing Vocabulary Problems

Using dolls can help you avoid the errors that sometimes occur when you and the child have different vocabularies and different understanding of the questions. Dolls give you a way to discuss sexual matters with children when you do not know their sexual vocabulary. They permit children who have their own vocabulary to show what certain words mean to them.

Showing What May be Difficult to Say

An interview can be overwhelming for young children. Even when they know the words, they may be too embarrassed to say them out loud to a stranger. With dolls, these children can point out and show things that are either difficult or even impossible for them to say. Dolls work because children find it easier to tell what happened by using something that is age-appropriate and familiar to them.

Common Criticisms of Interviews Using Dolls

Police, prosecutors, and others have been accused of not following accepted techniques for using dolls and of interviewing in a manner that encourages suggestion. Critics have said that anatomical dolls have no place in child sexual abuse interviews; dolls suggest fantasy to children, and exaggerated doll genitalia suggest sexual impropriety.

Dolls Suggest Abuse

Because most children's dolls normally do not have sexual parts, some commentators have complained that by showing anatomical dolls to children, a suggestion of sexual impropriety occurs. In addition, critics may say that children testifying in court are not testifying from their experience but rather from what they saw demonstrated with dolls during early interviews.

Dolls Can Be Used in Ways Contrary to Accepted Protocol

Another common criticism is that the interviewer did not use the dolls according to the manufacturer's intentions. Anatomical dolls often are shipped with complete instruction manuals. Enterprising critics might try to introduce these manuals into evidence and claim that since you did not follow the instructions, the results are invalid. As an alternative attack, an expert might testify that standard techniques for the use of dolls exist and you did not follow them.

Dolls Can Appear Bizarre

Dolls from different manufacturers may look quite different from each other. Some dolls have a look children find friendly, while others may appear menacing. Some dolls are completely out of scale, with disproportionately large sexual parts. The same is true in the child-adult size ratio. Some dolls are so bizarre looking that their use may unintentionally add humor to the case.

Planning the Interview

Interviewers have many techniques in addition to dolls when working with children. Often other methods will work better with a given child—crayons, pencils, coloring books, and drawings have been used. Sometimes nothing more than talking to the child is appropriate.

To decide what is best, plan the interview in advance, taking into account such things as the age of the child, whether or not there have been earlier interviews, and if so, the results of those interviews. If you decide to use dolls, inspect them before the interview, read any accompanying manuals, and be certain that the dolls are appropriate in looks and scale.

Age of Child

There is no set age range for using dolls in interviews. Usually, children 31/2 to 10 years old feel most comfortable with them. Teenagers, although embarrassed to talk about what happened to them, will say they don't want to show what happened to them by using dolls, especially if they hear that little children like using dolls.

Gathering the Facts

A good guideline is to introduce young children to the dolls during the get-acquainted part of the interview, then to use the dolls to aid in competency questions and to identify body parts. Later, when you are ready to discuss the facts, you should give the child the choice of describing things in the most comfortable way.

Earlier Interviews

If dolls have been used earlier in the case by others, there is a risk that things were done that may give rise to allegations that the earlier interview was done improperly.

If you discover that a child has had a previous interview, look, if possible, at the dolls that were used to determine if there is anything peculiar or suggestive about them. Talk to the previous interviewer to determine the techniques used and the manner in which the questions were asked. Do not use dolls repeatedly since multiple interviews of this kind provide the defense team with cross-examination opportunities, permitting the defense to ask the child how the dolls were shown the first time, how they were shown the second time, and so forth.

Therapist's Opinion

If dolls were used in a therapist's interview, check to see if the therapist's opinion regarding abuse was based on what the child said or on the child's interaction with the dolls. A current trend in diagnosis is observation of children playing with anatomical dolls and psychological analysis of the child's interaction. In this way, the therapist can diagnose whether the child has been sexually abused. This approach often is used with preverbal children or with those children too traumatized to describe what happened. Unfortunately, reliance on this type of diagnostic opinion may cause problems at trial.

Be aware that if the therapist's opinion reflects the child's interaction with the dolls rather than the child's description of what happened, that opinion may not be allowed in court under what is commonly known as the Frye rule, after *Frye* v. *United States,* 293 F.1013 (D.C. Cir. 1923). Under this rule, expert opinions regarding new scientific methods of proof are not allowed in court until after the prosecution has proved that the opinions are based on generally accepted and sound scientific knowledge.

Because the data are inconclusive about whether doll interaction diagnosis is accepted as reliable in the scientific community, it may not be possible for the prosecutor to show the court that the testimony is reliable before it is admitted into evidence.

This situation occurred in California in the recent case of *In re Amber B.,* 191 Cal. App.3d 682 (1987). That case ruled that the therapist's diagnosis from observation of the child interacting with the dolls was *inadmissible* in California unless the technique can be shown to be generally accepted as reliable in the scientific community in which it was developed.

Techniques for Using Anatomical Dolls

If, after weighing the pros and cons, you decide to use dolls, you should follow these techniques:

Introduce Dolls

Introduce the dolls fully clothed. Put them on the table where the interview is to be conducted so they are visible as the child comes into the room. This makes the dolls less threatening.

Begin by introducing yourself. Ask the child about school, pets, and any dolls he or she has at home. This gives children a chance to talk about themselves and allows you to measure how articulate and intelligent a particular child is. From here, you can ask competency questions using the dolls to show that the child understands concepts such as color or size.

As with all criminal justice interviews, the possibility exists that the defense will claim you coached or put words into the mouth of the child witness. Using dolls makes your case particularly vulnerable to the coaching

defense; whoever uses the dolls first may be accused of coaching. It may be claimed that the dolls were put into a suggestive position and the child was then asked, "Did that happen?"

If a witness is present during the interview, the witness can rebut the claim of coaching. The jury then has the benefit of hearing what the child said from another witness, and the claim of coaching has therefore made relevant what would otherwise be inadmissible hearsay.

The charge of coaching can also be rebutted by using audio or video taping. If you are comfortable with taping your interview, the jury can see and hear what may be a powerful recording of the child tearfully describing what the defendant did.

The technique of having a witness present or of taping the interview forces the defense to choose between foregoing the coaching defense or permitting powerful hearsay to be presented to the jury. It provides corroborating proof that your interview was proper and demonstrates the futility of the coaching claim.

Learn the Child's Sexual Vocabulary

After deciding that the child is a competent witness, find out what the child's words are for sexual parts. As will be discussed later, avoid pointing to or touching the doll's sexual parts when the child is telling what happened. However, pointing to and touching the dolls is appropriate when you are trying to learn the child's sexual vocabulary. You might say:

> "Okay, you're really good on colors. Do you know about parts of the body? (Picking up doll and pointing to her hair.) What's this?"

Continue in this way, going to easy, nonsexual things like hands, arms, feet. Then say something like this:

> "Why don't we take off the shirt and see what's there." (Taking off the doll's shirt and pointing to belly button.) "What's this?" (Taking off pants and pointing to genitals.) "What's this?" After the child answers, it is important to follow up with "Ever hear it called anything else?" "What?" "Who calls it that?"

These questions illustrate how to move from sexual part identification to the facts of the case in a nonleading, nontraumatic way. Often the offender will use and teach the child slang words and the child may not realize that these words are inappropriate. You can also make the transition when discussing the child doll's genitals and before showing the adult dolls. Ask if the child knows how children's sexual parts differ from those of adults. Before showing the adult dolls to the children, ask if they have ever seen an adult's sexual parts, and if so, whose?

Determine the Case Facts

Before going over what happened, ask the child if it would be easier to *tell* you what happened or to *show* you what happened using dolls. If the child wants to use dolls, then ask questions in an open-ended, nonleading manner:

> Q: "Mary, do you know why you are here?"
>
> A: "Uh-huh." (affirmative)
>
> Q: "Why?"
>
> A: "Frank (the suspect) did bad things to me."
>
> Q: "Can you tell me what he did?"
>
> A: (Silence, looking down to floor, eyes tearing.)
>
> Q: "Would it be easier for you to show me with the dolls?"
>
> A: (Nodding, taking dolls.) "I was here, and he was here" (placing adult doll on top of child doll).
>
> Q: "Where were you when this happened, Mary?"
>
> A: "In the bedroom."

Because children normally use dolls in play, and because this play often involves fantasy, critics may claim that what the children tell you is the product of fantasy encouraged by you, the interviewer. This can be a particular problem if you use terminology that makes it look as if you are encouraging fantasy. It is therefore unwise to say to the child: "Let's pretend that this girl-doll is you and this man-doll is Frank (name of suspect)." Other words or phrases to avoid: "Imagine," "make believe," "play act," "game," or "let's imagine that."

All pointing, touching, positioning, and describing of sexual acts must be done exclusively by the child. If you do any of these things, you may be accused of suggesting answers to the child. Even if the purpose of the pointing or touching is to confirm what the child said first, you may be accused of coaching. This is especially true if the interview was not taped because it may be impossible for the jury to understand the order of the touching.

Any arranging or touching of the dolls is very difficult to clarify for the jury since you will have to answer "Yes" to the question: "Did you put the dolls in the described sexual position?"

Properly Used, Dolls Serve a Useful Purpose

Anatomical dolls are just one of the many tools available to criminal justice practitioners. They may not be effective with very young children or with those approaching teenage years. They may be combined with other interviewing techniques like drawing or writing.

Although dolls can be useful in reducing stress, establishing rapport, determining competency, and learning the child's sexual vocabulary, they may also complicate the case. Police and prosecutors should examine carefully the potential problems before proceeding.

If you decide to use anatomical dolls for your interview, select appropriate ones, familiarize yourself with the manufacturer's accompanying manual, and plan the interview in advance.

Used properly, anatomical dolls can be an effective way of helping children explain what happened to them. Used improperly, dolls can block communication, inhibit you from making a proper case filing decision, cause severe case problems, and create the possibility of a civil lawsuit.

Discussion Questions

1. What were the facts of *Higgs* v. *District Court*, and how could the decision effect the prosecution of child abuse cases?

2. What is meant by the term *anatomical doll*?

3. What are the most common criticisms of using dolls to interview the victims of child sexual abuse? Which do you feel have merit?

4. Discuss the techniques being developed for interviewing children who have been the victims of sexual abuse. Do you think that children can accurately describe their feelings by applying their experiences to dolls?

Drugs and Crime

There is little question that one of the most important issues facing the American justice system today is control of the drug trade. There has been a massive and concerted effort to control the flow of narcotics into the United States for both political and social reasons. Most importantly, however, there is significant evidence that use of narcotics is strongly associated with criminality. One research effort found that about 75 percent of all arrestees test positively for drug use. Other research indicates that narcotics addicts are responsible for a significant amount of all criminal activity.

The effort to control the drug trade has been carried out on a number of different levels. One approach has been to stop the flow of drugs as it enters the United States from Latin America, Europe, and Asia. Federal enforcement agencies, the military, and the Coast Guard have been involved in surveillance and seizure operations. Some foreign governments have cooperated by arresting drug smugglers and destroying supplies. A recent survey prepared for the United States Customs Bureau found that state, local, and federal law enforcement agencies spend $6.2 billion annually on controlling the drug trade. State and local government agencies spent an additional $4.9 billion, or 18 percent of their operating budgets, on drug enforcement efforts.

Despite this massive campaign the efforts to stem the supply of drugs such as heroin, marijuana, and cocaine have not proven successful. There are over 12,000 miles of coastline in the United States that must be patrolled. Smugglers use ships, airplanes, and automobiles to smuggle. Despite increased funds and high-tech vigilence, the amount of drugs seized is only a small portion of the total.

There has also been an effort to destroy the raw materials for heroin, cocaine, and marijuana in the countries in which it is grown—Turkey, Afghanistan, Thailand, Burma, Columbia, Peru, Mexico, and Jamaica; however, source control is hard to achieve. Getting the cooperation of governments whose countries supply drugs is difficult. Though some South American and Asian governments have entered the fight against the drug trade, attempting to cut off the drug supply at its source, underdeveloped nations actually have an economic incentive to allow this lucrative cash crop to flourish. If drug crops are destroyed, their national economies will lose millions of dollars in foreign currency and their governments will face the displeasure of impoverished farmers. If the United States helps compensate for losses, other nations will be encouraged to get into the drug-producing business to cash in on this aid. The political scandal involving General Noriega of Panama, a national figure indicted for drug smuggling, highlights the problem.

Another suggested approach to drug control has been to legalize or decriminalize controlled substances and thereby remove them as a law enforcement issue.

This policy has been attempted in England, where private physicians and government clinics have the power to legally prescribe heroin. While some experts view the English approach as a viable solution to the heroin problem in the United States, it appears not to have been effective because massive importation of drugs hit Great Britain at the time it was implemented.

Identifying and treating drug users has also been tried as a control technique. Identification has been facilitated by mandatory drug testing programs in government and industry. About 25 percent of the country's largest companies, including IBM and AT&T, test job applicants for drugs. A number of different treatment strategies have been employed. In the United States, methadone maintenance has been used to treat drug addicts. Methadone is a drug similar to heroin, and addicts can be treated at clinics where they receive methadone under controlled conditions. Methadone programs have been undermined, however, because some users sell their methadone on the black market, while others supplement their dosages with illegally obtained heroin.

Controlling drugs by focusing on the user presents very difficult problems. In the United States and elsewhere, the drug user can be viewed more as a victim than a culprit of the drug trade. Many have had disturbed home lives and suffer from depression, alienation, and other indicators of social maladjustment. There is no known long-term "cure" for drug addiction.

The overwhelming problem associated with drug control is the enormous profits involved in the drug trade: 500 kilos of coca leaves worth $4,000 to a grower yields about 8 kilos of street cocaine valued at $500,000. A drug dealer who can move 100 pounds of coke into the United States can make $1.5 million in one shipment. An estimated sixty tons of cocaine are imported into the country each year with a street value of $17 billion. Government crackdowns simply serve to drive up the price of drugs and encourage more illegal entrepreneurs to enter the market. For example, the Hell's Angels motorcycle club has become one of the primary distributors of cocaine and amphetamines in the United States. Films and television shows like *Miami Vice* that depict the rise and fall of drug dealers may be viewed as cautionary tales showing the dangers of the drug trade, but in so doing they illustrate the lavish life-styles and unlimited cash supplies associated with life in the drug trade, which admiring lower-class youth can never hope to achieve through conventional means. The immense profit associated with the drug trade can even drive "respectable" businessmen like John DeLorean to get involved in drug trading as a quick cash fix for their ailing businesses (though of course DeLorean was acquitted on the defense of entrapment).

In sum, the tremendous profits in the drug trade, coupled with the emotional needs of users, make the control of illegal drugs an ongoing criminological dilemma. To remedy this situation the federal government has begun to make the arrest and conviction of drug traffickers a top priority. Between 1980 and 1986 the number of drug-related convictions in federal courts more than doubled, from 5,244 in 1980 to 12,285 in 1986. This 134 percent increase was significantly higher than the 27 percent increase in convictions for other federal crimes. In addition the percentage of convictees receiving a prison sentence increased from 71 percent to 77 percent and the average sentence increased from four to five years. Though it is often difficult to gain convictions in narcotics cases, many defendants receive probation or a short-term prison sentence. Nonetheless, the federal data seems to indicate a trend toward toughening criminal justice sentencing policy in an effort to limit the drug trade by incapacitating known suppliers and deterring potential ones.

This section contains a number of papers analyzing the nature and control of drug abuse. First, Marcia R. Chaiken and Bruce D. Johnson discuss their research findings on the characteristics of the different types of offenders who get involved in drug use and sales. The final three papers deal with drug enforcement strategies. Mary G. Graham discusses methods to control drug abuse and crime; Eric Wish presents an analysis of drug testing; and Mark Moore discusses some of the problems associated with reducing the flow of narcotics into the United States.

National Institute of Justice

Issues and Practices in Criminal Justice

Characteristics of Different Types of Drug-Involved Offenders

Marcia R. Chaiken, Abt Associates, Inc.
and Bruce D. Johnson, New York State Division of Substance Abuse Services

February 1988

Types of Drug-Involved Offenders

The types of adolescent and adult drug-involved offenders identified by researchers are briefly described in Tables 1 and 2. In general, those presented in Table 1 represent progression in drugs and crime involvement, though many low-level users and offenders never move to a more active type. Because juvenile and adult offenders are dealt with by separate divisions of the justice system,[1] studies of drug-involved offenders generally have concentrated on either adolescents or adults. Most types of adolescents described in this paper are not officially delinquents. Although researchers have learned about their involvement with drugs and other illegal activities through self-reports, the vast majority have never been apprehended by police or other law-enforcement agents.

The portraits of these young drug users presented here are not necessarily intended to encourage law-enforcement agencies to devote greater resources to adjudicating them. The troublesome behavior of most drug-involved youth is often attributable to inadequate adult supervision and is most often transitory; a majority stops committing illegal acts upon becoming adults. These youngsters are described to detail the widespread and pervasive nature of drug use and distribution among youngsters, and to encourage community organizations to provide supervised drug-free activities for teens.

Two types of adolescents described do require more juvenile justice resources: The small number of the most seriously drug-involved who are already coming to the frequent attention of police and juvenile authorities, and the few young high-rate violent dealers who evade arrest for most of their crimes. Unless they are identified and diverted into programs that provide the context and skills for more constructive lifestyles, research indicates both groups are more likely than any other type of delinquent to continue committing crimes as adults, including numerous violent offenses and vast numbers of drug deals.

Unlike adolescents, most adults who use drugs do not engage in other forms of illegal behavior.[2] Even among those who commit crimes, most adult drug-involved offenders are not violent and commit crimes at low rates. Yet they constitute the bulk of the population dealt with by police, prosecutors and other criminal justice practitioners. This report describes specific types of these criminals—including high-level dealers, women drug-involved offenders, and smugglers—and some of the special problems they present to the criminal justice system.

Two types of adults described here are older versions of the most seriously involved adolescents: The adult predatory offenders who are frequently arrested and the high-rate predatory offenders who rarely are caught. Although these types constitute only a small proportion of adult drug-involved offenders, they are responsible for a high proportion of violent crimes and thus justify intensive criminal justice attention.

Recent Findings About Adolescent Drug Use

The most recent findings about adolescent drug use reflect the enormous drug problem faced by the justice system. Over the past few decades, the number

Table 1 Types of drug-involved offenders

Type of offender	Typical drug use	Typical problems	Contact with justice system
Occasional users			
Adolescents	Light to moderate or single-substance, such as alcohol, marijuana, or combination use.	Driving under influence; truancy, early sexual activity; smoking.	None to little.
Adults	Light to moderate use of single substances such as hallucinogens, tranquilizers, alcohol, marijuana, cocaine, or combination use.	Driving under influence; lowered work productivity.	None to little.
Persons who sell small amounts of drugs			
Adolescents	Moderate use of alcohol and multiple types of drugs.	Same as adolescent occasional user; also, some poor school performance; some other minor illegal activity.	Minimal juvenile justice contact.
Adults	Moderate use of alcohol and multiple types of drugs including cocaine.	Same as adult occasional user.	None to little.
Persons who sell drugs frequently or in large amounts			
Adolescents	Moderate to heavy use of multiple drugs including cocaine.	Many involved in range of illegal activities including violent crimes; depends on subtype (see Table 2).	Dependent on subtype (see Table 2).
Adults	Moderate to heavy use of multiple drugs including heroin and cocaine.	Depends on subtype (see Table 2).	Dependent on subtype (see Table 2).

of adolescents using alcohol, marijuana, and other illicit drugs increased dramatically. Self-report data collected from children in the past 10 years found that over 25 percent of youngsters 13 to 17 used marijuana or other illicit drugs within the prior 12 months.[3] Over 35 percent of seniors in high school reported having had 5 or more drinks in a row within the prior 2 weeks. By 1981, two-thirds of high-school seniors reported having used marijuana or other illicit drugs sometime in their lives.

In recent years, the proportion of high school seniors who reported use of drugs dropped to 61 percent; however, this overall decline ended in 1985.[4] Moreover, the use of certain drugs, including cocaine, did not peak in the early 1980's; the proportion of

youngsters who used these drugs continued to rise.[5] Compared with other countries, even other technologically advanced nations, our children are more extensively involved with drugs and alcohol.[6]

In our country, adolescents most often begin using these substances between the ages of 13 and 15 when they are in grades 7, 8, and 9.[7] The primary factors that promote use are the general availability of alcohol or drugs, friends who are users, lack of parental supervision, and lack of attachment to school.[8] The involvement of adolescent users in other destructive behavior is strongly associated with the number and types of harmful substances they use; the more substances they use, the greater their chance of being involved in serious destructive or assaultive behavior.[9]

Table 2   Types of dealers who sell drugs frequently or in large amounts

Type of dealer	Typical drug use	Typical problems	Contact with justice system
Top-level dealers Adults (only)	None to heavy use of multiple types of drugs.	Major distribution of drugs; some other white-collar crime such as money laundering.	Low to minimal.
Lesser predatory Adolescents	Moderate to heavy drug use; some addiction; heroin and cocaine use.	Assaults; range of property crimes; poor school performance.	Low to moderate contact with juvenile or adult justice system.
Adult men	Moderate to heavy drug use; some addiction; heroin and cocaine use.	Burglary and other property crimes; many drug sales; irregular employment; moderate to high social instability.	Low to high contact with criminal justice system.
Adult women	Moderate to heavy drug use; some addiction; heroin and cocaine use.	Prostitution; theft; many drug sales; addicted babies; AIDS babies; high-risk children.	Low to moderate contact with criminal justice system.
Drug-involved violent predatory offenders: **The "losers"** Adolescents	Heavy use of multiple drugs; often addiction to heroin or cocaine.	Commit many crimes in periods of heaviest drug use including robberies; high rates of school dropout; problems likely to continue as adults.	High contact with both juvenile and adult criminal justice system.
Adults	Heavy use of multiple drugs; often addiction to heroin or cocaine.	Commit many crimes in periods of heaviest drug use including robberies; major source of income from criminal activity; low-status roles in drug hierarchy.	High contact with criminal justice system; high incarceration.
The "winners" Adolescents	Frequent use of multiple drugs; less frequent addiction to heroin and cocaine.	Commit many crimes; major source of income from criminal activity; take midlevel role in drug distribution to both adolescents and adults.	Minimal; low incarceration record.
Adults	Frequent use of multiple drugs; less frequent addiction to heroin and cocaine.	Commit many crimes; major source of income from criminal activity; take midlevel role in drug distribution to both adolescents and adults.	Minimal; low incarceration record.
Smugglers	None to high.	Provide pipelines of small to large quantities of drugs and money.	Variable contact.

Approximately half the adolescents who abuse substances consume only alcohol. However, close to one-third use both alcohol and marijuana, and over 10 percent use multiple types of drugs. Youngsters who use multiple drugs, such as PCP, barbiturates, amphetamines, cocaine, heroin, or psychedelics, are also likely to use marijuana and alcohol frequently.[10]

Girls' use of drugs differs from boys' in several ways. In general, girls are significantly less likely to be users.[11] Girls are more likely to use amphetamines and other drugs for weight control; they are less likely than boys to use cocaine, PCP, and most other drugs.[12] However, this difference lessened from 1975 to 1983. Recently, girls' use of alcohol has become more similar to boys,[13] and girls are almost as likely to report having a drug problem.[14] Among adolescents who report committing illegal acts, girls are just as likely as boys to report frequent consumption of many substances.[15]

Delinquency and Adolescent Use of Drugs

Although the pervasiveness of adolescent drug use is itself alarming, it also may indicate other forms of delinquency. Youngsters who use multiple drugs are generally more likely to be seriously delinquent than those who use only alcohol and marijuana.[16] However, both alcohol/marijuana and multiple drug users are more likely to practice health-threatening, risk-taking behavior. Those who use drugs—even only alcohol or marijuana—are more likely to smoke, be sexually active, and ride around in cars with drivers either drunk or on drugs.[17] Over 75 percent of boys who use alcohol and marijuana commit minor assaults, vandalism, or other public disorder offenses. Both boys and girls who drink and use marijuana or other drugs are more likely to be truant and to steal.[18] While these are a serious concern for educators and other community members, most adolescents who use drugs or commit occasional crimes do not come to the attention of the criminal or juvenile justice system.[19]

Although the use of most drugs has remained the same or declined among youth in recent years, cocaine use continues to rise.[20] Most youngsters on cocaine also use alcohol and marijuana several times a week; many also use other drugs such as psychedelics and stimulants.[21] This is a particular problem in urban areas in the Northeast and the West.[22] Unlike marijuana use, which

begins in junior high or early in high school for nearly 90 percent of users, cocaine use typically begins after ninth grade. Moreover, the proportion of youngsters who become regular users of cocaine after experimentation has grown.[23]

About half the youngsters who frequently use multiple drugs were delinquent before they began illicit drugs. Minor crimes such as theft often precede or coincide with serious drug involvement. Once frequent use of multiple types of drugs begins, however, chances are relatively high that these youngsters will commit a wide range of crimes, more and less serious. Boys tend to overt aggressive acts. Girls are more likely to be involved in more covert property crimes, such as shoplifting and petty theft.[24] Both boys and girls who use drugs are likely to sell drugs.

Adolescents Who Distribute Small Amounts of Drugs

Adolescents who distribute drugs are not necessarily involved in other or more serious criminal activity. Most sell marijuana, amphetamines, and tranquilizers less than once a month to support their own use.[25] Their buyers are almost always know to them—brothers and sisters, cousins, friends, or acquaintances of friends. Arrangements for sales are made over the phone, in school, or in places where youngsters congregate. However, they typically distribute drugs in homes or cars—not in public places.[26] Most of these adolescents do not consider these activities "serious" crimes. For example, a girl who used marijuana and other drugs, commented:

> … I don't consider it dealing. I'll sell hits of speed to my friends and joints and nickel bags [of marijuana] to my friends, but that's not dealing.[27]

This notion is reinforced by the relatively small probability of these transactions being treated as crimes.[28] Persistence in other, nondrug offenses is more likely to bring seriously drug-involved youngsters to the attention of the juvenile and criminal justice system. Most adolescents who sporadically distribute small amounts of drugs do not have a flagrantly delinquent lifestyle and therefore are rarely apprehended.[29]

Since these youths conceal their illicit behavior from most adults and are likely to participate in many conventional activities with children their age, criminal justice practitioners can take little direct action to prevent occasional adolescent sellers from distributing drugs and recruiting new users. However, in several jurisdictions police, sheriffs, and other practitioners are cooperatively developing educational programs to pro-vide other children with the skills to resist recruitment.[30]

Adolescents Who Frequently Sell Drugs

Although most youngsters who sporadically distribute small amounts of drugs are not seriously delinquent, a small number, most often multiple-drug users or heroin or cocaine users, are high-rate dealers[31] who link the adult world of drug distribution and the sporadic adolescent distributors. Although many of them are daily users of drugs, they may not meet the stereotype of the "strung-out junkie." Like many other adolescents, their lives revolve around getting out of school, hanging out and socializing, fast food, and movies. They also perform a central role among kids who regularly get high.

Youngsters who distribute drugs weekly often have an adult dealer who "fronts" or supplies them with drugs on credit. They in turn supply other youngsters who pay in cash. Most of the money is returned to the adult supplier; the rest is a commission that the youngster rapidly spends for cigarettes, beer, and other adolescent accoutrements.[32] Also, the youngster often keeps some drugs for personal use and shares drugs offered by the other adolescents he supplies.

For example, Gallo, a 17-year-old dealer, smokes about 10 joints of marijuana a day and frequently uses other drugs. His mother works and his home has become an after-school hangout and drug distribution point. According to Gallo,

> … [after school], there's about 10 people in my house. [After they buy drugs] they want to hang out. I'm getting high for free.[33]

Youngsters who distribute drugs weekly are more likely to sell drugs in public than children who sporadically sell small amounts. Although most drug distribution takes place in cars or homes, more public spots commonly used are schools, parks, swimming areas, and other places where teenagers congregate.[34] Typically, these transfers occur episodically; therefore, the probability of apprehension is low.[35]

Adolescents Who Distribute Drugs and Commit Many Other Types of Crimes

By far the most serious adolescent dealers are those who use multiple substances and commit both property and violent crimes at high rates. Only about 2 percent of all adolescents pursue serious criminality *and* use multiple types of illicit drugs. Such youths commit over 40 percent of the total robberies and assaults by adolescents. Additionally, they are responsible for over 60 percent of all teen-age felony thefts and drug sales.[36] They are more likely than any other type of juvenile offender to continue committing crimes as young adults.[37] Among multiple drug users, girls are as likely as boys to become high-rate persistent drug-involved offenders, whites as likely as blacks, and middle-class adolescents raised outside cities as likely as lower-class city children.[38]

Most research has focused on boys in cities. Seriously delinquent drug-involved city boys are frequently hired by adult or older adolescent street drug sellers as runners. Loosely organized into crews of 3 to 12, each boy generally handles relatively small quantities of drugs—for example, two or three packets or bags of heroin. They receive these units "on credit," "up front," or "on loan" from a supplier and are expected to return about 50 to 70 percent of the drug's street value.[39]

In addition to distributing drugs, these youngsters may act as lookouts, recruit customers, and guard street sellers from customer-robbers. They typically are users of marijuana and cocaine, but not heroin. Moreover, in some cities, dealers and suppliers prefer to hire distributors who do not "get high" during an operation.[40] But their employment as runners is not generally steady; it is interspersed with other crimes including robbery, burglary, and theft. When involved in selling drugs, they generally work long hours and facilitate many small transactions. They are rarely arrested for these activities since, when police approach, they and other runners flee in all directions.[41]

A relatively small number of youngsters who sell drugs develop excellent entrepreneurial skills. Their older contacts come to trust them, and they parlay this trust to advance in the drug business. By the time they are 18 or 19 they can have several years of experience in drug sales, be bosses of their own crews, and handle more than $500,000 a year. However, there is a high level of violence associated with the position of crew boss. Violent tactics are used both by and against crew bosses to regulate the trade.[42] But given the rewards, youngsters who achieve this position find the risk worthwhile.

For example, Darryl, a youngster in Harlem, started as a runner when he was 9 and was part of a clique of older major dealers before he was 19. He was the boss of a crew that sold heroin and cocaine. His income allowed him to indulge his taste for expensive clothes and cars; he simultaneously owned a Mercedes, BMW, and Cadillac.[43]

Youngsters like Darryl earn great respect among the other drug-involved adolescents in their community. Many work for him and dream of having his clothes, cars, and customers. However, most other youngsters who are integral to the street drug trade do not have the skills to succeed, and most either stop or become so dependent on drugs that they have continuing contacts with the justice system.

Adolescents Who Are Most Likely to Cycle in and out of the Justice System

Unlike youngsters who develop "successful" careers, crimes committed by other high-rate, delinquent, drug-involved urban boys are more opportunistic, less organized, and more likely to result in failure, including arrest.[44] Young offenders who are habitually and frequently high on a variety of drugs are especially likely to be caught doing crimes. Their high drug consumption effectively bars them from joining drug distribution networks except at the very lowest levels.

They may earn some drugs by steering customers to a seller in a "copping" area, "touting" or advertising drug availability for a dealer, or acting as a lookout; however, they are not often considered trustworthy enough to handle money or drugs. Not infrequently they bungle other criminal pursuits. For example:

> Buster is almost always stoned on ludes and beer. He is continually getting caught robbing and is in and out of treatment centers. Once he and another boy robbed [sic] a jewelry store. They smashed the window with a brick and the window fell on them, knocking both of them out. The store owner called the cops and an ambulance.[45]

Youngsters like Buster frequently start using drugs and committing serious crimes at much younger ages than most delinquents. Such boys often initiate property

and violent crimes, and such girls begin prostitution and theft, before they are 15. Yet juvenile authorities are more likely to intervene in the lives of these children after they have accumulated a record of a relatively large number of arrests. Ironically, by the time most seriously delinquent youngsters are judged to be in need of remedial or correctional action, they are approaching the age when the vast number of delinquents spontaneously stop committing crimes—or they are so deeply entrenched in a criminal, drug-involved lifestyle that ordinary measures taken to treat or deter them from crime in the future are largely ineffective.[46]

Drug-Involved Adolescents Who Continue to Commit Crime as Adults

Although over two-thirds of drug-using juvenile delinquents continue to use drugs as adults, close to half stop committing crimes.[47] More is known about the reasons why delinquents start using drugs and committing crimes than about why some stop and others continue. The few studies[48] that have followed delinquent youngsters into adulthood have shown that, in general, youngsters are most likely to continue to be offenders as adults if:

> they come from poor families,
> they have other criminals in their family,
> they do poorly in school,
> they started using drugs and committing other delinquent and antisocial acts at a relatively early age,
> they used multiple types of drugs and committed crimes frequently, and
> they have few opportunities in late adolescence to participate in legitimate and rewarding adult activities.[49]

There is some evidence that low nonverbal IQ and poor physical coordination also increase the probability of juvenile offenders continuing as adults.[50] However, researchers basically do not know why some of the most deeply involved adolescents drop out of crime while others continue as adults like Darryl or Buster.

Types of Adult Drug-Involved Offenders

Unlike adults who were persistent, serious, drug-involved delinquents as adolescents, most adults who use drugs do *not commit* crimes other than possessing illegal substances; however, they do create a substantial market for marijuana, amphetamines, and trendy drugs such as cocaine. Most adolescents who smoked marijuana regularly in high-school are likely to continue as young adults. For example, in New York 52 percent of men who used marijuana regularly in high school continued to use drugs as adults.[51] Moreover, after leaving high school, a substantial proportion of young people may start drinking heavily and at that point become involved with other drugs. Many young adults (ages 18 to 22) in college, at jobs in cities, or traveling away from parents increase their use of drugs and contacts with friends and acquaintances who use and sell drugs. As they assume greater responsibility for jobs, marry, or become parents, however, most greatly reduce their drug and alcohol consumption.[52]

Young adults, including middle-class and upper-class men and women, traditionally develop a unique subculture that emphasizes innovation and experimentation with the latest fads, including drugs. As specific drugs gain a reputation for dangerousness, they are dropped, and new drugs become fashionable. However, motivations and justifications for drug use appear to be similar. Reasons given for the 1980's use of cocaine echo the 1970's reasons for the use of PCP and the 1960's reasons for use of LSD—to experience altered states of thinking, seeing, and feeling.[53]

Although the use of drugs is hazardous to the physical, emotional and cognitive development of these young adults,[54] the vast majority do not threaten others with felonious acts. Even among young adults in treatment for drug use, most are not involved in serious or frequent criminal behavior.[55] Crimes are more likely to be committed by daily or almost daily users of cocaine or heroin than by other types of drug users.[56] Fortunately, less than 1 percent of young adults use heroin or cocaine so frequently.[57]

Most adult offenders who use drugs are involved in dealing drugs. However, many dealers also commit other types of crimes, not specializing in dealing alone. More typically, they commit *combinations* of crimes. Sellers who are primarily nonviolent supplement their dealing activities by shoplifting, forging checks, using stolen credit cards, and other property crimes. Some drug-selling offenders also burglarize homes and businesses in addition to committing theft and other property crimes.[58] The most serious drug-involved offenders, the violent predators, may also commit a range of more and less serious crimes including theft, drug sales, assaults, and robbery.[59]

Most offenders commit crimes less than once a month; however, a small number are very active, committing crimes every week or nearly every day they are free to do so.[60] Generally, the most active and violent criminals began committing crimes, including violent crimes, as young adolescents. These offenders frequently used heroin or multiple other drugs as youngsters, and they continue to use drugs daily or almost daily as adults. They are unlikely to be married or regularly employed as adults.[61] On the other hand, less active drug-involved offenders who confine their illicit activities to drug selling and property offenses are more likely to start doing crimes and using drugs as adults and to be more socially stable.[62]

The following sections describe some of the types of adult drug users/offenders studied by researchers. As with the discussion of adolescents, this examination is by no means exhaustive; rather it suggests the variety of patterns of drug use and criminal lifestyles associated with them.

Outwardly Respectable Adults Who Are Top-Level Dealers

Small drug sales among adult users are common; however, relatively few of these dealers distribute large quantities. Close to 10 percent of the young adults in this country sell drugs, mainly marijuana; about 5 percent sell other illegal drugs as well.[63] Most young adult sellers sell small quantities of drugs to a limited number of people. Their sales occur infrequently, usually less often than once a month, and privately. They are carried out less for monetary profit than to obtain drugs for the sellers' own use.[64] However, a small number of outwardly respectable young adult dealers sell large quantities of drugs to support themselves, some in luxurious lifestyles.[65]

Although many undergraduates at colleges and universities around the country know the one or two middle-level "pound dealers" on campus, most noncollegiate regional and wholesale distributors, for obvious reasons, are extremely cautious about their activities. Few studies have collected data about them. Even the handful of researchers who eventually came to know high-level dealers well found them at first superficially indistinguishable from noncriminal young professionals. However, dealers who distribute kilograms or more of drugs rarely are drawn from upscale professions, nor are they likely to have worked their way up from the streets.[66]

Unlike poor, minority-group members like Darryl, who consciously worked at becoming a dealer as a way to climb out of poverty,[67] wholesale dealers seem to drift into this line of work from many different walks of life. Most frequently they are drawn from professions and occupations with minimal stability, irregular work hours, and a high tolerance for drug abuse. Former graduate students, musicians, other performing artists, and barkeepers are among those who become dealers in their mid-20's.[68]

Prior to entering the trade, they are generally frequent users of drugs and attracted to the upper-level dealers' fast, extravagant lifestyle of partying, play, and cocaine snorting. Through friendships with people supplying them with drugs, they learn about the business and form connections with smugglers. Their first transactions are generally middle-level deals, limited to buying one to five pounds of cocaine. Initially, they are often apprehensive about the risks of arrest, but those who continue find such risks part of the job's allure.[69]

Top-level dealers usually buy drugs by the kilo and sell by the pound. In general, the higher the quantity of the drugs they sell, the lower the number of business contacts they have—and the more likely they are to distribute drugs only to people they know well and in whom they have a certain degree of trust.[70] Young adults like Darryl form the link between them and distributors who sell ounces, grams, or "bags" of drugs to consumers. Middlemen "lieutenants" also insulate top-level dealers against risk of arrest and carry out the violent tactics used to keep the low-level dealers and customers in order.[71] But, because the drug business is extremely competitive and loosely organized, few top-level dealers can maintain a consistent and relatively secure distribution network for a year or more.[72]

Although a few top-level dealers remain in the business 10 years or more, limited research suggests that stability at the top of the trade is quite rare. The fast life and cutthroat business tactics contribute to burnout in a relatively short time. However, even though they may turn to legitimate and less lucrative occupations for a while, former top dealers in legitimate jobs may miss the luxuries more accessible through illicit trade and return to dealing or turn to smuggling.[73]

Top-level dealers frequently cycle in and out of the trade until they are in their mid-or late 30's. Each time they return to the drug trade, they are likely to be a little less active. Many eventually shift over into a legitimate

"scam" that utilizes the business skills they developed selling drugs. Others continue to deal in smaller quantities for a relatively long time to supplement other legal income. A small number die from the physical effects of drugs or from a violent attack by a disgruntled competitor or customer.[74] Top-level dealers also may have their careers interrupted by a jail or prison term, but they are less likely to be incarcerated than dealers who also commit other types of crimes.[75]

Smugglers

Yet another group with whom criminal justice practitioners must deal are smugglers.[76] Research on drug smugglers has been limited to indepth studies of small numbers. Those about whom we know the most are generally men, approaching middle-age or older, who have excellent organizational skills, established connections, capital to invest, and a willingness to take large business risks. In general the business of smuggling is loosely organized, competitive, and populated by individual entrepreneurs. The specific people who are smugglers shift and change as old sources become the target of law enforcement, as new sources become available, or as smugglers tire of the corrupt practices endemic to illegal trade. Frequently top-level dealers move into the smuggling end of the drug trade and smugglers become top-level dealers.

The people who actually carry drugs into the country are extremely diverse. Depending on the drugs they handle and the country where the drugs originate, people who transport illegal drugs into the country vary widely in age, nationality, occupation, economic status, and the extent to which they personally use drugs.

Bulky drugs, such as marijuana, require relatively large containers during transport. Before the U.S. Drug Enforcement Agency slowed down the Mexican marijuana market, large numbers of relatively unskilled independent entrepreneurs could contract to drive drugs across the border. Currently marijuana is more often being transported long distances in large quantities using boats or planes by the more organized and skilled owners of these modes of transportation, the smugglers.

Concentrated drugs such as cocaine, on the other hand, are somewhat more easily transported. Thirty kilos of uncut cocaine can fit into two large suitcases. Smugglers hire a wide variety of people to actually transport heroin or cocaine. They include wealthy jetsetters who use drugs, or poor immigrants who do not use drugs but are willing to transport them in trade for airline tickets or money.

Adult Predatory Drug-Involved Offenders Who Are Frequently Arrested: "Losers"

Adults like Buster, who became deeply involved in predatory crime and drug use in early adolescence, are likely to be among the highest rate, most dangerous offenders who come to the attention of the criminal justice system.[77] They frequently use multiple types of illicit drugs, including heroin, cocaine, amphetamines, marijuana, and alcohol. Many are daily users. Because they did poorly in school, they have few skills for employment. They work off and on, but most of their money comes from family members or from crime. Most have been incarcerated as juveniles, many for robbery. The threat of incarceration does not appear to deter them from committing a variety of crimes, including robbery, assaults, burglary, theft, and drug sales.[78]

Being incarcerated—and committing different types of crimes almost every day they are free—is a way of life for them, their friends, and often their family members. A relatively large number have fathers or brothers who are also felons. They practice a range of different types of crimes. Although they stage a great number of robberies, they may commit an even greater number of burglaries, thefts, and drug sales. When apprehended, they thus are likely to be arrested for theft or for a small drug sale, although they may have robbed someone just a few days before.[79] Kit is one example of this type of violent predator.

> Kit is a 26-year-old robber-dealer who habitually uses heroin and cocaine. He was first incarcerated at age 15 for attempted murder. His activities for four days in April included: A street robbery in which he took the victim's watch and $150, then he shoplifted fruit, rice, beans and milk. The next day he sold 20 bags of heroin for which he received a commission of $175 cash, and $50 of heroin for his own use. The next day, he had 22 transactions of heroin and cocaine, for which he received a commission of $100 in heroin; he also beat up a man, for which he received $225 from the husband of the victim's girlfriend.
>
> Kit was arrested for burglary and spent three days in jail. He entered a guilty plea and was

fined $200. As soon as he was released, he got $250 in heroin, rebagged it, sold it for $550, and used most of the profit to pay his fine.[80]

Although Kit lives in New York City, the same type of drug-involved offenders operate in major cities around the country, including Los Angeles,[81] Miami,[82] New York,[83] Baltimore,[84] Chicago,[85] and Detroit.[86] To support their own drug use, they sell or help distribute hundreds of small units of drugs each year on the streets and in other public places. Additionally, each year they are free they are likely to commit other types of crimes—hundreds of thefts or many burglaries, and a few robberies and assaults. Others carry out weekly robberies, combined with several assaults, burglaries, or thefts.[87] Although arrested for only a small percent of the crimes they commit, they are also likely to begin committing many crimes as soon as they are released. Parole is not likely to deter them; they simply fail to report.[88]

Adult Predatory Drug-Involved Offenders Who Are Rarely Arrested: "Winners"

Perhaps more a problem than high-rate arrestees are the young high-rate "winners" who also commit hundreds of crimes each year but evade arrest for long periods.[89] More successful than offenders who get caught several times each year, they are likely to have started both property and violent crimes at very early ages—and even as youngsters they managed to evade arrest. Moreover, like Darryl, they are likely to advance rapidly in the drug trade and become lieutenants or crew-bosses.[90]

On the streets, they are known for their calculated violence. The assaults, robberies, or other crimes they commit are typically carefully planned and carried out. High rate "winners" are more likely to work with partners than high-rate offenders who are arrested frequently; they are more likely to hire lower-level offenders to act as guards and lookouts and to carry out parts of their crimes that are most visible and carry the highest risk of apprehension.[91] They are distinctively different from the high-rate losers, who are arrested frequently, in their use of drugs. Although "winners" are likely to use drugs such as marijuana and cocaine, they are not likely to be heroin users or daily users of other opiates.[92]

High-rate "winners" usually are younger than the predators who frequently are arrested. Ultimately, some lose control of their drug use and become addicted daily users. Eventually, some of them are arrested and convicted. Little is known about the careers of the majority of this type offender as they reach age 30 or more. However, their criminal careers may stretch from age 10 to age 24 or 25; 14 or 15 years, uninterrupted by the justice system.[93]

Less Predatory Adult Drug-Involved Offenders

Most adult drug-involved offenders are less serious criminals than robbers like Kit. They often have graduated from high school and have fairly regular legitimate employment. They usually commit thefts, pass bad checks, or break into cars and steal things, but they generally do not commit crimes that involve violence.[94]

Their participation in the drug trade is generally peripheral and transitory.[95] They provide short-term services for drug sellers to earn a few dollars or in return for drugs for their own use. They may bag drugs or inject an addict or provide temporary shelter for a dealer. Some run "shooting galleries" for addicts where they rent hypodermic needles and syringes, and occasionally they may sell small quantities of drugs.[96] Although they perform various jobs for dealers and other drug users, most don't seem to have the stomach or stamina to routinely face the incipient violence of the street trade. The number of crimes they commit depends on the amount and cost of drugs they use and the amount of drugs they receive in barter for their drug-related services. Even the users who are most addicted fluctuate in the amount of drugs they use. When they are using expensive drugs such as heroin daily or more, they are likely to commit several crimes a day.[97] For example,

> Nadine, 24, was a regular heroin user; she had two babies, and worked erratically. She supported her drug use with welfare money she received for her children, money she received from selling her food stamps and articles she lifted in shops, and money she stole in bars from men who left change on the counter. Her apartment was used as a shooting gallery by other addicts who shared their heroin with her.[98]

Nadine's high rate of petty theft is typical of many nonpredatory offenders—both women and men, especially middle-aged men—who are heroin users. Additionally, Nadine also represents the special problems of women who are seriously drug-involved.

Women Who Are Drug-Involved Offenders

Women who are drug-involved offenders constitute another distinct group with whom criminal justice practitioners must deal. In general women are far less likely than men to use almost all illicit drugs.[99] However women *offenders* are just as likely to be using drugs as male offenders.[100] These women are not likely to be high-rate robbers or assaulters,[101] but about one-third of addicted women offenders are prostitutes. Others, like Nadine, commit many thefts.[102]

Few become top-level or even mid-level drug dealers. Over half, however, play an active role in the lowest levels of the drug trade and facilitate as many sales as men who are also involved at the lowest levels.[103]

Many of these seriously drug-involved women have children; 70 percent of addicted women studied in San Francisco were mothers.[104] Women who continue to inject drugs during pregnancy may have infants born addicted. Additionally, because they frequently share needles with other addicts, a relatively high proportion of these women test seropositive for AIDS virus,[105] and infants of these seropositive women are at high risk of contracting AIDS. The children who survive early infancy, like Nadine's children, are often malnourished, neglected, and surrounded by high-rate dangerous criminals. There is little doubt that this environment increases the risk of these babies ultimately becoming criminals themselves.

Many of the highest-rate female offenders like Nadine avoid prostitution; others who are prostitutes have relatively frequent arrests. However even women who frequently come to the attention of the criminal justice system are less likely to receive effective drug treatment than men. Most programs available for drug-involved offenders have been structured to meet the needs of male offenders.[106] Moreover, the need to provide even minimal care for their children or fear of loss of custody prevents many women drug-involved offenders from entering residential treatment programs.[107]

What Can the Criminal Justice System Do?

It is not reasonable to expect criminal justice practitioners alone to put an end to sales of illicit drugs, given the diversity of the people involved in using, selling, and distributing them, the low visibility of the sites in which most transactions are made, the early age at which children start using drugs, and the loose and shifting organization of drug-involved offenders. It is even less reasonable to expect these practitioners to stop the use of illicit drugs.

A large proportion of drug users and drug-involved offenders are youngsters. Achieving even a substantial reduction in the use and sales of illicit drugs will require long-term concerted efforts by educators, health and mental health practitioners, and juvenile justice agencies to reduce availability of drugs, to counteract pressures for initiation of use, and to curtail continued abuse.[108]

The criminal justice system can have a significant impact on some of the worst problems associated with drug use—by effectively concentrating resources on the small number and particular types of offenders who are most seriously involved with drugs and who commit crimes at extremely high rates. Ideally, programs should address all users and offenders. Given limited resources, the emphasis necessarily must be on programs and practices that take drug distributors off the streets and reduce the amount of drugs they use. This in turn can reduce the numbers of violent predatory crimes and property crimes. Moreover, disrupting the activities of the most active dealers can also disrupt ongoing easy access to large quantities of drugs, and interrupt their distribution by youngsters in public urban drug markets.

Current knowledge suggests these methods for concentrating resources on the most active offenders:

■ Improving methods to identify high-rate dangerous drug-involved offenders;[109]

■ Replicating and testing programs previously found to effectively reduce their use of drugs;[110] and

■ Coordinating criminal justice system efforts to supervise and deal with these high-rate dangerous drug-involved offenders.

Improving Methods for Identifying High-Rate Dangerous Drug-Involved Offenders

Police, prosecutors, and other practitioners in many jurisdictions have formed special units or programs to increase arrests, convictions, and sentences of the highest-rate, most dangerous persistent offenders.[111] Some special units focus on people who sell drugs. Research

findings suggest that arrests of offenders who frequently sell drugs publicly are more likely to capture persistent high-rate and violent offenders than arrests of those who sell drugs in less visible settings.

Generally, police and prosecutors prefer to allocate scarce resources to dealing with crimes such as robbery or burglary that are publicly perceived as more serious than sale of a small amount of drugs[112] and can result in longer prison or jail sentences. Research shows that many convicted of robbery and burglary are persistent drug-involved criminals, and that a small number of them distribute drugs at very high rates.[113]

Although the small numbers who commit crimes at extremely high rates are likely to rob and sell drugs publicly, most people who are arrested for these crimes are not high-rate offenders. However, it is hard to accurately separate the highest-rate offenders from lower-rate offenders by examining their criminal records. Simple counts of all prior felony convictions or incarcerations and prior convictions for drug sales or possession *alone* are not adequate. This information is misleading because two types of offenders come to frequent criminal justice attention: Offenders whose frequency of apprehension reflects their high rates of crime, and offenders who are basically unprofessional, inept, low-rate offenders.[114]

Information that can help distinguish between them includes:

■ A prior conviction for robbery, burglary, arson, forcible rape, sex crime involving a child, kidnap, or murder;

■ Failure to complete a previous sentence (e.g. through escape); and

■ Pretrial release status (on bail or own recognizance) when arrested for a new crime.[115]

Information that is *not* routinely available but could significantly improve our ability to distinguish between high-rate and lower-rate drug-involved offenders includes:

■ Convictions for robbery as a juvenile,[116] and

■ Indications of persistent and frequent use of drugs.[117]

Analysis of arrestees' urine for specific drugs is already being routinely carried out in a small number of jurisdictions. However, a single "positive" is not evidence of either persistent or frequent drug use. Only repeated positive readings collected over time can be considered indicative of persistent or frequent drug use. Therefore, urinalysis results must be maintained on official records and applied only after a pattern of persistent or frequent drug consumption has been established.[118]

Replicating Programs Demonstrated to Reduce Drug Use

For many of the most serious offenders, regular involvement in crime and drugs, with intermittent incarceration, is a way of life. Simply arresting and incarcerating them is not likely to have a long-term effect on their drug use or behavior. Once released, many continue to use drugs and commit crimes.

However, most do not continuously commit crimes at high rates; the rates at which they sell drugs and commit other crimes appears to be closely associated with the intensity of their cocaine or heroin use.[119] The costs of drug use, in large part, are responsible for these fluctuations.[120] Criminal behavior is likely to desist or lessen during days of abstinence or greatly reduced consumption.[121]

Therefore, one realistic goal is to reduce the frequency of use and amount of drugs consumed by offenders who are regular users of heroin or cocaine. Studies of the effectiveness of treatment and rehabilitation programs for drug-involved offenders most generally have resulted in pessimistic findings.

Recently, however, more optimism has been generated by outcome studies of a small number of programs, including a few that take place in prisons and continue with care after release;[122] these prison-initiated programs do appear to reduce participants' involvement with drugs and crime.[123] Although it will be necessary to replicate these programs and evaluate their effectiveness for other offenders before confidently suggesting large-scale implementation, they hold the promise of reducing the amount of crime committed by drug-involved offenders.

Cooperative Efforts to Concentrate Resources on the Most Serious Offenders

The most effective concentration of resources on high-rate serious drug-involved offenders requires coordination between criminal justice agencies within and across jurisdictions. By working together to build strong cases, police and prosecutors can reduce the number of serious drug-involved criminals who are released after arrest because of procedural or evidentiary problems. Criminal history and drug-use records supplied by police and parole officers can be used by prosecutors and probation officers to provide judges with information needed to detain dangerous offenders before trial and to sentence convicted offenders to effective drug programs.

By working with program providers in the community, correctional staff in jails and prisons can increase the chance that released drug-involved offenders receive assistance in staying drug free. Parole and probation officers can reduce the numbers of recidivists who commit many crimes before they are rearrested, by cooperating with police. A concerted effort can do much to reduce the burden which seriously drug-involved offenders place on the criminal justice system, and allay the havoc they create for their families, communities, and country.

Discussion Questions

1. How is it possible for "outwardly respectable" adults to become drug dealers?
2. What is the relationship between drug use and crime? Do you believe that drug use causes crime, or vice versa?
3. What factors differentiate adult drug users who rarely get arrested ("winners") from those who are frequently apprehended ("losers")?
4. What steps can the criminal justice system take to reduce the incidence of drug use in the United States? Is the elimination of drugs a virtual impossibility?

Notes

1. Offenders who are 13, 14 or 15, if apprehended, are almost always handled by the juvenile justice system. Adolescents of high-school age, youngsters approximately 16 to 18, straddle the ages that are used to legally define offenders as adults or juveniles. In some States their crimes are handled by the criminal justice system; in other States the same offenses are handled by the juvenile justice system. Young adults, people in their late teens to mid-20's, are legally responsible for their own actions. However, when they are initially convicted of a crime in many jurisdictions, they are adjudicated as "first-time offenders," even if they were adjudicated for offenses as juveniles. Older people who have accumulated more years of legal responsibility, if not social responsibility, are referred to in this report as adults.

2. Compare Elliott et al., 1963; Kandel and Yamaguchi, 1985; DeLeon, 1984; Johnston, O'Malley, and Bachman, 1986.

3. See, for example, Elliott et al., 1985.

4. Johnston, O'Malley, and Bachman, 1985, 1986.

5.   Johnston, O'Malley, and Bachman, 1986; Miller, et al., 1982.

6.   Kandel, 1984; Johnston, O'Malley, and Bachman, 1986.

7.   Elliott and Huizinga, 1985; Johnston, O'Malley, and Bachman, 1986.

8.   Simcha-Fagan and Schwartz, 1986.

9.   Elliott and Huizinga, 1985.

10.   Elliott and Huizinga, 1985; Huizinga, 1986; Johnson and Wish, 1986a.

11.   Elliott and Huizinga, 1985; Johnston, O'Malley, and Bachman, 1986.

12.   Johnston, O'Malley, and Bachman, 1986; Kandel and Yamaguchi, 1985.

13.   Johnston, O'Malley, and Bachman, 1986.

14.   Elliott and Huizinga, 1985.

15.   Elliott and Huizinga, 1985; Huizinga, 1986; Kandel, Simcha-Fagan, and Davies, 1986.

16.   Elliott and Huizinga, 1985; Weis and Sederstrom, 1981; Huizinga, 1986.

17.   Jessor, 1982; Elliott and Morse, 1985; Elliott, Huizinga, and Ageton, 1985.

18.   Elliott et al., 1983; Huizinga, 1986.

19.   Huizinga and Dunford, 1985; Elliott, Dunford, and Huizinga, 1987.

20.   Johnston, O'Malley, and Bachman, 1986.

21.   Elliott and Huizinga, 1985; Johnston, O'Malley, and Bachman, 1986; Kandel, Murphy, and Kraus, 1985.

22.   Johnston, O'Malley, and Bachman, 1986.

23.   Johnston, O'Malley, and Bachman, 1986; Kozel and Adams, 1985; Abelson and Miller, 1985.

24.   Elliott and Huizinga, 1985; Kandel, Simcha-Fagan, and Davies, 1986; Simcha-Fagan and Schwartz, 1986; Weis and Sederstrom, 1981; Huizinga, 1986; Johnson and Wish, 1986a, 1986b; Dunford and Elliott, 1984; Dembo et al., 1987.

25.   Johnson and Wish, 1986a; Carpenter et al., 1988; Elliott and Huizinga, 1985.

26.   Carpenter et al., 1988.

27.   Carpenter et al., 1988.

28.   Huizinga and Dunford, 1985.

29.   Elliott et al., 1983; Huizinga, 1986; Dembo et al., 1987.

30.   DeJong, 1987; Burchard and Burchard, 1987.

31.   Elliott and Huizinga, 1985; Huizinga, 1986; Carpenter et al., 1988.

32.   Johnson et al., 1986; Carpenter et al., 1988.

33.   Carpenter et al., 1988.

34.   Carpenter et al., 1988.

35.   Carpenter et al., 1988; Huizinga and Dunford, 1985.

36.   Elliott and Huizinga, 1985; Johnson and Wish, 1986a, 1986b; Wish and Johnson, 1986.

37.   Elliott and Huizinga, 1985; Elliott, Dunford, and Huizinga, 1987; Elliott, Huizinga, and Morse, 1986; Kandel, Simcha-Fagan, and Davies, 1986.

38.   Huizinga, 1986; Huizinga and Elliott, 1987; Watters, Reinarman, and Fagan, 1985.

39.   Johnson et al., 1985; Mieczkowski, 1986; Williams and Kornblum, 1985.

40.   Mieczkowski, 1986.

41.   Williams and Kornblum, 1985; Mieczkowski, 1986.

42.   Mieczkowski, 1986; Goldstein, 1985; Fagan, Pieper, and Moore, 1986.

43.   Williams and Kornblum, 1985.

44.   Fagan, Pieper, and Moore, 1986; Fagan, Pieper, and Cheng, 1987; Fagan, Hansen, and Jang, 1983.

45.   Williams and Kornblum, 1985.

46.   Fagan, Pieper, and Moore, 1986; Fagan, Pieper, and Jang, 1983; Dembo et al., 1987.

47.   Kandel, Simcha-Fagan, and Davies, 1986; Huizinga and Elliott, 1985.

48.   See Blumstein, Farrington, and Moitra, 1985, for a review.

49.   Huizinga and Elliott, 1986, 1987; Fagan, Pieper, and Moore, 1986; Fagan, Hansen, and Jang, 1983; Blumstein et al., 1986.

50.   Blumstein, Farrington, and Moitra, 1985.

51.   Kandel and Andrews, 1987; Kandel and Logan, 1984; Kandel and Yamaguchi, 1987.

52.   Kandel and Yamaguchi, 1985, 1987; Kandel and Logan, 1984; Kandel et al., 1986; Johnston, O'Malley, and Bachman, 1986.

53.   Lerner and Burns, 1979; Carey, 1968; Goode, 1970; Johnston, O'Malley, and Bachman, 1985.

54.   Durell and Bukoski, 1984.

55.   DeLeon, 1984; Sells and Simpson, 1976.

56.   Ball et al., 1981, 1982; Johnson et al., 1985; Kandel, Murphy, and Kraus, 1985; Sanchez and Johnson, 1987.

57.   Kozel and Adams, 1985; Kandel and Yamaguchi, 1987; Kandel et al., 1986.

58.   Johnson et al., 1985; Chaiken and Chaiken, 1982, 1985, 1987.

59.   Chaiken and Chaiken, 1982, 1987; M. Chaiken, 1986; Johnson et al., 1985; Johnson and Wish, 1987.

60.   Ball et al., 1981, 1982; Ball, Shaffer and Nurco, 1983;

Ball, 1986; Johnson et al., 1985; Johnson and Wish, 1987; Sanchez and Johnson, 1987; Wish and Johnson, 1986.

61.   Chaiken and Chaiken, 1982, 1984; Fagan, Hansen, and Jang, 1983; Johnson et al., 1985.

62.   Chaiken and Chaiken, 1982.

63.   Blum, 1972; Johnson, 1973; Single and Kandel, 1978; Clayton and Voss, 1981; Elliott et al., 1983; Elliot and Huizinga, 1985; Johnson and Wish, 1986.

64.   Goode, 1970; Carey, 1968; Clayton and Voss, 1981; Carpenter et al., 1988.

65.   Waldorf, 1987; Adler, 1985; Reuter, 1987.

66.   Adler, 1985.

67.   Williams and Kornblum, 1985.

68.   Adler, 1985.

69.   Adler, 1985.

70.   Adler, 1985.

71.   Goldstein, 1985; Johnson et al., 1985; Johnson and Wish, 1987; Carpenter et al., 1988; Goode, 1970; Adler, 1985; Spunt et al., 1987; Waldorf et al., 1977; Waldorf, 1987; Johnson and Hamid, 1987.

72.   Adler, 1985.

73.   Adler, 1985.

74.   Adler, 1985.

75.   Adler, 1985; Reuter, 1987; Reuter and Kleiman, 1986; Chaiken and Chaiken, 1982, 1984, 1987.

76.   This section is based on Adler, 1985; Reuter and Kleiman, 1986; Reuter, 1987.

77.   Chaiken and Chaiken, 1982, 1984, 1985, 1987; Johnson et al., 1985; Hansen et al., 1985.

78.   Chaiken and Chaiken, 1982, 1984, 1985, 1987; Johnson et al., 1985; Hansen et al., 1985.

79.   Chaiken and Chaiken, 1982, 1984, 1985, 1987; M. Chaiken, 1986; Johnson et al., 1985.

80.   Johnson et al., 1985; Hanson et al., 1985.

81.   Klein and Moxen, 1986; Bullington, 1977.

82.   Inciardi, 1979; Inciardi, 1986; Inciardi and Pottieger, 1986.

83.   Johnson et al., 1985; Johnson and Wish, 1986a, 1986b, 1987; Sanchez and Johnson, 1987; Wish and Johnson, 1986.

84.   Ball, Shaffer, and Nurco, 1983; Ball et al., 1981, 1982.

85.   Weibel, 1986.

86.   Mieczkowski, 1986.

87.   M. Chaiken, 1986; Chaiken and Chaiken, 1982, 1985, 1987; Ball et al., 1981, 1982; Johnson et al., 1985; Wish and Johnson, 1986.

88.   Chaiken and Chaiken, 1987; Ball, 1986.

89.   Chaiken and Chaiken, 1985.

90.   Mieczkowski, 1986; Williams and Kornblum, 1985.

91.   Chaiken and Chaiken, 1985.

92.   Chaiken and Chaiken, 1985.

93.   Chaiken and Chaiken, 1985.

94.   Chaiken and Chaiken, 1982.

95.   Waldorf et al., 1977; Waldorf, 1987, Johnson et al., 1985.

96.   Johnson et al., 1985; Chaiken and Chaiken, 1982; Goldstein, 1981.

97.   Ball et al., 1981, 1982; Ball, 1986; Ball, Shaffer, and Nurco, 1983; Johnson et al., 1985; Speckart and Anglin, 1986a, 1986b; Chaiken and Chaiken, 1982; M. Chaiken, 1986; Sanchez and Johnson, 1987.

98.   Abstracted from Johnson et al., 1985: 154.

99.   Johnston, O'Malley, and Bachman, 1986; Miller et al., 1982.

100.   Sanchez and Johnson, 1987; Wish, Brady, and Cuadrado, 1986.

101.   Sanchez and Johnson, 1987; Inciardi, 1979.

102.   Sanchez and Johnson, 1987; Wish, Brady, and Cuadrado, 1986; Inciardi, 1979; Inciardi and Pottieger, 1986; Rosenbaum, 1981.

103.   Inciardi, 1979; Inciardi, 1986; Inciardi and Pottieger, 1986; Sanchez and Johnson, 1987; Datesman, 1981.

104.   Rosenbaum, 1981, 1982.

105.   Centers for Disease Control, 1987.

106.   Rosenbaum, 1981, 1982.

107.   Rosenbaum, 1982; Rosenbaum and Murphy, 1984.

108.   DeJong, 1987; Durell and Bukowski, 1984.

109.   Wish, Toborg, and Bellassai, 1987.

110.   Wexler, Lipton, and Johnson, 1988.

111.   See, for examples: Forst, 1983; Martin, 1986; Springer, Phillips, and Cannady, 1985; Chaiken and Chaiken, 1987.

112.   Center for Studies in Criminology and Criminal Law, 1980.

113.   Chaiken and Chaiken, 1982, 1984, 1985, 1987.

114.   Chaiken and Chaiken, 1985.

115.   Chaiken and Chaiken, 1987.

116.   Chaiken and Chaiken, 1985; Chaiken and Chaiken, 1987.

117.   See virtually all papers by Ball, Chaiken and Chaiken, Johnson, Nurco, and Shaffer.

118.   For a discussion of urinalysis, see Wish, Toborg, and Bellasai, 1987.

119.   Ball et al., 1981, 1982; Ball, Shaffer, and Nurco, 1983; Speckart and Anglin, 1986a, 1986b; Chaiken and Chaiken,

1982, 1984, 1985; M. Chaiken, 1986; Sanchez and Johnson, 1987.

120. Chaiken and Chaiken, 1982; M. Chaiken, 1986; Johnson et al., 1985.

121. Ball, et al., 1981, 1982; Ball, 1986; Speckart and Anglin, 1986a, b.

122. Wexler, Lipton, and Johnson, 1988; Wexler and Williams, 1986.

123. Johnson, Lipton, and Wish, 1986; Platt, 1986; Ross and Gendreau, 1980; Wexler, Lipton, and Johnson, 1988; Wexler and Lipton, 1985

References

Abelson, Herbert I., and Judith D. Miller, 1985. "A decade of trends in cocaine use in the household population": 35–49 in Nicholas J. Kozel and Edgar H. Adams, eds., *Cocaine Use in America: Epidemiologic and Clinical Perspectives.* Research Monograph Series 61. Rockville, Maryland, National Institute on Drug Abuse.

Alder, Patricia A., 1985. *Wheeling and Dealing: An Ethnography of Upper-Level Drug Dealing and Smuggling Communities.* New York, Columbia University Press.

Ball, John C., Lawrence Rosen, John A. Flueck, and David N. Nurco, 1981. "The criminality of heroin addicts when addicted and when off opiates": 39–65 in James A. Inciardi, ed., *The Drugs-Crime Connection.* Beverly Hills, Sage.

Ball, John C., Lawrence Rosen, John A. Flueck, and David N. Nurco, 1982. "Lifetime criminality of heroin addicts in the United States." *Journal of Drug Issues* 3: 225–239.

Ball, John C., John W. Shaffer, and David N. Nurco, 1983. "The day-to-day criminality of heroin addicts in Baltimore: A study in the continuity of offense rates. *Drug and Alcohol Dependence* 12 (1): 19–142.

Ball, John C., 1986. "The hyper-criminal opiate addict": 81–104 in Bruce D. Johnson and Eric Wish, eds., *Crime Rates Among Drug Abusing Offenders.* Final Report to the National Institute of Justice. New York, Narcotic and Drug Research, Inc.

Blum, Richard, 1972. *The Dream Sellers.* San Francisco, Jossey-Bass.

Blumstein, Alfred, Jacqueline Cohen, Jeffrey A. Roth, and Christy A. Visher, eds., 1986. *Criminal Careers and "Career Criminals."* Washington, D.C., National Academy Press.

Blumstein, Alfred, David P. Farrington, and Soumyo Moitra, 1985. "Delinquency careers: innocents, desisters, and persisters": 187–219 in Michael Tonry and Norval Morris, eds., *Crime and Justice: An Annual Review of Research* 6. Chicago, The University of Chicago Press.

Bullington, Bruce, 1977. *Heroin Use in the Barrio.* Lexington, Massachusetts, Lexington Books.

Burchard, John D., and Sara N. Burchard, 1987. *Prevention of Delinquent Behavior.* Beverly Hills, Sage.

Carey, James T., 1968. *The College Drug Scene.* Englewood Cliffs, Prentice Hall.

Carpenter, Cheryl, Barry Glassner, Bruce D. Johnson, and Julia Loughlin, 1988. *Kids, Drugs, Alcohol, and Crime.* Lexington, Massachusetts, Lexington Books, forthcoming.

Centers for Disease Control, 1987. *Morbidity and Mortality Weekly Report,* March 27.

Center for Studies in Criminology and Criminal Law, 1980. *National Survey of Crime Severity: Final National Level Geometric Means and Ratio Scores by Offense Stimuli Items.* Philadelphia, University of Pennsylvania.

Chaiken, Marcia R., 1986. "Crime rates and substance abuse among types of offenders": 12–54 in Bruce D. Johnson and Eric Wish, eds., *Crime Rates Among Drug-Abusing Offenders.* Final Report to the National Institute of Justice. New York, Narcotic and Drug Research, Inc.

Chaiken, Jan, and Marcia Chaiken, 1982. *Varieties of Criminal Behavior.* Santa Monica, Rand Corporation.

Chaiken, Marcia, and Jan M. Chaiken, 1984. "Offender types and public policy." *Crime and Delinquency* 30, 2: 195–226.

Chaiken, Marcia R., and Jan M. Chaiken, 1985. *Who Gets Caught Doing Crime?* Bureau of Justice Statistics Discussion Paper. Washington, D.C.

Chaiken, Marcia, and Jan M. Chaiken, 1987. *Selecting "Career Criminals" for Priority Prosecution.* Submitted to the National Institute of Justice. Waltham, Massachusetts, Brandeis University.

Clayton, Richard R., and Harwin L. Voss, 1981. *Young Men and Drugs in Manhattan: A Causal Analysis.* Rockville, Maryland, National Institute on Drug Abuse: 99–173.

Datesman, Susan K., 1981. "Women, crime and drugs": 85–104 in James A. Inciardi ed., *The Drugs-Crime Connection.* Beverly Hills, Sage.

DeJong, William, 1987. *Arresting the Demand for Drugs: Police and School Partnerships to Prevent Drug Abuse.* Washington, D.C., National Institute of Justice.

DeLeon, George, 1984. *The Therapeutic Community: Study of Effectiveness.* Rockville, Maryland, National Institute on Drug Abuse.

Dembo, Richard, Mark Washburn, Eric D. Wish, Horatio Yeung, Alan Getreu, Estrellita Berry, and William R. Blount, 1987. "Heavy marijuana use among youths entering a juvenile detention center." *Journal of Psychoactive Drugs* 19, 1: 47–56.

Deren, Sherry, 1986. "Children of substance abusers: A review of the literature." *Journal of Substance Abuse Treatment,* 3:77–94.

Dunford, Franklyn W., and Delbert S. Elliott, 1984. "Identifying career offenders with self-reported data." *Journal of Research in Crime and Delinquency,* 21: 57–86.

Durell, Jack, and William Bukoski, 1984. "Preventing substance abuse: The state of the art." *Public Health Reports* 1: 23–3.

Elliott, Delbert S., Susanne S. Ageton, David Huizinga, Brian Knowles, and Rochelle J. Canter, 1983. *The Prevalence and Incidence of Delinquent Behavior, 1976–1980.* Boulder, Colorado, Behavioral Research Institute.

Elliott, Delbert S., and David Huizinga, 1985. "The relationship between delinquent behavior and ADM problems." Proceedings of the ADAMHA/OJJDP research conference on juvenile offenders with serious drug, alcohol, and mental health problems. Washington, D.C., OJJDP.

Elliott, Delbert S., and Barbara Morse, 1985. "Drug use, delinquency, and sexual activity." In C. Jones and E. McAnarney eds. *Drug Abuse and Adolescent Sexual Activity, Pregnancy, and Parenthood.* Washington, D.C., U.S. Government Printing Office.

Elliott, Delbert S., David Huizinga, and Barbara Morse, 1986. "Self-reported violent offending: A descriptive analysis of juvenile violent offenders and their offending careers." *Journal of Interpersonal Violence* 1, 4: 472–514.

Elliott, Delbert S., Franklyn W. Dunford, and David Huizinga, 1987. "The identification and prediction of career offenders utilizing self-reported and official data": 90–121 in John D. Burchard and Sara N. Burchard, eds., *Prevention of Delinquent Behavior.* Beverly Hills, Sage.

Fagan, Jeffrey, Elizabeth Pieper, and Yuteh Cheng, 1987. "Contributions of victimization to delinquency in inner cities." *Journal of Criminal Law and Criminology* (forthcoming).

Fagan, Jeffrey, Karen Hansen, and Michael Jang, 1983. "Profiles of chronically violent delinquents: An empirical test of integrated theory of violent delinquency": 91–120 in James Kleugal, ed., *Evaluating Juvenile Justice.* Beverly Hills, Sage.

Forst, Brian, 1983. "The prosecutor's case selection problem: 'career criminals' and other concerns," in Daniel McGillis, Susan Estrich, and Mark Moore, eds., *Dealing with Dangerous Offenders, Volume II.* Cambridge, Harvard University.

Goldstein, Paul J., 1981. "Getting over: Economic alternatives to predatory crime among street drug users": 67–84 in James A. Inciardi, ed., *The Drugs/Crime Connection.* Beverly Hills, Sage.

Goldstein, Paul J., 1985. "Drugs and violent behavior." *Journal of Drug Issues* (Fall): 493–506.

Goode, Erich, 1970. *The Marijuana Smokers.* New York: Basic Books.

Hanson, Bill, George Beschner, James M. Walters, and Elliott Bovelle, 1985. *Life With Heroin: Voices From the Inner City.* Lexington, Massachusetts, Lexington Books.

Huizinga, David, 1986. "Relationships between delinquent and drug-use behaviors in a national sample of youths": 145–194 in Bruce D. Johnson and Eric D. Wish, eds., *Crime Rates Among Drug Abusing Offenders.* New York, Narcotic and Drug Research, Inc.

Huizinga, David, and Franklyn W. Dunford, 1985. "The delinquent behavior of arrested individuals." Paper presented at the Academy of Criminal Justice Sciences. Las Vegas, Nevada, April.

Huizinga, David and Delbert S. Elliott, 1986. "Reassessing the reliability and validity of self-report delinquency measures." *Journal of Quantitative Criminology* 2, 4: 292–327.

Huizinga, David and Delbert S. Elliott, 1987. "Juvenile offenders: Prevalence, offender incidence, and arrest rates by race." *Crime and Delinquency* 33, 2: 206–223.

Inciardi, James A., 1979. "Heroin use and street crime." *Crime and Delinquency* July: 335–46.

Inciardi, 1986. *The War on Drugs. Heroin, Cocaine, Crime and Public Policy.* Palo Alto, California, Mayfield Publishing Company.

Inciardi, James A., and Anne E. Pottieger, 1986. "Drug use and crime among women narcotics users: An empirical assessment." *Journal of Drug Issues* 16, 1: 91–106.

Jessor, Richard, 1982. "Critical Issues in Research on Adolescent Health Promotion" in T.J. Coates, A.C. Peterson, and C. Perry, eds., *Promoting Adolescent Health.* New York, Academic Press.

Johnson, Bruce D., 1973. *Marijuana Users and Drug Subcultures.* New York, Wiley-Interscience.

Johnson, Bruce D., and Ansley Hamid, 1987. "Critical dimensions of crack distribution." Paper presented at the American Society of Criminology, Montreal, Canada, November.

Johnson, Bruce D., Paul Goldstein, Edward Preble, James Schmeidler, Douglas S. Lipton, Barry Spunt, and Thomas Miller, 1985. *Taking Care of Business: The Economics of Crime By Heroin Abusers.* Lexington, Massachusetts, Lexington Books.

Johnson, Bruce D., Barry Glassner, Julia Loughlin, and Cheryl Carpenter, 1986. "Drugs and Alcohol in Adolescent Delinquency." Final Report to the National Institute of Justice. New York, Interdisciplinary Research Center and Narcotic and Drug Research, Inc.

Johnson, Bruce D., and Eric D. Wish, 1986a. "Crime Rates Among Drug-Abusing Offenders." Final Report to National Institute of Justice. New York, Narcotic and Drug Research, Inc.

Johnson, Bruce D., and Eric D. Wish, 1986b. "Highlights from Research on Drug and Alcohol Abusing Criminals." Summary report to the National Institute of Justice. New York, Narcotic and Drug Research, Inc.

Johnson, Bruce D. and Eric D. Wish, 1987. *Criminal Events Among Seriously Criminal Drug Abusers.* Final Report to the

National Institute of Justice. New York: Narcotic and Drug Research, Inc.

Johnston, Lloyd D., Patrick M. O'Malley, and Jerald G. Bachman, 1985. *Use of Licit and Illicit Drugs by America's High School Students, 1975–1984.* Rockville, Maryland, National Institute on Drug Abuse.

Johnston, Lloyd D., Patrick M. O'Malley, and Jerald G. Bachman, 1986. *Drug Use Among American High School Students, College Students, and Other Young Adults, National Trends Through 1985.* Rockville, Maryland, National Institute on Drug Abuse.

Kandel, Denise B., 1984. "Substance abuse by adolescents in Israel and France: A cross-cultural perspective." *Public Health Reports* 99, 3: 277–283.

Kandel, Denise B., and John A. Logan, 1984. "Periods of drug use from adolescence to young adulthood: I. Periods of risk for initiation, continued use, and discontinuation." *American Journal of Public Health* 74, 7: 660–666.

Kandel, Denise B., Debra Murphy, and Daniel Kraus, 1985. "Cocaine use in young adulthood: Patterns of use and psychosocial correlates": 70–110 in Nicholas J. Kozel and Edgar Adams, eds., *Cocaine Use in America.* Research Monograph 61. Rockville, Maryland, National Institute on Drug Abuse.

Kandel, Denise B., and Kazuo Yamaguchi, 1985. "Developmental patterns of use of legal, illegal, and medically prescribed psychotropic drugs from adolescence to adulthood": 193–235 in C.L. Jones and R. J. Battjes, eds., *Etiology of Drug Abuse: Implications for Prevention.* Research Monograph 56. Rockville, Maryland, National Institute on Drug Abuse.

Kandel, Denise B., Mark Davies, Dan Kraus, and Kazuo Yamaguchi, 1986. "The consequences for young adulthood of adolescent drug involvement." *Archives of General Psychiatry* 43: 746–754.

Kandel, Denise B., Ora Simcha-Fagan, and Mark Davies, 1986. "Risk factors for delinquency and illicit drug use from adolescence to young adulthood." *Journal of Drug Issues,* Winter: 67–90.

Kandel, Denise B., and Kenneth Andrews, 1987. "Processes of adolescent socialization by parents and peers." *International Journal of Addictions* 22, 4: 319–342.

Kandel, Denise B., and Kazuo Yamaguchi, 1987. "Job mobility and drug use: An event history analysis." *American Journal of Sociology* 92, 4: 836–78.

Klein, Malcolm W., and Cheryl Moxen, 1986. *Gang Involvement in Cocaine "Rock Trafficking."* Grant Application to the National Institute of Justice. Los Angeles, University of Southern California.

Kozel, Nicholas J., and Edgar H. Adams, eds., 1985. *Cocaine Use in America: Epidemiologic and Clinical Perspectives.* Research Monograph 61. Rockville, Maryland, National Institute on Drug Abuse.

Lerner, Steven E., and R. Stanley Burns, 1979. "Youthful phencyclidine (PCP) users," Chapter 14 in George Beschner and Alfred S. Friedman, *Youth Drug.* Lexington, Massachusetts, Lexington Books.

Martin, Susan E. and Lawrence W. Sherman, 1986. *Catching Career Criminals, The Repeat Offender Project.* Washington, D.C., Police Foundation.

Mieczkowski, Thomas, 1986. "Geeking up and throwing down: Heroin street life in Detroit." *Criminology* 24, 4: 645–666.

Miller, Judith D., Ira Cifin, H. Gardner-Keaton, P.W. Wirtz, Herbert I. Abelson, and Patricia M. Fishburne, 1982. *National Survey on Drug Abuse: Main Findings.* Washington, D.C.: U.S. Government Printing Office.

Platt, Jerome J., 1986. *Heroin Addiction: Theory, Research and Treatment (second edition).* Malabar, Florida, Krieger.

Reuter, Peter, 1987. Personal communication based on NIJ-sponsored research in progress.

Reuter, Peter, and Mark A.R. Kleiman, 1986. "Risks and prices: An economic analysis of drug enforcement": 289–340 in Michael Tonry and Norval Morris, eds., *Crime and Justice* 7. Chicago, University of Chicago Press.

Rosenbaum, Marsha, 1981. "Women addicts' experience of the heroin world: Risk, chaos, and inundation." *Urban Life* 10(1) 1: 65–91.

Rosenbaum, Marsha, 1982. "Getting on methadone: the experience of the woman addict." *Contemporary Drug Problems,* spring: 113–143.

Rosenbaum, Marsha, and Sheigla Murphy, 1984. "Always a junkie?: The arduous task of getting off methadone maintenance." *Journal of Drug Issues* (summer): 527–552.

Ross, Robert R. and Paul Gendreau, 1980. *Effective Correctional Treatment.* Toronto, Canada, Butterworths.

Sanchez, Jose E., and Bruce D. Johnson, 1987. "Women and the drugs-crime connection: Crime rates among drug-abusing women at Rikers Island." *Journal of Psychoactive Drugs* 19, 2: 205–216.

Sells, Saul B. and D. Dwayne Simpson, 1976. *Effectiveness of Drug Treatment.* V. III, IV, V. Cambridge, Massachusetts: Ballinger.

Simcha-Fagan, Ora and Joseph E. Schwartz, 1986. "Neighborhood and delinquency: An assessment of contextual effects." *Criminology* 24, 4: 667–695.

Single, Eric and Denise Kandel, 1978. "The role of buying and selling in illicit drug use": 118–128 in Arnold S. Trebach, Ed., *Drugs, Crime, and Politics.* New York: Praeger.

Speckart, George and M. Douglas Anglin, 1986a. "Narcotics use and crime: A causal modeling approach." *Journal of Quantitative Criminology,* 2: 3–28.

Speckart, George and M. Douglas Anglin, 1986b. "Narcotics use and crime: An overview of recent research advances."

Presented to Drugs, Alcohol, and Crime Conference, sponsored by National Institute of Justice, San Francisco, California.

Springer, J. Fred, Joel Phillips, and Lynne Cannady. *The Effectiveness of Selective Prosecution by Career Criminal Programs.* Executive Summary. Sacramento, California: EMT Associates.

Spunt, Barry J., Paul J. Goldstein, Douglas S. Lipton, Patricia Bellucci, Thomas Miller, Nilda Cortez, Mustapha Khan, and Andrea Kale, 1987. "Systemic violence among street drug distributors." Presented at American Society of Criminology, Montreal, Canada, November.

Waldorf, Dan, Shiegla Murphy, Craig Reinarman, and Briget Joyce, 1977. "An Ethnography of Cocaine Snorters." Washington, D.C., Drug Abuse Council.

Waldorf, Dan, 1987. "Business practices and social organization of cocaine sellers." Presented at the American Society of Criminology, Montreal, Canada, November.

Watters, John K., Craig Reinarman, and Jeffrey Fagan, 1985. "Causality, context, and contingency: Relationships between drug use and delinquency." *Journal of Contemporary Drug Problems* (December).

Weibel, Wayne, 1986. Personal communication.

Weis, Joseph G. and John Sederstrom, 1981. "The prevention of serious delinquency: What to do?" Washington, D.C., National Institute for Juvenile Justice and Delinquency Prevention.

Wexler, Harry K. and Douglas S. Lipton, 1985. "Prison drug treatment: The critical 90 days of re-entry." Presented at American Society of Criminology, San Diego, California, November.

Wexler, Harry K. and Ronald Williams, 1986. "The 'Stay 'N' Out' therapeutic community: Prison treatment for substance abusers." *Journal of Psychoactive Drugs* 18, 3: 221–230.

Wexler, Harry K., Douglas S. Lipton, and Bruce D. Johnson, 1988. "A criminal justice strategy for treating drug offenders in custody." Washington, D.C., National Institute of Justice, forthcoming.

Williams, Terry M., and William Kornblum, 1985. *Growing Up Poor.* Lexington, Massachusetts, Lexington Books.

Wish, Eric D., Mary A. Toborg, and John P. Bellassai, 1987. "Identifying Drug Users and Monitoring Them During Conditional Release." Washington, D.C., National Institute of Justice.

Wish, Eric D., Elizabeth Brady, and Mary Cuadrado, 1986. "Urine Testing of Arrestees: Findings from Manhattan." New York: Narcotic and Drug Research, Inc.

Wish, Eric D., and Bruce D. Johnson, 1986. "The impact of substance abuse on criminal careers": 52–88 in Alfred Blumstein, Jacqueline Cohen, Jeffrey A. Roth, and Christy A. Visher, eds., *Criminal Careers and "Career Criminals."* V. II. Washington, D.C., National Academy Press.

National Institute of Justice

Research in Action

Controlling Drug Abuse and Crime: A Research Update

Mary G. Graham, National Institute of Justice

March/April 1987

Drug trafficking and abuse wreak enormous damage on society each year. Lives destroyed or seriously impaired, crime losses, decreased productivity, treatment costs—all contribute to the $59 billion annual toll exacted by illicit drug use and related crime. These social and economic repercussions explain why drugs and crime rank high on the list of public concerns in poll after poll.

Dramatic increases in cocaine use across all age groups and in all parts of the country have contributed to the alarm over drugs. Even as heroin and marijuana use has leveled off since 1980, cocaine-related cases in hospital emergency rooms have tripled since 1981. Emergence of "crack," a new, low-cost smokable cocaine, has resulted in more widespread use especially among the young—and more rapid dependence. A recent survey conducted for the National Institute on Drug Abuse by University of Michigan researchers indicates that 4.1 percent of high school seniors used "crack" during 1986. Addiction to "crack" can occur within several months, as opposed to the 3 or 4 years for typical cocaine "snorting."

This article reviews research by the National Institute of Justice that is changing the way we look at drug abuse and its relationships to crime. It also describes promising options for attacking drug trafficking and suppressing demand for drugs by criminals.

Building New Knowledge

Much of our previous knowledge about the extent of drug use among criminals has been based on reports by offenders themselves. Research on drug testing of arrestees is revealing the true dimensions of the drug problem, outstripping estimates based on self-report data.

Drug Abuse by Criminals

More than 14,000 arrestees were tested in Washington, D.C., and New York City in 1984, using highly accurate urinalysis technology. More than half those arrested in both cities tested positive for illegal drugs—double the number expected. The results also showed the prevalence of multiple drug use. Nearly a third of the arrestees testing positive in the District of Columbia had used more than one drug. The findings confirmed that without drug testing most drug use will go undetected. Only half of those who tested positive actually admitted using drugs.

More recent data from the two cities show that drug use by arrested persons is on the rise. By September 1986, nearly three out of four Washington, D.C., arrestees tested positive, compared with 56 percent in March 1984 when testing began.

New findings in New York City reflect the surge in cocaine use. Of 400 people processed through Manhattan Central Booking in September and October 1986, more than 80 percent tested positive for cocaine, compared with 42 percent in 1984. The increase was found among all ages, but it was especially large among young people between 16 and 20 years old—from 28 percent in 1984 to 71 percent last fall.

Drug-Crime Connections

Evidence of close relationships between drugs and crime continues to mount. The 1984 drug testing re-

Fighting Drug Trafficking with Forfeiture Sanctions

Forfeiture is a legal procedure that enables a government to seize property used in the commission of a crime and, in some jurisdictions, assets traceable to criminal profits. Federal prosecutors are successfully wielding forfeiture sanctions as a powerful weapon against drug traffickers. In fiscal year 1986, total income to the Department of Justice Assets Forfeiture Fund was some $90 million. And, under the provisions of the 1984 Comprehensive Crime Control Act, approximately $25 million in cash and property forfeited in Federal cases in 1986 was shared with the State and local criminal justice agencies that participated in those cases.

Used effectively, forfeiture sanctions can cripple an ongoing criminal enterprise by seizing the tools of the drug trafficking trade—planes, vessels, cars, and trucks—as well as cash, bank accounts, and other goods used in criminal activity or obtained with illicit profits. The risk of losing such assets raises the stakes considerably for criminal enterprises such as drug trafficking. For example, Federal prosecutors in California seized land that had been used to grow marijuana. The prospect of losing prime real estate may well serve as a powerful deterrent to others contemplating an illegal harvest.

An additional advantage of forfeiture for jurisdictions is the financial windfall gained through successful forfeiture proceedings. In most States, proceeds from the sale of property seized go to the State or local treasury. Some States, however, allow law enforcement agencies to keep the funds or forfeited property for official use. Seized vehicles, for example, can be used in undercover operations, and cash can supplement the undercover drug "buy" fund.

Despite the potential of forfeiture as a drug enforcement strategy, its use remains relatively limited at the State and local levels. Two complementary efforts, sponsored by the National Institute of Justice and the Bureau of Justice Assistance, aim to change that picture.

With funds from the National Institute of Justice, the National Criminal Justice Association (NCJA), in conjunction with the Police Executive Research Forum (PERF), will develop an instruction manual on establishing and maintaining an asset seizure and forfeiture program at the State level. The project will also devise and pilot test a model training curriculum.

In a survey conducted by NCJA as part of a 1986 pilot program on asset seizure and forfeiture, every responding jurisdiction reported the need for training in this area. Existing forfeiture statutes were viewed as ambiguous and lacking procedural guidelines for implementation.

Police and prosecutors were reluctant to use forfeiture sanctions in drug trafficking cases without firm knowledge and understanding of relevant statutes and procedures, and State officials were concerned about managing seized assets.

The manual is intended to guide development of a State asset seizure and forfeiture program. It will discuss recent developments in forfeiture laws and procedures—establishment of a seizure and forfeiture capability, management of an inventory of forfeited assets, cooperative enforcement and prosecution efforts, and the resource requirements of maintaining such a program. It will also cover investigative tools for forfeiture cases, with an emphasis on financial investigations.

The core document for the training curriculum, the manual is also designed to be an independent, "stand-alone" resource for officials who want to establish or review forfeiture programs.

---

search in Manhattan showed, for example, that more than half those charged with murder, manslaughter, robbery, and burglary tested positive for one or more drugs. And the more recent 1986 data on two samples of arrestees in Manhattan showed that between 59 percent and 92 percent of those charged with robbery tested positive for cocaine, as did more than 70 percent of those charged with burglary.

Drug abuse has also been shown to be one of the best indicators of serious criminal careers. Institute-sponsored research found that a majority of the "violent predators" among prison and jail inmates had histories of heroin abuse, frequently in combination with alcohol and other drugs. California prison and jail inmates who were addicted to heroin reported committing 15 times as many robberies, 20 times as many burglaries, and 10 times as many thefts as non-drug users.

NIJ research indicates that drug use accelerates criminal behavior. Studies in Baltimore showed addicts committed four to six times more crime during periods of heavy drug use than when they were relatively drug free. And, contrary to what was previously believed, research in New York City indicates that drug abusers are at least as violent, and perhaps more violent, than their non-drug-using counterparts. Heroin abusers are as likely to commit crimes such as homicide and sexual assault and even more likely to commit robbery and weapons offenses.

A growing number of homicides in major cities are suspected to be drug related. Research in progress is compiling data on the presence of drugs in the victim or killer, drugs or paraphernalia found at the scene of the crime, and the victim and murderer's known drug connections. The findings will lead to guidelines for revised police reporting of homicides so that more accurate and complete information on the extent of drug involvement in killings can be recorded. These statistics may advance our understanding of drugs as a catalyst for violence.

Cutting Supply and Reducing Demand

The growing evidence of drug-crime connections has spurred efforts to develop new law enforcement tools for cutting both the supply and the demand for illegal drugs.

Disrupting Supplies

Huge profits generated by the illegal drug market have created a web of suppliers. NIJ research is focusing on the best combination of strategies to disrupt various types of distribution networks.

Strategies to incapacitate the middle-level retail cocaine and heroin wholesaler are expected from a study now under way in Arlington County, Virginia; Broward County, Florida; Baltimore, Maryland; and Phoenix, Arizona.

Researchers are collecting data on drug unit policies and operations and on the characteristics and vulnerabilities of wholesalers. The information is drawn from police records, files of closed cases, and interviews with investigators in the four jurisdictions, all of which have active enforcement policies against wholesalers. The study will analyze when the dealers were first detected, how much intelligence had been gathered, and what conditions led to major arrests and prosecutions.

In California, street gangs have become increasingly active in selling cocaine. Research in progress is studying how the youth gangs acquire cocaine, how they distribute the drug, and the customers they sell to.

The study is expected to offer new ideas for breaking these networks, reducing both trafficking and violence.

Attacking the financial underpinnings of drug traffickers is another weapon in deterring suppliers. NIJ has analyzed the potential of asset seizure and forfeiture provisions in Federal and State laws as a tool for eliminating the trafficker's working capital.

Profits from illegal drugs often find their way into the legitimate economy. Before dealers can make use of their profits, the funds must be "laundered." Federal investigators have become experienced in tracing the money narcotics dealers and other organized crime elements shift into apparently legitimate channels. The National Institute of Justice is preparing a handbook showing how the Federal experience can be adapted by State and local agencies initiating programs to investigate and prosecute money laundering operations.

Drug Testing

Court-supervised drug testing is giving criminal justice a new tool to reduce demand for drugs by offenders and to help control crime.

The potential of mandatory drug testing of those released before trial was demonstrated in an NIJ-sponsored experiment in Washington, D.C. As a result of the research, the city has made drug testing of arrestees a standard part of its pretrial release programs. Judges in D.C. Superior Court use the objective information about an offender's drug habits to decide what conditions should be imposed on those released pending trial. Drug-using defendants can be ordered to report for periodic testing while on release.

Replication of the successful D.C. pretrial drug-testing program is planned in three or more cities. The Bureau of Justice Assistance of the Office of Justice Programs will fund operation of the program in participating jurisdictions, and the National Institute of Justice will support evaluation of the results.

New NIJ research is exploring other ways that drug testing of offenders can counter drug abuse and crime.

Public Safety and Offender Supervision

Research in Washington, D.C., and New York revealed that arrestees who use drugs were more likely to be rearrested while on release and to fail to appear for trial. Mandatory drug testing is the best available method to ensure that released defendants remain drug free and thus less likely to jeopardize public safety.

Drug Detection Through Hair Analysis: Developing Future Capabilities

Since all drug testing methods have inherent limitations, the National Institute of Justice is interested in developing new screening capabilities that complement those already available. Urinalysis provides an objective and efficient large-scale tool for rapidly screening criminal justice populations for drug use. Its power to detect is limited, however, to drugs consumed within the previous 2 to 3 days. Analysis of a few strands of human hair, on the other hand, offers the potential to detect drugs absorbed by the growing hair over a much longer period.

Hair analysis promises a complementary type of drug detection for various criminal justice and forensic applications. At present, however, it is still in the developmental stage and may be a few years from wide-scale field applications.

An NIJ pilot study will explore whether present laboratory capabilities can be transferred into operational environments. The research will monitor a sample of Los Angeles parole and probation clients over a 1-year period for compliance with abstinence from serious drugs as a condition of release. The results obtained with radioimmunoassay of hair (RIAH) will be compared to those obtained from urine samples.

Monitoring Methods

Current drug detection methods primarily monitor two types of effects. The first are *short-term behavioral impacts* on speech, eye movements, and coordination of motion. These stem from the effects of drugs or alcohol on the brain and typically start within several seconds or minutes after the drug or alcohol is consumed. They are generally over within a few hours. Drunk driving and violent assaults are the most common instances where offenders are likely to be apprehended and tested while these effects are still present.

A second type of possible indicators of drug usage are the *short-term metabolic effects* evidenced in changes in the breath, blood, and urine. These effects begin within about a half-hour and end within 2 to 4 days for heroin or cocaine. Other drugs such as marijuana and PCP may be detectable in trace amounts for up to 2 to 3 weeks. But the body's processing eliminates so much within a few days that urine tests become impractical beyond that period.

A third set of possible diagnostic indicators exists. *Long-term organic effects* result when drug molecules are absorbed by growing body tissues such as hair and nails. Drugs become detectable within the hair about 3 to 4 days after consumption. Thus, hair analysis cannot reveal recent usage. But after 3–4 days, the portion of the growing hair nearest the scalp has entrapped detectable drug molecules that remain for the entire life of the hair shaft. As the hair grows, it records the individual's pattern of drug consumption much as a recorded tape retains a pattern of the signals

In Washington, D.C., for example, the pretrial rearrest rate for drug users was 50 percent higher than for nonusers. Among defendants who reported regularly for court-mandated drug tests, however, the rate of pretrial arrests was 14 percent—the same as that for defendants who did not use drugs. Thus, drug testing also benefits the defendants. Those who test clean while under supervision have the opportunity to remain in the community pending trial.

Drug testing also can provide greater control over offenders free in the community on probation and parole. New research will assess the potential of drug screening for reducing the risk posed by regular probationers and by convicted felons in intensive probation supervision programs.

Another study is analyzing probation and parole supervision of addicted offenders. The effects of varying levels of supervision are being tracked to find better ways to match various types of addicts with different degrees of supervision and control.

National Institute of Justice research is also focusing on young people not yet heavily committed to drug use or dangerous criminal careers. Evaluators will assess a program begun in Washington, D.C., with funds from the Bureau of Justice Assistance. The new program is one of the first in the Nation to require all juveniles arrested for serious crimes to be given urine tests to detect drug use. The goal is to break their drug habits before they become well established and thus reduce the youngsters' criminal activity.

Forecasting

Information about national drug consumption patterns comes primarily from surveys of various population

Drug Detection Through Hair Analysis: Developing Future Capabilities—Continued

imposed on it. Hair on the head grows about one-half inch per month. A 2–3 inch strand of hair, for example, would contain a record of the last 4–6 months of drug usage. Any body hair is potentially usable in tests, but hair on the head offers the advantages of relatively rapid growth and minimal intrusiveness.

The techniques of hair analysis are essentially the same as those of radioimmunoassay of urine and offer the same general detection sensitivity. Because hair analysis involves additional steps, however, it is inherently more time consuming and more costly per test. But detecting a probationer's abstention or drug usage over a prolonged period, for example, may require only periodic sampling—testing hair every month or two rather than conducting much more frequent urine tests. The result may be not only greater reliability but reduced expense for long-term monitoring. Hair analysis capabilities could also minimize some concerns associated with urinalysis:

■ Hair samples can be readily obtained from either sex in public without violating privacy and without the invasiveness related to blood or urine as monitoring mediums.

■ Subjects cannot claim they are "unable" to provide a sample while being observed.

■ Subjects cannot attempt to avoid detection by "flushing" the system with large quantities of fluids to dilute urine samples or by "staying clean" for a few days or weeks before a scheduled test.

Hair analysis also means that additional samples can be acquired and tested. This retesting capability would be valuable to confirm a positive result, as is now done with positive urine samples. It also would permit acquisition of a totally new sample to verify or refute original test findings. This would overcome, in ways not now possible, the legal and operational challenges presented by offenders' claims of "That's not my sample," "Somebody must have put something in it," and "I haven't taken anything at any time."

For the long term, it appears that present laboratory-based hair analysis methods will be refined and made more amenable to larger scale applications. When this occurs, hair analysis will become a technique complementary to urinalysis, expanding the criminal justice system's ability to detect and monitor illicit drug abuse.

groups about their admitted drug use, hospital admissions for overdose, or applications to treatment programs. These indicators show up well after the introduction of a new drug like "crack" or increases in use of a particular drug like PCP. Changes in drug use patterns among arrestees, however, appear to precede such changes in the general population.

To detect drug use changes accurately and objectively, the National Institute of Justice has launched a national Drug Use Forecasting program (DUF) that will test arrestees in 10 cities across the country. Indianapolis, New York, and Washington, D.C., are the first cities in the system, which will be funded jointly by the National Institute of Justice and the Bureau of Justice Assistance. Each participating city will test samples of arrestees four times a year. The results will provide information useful in planning and evaluating drug control tactics and signaling early warnings about use of

a particular drug to health, education, and treatment programs.

Extending Drug-Testing Capabilities

The availability of more accurate technology has made urinalysis a reliable indicator of objective information on an offender's recent drug use. At the same time, the National Institute is exploring other screening methods that can add to the ability to detect drug use even more accurately and at lower cost. One method currently under study tests hair samples, which provide a more permanent record of an individual's drug use.

Enforcement

An NIJ study in Lynn, Massachusetts, is assessing the merits of police crackdowns on street-level

Police Crack Down on Heroin Market in Lynn, Massachusetts

In 1983, a virtual drug bazaar operated each day just four blocks from the downtown business district of Lynn, Massachusetts. Drug dealers openly competed for business, sending "runners" out to hawk their wares to both pedestrians and drivers passing by. The easy and consistent availability of high-potency drugs made Lynn the preferred place to buy heroin for drug users all over the North Shore of Massachusetts.

Lynn, with a population of 80,000, had the second highest crime rate of all Massachusetts cities and a police department whose sworn strength had fallen by about one-third due to fiscal pressures. Understaffed, it had no resources it could dedicate solely to narcotics work.

Chronic complaints from residents and merchants brought Lynn's drug trade to the attention of the newly organized county Drug Task Force. When it began operations in September 1983, the Task Force's objective was to make the streets of Lynn an unattractive place for heroin buyers and sellers to meet. And, it was hoped, retail heroin enforcement would lead not only to a reduction of drug sales but also to a reduction in the area's property crime.

The National Institute of Justice assessed the results of the Task Force effort. By every available measure, the heroin market in Lynn shrank substantially. What was a bustling street drug market became placid and ordinary looking, with no report of substitute drug markets developing.

In the first 10 months, 186 arrests were made on a total of 227 charges. Ninety-six defendants were convicted or pleaded guilty, including 10 on felony heroin charges. Nominal minimum sentences on all charges totaled 110 years.

The effect on non-drug crime was also dramatic. A year after the enforcement effort began, robberies dropped 18.5 percent and reported burglaries were down 37.5 percent compared to the previous 12 months. A year later, even after drug enforcement manpower in Lynn was reduced due to a shift in personnel, reported burglaries remained at their new, lower level. Reported robberies declined still further, to a level 30 percent below the 1983–84 period.

Two Types of Enforcement

In many cities, police departments have assigned retail drug traffic enforcement to a separate vice or narcotics unit staffed by detectives. Traditionally, those units have been devoted to catching the "kingpins" of the drug trade and have accorded little value to street arrests. At the same time, policies designed to ensure rapid response to calls for service and to prevent corruption have insulated retail drug markets from the uniform patrol force.

The two types of enforcement—one for high-level drug dealers, the other for street dealers and users—produce different effects on the drug trade.

If risk increases due to more vigorous enforcement, some high-level dealers may quit, cut back, or refuse to expand when the opportunity arises. This shift will generate higher prices. Higher prices mean users may commit more crime just to meet the cost of the drug.

When street-level enforcement becomes more vigorous, though, heroin buyers are likely to face increased difficulty in "scoring" (as well as increased risk of arrest for possession) rather than just higher dollar prices. Thus, street-level enforcement increases the time and risk involved in buying heroin rather than its money price. In Lynn, the increase in transaction time and risk cut both drug and non-drug crime.

While the Lynn results indicate the impact enhanced street enforcement can have, some questions remain. Is the drug trade and related crime really decreased or just displaced to other locations by street-level enforcement? What about the scale, timing, and duration of such efforts? Police managers need to think through the possible resource needs for launching retail drug enforcement efforts. Further analysis of the Lynn program data and evaluation of a similar effort in Lawrence, Massachusetts, will help answer some of these questions.

(This summary was drawn from the report *Bringing Back Street-Level Heroin Enforcement* by Mark A.R. Kleiman, who is a Research Fellow in Criminal Justice at the Kennedy School of Government, Harvard University. He is evaluating the Lynn and Lawrence programs for the National Institute of Justice.)

heroin trafficking. The results indicate that disruption at the point of purchase meant fewer customers for street dealers and also reduced robberies and burglaries in the target areas. (See box on this page for more details.)

New research planned by the National Institute of Justice will examine these and other street-level enforcement tactics.

The "drug culture," reinforced by marketing of drug use paraphernalia, may spur demand. A National

Institute study found that enactment of the Drug Enforcement Administration's Model Drug Paraphernalia Act by a majority of States has significantly reduced "head shop" operations and the ready availability of "hard-core" paraphernalia. In response to the legislation, the drug paraphernalia industry has placed new emphasis on "dual-use" items and on mail-order sales. Advertising has become more sophisticated and frequently includes disclaimers and announcements that the objects are sold for use with legal substances only.

State laws are currently the most effective means of controlling the sale of drug paraphernalia, but adequate resources are a prerequisite for effective enforcement. Lack of resources was reported as the primary reason for nonenforcement of the laws.

Prevention and Treatment

Drug prevention and treatment programs primarily fall within the responsibility of agencies other than the Department of Justice. Because law enforcement can contribute to such efforts, however, NIJ research is analyzing approaches that appear promising and is assessing the impact of treatment on drug-abusing criminals.

DARE

Drug Awareness Resistance Education (DARE) involves police and public schools as partners in teaching younger children to resist offers to try drugs. A model program started in Los Angeles, the DARE concept has now been transferred to schools in Virginia, Massachusetts, New York City, and Washington, D.C. An NIJ report will document the approaches used in the four jurisdictions to plan, design, and implement drug education programs for elementary schools. The programs feature joint efforts by law enforcement and public schools to present materials on the dangers of using drugs, ways of resisting peer pressure to take drugs, and students' self-esteem. The report will describe the joint agreements between agencies, curriculums, selection and training of police officers—and in one site, prosecutors—and the results of short-term evaluations of the efforts.

Treatment Effects

Many of the effects of treatment programs are still unknown. NIJ research is providing some answers to questions about the impact of treatment programs on crime rates, the economic costs imposed by drug abus-

ers' criminal activity, and the cost-benefit ratio for various types of treatment.

Using a national sample of clients in the Treatment Outcome Prospective Study (TOPS), an NIJ study found that, by virtually all economic measures, crime is lower after treatment than before. The savings in crime-related costs are at least as great as the cost of the treatment programs. Residential treatment appears to have the greatest economic return in comparison to methadone maintenance for narcotics addicts or outpatient drug treatment.

The study results also indicate that the longer the time in treatment, the better. Clients staying in treatment for longer periods are more likely to change their drug lifestyles than those who undergo treatment for shorter episodes. The criminal justice system can help get drug abusers into treatment and keep them there for longer periods. The researchers concluded that "there are real returns to society and law abiding citizens" from longer terms of treatment for offenders required to enroll in drug treatment as part of their sentence.

Opportunities for intervention with drug-abusing delinquents are being explored in inner city neighborhoods in California. The study is examining how drugs figure in the commission of violent crime by juveniles and the social-psychological and demographic characteristics of high-risk delinquents. The analysis should help improve classification and potential treatment for various types of juvenile offenders.

Looking Ahead

Research will continue to play a vital role in developing information that can serve as a foundation for more effective public policies against drugs and crime. The National Institute of Justice has expanded funding for research that will help improve criminal justice strategies for stemming drug abuse and trafficking. The research on drug and alcohol abuse and related crimes is. . . aimed at identifying more effective public policy responses as well as more complete and accurate measurement of the extent of drug abuse, drug-related crime, and the social costs they impose on us all.

Discussion Questions

1. How can a forfeiture strategy reduce the attractiveness of competing in the drug trade?

2. What are some of the treatment efforts that seem to reduce recidivism among drug addicts, and why do you think they are successful?

3. Which law enforcement strategy—street level or high level—appears to have the greatest impact on the drug trade?

4. Do you think that ex-offenders would be more successful in treating current users than professional clinicians?

National Institute of Justice / CRIME FILE

Drug Testing

Eric Wish, Visiting Fellow, National Institute of Justice

1986

Introduction

In the current atmosphere of heightened concern about drug abuse in America, there is growing interest in the use of chemical tests, especially urine tests, for identifying drug users. Public debate, often heated, has focused on the advisability and legality of using urine tests to identify drug use in athletes, celebrities, and employees performing sensitive jobs. However, less attention has been given to the uses of urine testing for persons who have been arrested or are under the supervision of the criminal justice system, despite the high prevalence of drug abuse and associated health problems in criminals.

Why Identify the Drug Abuser?

To target active criminals. Researchers have found that drug-abusing offenders are among the most active criminals. Addicts commit more crimes during periods when they are using drugs frequently than during periods of lesser drug use. The association between high rates of offending and drug abuse has been found predominantly in persons who use expensive dependence-producing drugs like cocaine and heroin. Less is known about the criminal activities of people who abuse PCP or other nonaddictive illicit drugs. In youths, however, heavy marijuana use is also associated with problem behavior and is often accompanied by the use of other illicit drugs.

There are a number of reasons why drug abuse and crime are associated. Some people are so dependent upon drugs that they are driven to commit income-generating crimes like theft, robbery, drug selling, and prostitution. For other people, drug abuse appears to be merely one of many deviant behaviors they engage in: for still others, crime may be the result of a violent, bizarre reaction to a drug. In planning effective responses for each person, it may be necessary to understand which of the above relations between drug use and crime applies.

To protect the public from crimes by persons released to the community. Judges are often faulted when persons they have released pending trial or on probation are found to have committed another crime, especially a violent crime. If persons who are released to the community before trial or under probation or parole supervision were tested for illicit drug use, it might be possible to initiate treatment or urine monitoring for those who test positive. Because of the association between drug use and offending, effective programs for controlling or monitoring drug use may be a means of reducing crimes of released arrestees and offenders.

To reduce jail or prison crowding. Jail and prison populations in large cities contain substantial numbers of drug-dependent persons. By identifying drug-dependent persons and placing them in residential treatment programs or urine monitoring programs, we may be able to reduce jail and prison populations and to lessen future drug abuse and crime. One jurisdiction in Indiana is adopting a program in which arrestees charged with minor offenses can be released without bail if they agree to participate in a urine monitoring program. The cost of testing is charged to the defendant but is less than the amount for bail and should result in the early release of more defendants. Judges in Washington, D.C., report that because of their pretrial testing program, they are more likely to release suspected drug users because they know that their drug problems are being addressed.

To reduce drug abuse and crime.   There is growing evidence that criminal justice referral of offenders to drug abuse treatment programs, often accompanied by urine monitoring, can lead to a longer treatment period and to reductions in both drug abuse and crime. Because younger offenders are less likely than older offenders to inject hard drugs and to use heroin, identification of youthful offenders who are abusing drugs such as marijuana, PCP, or cocaine may hold promise for preventing more extensive drug use.

To address public health problems.   Abusers of hard drugs, especially persons who inject drugs, are at high risk for health problems. Intravenous drug users are especially at high risk for contracting AIDS by sharing dirty needles that contain blood from infected fellow addicts. Prostitutes are also likely to have serious drug abuse and associated health problems. More than two-thirds of the arrestees in Washington, D.C., and New York City have been found to test positive by urinalysis for one or more drugs. The criminal justice system may have an unusual opportunity to identify persons with health problems.

To monitor community drug use trends.   As illicit drugs become available in a community, the more deviant persons can be expected to be among those who first use them. Thus, an ongoing urine testing program may provide warning of drug epidemics and information on changing patterns of drug availability. The results from a current urine testing program for arrestees in Washington, D.C., have been useful for tracking the rising trend of heroin use in the 1970's and of cocaine in the 1980's.

How Do We Identify Drug Users?

A variety of methods are available for identifying drug users in the criminal justice system. Urine testing is the most commonly used method and much of the current policy debate focuses primarily on urine testing. Other forms of drug use testing are now under development— including testing of drug traces in hair samples—that may be less intrusive and, perhaps as a result, less controversial.

Offenders' self-reports.   Social science research has amply documented that people are willing to disclose sensitive information about their drug use if the information is collected voluntarily, for research purposes only, and if confidentiality is assured. These conditions do not exist for persons detained and processed by the criminal justice system. Many detainees will conceal their recent drug use, even in a voluntary, confidential, research interview. Estimates of recent drug use obtained by self-reports from arrestees generally identify about half as many drug users as urine tests do.

Criminal justice records.   The criminal justice system maintains extensive files on offenders. However, because much of the information in the files is obtained from the offender, the records provide only limited information about an offender's involvement with drugs. Furthermore, drug users are arrested for a variety of offenses; relying solely on the filing of a drug-related charge at arrest to identify drug users will also underdetect users.

Urinalysis tests.   Although urine tests have long been used by the criminal justice system, only with the advent of more accurate and less expensive technology has urine testing become a viable option for screening large numbers of offenders. Primarily because of their low cost (under $5 for each drug tested) and ease of use, the EMIT™ (enzyme multiplied immune test) tests are the most commonly used urine tests today. These tests depend on a chemical reaction between the specimen and an antibody designed to react to a specific drug. The chemical reaction causes a change in the specimen's transmission of light, which is measured by a machine. If the reading is higher than a given standard, the specimen is positive for the drug. Because the determination of a positive is based on specific numbers, the level of subjectivity required by the EMIT test is less than that required by most other tests.

The growing popularity of the EMIT tests has made them the object of several legal challenges. The primary criticism is that the EMIT tests have too high a rate of false-positive errors. That is, the tests too often falsely indicate the presence of a drug. Much of the debate surrounds the possibility that some common *licit* drugs can cross-react with the test's reagents to produce a positive result. The ingestion of poppy seed bagels has been found to produce a positive test result for opiates, for instance. Furthermore, the EMIT test for opiates will detect prescribed drugs such as codeine as well as heroin (morphine). Sloppy recording procedures by laboratory staff and failure to maintain careful controls over the chain of custody of the specimen can also produce serious test errors.

The future of urine testing in the criminal justice system will probably depend on a satisfactory solution to the problem of false-positive errors. Preliminary Federal guidelines for testing specify that all positive test results from immunoassay tests, like EMIT, should be confirmed by gas chromatography/mass spectroscopy (GC/MS). GC/MS is the most accurate technique available for identifying drugs in the urine, but it costs $70 to $100 per specimen. It seems appropriate to require such a procedure when a single test result may end in loss of a person's job or liberty. However, when a test result is used to trigger further investigation to determine if a person is involved in drug use, confirmation by other methods (urine monitoring or diagnostic interview) may be equally acceptable. The courts have yet to decide this issue.

Who Should Be Tested?

Arrestees. By testing arrestees one can screen for drug abusers in the largest and most diverse criminal justice population, in contrast with the much smaller populations reached by programs which test only persons who have been placed on probation or parole. There are, however, special legal concerns regarding testing and monitoring of persons at the pretrial stage, before a determination of guilt or innocence has been made. In some States a judge has statutory authority to decide the defendant's pretrial release status solely on the basis of information regarding the defendant's risk of failure-to-appear in court (FTA). The judge's authority to order urine screening or to set pretrial release conditions aimed at monitoring drug use, or requiring treatment, may depend in these States on the existence of a link between drug abuse and FTA. Prior research has suggested such a link, and research being completed in New York City has found that arrestees who tested positive for drugs and admitted current drug dependence, or a need for treatment, were at high risk for FTA.

While a number of jurisdictions are considering implementing pretrial testing programs, Washington, D.C., is the only jurisdiction with an operating program. Judges use urinalysis results and information from a brief cellblock interview about prior drug use to determine conditions of pretrial release. The judge may refer arrestees who test positive to a treatment program or to continued urine monitoring.

Probationers and parolees. Probation and parole are suitable times for screening for drug use, primarily because abstinence from illicit drugs is typically a condition of postconviction release. Testing would probably be constructive, however, only in programs with manageable case loads so that the tests can be used as part of a comprehensive program of assessment and treatment. Adequate resources must be available for treatment and monitoring.

Juveniles. Adult offenders tend to have begun their illicit drug use as youths. There is hope that by identifying juvenile detainees who use such drugs as marijuana and PCP, and intervening with them, it may be possible to prevent their progression to injection of harder drugs.

Female detainees. Much less attention has been given to the drug use and crime of female offenders than of males. This is true in spite of the evidence that female arrestees are more likely than males to test positive for drugs and to have associated health problems. Many female offenders engage in prostitution and inject drugs, making them a high risk group for transmission of the disease AIDS.

Why Not Test?

It is clear from experience with the Washington testing program that many of the issues and criticisms that have been raised about drug testing in the workplace will be raised about testing offenders. This section reviews briefly some of the more significant legal and practical issues relevant to offender urine testing programs.

Fourth amendment rights against illegal search and seizure. Does the government have the right to impose mandatory testing on a person in the absence of individualized suspicion? It is argued that the invasion of privacy, the costs, and the intrusiveness of urine testing are too great to justify the testing of persons at random, when there is no clear suspicion that the person is using drugs. In some instances, mandatory urine testing has been sustained by the courts when unique institutional requirements existed. For example, such tests have been upheld for jockeys, in the context of regulation and reduction of criminal influence in the racetrack industry, as well as for prison inmates to promote security, and in the military.

A Federal appeals court overturned a lower court's decision staying the U.S. Customs Service program from testing employees transferring to sensitive jobs. The appeals court found that the particular method by which the program operated was limited in its intrusiveness and that there was a strong and legitimate governmental interest in not employing drug users in the positions in question. It is not clear how these legal precedents will apply to programs for screening large numbers of offenders.

Critics of mandatory urine testing argue that the need to watch the person providing the specimen is an unacceptable infringement of privacy. When an employee or offender who has received advance notice is tested, special precautions must be made to ensure that the person does not substitute someone else's urine. When arrestees have no time to plan for the urine test, there may be less need to observe the voiding. Under these circumstances, the test may be no more intrusive than conditions that already exist in using public restrooms or toilet facilities in local jails.

The legality of mandatory testing of offenders will probably depend on the stage at which testing is introduced. Some believe that it is important to require tests of persons at the pretrial stage when they are presumed to be innocent. Others argue that because an arrest results from probable cause to believe that the person has committed a crime, and because arrestees have reduced fourth amendment rights, it is legal to require testing of arrestees. Probation officers often have the authority to require urine tests to enforce the conditions of probation requiring abstention from illicit drug use. Similar authority may also apply to parole officers.

Fourteenth amendment due process rights. Considerable litigation has occurred over the accuracy of urine tests and whether punitive actions taken against a person on the basis of a single unconfirmed urine test violate the 14th amendment's guarantees of due process. Because of the extensive use of the EMIT test, most of this discussion has concerned the accuracy of that particular test.

It is clear that the acceptability of results of EMIT tests of criminal justice detainees varies from jurisdiction to jurisdiction. Some courts have ruled that a single unconfirmed EMIT result is sufficient for revoking probation or imposing sanctions on prisoners, while other courts have ruled that the test must be confirmed. There is, however, little agreement on the type of confirmatory test required. In some instances, courts have ruled that repeating the EMIT test is sufficient,

while other courts have required that an alternative method such as TLC (thin layer chromatography) or GC/MS be used.

When persons are tested repeatedly, other issues become relevant. For example, a contempt of court ruling for a person on pretrial release in Washington, D.C., who tested positive for PCP on 16 tests over a 60-day period was denied when expert witnesses could not specify the length of time that PCP could be detected in urine. Unlike cocaine and opiates, which are eliminated from the body within days after ingestion, PCP and marijuana may be stored and released weeks after use. The Washington judge could not therefore rule out the defendant's claim that all of the positive tests were the result of use of PCP before the pretrial period began. There is a critical need for the creation of a national system for evaluating laboratory proficiency and establishing appropriate guidelines for the use and interpretation of urine tests by the criminal justice system.

Other relevant issues. A number of other legal and ethical issues have been raised. Among the most important is whether the testing program could result in additional harm to the offender. Persons arrested for a minor offense might find themselves in more trouble with the court by participating in a drug testing program (if they repeatedly test positive), than they would have been for the original arrest charge. Penalties could also result from refusal to take a test.

Another important issue is the confidentiality of test result information. For example, is information about drug use at arrest to be made available at the time of sentencing or parole? A person labeled a drug user can suffer adverse consequences from that label for some time after a positive test result is obtained.

Perhaps the greatest danger posed by urine testing programs is the belief that use of the tests will somehow solve the drug abuse problem. Testing will uncover the magnitude of the drug problem in a jurisdiction and identify some of the affected persons. However, in the absence of well-developed plans on how to assess a person's level of drug involvement and how to plan effective responses, the testing program will fail to achieve its goals. A program that does nothing more than increase detentions will only add to jail and prison crowding. Drug abuse treatment facilities in most large cities are filled to capacity and will require new resources if they are to handle an influx of criminal justice referrals. A comprehensive strategy for handling the test results should be in place *before* urine testing is adopted.

Discussion Questions

1. Should criminal justice system officials be permitted to test arrestees for drug use? Probationers? Parolees?
2. Should testing of arrestees for current drug use be limited to people who have been charged with drug-related crimes? Why or why not?
3. Should testing for drug use be permitted for all arrestees (or probationers or parolees) or only in cases where there is probable cause to believe that the arrestees are current users of illicit drugs?
4. Should the rules governing administration of drug use testing and confirmation of positive results be stricter for arrestees, whose positive result may lead to loss of pretrial freedom, or for employees, whose positive result may lead to loss of a job?
5. If you were chief judge of an urban court, would you establish a program of drug use tests for all arrestees? Why or why not?

References

Carver, John A. 1986. "Drugs and Crime: Controlling Use and Reducing Risk Through Testing." *NIJ Reports* SNI: 199 September/October.

Hawks, Richard L., and C. Nora Chiang, eds. 1986. *Urine Testing for Drugs of Abuse*. Washington, D.C.: U.S. Department of Health and Human Services, National Institute on Drug Abuse.

Stitzer, Maxine, and Mary E. McCaul. Forthcoming. "Criminal Justice Interventions with Drug and Alcohol Abusers: The Role of Compulsory Treatment." In *Behavioral Approaches to Crime and Delinquency*, edited by Curtis J. Braukman and Edward K. Morris. New York: Plenum Press.

Wish, Eric D., and Bruce D. Johnson. 1986. "The Impact of Substance Abuse on Criminal Careers." In *Criminal Careers and Career Criminals, Volume II*, edited by Alfred Blumstein, Jacqueline Cohen, Jeffrey A. Roth, and Christy A. Visher. Washington, D.C.: National Academy Press.

Cases

National Treasury Employees Union v. William Von Raab, Commissioner. 41 CrL 2097 (5th Cir. May 6, 1987).

Peranzo v. Coughlin, 608 F. Supp. 1504 (S.D.N.Y. 1985).

Wykoff v. Resig, 613 F. Supp. 1504 (N.D. Ind. 1985).

National Institute of Justice   *CRIME FILE*

Drug Trafficking

Mark Moore, Harvard University

1988

The widespread use of drugs such as heroin, cocaine, and marijuana is commonly viewed as an important social problem. In the public mind, drugs are linked to three social problems.

Drugs and crime. Very large proportions of those arrested for street crimes such as robbery, burglary, and larceny are drug users. The addict's need for money to finance his habit and the mechanisms of addiction establish a link between drugs and crime. Insofar as drug use itself is illegal, society has linked drugs to crime directly. Any possession or use is, by definition, criminal conduct.

Drugs and social dependence. To many people, drug dependence in itself is a serious social problem. Persons who willfully drug themselves, particularly when they do this repeatedly, become social dependents. They have violated their obligation to remain sober and responsible by surrendering their judgment and their faculties to drugs.

A predictable set of consequences is commonly believed to flow from the compulsive use of drugs. These include early death, elevated morbidity, frequent unemployment, deep poverty, incapacity to meet responsibilities to spouses and children, and social isolation. Insofar as society accepts responsibility for meeting the health and economic needs of its citizens, drug users' inability to care for themselves and their dependents becomes a social problem.

Drugs as traps for children. A particularly troubling aspect of drug use is the notion that many children who would otherwise remain on a path toward responsible citizenship are deflected by drug use. Casual experimentation leads to more frequent use which, in turn, leads to reduced performance in school, tragic accidents, and reduced life chances.

Although this last image may be more a product of parental fears than of reality, some important facts lie behind it. Early drug use *is* correlated with more serious later drug use, with difficulties in schools, and with crime. One of the worst aspects of drug use may be its attraction to youths in urban ghettos, for it robs many of their chance for upward mobility. With that, some of the promise and justice of a democratic society is lost.

Perspectives on Drug Trafficking

It seems wrong—even evil—for drug traffickers to supply drugs to users, and it seems unjust that drug traffickers grow rich and powerful on their ill-gotten gains. These simple intuitions establish two quite different perspectives for looking at drug trafficking.

Drug trafficking as drug supply. From the perspective of drug control policy, the worst thing about drug traffickers is that they supply drugs. Too many drugs reach illicit users in the United States. The objective of drug trafficking policies should be to minimize the supply capacity of the distribution systems so that the smallest possible volume of drugs reaches users.

Drug trafficking as organized crime. Some criminal organizations engaged in drug trafficking grow rich and powerful. This situation, in turn, undermines citizens' confidence in their government. When drug trafficking is viewed as an organized crime problem, the objective of control efforts is to arrest and punish rich traffickers and to prevent new groups from arising.

To a degree, these perspectives and objectives are congruent. A principal means for minimizing the flow of drugs to the United States is to immobilize major trafficking organizations. In some circumstances, however, these objectives diverge. Aggressive law enforcement efforts directed at marginal trafficking organizations might well reduce the overall supply of drugs to illicit markets. But these efforts, by eliminating marginal traffickers, may increase the wealth and power of the drug trafficking organizations that remain by allowing them to gain effective control over the market.

Alternative Approaches

Choices between approaches for dealing with drug trafficking will depend on which aspects of the trafficking problem are deemed most important and on the costs and efficacy of particular policies.

Legalization. The most radical approach to dealing with drug trafficking is to legalize the drugs. Legalization can mean many different things. At one extreme, it can mean complete elimination of any legal restrictions on the production, distribution, possession, or use of any drug. At the other extreme, it can mean allowing some limited uses of some particular drugs, producing the drugs only under government auspices, distributing them through tightly regulated distribution systems, and punishing with severe criminal penalties any production or use outside the authorized system.

The goal of legalizing drugs is to bring them under effective legal control. If it were legal to produce and distribute drugs, legitimate businessmen would enter the business. There would be less need for violence and corruption since the industry would have access to the courts. And, instead of absorbing tax dollars as targets of expensive enforcement efforts, the drug sellers might begin to pay taxes. So, legalization might well solve the organized crime aspects of the drug trafficking problem.

On average, drug use under legalization might not be as destructive to users and to society as under the current prohibition, because drugs would be less expensive, purer, and more conveniently available. However, by relaxing opposition to drug use, and by making drugs more freely available, legalization might fuel a significant increase in the level of drug use. It is not unreasonable to assume that the number of people who become chronic, intensive users would increase substantially. It is this risk, as well as a widespread perception that drug use is simply wrong, that militates against outright legalization.

An alternative is to choose a system more restrictive than outright legalization but one that still leaves room for legitimate uses of some drugs. Arguably, such a policy would produce some of the potential benefits of legalization without accelerating growth in the level of drug use. The difficulty is that wherever the boundary between the legitimate and illicit use of drugs is drawn, an illicit market will develop just outside the boundary. Indeed, the more restrictive the boundary, the larger and more controlled by "organized crime" the resulting black market.

The existing drug laws in the United States establish a regulatory rather than a prohibitionist regime. While most uses of heroin and marijuana are illegal, some research uses of these drugs are authorized under the current laws, and there is discussion of the possible use of these drugs for medical purposes such as the treatment of terminal cancer patients. Cocaine is legal for use as a local anesthetic by dentists. And barbiturates, amphetamines, and tranquilizers are legalized for a variety of medical purposes and distributed through licensed pharmacists and physicians.

That there are some legal uses of these drugs has not eliminated illicit trafficking. For marijuana, heroin, and cocaine, the restrictions are so sharp relative to the current demand for the drugs that virtually the entire distribution system remains illicit and depends on drug trafficking. For amphetamines, barbiturates, and tranquilizers, the restrictions are fewer, so a larger portion of the demand is met from legitimate illicit distribution. Distribution of these drugs takes the form of diversion from legitimate channels rather than wholly illicit production and distribution.

Source country crop control. A second approach to dealing with drug trafficking is to try to eliminate the raw materials that are used to produce the drugs. For heroin, cocaine, and marijuana, this means controlling opium, coca leaf, and marijuana crops in countries such as Turkey, Afghanistan, Thailand, Bolivia, Colombia, Peru, Mexico, and Jamaica. For marijuana, illicit domestic production is also important.

Efforts to control these foreign crops generally take one of two forms. Governments either try to induce farmers to stop producing the crops for illicit markets or attempt to destroy those crops that can be located. Sometimes the inducement takes the form of subsidies for growing other crops. Other times foreign crops are bought and burned before they reach illicit channels. Eradication may also be accomplished by airborne chemical spraying (which has the advantage of being controlled by a relatively small number of people, and the disadvantage of doing a great deal of collateral damage to legitimate crops), or by ground-level destruction of crops through cutting and digging (which has the disadvantage of relying on large numbers of people and of being quite visible well in advance of the operations).

In general, these efforts suffer from two major difficulties. First, there seems to be no shortage of locations where the crops may be grown. If Turkey stops growing opium poppies, Mexico, Afghanistan, and Southeast Asia can eventually take up the slack. If Colombia stops growing coca, Peru can replace it. If Mexico eliminated marijuana production, the hills of California would be even more densely filled with marijuana plants than they now are.

The second problem is that foreign governments cannot always be relied on to pursue crop control policies vigorously. Sometimes the difficulty is that the crops lie in parts of the country that are not under effective governmental control. Other times the problem is inefficiency or corruption in the agencies that are managing the programs. In the worst cases, the crops are sufficiently important to the domestic economy (or the personal well-being of high government officials) that the government prefers not to act at all.

When foreign governments are reluctant to cooperate, the United States Government must balance its interest in advancing its drug policy objectives against other foreign policy objectives. One particularly perplexing problem is posed by governments that are important to the United States as regional bulwarks against communist expansion and are also acquiescent in drug trafficking. The United States Government may feel required to overlook drug trafficking in order to maintain that government's anti-communist activities.

These observations do not imply that crop control policies can never be effective. In the early 1970's, more effective control of opium poppies in Turkey produced a 2-to 3-year reduction in the supply of heroin to the U.S. East Coast and an observable reduction in the rate at which new people were becoming addicted.

These observations do suggest, however, that crop control programs cannot be counted on as long-term solutions; they will take place sporadically and unpredictably. This suggests that an effective way to manage our crop control efforts is to position ourselves in foreign countries to notice and exploit opportunities when they arise but not to rely on this approach as our major initiative for controlling drug trafficking.

Interdiction. Interdiction efforts aimed at stopping illicit drugs at the border are appealing. First, the imagery is compelling. If we cannot rely on foreign countries to help us with our drug problem, we will do it ourselves by establishing defenses at the border.

Second, Government agencies have special powers to search at the border, which should make it easier to find illicit drugs. Forces of the U.S. Customs Agency and the U.S. Immigration and Naturalization Service inspect people and goods passing through official "ports of entry," and they patrol between "ports of entry," to ensure that no one can cross the border without facing inspection. The Coast Guard, the military, and civilian aviation authorities all have capabilities that allow the Government to detect who is crossing the border and to prevent illegal crossings.

There are, however, two problems with interdiction. One is the sheer size of the inspection task. More than 12,000 miles of international boundary must be patrolled. Over 420 billion tons of goods, and more than 270 million people, cross these boundaries each year, yet the quantities of drugs are small—a few hundred tons of marijuana and less than 20 tons of heroin or cocaine. Moreover, the heroin and cocaine arrive in lots of less than a hundred pounds.

That the volume of heroin and cocaine imported is much less than the volume of marijuana points to the second problem with interdiction. It is a strategy that is more successful with marijuana than with heroin or cocaine. Marijuana's bulkiness makes it more vulnerable to interdiction efforts.

This situation is unfortunate because, in the eyes of many, marijuana presents fewer problems than heroin and cocaine. Moreover, marijuana can be grown easily in the United States. If foreign supplies are kept out, the supply system can adjust by growing more marijuana domestically.

That seems to be what has happened. Current estimates indicate that interdiction efforts are successful in seizing about a third of the marijuana destined for the United States. Yet, except for a few local areas, the impact on the price and availability of the drug has been minimal. Worse, the current U.S.-grown marijuana is more potent than the imported marijuana.

High-level enforcement. A fourth attack on illicit trafficking is directed at the organizations responsible for producing, importing, and distributing drugs. The basic aim is to immobilize or destroy the trafficking networks.

In the past, enforcement agencies have tended to view this problem as "getting to Mr. Big"—the individual kingpin who, it was assumed, controlled an organization's capacity to distribute drugs. If that person could be arrested, prosecuted, and imprisoned, the network would fall apart.

More recently, the law enforcement community has become less certain that this strategy can succeed. Even when "Mr. Big" is in prison, he can continue to manage the distribution of drugs. Moreover, the organizations seem less dependent on single individuals than enforcement officials once assumed. Finally, the whole drug distribution system is less centralized than was once assumed. Relatively small and impermanent organizations—freelance entrepreneurs—supply a large proportion of illicit drugs.

To deal with this decentralization, enforcement aims have shifted from stopping individual dealers to destroying whole networks. Federal investigators have been granted special powers to seize drug dealers' assets, including boats, cars, planes, houses, bank accounts, and cash.

The main problem with attacking illicit trafficking organizations is that it is enormously expensive. Convincing evidence can be produced only through sustained efforts to recruit informants, establish electronic surveillance, and insinuate undercover agents. It is difficult for prosecutions to succeed because of the complexity of conspiracy laws and the particularly intrusive investigative methods that must be used to gather evidence.

Street-level enforcement.   A fifth line of attack is to go after street-level dealing through the use of physical surveillance or "buy and bust" operations. In the recent past, this approach has been deemphasized. It seemed to have no impact on the overall supply because dealers who were arrested were jailed only intermittently and when they were, they were easily replaced. At best, drug dealing was driven off the street temporarily, or to a different street. Many hours were spent to produce small, transient results, and these operations seemed to invite abuses of authority and corruption. As a result, many police were removed from street-level enforcement.

Recently, police have renewed street-level enforcement efforts, but they have altered their objectives. To the extent that street-level enforcement increases the "hassle" associated with using drugs, it can make a contribution to the objective of reducing drug use. If drugs, already expensive, can be made inconvenient to purchase, some nonaddicted users may be persuaded to abandon drugs. More experienced users can benefit if treatment programs are available.

Street-level enforcement can contribute to other objectives. It can encourage criminally active drug users to reduce their consumption, or draw them into treatment programs. It can contribute to the objective of immobilizing major traffickers by identifying defendants who can provide information about major trafficking networks. Ultimately, it can contribute to the quality of life in neighborhoods by returning the streets to community control.

These rationales give street-level enforcement some plausibility. What gives it real force is that it seems to work. A small task force committed to street-level drug enforcement in Lynn, Massachusetts, cut robberies by 18 percent and burglaries by 37 percent while it was in operation. Operation Pressure Point, carried out on the Lower East Side of Manhattan, reduced robberies by 40 percent and burglaries by 27 percent.

There have also been some important failures. An operation in Lawrence, Massachusetts, modeled after the Lynn program, failed to produce any important effect on levels of crime or drug use in that community. The reasons seem to be that the effort was too small relative to the size of the opposing trafficking networks and that the effort was focused on cocaine rather than heroin. An operation in Philadelphia failed to produce anything other than angry citizens and a stern rebuke by the courts because it was carried out without any consultation with the community, and without any regard for evidentiary standards.

Subsequent discussions of these results among academics and practitioners have produced several guidelines for successful street-level enforcement. First, the scale of the enforcement effort should be in some sense proportionate to the effective size of the trafficking network. Second, police should carry out the operation after obtaining widespread community support, and with scrupulous attention to the niceties of search and seizure. Otherwise, the operation will lack the legitimacy necessary to sustain continued support. Third, it is important to complement the street-level enforcement effort with other investments, not only in the criminal justice system, but also in the treatment system. Otherwise the opportunities created by street-level enforcement will not be fully realized.

Discussion Questions

1. Why should drug use be prohibited? Is it to reduce crime or to achieve a social welfare objective? Are the drug laws an appropriate use of the criminal sanction?

2. What should society's objective be in confronting drug trafficking? Should the primary objective be to minimize the supply of drugs, or to attack powerful criminal organizations, or something else?

3. What are the relative strengths and weaknesses of the four major drug trafficking policies: crop control, interdiction, high-level enforcement, street-level enforcement?

References

Grinspoon, Lester, and James B. Bakalar. 1985. *Cocaine: A Drug and its Social Evolution.* Revised Edition. New York: Basic Books.

Kaplan, John. 1983. *The Hardest Drug: Heroin and Public Policy.* Chicago: University of Chicago Press.

Kleiman, Mark A.R. 1986. "Bringing Back Street Level Heroin Enforcement." Program in Criminal Justice Policy and Management, Cambridge, Mass.: Harvard University, Kennedy School of Government.

Mills, James. 1986. *The Underground Empire.* New York: Doubleday.

Moore, Mark H. 1977. *Buy and Bust: The Effective Regulation of an Illicit Market in Heroin.* Lexington, Mass.: D.C. Heath.

Reuter, Peter, and Mark Kleiman. 1986. "Risks and Prices: An Economic Analysis of Drug Enforcement." In *Crime and Justice: An Annual Review of Research,* vol. 7, edited by Michael Tonry and Norval Morris. Chicago: University of Chicago Press.

3

The Criminal Justice System

The Police and Law Enforcement

Introduction

Law enforcement agencies have traditionally been charged with maintaining public order, enforcing the criminal law, preventing and detecting crime, and apprehending and arresting criminal suspects. As our society has evolved, new and complex functions have been required of police officers. Today, law enforcement agencies work actively with community leaders to prevent criminal behavior; they divert juveniles, alcoholics, and drug addicts from the criminal justice system; they participate in specialized crime prevention projects such as drug awareness projects in local schools; they resolve family conflicts; they facilitate the movement of people and vehicles; and they provide social services, such as preserving civil order on an emergency basis, finding shelter for the homeless, and helping those with special needs.

Because of these expanded responsibilities, greater professionalism is required of police officers. The of-

ficer must not only be technically competent to investigate crimes and make an arrest but also be aware of the rules and procedures associated with arrest, apprehension, and investigation of criminal activity. The police officer must be in possession of a wide variety of skills, from using technological advances such as computers, to developing the proper contacts with social service agencies in order to give aid to an abused or homeless child.

The police officer's role is established by the boundaries of the criminal law. While the officer sets the criminal justice system in motion by his or her authority to arrest, and this authority is vested in the law, it is neither final nor absolute. The police officer's duty requires discretion in dealing with a variety of situations, victims, criminals, and citizens. The officer must determine when an argument becomes disorderly conduct or criminal assault; whether it is appropriate to arrest a juvenile or refer him or her to a social agency; or when to assume that probable cause exists to arrest a suspect for a crime.

The first two papers in this section, by George L. Kelling and by Mark H. Moore and Robert C. Trojanowicz, focus on the community policing concept, which has become one of the most talked about law enforcement strategies in recent years. The final two articles deal with the police response to special needs. First, Peter E. Finn and Monique Sullivan discuss how police agencies have responded to the needs of special populations—the mentally ill, homeless, and public inebriate. Then Theodore M. Hammett reviews how dealing with AIDS-infected suspects has influenced law enforcement.

National Institute of Justice

Perspectives on Policing

Police and Communities: The Quiet Revolution

George L. Kelling, Northeastern University

June 1988

Introduction

A quiet revolution is reshaping American policing.

Police in dozens of communities are returning to foot patrol. In many communities, police are surveying citizens to learn what they believe to be their most serious neighborhood problems. Many police departments are finding alternatives to rapidly responding to the majority of calls for service. Many departments are targeting resources on citizen fear of crime by concentrating on disorder. Organizing citizens' groups has become a priority in many departments. Increasingly, police departments are looking for means to evaluate themselves on their contribution to the quality of neighborhood life, not just crime statistics. Are such activities the business of policing? In a crescendo, police are answering yes.

True, such activities contrast with popular images of police: the "thin blue line" separating plundering villains from peaceful residents and storekeepers, and racing through city streets in high-powered cars with sirens wailing and lights flashing. Yet, in city after city, a new vision of policing is taking hold of the imagination of progressive police and gratified citizens. Note the 1987 report of the Philadelphia Task Force. Dismissing the notion of police as Philadelphia's professional defense against crime, and its residents as passive recipients of police ministrations, the report affirms new police values:

> Because the current strategy for policing Philadelphia emphasizes crime control and neglects the Department's need to be accountable to the public and for a partnership with it, the task force recommends: The police commis-

sioner should formulate an explicit mission statement for the Department that will guide planning and operations toward a strategy of *"community"* or *"problem solving"* policing. Such a statement should be developed in consultation with the citizens of Philadelphia and should reflect their views. (Emphases added.)

These themes—problem solving, community policing, consultation, partnership, accountability—have swept through American policing so swiftly that Harvard University's Professor Mark H. Moore has noted that "We in academe have to scramble to keep track of developments in policing." Professor Herman Goldstein of the University of Wisconsin sees police as "having turned a corner" by emphasizing community accountability and problem solving.

The New Model of Policing

What corner has been turned? What are these changes that are advancing through policing?

Broken Windows

In February 1982, James Q. Wilson and I published an article in *Atlantic* known popularly as "Broken Windows." We made three points.

1. Neighborhood disorder—drunks, panhandling, youth gangs, prostitution, and other urban incivilities—creates citizen fear.

2. Just as unrepaired broken windows can signal to people that nobody cares about a building and lead

to more serious vandalism, untended disorderly behavior can also signal that nobody cares about the community and lead to more serious disorder and crime. Such signals—untended property, disorderly persons, drunks, obstreperous youth, etc.—both create fear in citizens and attract predators.

3. If police are to deal with disorder to reduce fear and crime, they must rely on citizens for legitimacy and assistance.

"Broken Windows" gave voice to sentiments felt both by citizens and police. It recognized a major change in the focus of police. Police had believed that they should deal with serious crime, yet were frustrated by lack of success. Citizens conceded to police that crime was a problem, but were more concerned about daily incivilities that disrupted and often destroyed neighborhood social, commercial, and political life. "We were trying to get people to be concerned about crime problems," says Darrel Stephens, former Chief in Newport News and now Executive Director of the Police Executive Research Forum, "never understanding that daily living issues had a much greater impact on citizens and commanded their time and attention."

Many police officials, however, believed the broken windows metaphor went further. For them, it not only suggested changes in the focus of police work (disorder, for example), it also suggested major modifications in the overall strategy of police departments. What are some of these strategic changes?

Defense of a Community

Police are a neighborhood's primary defense against disorder and crime, right? This orthodoxy has been the basis of police strategy for a generation. What is the police job? Fighting crime. How do they do this? Patrolling in cars, responding to calls for service, and investigating crimes. What is the role of citizens in all of this? Supporting police by calling them if trouble occurs and by being good witnesses.

But using our metaphor, let us again ask the question of whether police are the primary defense against crime and disorder. Are police the "thin blue line" defending neighborhoods and communities? Considering a specific example might help us answer this question. For example, should police have primary responsibility for controlling a neighborhood youth who, say, is bullying other children?

Of course not. The first line of defense in a neighborhood against a troublesome youth is the youth's family. Even if the family is failing, our immediate answer would not be to involve police. Extended family—aunts, uncles, grandparents—might become involved. Neighbors and friends (of both the parents and youth) often offer assistance. The youth's church or school might become involved.

On occasion police will be called: Suppose that the youth is severely bullying other children to the point of injuring them. A bullied child's parents call the police. Is the bully's family then relieved of responsibility? Are neighbors? The school? Once police are called, are neighbors relieved of their duty to be vigilant and protect their own or other neighbors' children? Does calling police relieve teachers of their obligation to be alert and protect children from assault? The answer to all these questions is no. We expect families, neighbors, teachers, and others to be responsible and prudent.

If we believe that community institutions are the first line of defense against disorder and crime, and the source of strength for maintaining the quality of life, what should the strategy of police be? The old view was that they were a community's professional defense against crime and disorder: Citizens should leave control of crime and maintenance of order to police. The new strategy is that police are to stimulate and buttress a community's ability to produce attractive neighborhoods and protect them against predators. Moreover, in communities that are wary of strangers, police serve to help citizens tolerate and protect outsiders who come into their neighborhoods for social or commercial purposes.

But what about neighborhoods in which things have gotten out of hand—where, for example, predators like drug dealers take over and openly and outrageously deal drugs and threaten citizens? Clearly, police must play a leading role defending such communities. Should they do so on their own, however?

Police have tried in the past to control neighborhoods plagued by predators without involving residents. Concerned, for example, about serious street crime, police made youths, especially minority youths, the targets of aggressive field interrogations. The results, in the United States during the 1960's and more recently in England during the early 1980's, were disastrous. Crime was largely unaffected. Youths already hostile to police became even more so. Worst of all, good citizens became estranged from police.

Citizens in neighborhoods plagued by crime and disorder were disaffected because they simply would not have police they neither knew nor authorized whizzing in and out of their neighborhoods "takin' names and kickin' ass." Community relations programs were beside the point. Citizens were in no mood to surrender control of their neighborhoods to remote and officious police who showed them little respect. Police are the first line of defense in a neighborhood? Wrong—citizens are!

Defending Communities—From Incidents to Problems

The strategy of assisting citizens maintain the quality of life in their neighborhoods dramatically improves on the former police strategy. To understand why, one has to understand in some detail how police work has been conducted in the past. Generally, the business of police for the past 30 years has been responding to calls for service.

For example, a concerned and frightened citizen calls police about a neighbor husband and wife who are fighting. Police come and intervene. They might separate the couple, urge them to get help, or, if violence has occurred, arrest the perpetrator. But basically, police try to resolve the incident and get back into their patrol cars so they are available for the next call. Beat officers may well know that this household has been the subject of 50 or 100 calls to the police department during the past year. In fact, they have known intuitively what researchers Glenn Pierce in Boston and Lawrence Sherman in Minneapolis have confirmed through research: fewer than 10 percent of the addresses calling for police service generate over 60 percent of the total calls for service during a given year.

Indeed, it is very likely that the domestic dispute described above is nothing new for the disputing couple, the neighbors, or police. More likely than not, citizens have previously called police and they have responded. And, with each call to police, it becomes more likely that there will be another.

This atomistic response to incidents acutely frustrates patrol officers. Herman Goldstein describes this frustration: "Although the public looks at the average officer as a powerful authority figure, the officer very often feels impotent because he or she is dealing with things for which he or she has no solution. Officers believe this makes them look silly in the eyes of the public." But, given the routine of police work, officers

have had no alternative to their typical response: Go to a call, pacify things, and leave to get ready for another call. To deal with the problem of atomistic responses to incidents, Goldstein has proposed what he calls "problem-oriented policing."

Stated simply, problem-oriented policing is a method of working with citizens to help them identify and solve problems. Darrel Stephens, along with Chief David Couper of Madison, Wisconsin, and Chief Neil Behan of Baltimore County, Maryland, has pioneered in problem-oriented policing. Problems approached via problem-oriented policing include sexual assault and drunk driving in Madison, auto theft, spouse abuse, and burglary in Newport News, and street robbery and burglary in Baltimore County.

Stephens's goal is for "police officers to take the time to stop and think about what they were doing." Mark Moore echoes Stephens: "In the past there were a small number of guys in the police chief's office who did the thinking and everybody else just carried out their ideas. Problem solving gets thousands of brains working on problems."

The Drive to Change

Why are these changes taking place now? There are three reasons:

1. Citizen disenchantment with police services;
2. Research conducted during the 1970's; and,
3. Frustration with the traditional role of the police officer.

1. ***Disenchantment with police services***—At first, it seems too strong to say "disenchantment" when referring to citizens' attitudes towards police. Certainly citizens admire and respect most police officers. Citizens enjoy contact with police. Moreover, research shows that most citizens do not find the limited capability of police to prevent or solve crimes either surprising or of particular concern. Nevertheless, there is widespread disenchantment with police tactics that continue to keep police officers remote and distant from citizens.

    Minority citizens in inner cities continue to be frustrated by police who whisk in and out of their neighborhoods with little sensitivity to community norms and values. Regardless of where one asks, minorities want both the familiarity and accountability that characterize foot patrol. Working-and middle-class communities of all races are demanding increased collaboration with police in the determination of police priorities in their neighborhoods. Community crime control has become a mainstay of their sense of neighborhood security and a means of lobbying for different police services. And many merchants and affluent citizens have felt so vulnerable that they have turned to private security for service and protection. In private sector terms, police are losing to the competition—private security and community crime control.

2. *Research*—The 1970's research about police effectiveness was another stimulus to change. Research about preventive patrol, rapid response to calls for service, and investigative work—the three mainstays of police tactics—was uniformly discouraging.

   Research demonstrated that preventive patrol in automobiles had little effect on crime, citizen levels of fear, or citizen satisfaction with police. Rapid response to calls for service likewise had little impact on arrests, citizen satisfaction with police, or levels of citizen fear. Also, research into criminal investigation effectiveness suggested that detective units were so poorly administered that they had little chance of being effective.

3. *Role of the patrol officer*—Finally, patrol officers have been frustrated with their traditional role. Despite pieties that patrol has been the backbone of policing, every police executive has known that, at best, patrol has been what officers do until they become detectives or are promoted.

   At worst, patrol has been the dumping ground for officers who are incompetent, suffering from alcoholism or other problems, or simply burned out. High status for police practitioners went to detectives. Getting "busted to patrol" has been a constant threat to police managers or detectives who fail to perform by some standard of judgment. (It is doubtful that failing patrol officers ever get threatened with being busted to the detective unit.)

   Never mind that patrol officers have the most important mission in police departments: They handle the public's most pressing problems and must make complex decisions almost instantaneously. Moreover, they do this with little supervision or training. Despite this, police administrators treat patrol officers as if they did little to advance

the organization's mission. The salaries of patrol officers also reflect their demeaned status. No wonder many officers have grown cynical and have turned to unions for leadership rather than to police executives. "Stupid management made unions," says Robert Kliesmet, the President of the International Union of Police Associations AFL-CIO.

The Basis for New Optimism

Given these circumstances, what is the basis of current optimism of police leaders that they have turned a corner? Optimism arises from four factors:

1. Citizen response to the new strategy;
2. Ongoing research on police effectiveness;
3. Past experiences police have had with innovation; and
4. The values of the new generation of police leaders.

1. *Citizen response*—The overwhelming public response to community and problem-solving policing has been positive, regardless of where it has been instituted. When queried about how he knows community policing works in New York City, Lt. Jerry Simpson responds: "The District Commanders' phones stop ringing." Simpson continues: "Commanders' phones stop ringing because problems have been solved. Even skeptical commanders soon learn that most of their troubles go away with community policing." Citizens like the cop on the beat and enjoy working with him/her to solve problems. Crisley Wood, Executive Director of the Neighborhood Justice Network in Boston—an agency that has established a network of neighborhood crime control organizations—puts it this way: "The cop on the beat, who meets regularly with citizen groups, is the single most important service that the Boston Police Department can provide."

   Testimonies aside, perhaps the single most compelling evidence of the popularity of community or problem-solving policing is found in Flint, Michigan, where, it will be recalled, citizens have twice voted to increase their taxes to maintain neighborhood foot patrols—the second time by a two-to-one margin.

2. *New research on effectiveness*—Research conducted during the early and mid-1970's frustrated police executives. It generally showed what did not

work. Research conducted during the late 1970's and early 1980's was different. By beginning to demonstrate that new tactics did work, it fueled the move to rejuvenate policing. This research provided police with the following guidance:

Foot patrol can reduce citizen fear of crime, improve the relationship between police and citizens, and increase citizen satisfaction with police. This was discovered in Newark, New Jersey, and Flint. In Flint, foot patrol also reduced crime and calls for service. Moreover, in both cities, it increased officer satisfaction with police work.

The productivity of detectives can be enhanced if patrol officers carefully interview neighborhood residents about criminal events, get the information to detectives, and detectives use it wisely, according to John Eck of PERF.

Citizen fear can be substantially reduced, researcher Tony Pate of the Police Foundation discovered in Newark, by police tactics that emphasize increasing the quantity and improving the quality of citizen-police interaction.

Police anti-fear tactics can also reduce household burglaries, according to research conducted by Mary Ann Wycoff, also of the Police Foundation.

Street-level enforcement of heroin and cocaine laws can reduce serious crime in the area of enforcement, without being displaced to adjacent areas, according to an experiment conducted by Mark Kleiman of Harvard University's Program in Criminal Justice Policy and Management.

Problem-oriented policing can be used to reduce thefts from cars, problems associated with prostitution, and household burglaries, according to William Spelman and John Eck of PERF.

These positive findings about new police tactics provide police with both the motive and justification for continued efforts to rejuvenate policing.

3. *Experience with innovation*—The desire to improve policing is not new with this generation of reformers. The 1960's and 1970's had their share of reformers as well. Robert Eichelberger of Dayton innovated with team policing (tactics akin in many ways to problem solving) and public policymaking; Frank Dyson of Dallas with team policing and

generalist/specialist patrol officers; Carl Gooden with team policing in Cincinnati; and there were many other innovators.

But innovators of this earlier era were handicapped by a lack of documented successes and failures of implementation. Those who experimented with team policing were not aware that elements of team policing were simply incompatible with preventive patrol and rapid response to calls for service. As a result, implementation of team policing followed a discouraging pattern. It would be implemented, officers and citizens would like it, it would have an initial impact on crime, and then business as usual would overwhelm it—the program would simply vanish.

Moreover, the lessons about innovation and excellence that Peters and Waterman brought together in *In Search of Excellence* were not available to police administrators. The current generation of reformers has an edge: They have availed themselves of the opportunity to learn from the documented successes and failures of the past. Not content with merely studying innovation and management in policing, Houston's Chief Lee Brown is having key personnel spend internships in private sector corporations noted for excellence in management.

4. *New breed of police leadership*—The new breed of police leadership is unique in the history of American policing. Unlike the tendency in the past for chiefs to be local and inbred, chiefs of this generation are urbane and cosmopolitan.

Chief Lee Brown of Houston received a Ph.D. in criminology from the University of California-Berkeley; Chief Joseph McNamara of San Jose, California, has a Ph.D. from Harvard University, and is a published novelist; Hubert Williams, formerly Director of the Newark Police Department and now President of the Police Foundation, is a lawyer and has studied criminology in the Law School at Harvard University; Benjamin Ward, Commissioner of the New York City Police Department, is an attorney and was Commissioner of Corrections in New York State.

These are merely a sample. The point is, members of this generation of police leadership are well educated and of diverse backgrounds. All of those noted above, as well as many others, have sponsored research and experimentation to improve policing.

Problems

We have looked at the benefits of community policing. What is the down side? What are the risks?

These questions led to the creation of the Executive Session on Community Policing in the Program in Criminal Justice Policy and Management of Harvard University's John F. Kennedy School of Government. Funded by the National Institute of Justice and the Charles Stewart Mott and Guggenheim Foundations, the Executive Session has convened police and political elites with a small number of academics around the issue of community policing. Francis X. Hartmann, moderator of the Executive Session, describes the purpose of the meetings: "These persons with a special and important relationship to contemporary policing have evolved into a real working group, which is addressing the gap between the realities and aspirations of American policing. Community policing is a significant effort to fill this gap."

Among the questions the Executive Session has raised are the following:

1. Police are a valuable resource in a community. Does community policing squander that resource by concentrating on the wrong priorities?
2. How will community policing fit into police departments given how they are now organized? and,
3. Will community policing open the door to increased police corruption or other inappropriate behavior by line officers?

Will Community Policing Squander Police Resources?

This question worries police. They understand that police are a valuable but sparse resource in a community. Hubert Williams, a pioneer in community policing, expresses his concern. "Are police now being put in the role of providing services that are statutorily the responsibilities of some other agencies?" Los Angeles's Chief Gates echoes Williams: "Hubie's (Williams is) right—you can't solve all the problems in the world and shouldn't try." Both worry that if police are spread too thin, by problem-solving activities for example, that they will not be able to properly protect the community from serious crime.

This issue is now being heatedly debated in Flint. There, it will be recalled, citizens have passed two bills

funding foot patrol—the second by a two-to-one majority. A report commissioned by city government, however, concludes: "The Cost of the Neighborhood Foot Patrol Program Exceeds the Benefit It Provides the Citizens of Flint," and recommends abandoning the program when funding expires.

Why, according to the report, should foot patrol be abandoned? So more "effective" police work can be done. What is effective police work? Quick response to calls for service, taking reports, and increased visibility by putting police officers in cars. "It is simply wrong," says Robert Wasserman, noted police tactician and Research Fellow in the Program in Criminal Justice at Harvard, "to propose abandoning foot patrol in the name of short response time and visibility vis-a-vis patrolling in cars. Every shred of evidence is that rapid response and patrolling in cars doesn't reduce crime, increase citizen satisfaction, or reduce fear. Which is the luxury," Wasserman concludes, "a tactic like foot patrol that gives you two, and maybe three, of your goals, or a tactic like riding around in cars going from call to call that gives you none?" Experienced police executives share Wasserman's concerns. Almost without exception, they are attempting to find ways to get out of the morass that myths of the efficacy of rapid response have created for large-city police departments. It was Commissioner Ben Ward of New York City, for example, who put a cap on resources that can be used to respond to calls for service and is attempting to find improved means of responding to calls. Commissioner Francis "Mickey" Roache expresses the deep frustration felt by so many police: "I hate to say this, but in Boston we run from one call to another. We don't accomplish anything. We're just running all over the place. It's absolutely insane."

A politician's response to the recommendation to end Flint's foot patrol program is interesting. Daniel Whitehurst, former Mayor of Fresno, California, reflects: "I find it hard to imagine ending a program that citizens not only find popular but are willing to pay for as well."

"The overwhelming danger," Mark Moore concludes, "is that, in the name of efficiency, police and city officials will be tempted to maintain old patterns. They will think they are doing good, but will be squandering police resources." "Chips" Stewart emphasizes the need to move ahead: "As comfortable as old tactics might feel, police must continue to experiment with methods that have shown promise to improve police effectiveness and efficiency."

Will Community Policing Fit Within Policing as it is Now Organized?

Many police and academics believe this to be the most serious problem facing cities implementing community policing. Modern police departments have achieved an impressive capacity to respond quickly to calls for service. This has been accomplished by acquiring and linking elaborate automobile, telephone, radio, and computer technologies, by centralizing control and dispatch of officers, by pressing officers to be "in service" (rather than "out of service" dealing with citizens), and by allocating police in cars throughout the city on the basis of expected calls for service.

Community policing is quite different: it is not incident-or technology-driven; officers operate on a decentralized basis, it emphasizes officers being in regular contact with citizens, and it allocates police on the basis of neighborhoods. The question is, how reconcilable are these two strategies? Some (Lawrence Sherman of the University of Maryland is one example) have taken a strong stance that radical alterations will be required if police are to respond more effectively to community problems. Others (Richard Larson of the Massachusetts Institute of Technology, for example) disagree, believing that community policing is reconcilable with rapid response technology—indeed Professor Larson would emphasize that current computer technology can facilitate community policing.

Will the Community Policing Strategy Lead to Increased Police Corruption and Misbehavior?

The initial news from Houston, New York, Flint, Newark, Los Angeles, Baltimore County, and other police departments which have experimented with community policing is good. Community policing has not led to increased problems of corruption or misbehavior.

Why is it, however, that policymakers fear that community policing has the potential to increase the incidents of police running amok? The answer? Community policing radically decentralizes police authority; officers must create for themselves the best responses to problems; and, police become intimately involved with citizens.

These ingredients may not sound so troublesome in themselves—after all, many private and public sector organizations radically decentralize authority, encourage creativity, and are characterized by relative intimacy between service providers and consumers. Nevertheless, in police circles such ingredients violate the orthodox means of controlling corruption. For a generation, police have believed that to eliminate corruption it is necessary to centralize authority, limit discretion, and reduce intimacy between police and citizens. They had good reason to: Early policing in the United States had been characterized by financial corruption, failure of police to protect the rights of all citizens, and zealotry.

But just as it is possible to squander police resources in the name of efficiency, it is also possible to squander police resources in the quest for integrity. Centralization, standardization, and remoteness may preclude many opportunities for corruption, but they may also preclude the possibility of good policing. For example, street-level cocaine and heroin enforcement by patrol officers, now known to have crime reduction value, has been banned in cities because of fear of corruption. It is almost as if the purpose of police was to be corruption free, rather than to do essential work. If, as it appears to be, it is necessary to take risks to solve problems, then so be it: police will have to learn to manage risks as well as do managers in other enterprises.

Does this imply softening on the issue of police corruption? Absolutely not. Police and city managers will have to continue to be vigilant: community policing exposes officers to more opportunities for traditional financial corruption; in many neighborhoods police will be faced with demands to protect communities from the incursions of minorities; and, police will be tempted to become overzealous when they see citizens' problems being ignored by other agencies.

These dangers mean, however, that police executives will have to manage through values, rather than merely policies and procedures, and by establishing regular neighborhood and community institution reporting mechanisms, rather than through centralized command and control systems.

Each of these issues—use of police resources, organizational compatibility, and corruption—is complicated. Some will be the subject of debate. Others will require research and experimentation to resolve. But most police chiefs will begin to address these issues in a new way. They will not attempt to resolve them in the ways of the past: in secret, behind closed doors. Their approach will reflect the values of the individual neighborhoods as well as the community as a whole.

Policing is changing dramatically. On the one hand, we wish policing to retain the old values of police integrity, equitable distribution of police resources throughout a community, and police efficiency which characterized the old model of police. But the challenge of contemporary police and city executives is to redefine these concepts in light of the resurgence of neighborhood vitality, consumerism, and more realistic assessments of the institutional capacity of police.

The quiet revolution is beginning to make itself heard: citizens and police are joining together to defend communities.

Discussion Questions

1. What does the term *community policing* refer to, and how has it changed the scope of law enforcement in the United States?

2. What are the three concepts that make up the "broken windows" approach? Should police be responsible for the general well-being of a neighborhood? Are they adequately trained for such activities?

3. Should police become community problem solvers? How can they identify the "real" problems of a community? Who defines what a community actually is and who is responsible for articulating its problems?

National Institute of Justice   *Perspectives on Policing*

Policing and the Fear of Crime

Mark H. Moore, Harvard University
and Robert C. Trojanowicz, Michigan State University

June 1988

When crimes occur—when a ghetto teenager is shot to death in a gang war, when an elderly woman is mugged for her social security check, when a nurse is raped in a hospital parking lot, when one driver is punched by another in a dispute over a parking place, when a black family's new home is vandalized—society's attention is naturally focused on the victims and their material losses. Their wounds, bruises, lost property, and inconvenience can be seen, touched, and counted. These are the concrete signs of criminal victimization.

Behind the immediate, concrete losses of crime victims, however, is a different, more abstract crime problem—that of fear. For victims, fear is often the largest and more enduring legacy of their victimization. The raped nurse will feel vulnerable long after her cuts and bruises heal. The harassed black family suffers far more from the fear of neighborhood hostility than the inconvenience of repairing their property.

For the rest of us—the not-recently, or not-yet victimized—fear becomes a contagious agent spreading the injuriousness of criminal victimization. The gang member's death makes parents despair of their children's future. The mugging of the elderly woman teaches elderly residents to fear the streets and the teenagers who roam them. The fight over the parking place confirms the general fear of strangers. The harassment of the black family makes other minorities reluctant to claim their rights. In these ways, fear extends the damage of criminal victimization.

Of course, fear is not totally unproductive. It prompts caution among citizens and thereby reduces criminal opportunities. Too, it motivates citizens to shoulder some of the burdens of crime control by buying locks and dogs, thereby adding to general deterrence. And fear kindles enthusiasm for publicly supported crime control measures. Thus, reasonable fears, channeled in constructive directions, prepare society to deal with crime. It is only when fear is unreasonable, or generates counterproductive responses, that it becomes a social problem.

This paper explores fear as a problem to be addressed by the police. It examines current levels and recent trends in the fear of crime; analyzes how fear is linked to criminal victimization; considers the extent to which fear is a distinct problem that invites separate control strategies; and assesses the positive and negative social consequences of fear. It then turns to what is known about the efficacy of police strategies for managing fear, i.e., for reducing fear when it is irrational and destructive, and for channeling fear along constructive paths when it is reasonable and helpful in controlling crime.

The Fear of Crime

Society does not yet systematically collect data on fear. Consequently, our map of fear—its levels, trends, and social location—is sketchy. Nonetheless, its main features are easily identified.

First, fear is widespread. The broadest impact was registered by "The Figgie Report on Fear of Crime" released in 1980. Two-fifths of Americans surveyed reported that they were "highly fearful" they would become victims of violent crime.[1] Similar results were reported by the Harris poll of 1975, which found that 55 percent of all adults said they felt "uneasy" walking their own streets.[2] The Gallup poll of 1977 found that about 45 percent of the population (61 percent of the women and 28 percent of the men) were afraid to walk alone at night.[3] An eight-city victimization survey published in 1977 found that 45 percent of all respondents limited their activities because of fear of crime.[4] A statewide study in Michigan reported that 66 percent of respondents avoided certain places because of fear of crime.[5] Interviews with a random sample of Texans in 1978 found that more than half said that they feared becoming a serious crime victim within a year.[6]

Second, fear of crime increased from the late 1960's to the mid-1970's, then began decreasing during the mid-1970's. According to the 1968 Gallup poll, 44 percent of the women and 16 percent of the men said that they were afraid to walk alone at night. In 1977, when a similar question was asked, 61 percent of the women and 28 percent of the men reported they were afraid to walk alone at night—an increase of 17 percent for women and 12 percent for men.[7] In 1975, a Harris poll found that 55 percent of all adults felt "uneasy" walking their own streets. In 1985, this number had fallen to 32 percent—a significant decline.[8]

Third, fear is not evenly distributed across the population. Predictably, those who feel themselves most vulnerable are also the most fearful. Looking at the distribution of fear across age and sex categories, the greatest levels of fear are reported by elderly women. The next most frightened group seems to be all other women. The least afraid are young men.

Looking at race, class, and residence variables, blacks are more afraid of crime than whites, the poor more afraid than the middle class or wealthy, and inner-city dwellers more afraid than suburbanites.[9]

Indeed, while the current national trend may show a decline in fear, anecdotal evidence suggests that this trend has not yet reached America's ghettos. There, fear has become a condition of life. Claude Brown describes Harlem's problem in 1985:

> ... In any Harlem building, ... every door has at least three locks on it. Nobody opens a door without first finding out who's there. In the early evening, ... you see people ... lingering outside nice apartment houses, peeking in the lobbies. They seem to be casing the joint. They are actually trying to figure out who is in the lobby of *their* building. "Is this someone waiting to mug me? Should I risk going in, or should I wait for someone else to come?"
>
> If you live in Harlem, USA, you don't park your automobile two blocks from your apartment house because that gives potential muggers an opportunity to get a fix on you. You'd better find a parking space within a block of

your house, because if you have to walk two blocks, you're not going to make it. . . .

> In Harlem, elderly people walking their dogs in the morning cross the street when they see some young people coming. . . . And what those elderly men and women have in the paper bags they're carrying is not just a pooper scooper—it's a gun. And if those youngsters cross the street, somebody's going to get hurt.[10]

These findings suggest that one of the most important privileges one acquires as one gains wealth and status in American society is the opportunity to leave the fear of crime behind. The unjust irony is that "criminals walk city streets, while fear virtually imprisons groups like women and the elderly in their homes."[11] The important long-run consequence of this uneven distribution of fear for the economic development of our cities [is this]: if the inner-city populations are afraid of crime, then commerce and investment essentially disappear, and with them, the chance for upward social mobility.[12] If Hobbes is correct in asserting that the most fundamental purpose of civil government is to establish order and protect citizens from the fear of criminal attack that made life "nasty, brutish and short" in the "state of nature," then the current level and distribution of fear indicate an important governmental failure.[13]

The Causes of Fear

In the past, fear was viewed as primarily caused by criminal victimization. Hence, the principal strategy for controlling crime was reducing criminal victimization. More recently, we have learned that while fear of crime is associated with criminal victimization, the relationship is less close than originally assumed.[14]

The association between victimization and fear is seen most closely in the aggregate patterns across time and space. Those who live in areas with high crime rates are more afraid and take more preventive action than people living in areas where the risk of victimization is lower.[15] The trends in levels of fear seem to mirror (perhaps with a lag) trends in levels of crime.

Yet, the groups that are most fearful are not necessarily those with the highest victimization rates; indeed, the order is exactly reversed. Elderly women, who are most afraid, are the least frequently victimized. Young men, who are least afraid, are most often victimized.[16]

Even more surprisingly, past victimization has only a small impact on levels of fear; people who have heard about others' victimizations are almost as fearful as those who have actually been victimized.[17] And when citizens are asked about the things that frighten them, there is little talk about "real crimes" such as robbery, rape, and murder. More often there is talk about other signs of physical decay and social disorganization such as "junk and trash in vacant lots, boarded-up buildings, stripped and abandoned cars, bands of teen-agers congregating on street corners, street prostitution, panhandling, public drinking, verbal harassment of women, open gambling and drug use, and other incivilities."[18]

In accounting for levels of fear in communities, Wesley Skogan divides the contributing causes into five broad categories: (1) actual criminal victimization; (2) second-hand information about criminal victimization distributed through social networks; (3) physical deterioration and social disorder; (4) the characteristics of the built environment (i.e., the physical composition of the housing stock); and (5) group conflict.[19] He finds the strongest effects on fear arising from physical deterioration, social disorder, and group conflict.[20] The impact of the built environment is hard to detect once one has subtracted the effects of other variables influencing levels of fear. A review article by Charles Murray also found little evidence of a separate effect of the built environment on fear. The only exception to this general conclusion is evidence indicating that improved street lighting can sometimes produce significant fear reductions.[21]

The important implication of these research results is that fear might be attacked by strategies other than those that directly reduce criminal victimization. Fear might be reduced even without changes in levels of victimization by using the communications within social networks to provide accurate information about risks of criminal victimization and advice about constructive responses to the risk of crime; by eliminating the external signs of physical decay and social disorder; and by more effectively regulating group conflict between young and old, whites and minority groups, rich and poor. The more intriguing possibility, however, is that if fear could be rationalized and constructively channeled, not only would fear and its adverse consequences be ameliorated, but also real levels of victimization reduced. In this sense, the conventional understanding of this problem would be reversed: instead of controlling victimization to control fear, we would manage fear to reduce victimization. To understand this possibility, we must explore the consequences of fear—not only as ends in themselves, but also as means for helping society deal with crime.

The Economic and Societal Consequences of Fear: Costs and Benefits

Fear is a more or less rational response to crime. It produces social consequences through two different mechanisms. First, people are uncomfortable emotionally. Instead of luxuriating in the peace and safety of their homes, they feel vulnerable and isolated. Instead of enjoying the camaraderie of trips to school, grocery stores, and work, they feel anxious and afraid. Since these are less happy conditions than feeling secure, fear produces an immediate loss in personal well-being.

Second, fear motivates people to invest time and money in defensive measures to reduce their vulnerability. They stay indoors more than they would wish, avoid certain places, buy extra locks, and ask for special protection to make bank deposits. Since this time, effort, and money could presumably be spent on other things that make people happier, such expenditures must also be counted as personal costs which, in turn, become social costs as they are aggregated.

These are far from trivial issues. The fact that two-fifths of the population is afraid and that the Nation continues to nominate crime as one of its greatest concerns means that society is living less securely and happily than is desirable. And if 45 percent of the population restricts its daily behavior to minimize vulnerability, and the Nation spends more than $20 billion on private security protection, then private expenditures on reducing fear constitute a significant component of the national economy.[22] All this is in addition to the $40 billion that society spends publicly on crime control efforts.[23] In short, fear of crime claims a noticeable share of the Nation's welfare and resources.

Fear has a further effect. Individual responses to fear aggregate in a way that erodes the overall quality of community life and, paradoxically, the overall capacity of society to deal with crime.[24] This occurs when the defensive reactions of individuals essentially compromise community life, or when they exacerbate the disparities between rich and poor by relying too much on private rather than public security.

Skogan has described in detail the mechanisms that erode community life:

> Fear ... can work in conjunction with other factors to stimulate more rapid neighborhood decline. Together, the spread of fear and other local problems provide a form of positive feedback that can further increase levels of crime. These feedback processes include (1) physical and psychological withdrawal from community life; (2) a weakening of the informal social control processes that inhibit crime and disorder; (3) a decline in the organizational life and mobilization capacity of the neighborhood; (4) deteriorating business conditions; (5) the importation and domestic production of delinquency and deviance; and (6) further dramatic changes in the composition of the population. At the end lies a stage characterized by demographic collapse.[25]

Even if fear does not destroy neighborhood life, it can damage it by prompting responses which protect some citizens at the expense of others, thereby leading to greater social disparities between rich and poor, resourceful and dependent, well-organized and anomic communities. For example, when individuals retreat behind closed doors and shuttered windows, they make their own homes safer. But they make the streets more dangerous, for there are fewer people watching and intervening on the streets. Or, when individuals invest in burglar alarms or private security guards rather than spending more on public police forces, they may make themselves safer, but leave others worse off because crime is deflected onto others.

Similarly, neighborhood patrols can make residents feel safe. But they may threaten and injure other law-abiding citizens who want to use the public thoroughfares. Private security guards sometimes bring guns and violence to situations that would otherwise be more peaceably settled. Private efforts may transform our cities from communities now linked to one another through transportation, commerce, and recreation, to collections of isolated armed camps, shocking not only for their apparent indifference to one another, but also ultimately for their failure to control crime and reduce fear. In fact, such constant reminders of potential threats may actually increase fear.

Whether fear produces these results or not depends a great deal on how citizens respond to their fears. If they adopt defensive, individualistic solutions, then the risks of neighborhood collapse and injustice are increased. If they adopt constructive, community-based responses, then the community will be strengthened not only in terms of its ability to defend itself, but also as an image of civilized society. Societies built on communal crime control efforts have more order, justice, and freedom than those based on individualistic responses. Indeed, it is for these reasons that social control and the administration of justice became public rather than private functions.

Police Strategies for Reducing Fear

If it is true that fear is a problem in its own right, then it is important to evaluate the effectiveness of police strategies not only in terms of their capacity to control crime, but also in terms of their capacity to reduce fear. And if fear is affected by more factors than just criminal victimization, then there might be some special police strategies other than controlling victimization that could be effective in controlling the fear of crime.

Over the last 30 years, the dominant police strategy has emphasized three operational components: motorized patrol, rapid response to calls for service, and retrospective investigation of crimes.[26] The principal aim has been to solve crimes and capture criminals rather than reduce fear. The assumption has been that if victimization could be reduced, fear would decrease as well. Insofar as fear was considered a separate problem, police strategists assumed that motorized patrol and rapid response would provide a reassuring police omnipresence.[27]

To the extent that the police thought about managing citizens' individual responses to crime, they visualized a relationship in which citizens detected crime and mobilized the police to deal with it—not one in which the citizens played an important crime control role. The police advised shopkeepers and citizens about self-defense. They created 911 telephone systems to insure that citizens could reach them easily. And they encouraged citizens to mark their property to aid the police in recovering stolen property. But their primary objective was to make themselves society's principal response to crime. Everything else was seen as auxiliary.

As near monopolists in supplying enhanced security and crime control, police managers and union leaders were ambivalent about the issue of fear. On the one hand, as those responsible for security, they felt some obligation to enhance security and reduce fear.

That was by far the predominant view. On the other hand, if citizens were afraid of crime and the police were the solution, the police department would benefit in the fight for scarce municipal funds. This fact has tempted some police executives and some unions to emphasize the risks of crime.[28]

The strategy that emphasized motorized patrol, rapid response, and retrospective investigation of crimes was not designed to reduce fear other than by a reduction in crime. Indeed, insofar as the principal objective of this strategy was to reduce crime, and insofar as citizens were viewed as operational auxiliaries of the police, the police could increase citizens' vigilance by warning of the risks of crime. Nevertheless, to the extent that reduced fear was considered an important objective, it was assumed that the presence and availability of police through motorized patrols and response to calls would achieve that objective.

The anticipated effects of this strategy on levels of fear have not materialized. There have been some occasions, of course, when effective police action against a serial murderer or rapist has reassured a terrorized community. Under ordinary circumstances, however, success of the police in calming fears has been hard to show. The Kansas City experiment showed that citizens were unaware of the level of patrol that occurred in their area. Consequently, they were neither reassured by increased patrolling nor frightened by reduced levels of patrol.[29] Subsequent work on response times revealed that fast responses did not necessarily reassure victims. Before victims even called the police, they often sought assistance and comfort from friends or relatives. Once they called, their satisfaction was related more to their expectations of when the police would arrive than to actual response time. Response time alone was not a significant factor in citizen satisfaction.[30] Thus, the dominant strategy of policing has not performed particularly well in reducing or channeling citizens' fears.

In contrast to the Kansas City study of *motorized* patrol, two field experiments have now shown that citizens are aware of increases or decreases in levels of *foot* patrol, and that increased foot patrol reduces citizens' fears. After reviewing surveys of citizens' assessments of crime problems in neighborhoods that had enhanced, constant, or reduced levels of foot patrol, the authors of *The Newark Foot Patrol Experiment* concluded:

> ... persons living in areas where foot patrol was created perceived a notable decrease in the severity of crime-related problems.[31]

And:

> Consistently, residents in beats where foot patrol was added see the severity of crime problems diminishing in their neighborhoods at levels greater than the other two [kinds of] areas.[32]

Similarly, a foot patrol experiment in Flint, Michigan, found the following:

> Almost 70 percent of the citizens interviewed during the final year of the study felt safer because of the Foot Patrol Program. Moreover, many qualified their response by saying that they felt especially safe when the foot patrol officer was well known and highly visible.[33]

Whether foot patrol can work in less dense cities, and whether it is worth the cost, remain arguable questions. But the experimental evidence clearly supports the hypothesis that fear is reduced among citizens exposed to foot patrol.

Even more significantly, complex experiments in Newark and Houston with a varied mix of fear reduction programs showed that at least some programs could successfully reduce citizens' fears. In Houston, the principal program elements included:

1. a police community newsletter designed to give accurate crime information to citizens;
2. a community organizing response team designed to build a community organization in an area where none had existed;
3. a citizen contact program that kept the same officer patrolling in a particular area of the city and directed him to make individual contacts with citizens in the area;
4. a program directing officers to re-contact victims of crime in the days following their victimization to reassure them of the police presence; and
5. establishing a police community contact center staffed by two patrol officers, a civilian coordinator, and three police aids, within which a school program aimed at reducing truancy and a park program designed to reduce vandalism and increase use of a local park were discussed, designed, and operated.[34]

In Newark, some program elements were similar, but some were unique. Newark's programs included the following:

1. a police community newsletter;
2. a coordinated community policing program that in-

cluded a directed police citizen contact program, a neighborhood community police center, neighborhood cleanup activities, and intensified law enforcement and order maintenance;

3. a program to reduce the signs of crime that included: a) a directed patrol task force committed to foot patrol, radar checks on busy roads, bus checks to enforce city ordinances on buses, and enforcement of disorderly conduct laws; and b) a neighborhood cleanup effort that used police auspices to pressure city service agencies to clean up neighborhoods, and to establish a community work program for juveniles that made their labor available for cleanup details.[35]

Evaluations of these different program elements revealed that programs "designed to increase the quantity and improve the quality of contacts between citizens and police" were generally successful in reducing citizens' fears.[36] This meant that the Houston Citizen Contact Patrol, the Houston Community Organizing Response Team, the Houston Police Community Station, and the Newark Coordinated Community Policing Program were all successful in reducing fear.

Other approaches which encouraged close contact, such as newsletters, the victim re-contact program, and the signs-of-crime program, did not produce clear evidence of fear reduction in these experiments. The reasons that these programs did not work, however, may have been specific to the particular situations rather than inherent in the programs themselves. The victim re-contact program ran into severe operating problems in transmitting information about victimization from the reporting officers to the beat patrol officers responsible for the re-contacts. As a result, the contacts came far too long after the victimization. Newsletters might be valuable if they were published and distributed in the context of ongoing conversations with the community about crime problems. And efforts to eliminate the signs of crime through order maintenance and neighborhood cleanup might succeed if the programs were aimed at problems identified by the community. So, the initial failures of these particular program elements need not condemn them forever.

The one clear implication of both the foot patrol and fear reduction experiments is that closer contact between citizens and police officers reduces fear. As James Q. Wilson concludes in his foreword to the summary report of the fear reduction experiment:

In Houston, … opening a neighborhood police station, contacting the citizens about their problems, and stimulating the formation of neighborhood organizations where none had existed can help reduce the fear of crime and even reduce the actual level of victimization.[37]

In Newark, many of the same steps—including opening a storefront police office and directing the police to make contacts with the citizens in their homes—also had beneficial effects.

The success of these police tactics in reducing fear, along with the observation that fear is a separate and important problem, suggests a new area in which police can make a substantial contribution to the quality of life in the Nation's cities. However, it seems likely that programs like those tried in Flint, Newark, and Houston will not be tried elsewhere unless mayors and police administrators begin to take fear seriously as a separate problem. Such programs are expensive and take patrol resources and managerial attention away from the traditional functions of patrol and retrospective investigation of crimes. Unless their effects are valued, they will disappear as expensive luxuries.

On the other hand, mayors and police executives could view fear as a problem in its own right and as something that inhibits rather than aids effective crime control by forcing people off the streets and narrowing their sense of control and responsibility. If that were the case, not only would these special tactics become important, but the overall strategy of the department might change. That idea has led to wider and more sustained attacks on fear in Baltimore County and Newport News.

In Baltimore County, a substantial portion of the police department was committed to the Citizen Oriented Police Enforcement (COPE) unit—a program designed to improve the quantity and quality of contacts between citizens and the police and to work on problems of concern to citizens.[38] A major objective was to reduce fear. The effort succeeded. Measured levels of fear dropped an average of 10 percent for the various projects during a 6 month period.[39] In Newport News, the entire department shifted to a style of policing that emphasized problem-solving over traditional reactive methods.[40] This approach, like COPE, took citizens' fears and concerns seriously, as well as serious crime and calls for service.

These examples illustrate the security-enhancing potential of problem-solving and community approaches to policing. By incorporating fear reduction as an important objective of policing, by changing the activities of the police to include more frequent, more sustained contacts with citizens, and by consultation and joint planning, police departments seem to be able not only to reduce fear, but to transform it into something that helps to build strong social institutions. That is the promise of these approaches.

Conclusion

Fear of crime is an important problem in its own right. Although levels of fear are related to levels of criminal victimization, fear is influenced by other factors, such as a general sense of vulnerability, signs of physical and social decay, and inter-group conflict. Consequently, there is both a reason for fear and an opportunity to work directly on that fear, rather than indirectly through attempts to reduce criminal victimization.

The current police strategy, which relies on motorized patrol, rapid responses to calls for service, and retrospective investigations of crime, seems to produce little reassurance to frightened citizens, except in unusual circumstances when the police arrest a violent offender in the middle of a crime spree. Moreover, a focus on controlling crime rather than increasing security (analogous to the medical profession's focus on curing disease rather than promoting health) leads the police to miss opportunities to take steps that would reduce fear independently of reducing crime. Consequently, the current strategy of policing does not result in reduced fear. Nor does it leave much room for fear reduction programs in the police department.

This is unfortunate, because some fear reduction programs have succeeded in reducing citizens' fears. Two field experiments showed that foot patrol can reduce fear and promote security. Programs which enhance the quantity and quality of police contacts with citizens through neighborhood police stations and through required regular contacts between citizens and police have been successful in reducing fear in Houston and Newark.

The success of these particular programs points to the potential of a more general change in the strategy of policing that (1) would make fear reduction an important objective and (2) would concentrate on improving the quantity and quality of contacts between citizens and police at all levels of the department. The success of these approaches has been demonstrated in Baltimore County and Newport News.

Based on this discussion, it is apparent that a shift in strategy would probably be successful in reducing fear, and that that would be an important accomplishment. What is more speculative (but quite plausible) is that community policing would also be successful in channeling the remaining fear along constructive rather than destructive paths. Criminal victimization would be reduced, and the overall quality of community life enhanced beyond the mere reduction in fear.

Discussion Questions

1. What causes the fear of crime in a neighborhood? Which crime patterns provoke the most fear?

2. What are the economic and social costs of fear? Can neighborhood patrols and self-defense forces counteract fear?

3. What can law enforcement agencies do to counteract fear? Can such strategies as foot patrol really make a difference?

4. Consider the benefits of a "high-tech," motorized, computer-equipped patrol force. What advantages could a police community organizing effort have over modern technology?

Notes

1. *The Figgie Report on Fear of Crime: America Afraid, Part 1: The General Public* (Research and Forecasts, Inc., Sponsored by A-T-O, Inc., Willoughby, Ohio, 1980), p. 29.

2. Louis Harris, "Crime Rates: Personal Uneasiness in Neighborhoods," *Chicago Tribune*, 6 June 1975.

3. *Gallup Poll Public Opinion*, Vol. 5: 1977 (New York: Random House, 1977), pp. 1240–41.

4. James Garofalo, *Public Opinion About Crime: The Attitudes of Victims and Non-Victims in Selected Cities* (Washington, D.C.: U.S. Government Printing Office, 1977).

5. "The Michigan Public Speaks Out on Crime" (Detroit, Michigan: Market Opinion Research, 1977).

6. R.H.C. Teske, Jr., and N.L. Powell, "Texas Crime Poll— Spring 1978," *Survey* (Huntsville, Texas: Sam Houston State University Criminal Justice Center, 1978), p. 19.

7. *Gallup Poll Public Opinion*, Vol. 3: 1935–1971 (New York: Random House, 1972), pp. 2164–65. *Gallup Poll Public Opinion*, Vol. 5: 1977 (New York: Random House, 1977), pp. 1240–41.

8. Louis Harris, "Crime Rates: Personal Uneasiness in Neighborhoods," *Chicago Tribune*, 6 June 1975. Louis Harris, "Crime Fears Decreasing," *Harris Survey* (Orlando, Florida: Tribune Media Services, Inc., 21 March 1985).

9. Wesley G. Skogan and Michael G. Maxfield, *Coping With Crime: Individual and Neighborhood Reactions*, Vol. 124 (Beverly Hills, California: Sage Publications, 1981), pp. 74–77.

10. Claude Brown in "Images of Fear," *Harper's*, Vol. 270, No. 1620 (May 1985), p. 44.

11. Robert C. Trojanowicz et al., "Fear of Crime: A Critical Issue in Community Policing" (Unpublished paper, Program in Criminal Justice Policy and Management, John F. Kennedy School of Government, Harvard University, Cambridge, 29 September 1987), p. 1.

12. James K. Stewart, "The Urban Strangler: How Crime Causes Poverty in the Inner City," *Policy Review*, No. 37 (Summer 1986), pp. 6–10.

13. Thomas Hobbes, *Leviathan* (New York: Penguin Publishing, 1981).

14. Wesley Skogan, "Fear of Crime and Neighborhood Change," in Albert J. Reiss, Jr., and Michael Tonry, *Communities and Crime*, Vol. 8 of *Crime and Justice: A Review of Research* (Chicago: The University of Chicago Press, 1986), p. 210.

15. Skogan and Maxfield, *Coping with Crime*, pp. 194–98.

16. Skogan and Maxfield, *Coping with Crime*, Chapter 5.

17. Skogan, "Fear of Crime and Neighborhood Change," p. 211.

18. Ibid., p. 212.

19. Ibid., pp. 210–15.

20. Ibid., p. 222.

21. Charles A. Murray, "The Physical Environment and Community Control of Crime," in James Q. Wilson, ed., *Crime and Public Policy* (San Francisco: Institute for Contemporary Studies, 1983), p. 115.

22. William C. Cunningham and Todd Taylor, *The Hallcrest Report: Private Security and Police in America* (Portland, Oregon: Chancellor Press, 1985).

23. National Institute of Justice, *Crime and Protection in America: A Study of Private Security and Law Enforcement Resources and Relationships* (Washington, D.C.: U.S. Department of Justice, May 1985).

24. For a discussion of the importance of "eyes on the street," see Jane Jacobs, *The Death and Life of Great American Cities* (New York: Random House, 1961).

25. Skogan, "Fear of Crime and Neighborhood Change," p. 215.

26. George L. Kelling and Mark H. Moore, "From Political to Reform to Community: The Evolving Strategy of Police," Working Paper #87-05-08 (Program in Criminal Justice Policy and Management, John F. Kennedy School of Government, Harvard University, Cambridge, October 1987).

27. O.W. Wilson, *Distribution of Police Patrol Forces* (Chicago: Public Administration Service, 1941).

28. For an example of the use of fear to build support for the police, see the discussion of the "fear city" campaign in *The Newark Foot Patrol Experiment* (Washington, D.C.: Police Foundation, 1981), pp. 120-21.

29. Kelling et al., *Kansas City Preventive Patrol Experiment*.

30. Antony Pate et al., *Police Response Time: Its Determinants and Effects* (Washington, D.C.: Police Foundation, 1987).

31. *The Newark Foot Patrol Experiment*, p. 72.

32. Ibid., p. 123.

33. Robert Trojanowicz, *An Evaluation of the Neighborhood Foot Patrol Program in Flint, Michigan* (East Lansing: Michigan State University, 1982), p. 86.

34. Antony Pate et al., *Reducing Fear of Crime in Houston and Newark*, pp. 7–10.

35. Ibid., pp. 10–18.

36. Ibid., p. 35.

37. James Q. Wilson, in Pate et al., *Reducing Fear of Crime in Houston and Newark*, p. ii.

38. Philip B. Taft, Jr., "Fighting Fear: The Baltimore County COPE Project" (Washington, D.C.: Police Executive Research Forum, February 1986).

39. Ibid., p. 20.

40. John E. Eck and William Spelman, "Solving Problems: Problem-Oriented Policing in Newport News" (Washington, D.C.: Police Executive Research Forum, January 1987).

National Institute of Justice   *Research in Action*

Police Response to Special Populations

Handling the Mentally Ill, Public Inebriate, and the Homeless

Peter E. Finn, Abt Associates, Inc.
and Monique Sullivan, Abt Associates, Inc.

January 1988

■ *Two police officers are dispatched to a housing project to handle a disturbance call. The officers find a terrified man hurling rocks at neighbors he says are trying to kill him with ray guns. A check by the officers fails to find any nearby family members or close friends.*

■ *A deputy sheriff cruising a suburban shopping mall is stopped by a store manager and asked to get rid of two public inebriates sitting next to a dumpster behind the store. The merchant says the two have been accosting passers-by for "spare change."*

■ *A bus terminal manager calls the police to have several homeless people evicted from the waiting area where they have piled up their belongings on the seats.*

The public repeatedly calls on law enforcement officers for assistance with people who are mentally ill, drunk in public, and homeless. They do so because peace officers are unique in providing free, around-the-clock service, mobility, a legal obligation to respond, and legal authority to detain.

In recent years, these requests have increased. Laws making it more difficult to commit the mentally ill have left many disturbed people on the streets, while the deinstitutionalization policies of the 1960's and 1970's have led to the release of thousands of mentally ill individuals from mental hospitals.

Jail crowding and the decriminalization of public intoxication have left more inebriates in public view. Various changes in employment patterns and public assistance programs and decreased availability of low-income housing have increased the number of homeless. At the same time, the number of facilities to assist these groups has either declined or not kept pace with the increasing need.

To help lessen the burden on police officers and deputy sheriffs who must handle special populations, some jurisdictions have created formal networks between law enforcement and social service agencies.

Challenge to Law Enforcement

The mentally ill. Handling the mentally ill is perhaps the single most difficult type of call for law enforcement officers.[1] Today, these encounters are becoming more frequent. In one urban police department, 8 percent of more than 1,000 police-citizen encounters involved dealing with mentally ill persons, according to a study funded by the National Institute of Justice and the National Institute of Mental Health.[2]

In most of these situations—nearly 72 percent—police used informal dispositions, such as calming the person down or taking the person home. Less than 12 percent of the mentally ill were hospitalized. Nearly 17 percent were arrested.

Regardless of disposition, police officers usually found themselves saddled with sole responsibility for suspected mentally ill persons whose public behavior warranted some form of social intervention.

The public inebriate. Police officers also have to cope largely on their own with people found drunk in public. A recent National Institute of Justice study[3] found that limited bed space and selective admission practices at detoxification and other alcoholism facilities have curtailed the ability of the police to transport public inebriates to health care facilities.

Jail crowding and the perception that the station-house lockup is an inappropriate place to take the public drunk increasingly limit other police alternatives.

The homeless.   Police are often called on to remove the homeless from streets and parks. The homeless have a dampening effect on business, and they invite crime by creating an appearance of community neglect. The homeless are often a danger to themselves, particularly in subfreezing weather. Law enforcement officers dealing with the homeless on the street have few options: Not only is shelter space limited, but most shelters refuse to admit the large percentage of homeless who are also mentally ill or alcoholic.

Networks with Social Service Agencies

One way of expanding the options for handling these populations is to share responsibility for them with the social service system. Networks between law enforcement agencies and human services agencies can yield substantial benefits not only for the agencies involved, but for individuals who need help.

This research describes the benefits and principal features of 12 such networks, drawing on the experience of those who participated. The lessons learned can help other jurisdictions to improve their procedures for dealing with special populations.

Table 1 presents selected features of all 12 networks summarized in this paper.

Table 1   Selected features of twelve networks

	Birmingham	Boston	Erie	Fairfax County	Galveston County	Los Angeles
Target group(s)	mentally ill — —	— inebriates homeless	mentally ill — —	mentally ill — —	mentally ill — —	mentally ill — —
Demography: population square miles	283,000 100 sq. mi.	NA 7 sq. mi.[a]	117,000 22 sq. mi.	700,000 400 sq. mi.	194,000 400 sq. mi.	3,000,000 465 sq. mi.
Land agency or agencies	police department	shelter and police department	private mental health emergency service	community mental health center	sheriff's department	police department and County Dept. of Mental Health
Law enforcement agency/ agencies involved: type	city police	city police	city police	county police	sheriff's department and others	city police
size (sworn officers)	497	241[a]	210	950	287	7,000
Annual funding: amount source(s)	$200,000 • city	$148,000 • state	$225,000 • state $25,000 • city	$391,000 • county • regional mental health center	$434,000 • regional mental health center	none NA
Date network began	1977	1985	1972	1977	1975	1985

Continued on next page

Common Network Features

Although the networks vary considerably in their organization, operations, personnel, and funding, they all have the same goals and basic structure and provide similar benefits.

Goals.   The networks have three common objectives.

1. To relieve police officers and deputy sheriffs from having to deal with individuals whose problems are primarily psychiatric, medical, or economic.
2. To ensure that law enforcement officers refer only those special populations that facilities are mandated to assist.

3. To provide the assistance these populations need to prevent their coming to the attention of the criminal justice system again.

Basic network structure.   Networks that focus on the mentally ill all have special units on duty or on call 24 hours a day, that:

■ screen individuals for the most advisable disposition;
■ identify the most appropriate facility to refer them to; and
■ provide on-scene emergency assistance when necessary.

In some sites the unit consists of trained law enforcement officers; in others, the law enforcement agency

Table 1   Continued

	Madison	Montgomery County	New York/ Jersey City	Portland	San Diego	Washtenaw County
Target group(s)	mentally ill inebriates —	mentally ill — —	— — homeless	— — —	— inebriates —	mentally ill inebriates —
Demography: population square miles	180,000 58 sq. mi.	650,000 500 sq. mi.	NA[b] NA[b]	562,640 431 sq. mi.	960,000 322 sq. mi.	265,000 575 sq. mi.
Land agency or agencies	police department	private, nonprofit psychiatric hospital	quasi-private transportation authority	detoxication center	County Alcohol Program	sheriff's department and county mental health center
Law enforcement agency/ agencies involved: type	city police	52 police agencies	transportation authority police	city police and others	city police and others	county sheriff
size (sworn officers)	295	2,150	1,200	750	1,576	150
Annual funding: amount source(s)	$35,000 • city	$170,000 • county $2000 • city police	$915,665 • Port Authority • cities (New York, Jersey City)	$775,000 • county	$240,000 • county	none
Date network began	1973	1974	1985	1975	1976	1978

[a]For police precinct only.

[b]Data not available; the Port Authority serves transportation facilities in two states.

[c]An unknown, but small, amount of extra funding was needed to hire consultants to help train network participants and perform some of the work which County Department of Mental Health staff who were assigned to the network had been doing.

hires social workers to perform these functions. In still other networks a social service agency provides the special unit.

Depending on the arrangement, screening and referral may take place on the phone, at the scene of the incident, or at the unit's facility. In some jurisdictions, the unit assists with all encounters between law enforcement officers and the mentally ill; in other communities, patrol officers are trained to handle routine cases themselves and instructed to call on the special unit only in emergencies.

Most networks for the public inebriate or the homeless have forged an arrangement directly between the law enforcement agency and one or more detoxification facilities or homeless shelters. Typically, the parties involved agree to strict referral and admission procedures.

Benefits of Networking

Each of the 12 networks has been careful to incorporate benefits for every participating agency. This helps ensure the wholehearted involvement of each participant and overcome perhaps the most serious stumbling block to networking—increased costs.

Police officers and deputy sheriffs gain several benefits from networking:

More time for law enforcement.   Networking significantly reduces the time spent stabilizing the situation at the scene, locating a facility willing to accept the person, waiting at the facility, and making repeat runs—sometimes on the same shift—to handle the same problem all over again.

Reduced danger.   In most networks, trained staff either advises officers by phone about how to defuse volatile situations or comes to the scene of an incident and takes over the case. Social workers often let responding officers know whether a suspected mentally ill individual has a history of violent behavior.

Increased job satisfaction.   Several sites report reduced criticism from the media, public, and political officials for allegedly mishandling or ignoring special populations. By informing officers in writing about the treatment plan developed for each referral, some networks give officers a feeling of closure on the case and explain why a less-than-ideal disposition was used.

Networking also benefits the social service system. In fact, social service agencies initiated several of the networks to help ease their task. Emergency care staff spends less time unnecessarily evaluating, treating, or transferring inappropriate police referrals. A network prescreens these populations and either diverts them to outpatient treatment facilities or takes them to a facility appropriate to their needs. In addition, police give priority to responding to calls from human service providers for emergency assistance with combative clients in a facility or in the home.

Local government officials find a network demonstrates their concern about a serious community problem. Furthermore, by assigning specially trained individuals to handle the mentally ill and public inebriate, county and municipal officials reduce their vulnerability to lawsuits and to criticism in the media by preventing tragedies and providing appropriate assistance. Finally, by diverting these groups to treatment programs and shelters, jail crowding can be reduced.

Establishing the Network

Network organizers need a clear understanding of each agency's problems in handling the mentally ill, the public inebriate, or the homeless. For example, law enforcement officials in several sites found that asking mental health facilities to provide crisis intervention can intimidate some human service providers, because many of them have not been trained to give emergency psychiatric care.

Law enforcement agencies also need to realize that most social service agencies require time to change their policies to participate in a new arrangement. Law enforcement agencies can often act swiftly to change their in-house procedures.

Involving every group.   The most effective way to form a network is to involve every relevant group in planning the arrangement. The Los Angeles Police Department, for example, assembled a task force with representatives from the County Sheriff's Department, the County Department of Mental Health, the County Department of Health Services, the City Fire Department, the District Attorney's Office, the City Attorney Office, the Superior Court, the Los Angeles County Alliance for the Mentally Ill, and seven regional centers serving the developmentally disabled.

There is no single best way to involve all the needed groups. Sometimes not every pertinent group can be involved in the initial planning stages, but all can be invited to join later. Planners in Fairfax County, Virginia, and Portland, Oregon, found they eventually had to add the local emergency medical services (EMS) provider to their network to avoid conflict and duplication of effort in responding to mentally ill persons or public inebriates with emergency medical problems.

In most sites, the task force and one-on-one meetings to develop the network involved high-ranking administrators capable of committing their organizations to a formal agreement or going directly to a higher authority who could authorize participation. Involving individuals within each organization who will actually implement the arrangement is also important. In law enforcement agencies, it is particularly critical to gain the support of watch commanders, who can in turn influence line officers.

Developing written agreements.   Explicit written statements of roles and responsibilities exist in nearly all the sites. When administrators make a commitment in writing, they are usually careful to agree to perform only those activities they are truly prepared to undertake. A written document also reduces misunderstandings and uncertainty over each party's role and responsibilities.

A number of agencies also prepared written networking instructions for their own staff. Law enforcement agency protocols are typically incorporated into the department's general orders. Six pages of the Washtenaw County Sheriff's Department Policy and Procedures Manual give instructions for "Handling Persons in Need of Mental Health Services."

The programs also use monitoring and evaluation to help sustain the arrangement. Problem areas in need of attention can be pinpointed and the value of the network can be documented.

For example, an evaluation of the Montgomery County, Pennsylvania, network documented that the Mental Health/Mental Retardation Emergency Service ambulance saved police 218 hours in just 1 month by transporting mentally ill individuals for evaluation, medical care, and other needs.

Effective Communication

One of the most important communication techniques is training. Most networks provide training to promote proper use of the network, change attitudes that inhibit collaboration, and develop skills in handling special populations.

The sites use a wide variety of training methods:

■ Crosstraining. In Madison, Wisconsin, social workers train the police, and police train the social workers. Crosstraining results in a clear understanding of what each participant can contribute to—and expect from—the network. When the San Diego Inebriate Reception Center kept calling the police to arrest combative patients, an officer met with the staff to explain why officers could not arrest patients for misdemeanors—and how staff members themselves could make a citizen's arrest that would permit an officer to bring a patient to the jail.

■ Academy training. Coursework at the regional police academy in San Diego incorporates information on how to use the Inebriate Reception Center.

■ Inservice workshops. In Montgomery County, Pennsylvania, network participants create a master training schedule each year to make sure that all 52 county police departments are updated on the network's services and to teach new officers how to recognize and handle the mentally ill.

■ Coursework. Galveston County's Mental Health Deputies take a 9-month course to become emergency medical technicians. This is followed by 9 months of service in casework with the Regional Mental Health/Mental Retardation Center, focusing on crisis intervention and handling the mentally ill.

■ Field trips. Police academy classes in Portland visit the Hooper Detoxification Center and observe its operations.

Most sites combine several training methods. This ensures that all network participants are reached and reinforces what they learn.

Task forces set up to initiate a network often continue to meet to address unresolved or new problems with the arrangement. The Psychiatric Emergency Coordinating Committee in Los Angeles that developed the Memorandum of Agreement is still working on ways to address the lack of 24-hour emergency facilities for the developmentally disabled.

The Role of Civil Statutes

State civil codes play a significant role in facilitating or hampering some networks. Most of the relevant legislation relates to the handling of the mentally ill, but some codes address the public inebriate as well.

Law enforcement's involvement in a network focusing on the mentally ill is simplified when judicial approval is not required to detain these individuals and when a broad range of behavior justifies involuntary detention. The need for a magistrate's warrant discourages some officers from dealing with this population because of the extra time involved in securing the warrant. To solve this problem, the crisis units in some networks take responsibility for obtaining judicial approval. For example, when family members are not available in Fairfax County to petition for involuntary detention, crisis unit staff, rather than police, fills out and signs the petition, and telephones a magistrate for a verbal order of detention. This approach also makes it unnecessary for the detaining officers to testify the following day at the preliminary hearing.

The most serious networking problems occur because many social service facilities have difficulties providing 24-hour emergency care. Several networks have been helped in overcoming this barrier by relying on civil codes that mandate 24-hour emergency evaluation and care of suspected mentally ill individuals.

Civil codes in California, Oregon, and Wisconsin require certified detoxification facilities to accept incapacitated public inebriates brought in by peace officers for involuntary detention. Police officers in Madison and Portland can therefore leave within a few minutes of transporting inebriates to the designated detoxification facility.

In order that civil codes facilitate and not hamper networking, participants are typically instructed in what the law permits and requires. This instruction usually addresses confidentiality statutes, as well as emergency detention and emergency care legislation.

If the statutes are complicated, it is difficult to explain them adequately to all police officers or deputy sheriffs in a large law enforcement agency or to all emergency staff in a large health-care facility. As a result, Los Angeles and Erie thoroughly trained their special mental illness unit staff to answer legal questions. The units respond around the clock to questions from any patrol officer or mental health professional. Los Angeles' Mental Evaluation Unit (along with other participating agencies in the network) in turn has a 24-hour hotline to the District Attorney's Psychiatric Section for immediate legal opinions regarding handling of the mentally ill.

Funding: Luxury or Necessity?

A critical issue in initiating and sustaining the networks has been whether—and how much—additional funding is needed. In fact, every site but one required extra funds to initiate its arrangement; however, two sites have not needed special funding to maintain their network.

Washtenaw County secured a Federal grant when it first began in 1978 but was careful not to use any of the funds for operational expenses so the network would be self-sufficient. The funds were used only to evaluate the arrangement. Los Angeles has required very little additional funding despite an ambitious networking arrangement. The County Department of Mental Health had to hire consultants to help train the network participants and to perform some tasks previously handled by network staff.

Montgomery County's network in Pennsylvania needed $650,000 a year to operate initially but then became increasingly self-sufficient through third-party insurance reimbursements. Currently, its expenses include $22,000 for a network liaison position, $10,000 to cover ambulance runs for indigent people without third-party insurance coverage, and $140,000 for hospitalization expenses of involuntarily committed mentally ill persons without insurance coverage. (Without the hospitalization funds, many mentally ill persons would either be left on the street or placed in jail, since other hospitals are unwilling to accept indigent county patients.) The $172,000 total cost is modest in relation to the major hospitalization services and on-scene assistance the network provides.

Networks can be initiated or operated without additional funds, or with minimal extra money, when network participants can free up resources for the network through operating efficiencies. The Los Angeles County Department of Mental Health encourages facilities to screen nonemergency admissions more carefully, reduce (where appropriate) the time mental patients are hospitalized, and provide increased aftercare to reduce readmissions.

Expenses can also be minimized when social service and law enforcement agencies can reassign resources to network functions. The Galveston County network requires the principal participating hospital to allocate any available bed—including medical beds—to law enforcement referrals.

Finally, several networks have achieved savings for members that offset part or all of their increases in expenditures. Although many public inebriates in San

Diego would probably have been ignored rather than taken to jail, the $8.00 expense to handle each drunk person at the Inebriate Reception Center is unquestionably cheaper than increasing cell space at the jail to accommodate the 25,000 inebriates diverted to the Center each year.

The sites have used three techniques for approaching potential funding sources. Rather than burdening one agency with the entire expense, several agencies are usually approached to contribute smaller amounts. Thus, the arrangement in New York/Jersey City is paid for by the Port Authority of New York and New Jersey, the New York City Department of Mental Health, and the Jersey City Housing Authority.

Requests for additional funds are softened by securing free services to supplement paid assistance. Churches in New Jersey have established homeless shelters and links to social services for Port Authority referrals. In addition, the Jersey City Department of Housing and Economic Development personally donated or secured a number of in-kind services for a homeless shelter and drop-in center, including underwriting insurance, improvements to meet fire codes, additional telephone lines, and training of shelter volunteers.

Networks in Birmingham and Montgomery County have documented how funding the arrangement enables police officers and deputy sheriffs to redirect a large number of hours from mental illness incidents to more urgent law enforcement needs. During one 3-month period, the Birmingham network saved officers the equivalent of 21 person shifts. The Montgomery County arrangement spared officers 27 shifts in 1 month alone.

How Four Networks Solved Problems

The following examples describe four of the network sites. These four illustrate how very different jurisdictions can come up with an arrangement that works.

Los Angeles, California. The Los Angeles Police Department requires all 7,000 police officers to call an emergency Mental Evaluation Unit for 24-hour-a-day assistance in handling, screening, and transporting suspected mentally ill people. The unit is staffed by nine detectives and receives 550 to 600 calls a month from patrol officers.

A unit detective prescreens each case over the phone and suggests how to handle the individual. The detective then either goes to the scene to take over the case or, more typically, tells the patrol officers to bring the individual to the Mental Evaluation Unit office. Whether in the office or on-scene, the unit officer assesses the person's condition and, if appropriate, tells the patrol officers to take the person to the hospital.

An emergency ward psychiatrist evaluates the person quickly, confident that if a Mental Evaluation Unit detective has made the referral, the patient probably needs to be hospitalized. If so, the facility either admits the patient or finds a bed at another facility. The patrol officers will have spent 30 minutes on the case, and the Mental Evaluation Unit detective 15 minutes.

The Los Angeles network is spelled out in a seven-page Memorandum of Agreement signed by the Chief of the Los Angeles Police Department, the Director of the Los Angeles County Department of Mental Health, and the heads of 14 other pertinent agencies and organizations. In addition to requiring the Police Department to set up the mental health emergency command post, the memorandum requires the Department of Mental Health to maintain a 24-hour resource accessible to the police and responsible for immediately resolving urgent situations.

Development of the network was facilitated by a recent amendment to California's Welfare and Institutions Code which forbids mental health professionals from using lack of bed space as a reason for refusing to assess whether a person brought in by police needs to be evaluated and treated. A second amendment requires that the officer not be kept waiting longer than is necessary to complete the required paperwork and a safe and orderly transfer of physical custody to the facility.

Boston, Massachusetts. Police in a downtown Boston police precinct may take homeless people (including intoxicated and mentally ill street people) to the Pine Street Inn at any hour of the night. The Inn is the largest shelter for the homeless in the city.

The precinct captain keeps his officers informed about the small number of individuals (principally, those who are violent or have serious medical problems) whom the Inn will not accept. The captain also instructs officers to wait a few minutes at the Inn until staff admits the referral, rather than, as in the past, leaving the person at the door and driving off.

The State Department of Public Welfare spends $148,000 a year to station an off-duty officer at the Inn during each shift. The special duty officers often show other officers how to handle homeless people without inciting trouble, and they often double-check to make sure only appropriate referrals are brought in by on-duty officers. The police presence also helps keep the atmosphere calm at Pine Street.

San Diego, California.   The San Diego County Alcohol Program contracts with the Volunteers of America to run the Inebriate Reception Center, in which up to 80 drunk people at one time can sober up. The San Diego Police Department requires its officers to bring all public inebriates to the center. Officers leave within 7 minutes, compared with up to an hour to book inebriates into the jail.

The San Diego Police Department brings nearly 25,000 inebriates a year to the center; 15 other law enforcement agencies in the county bring over 1,000. The county pays $240,000 for center operations, an average of $8.00 for each public inebriate referred.

Washtenaw County, Michigan.   The 150 sheriff's deputies in Washtenaw County have 24-hour access to the County Community Mental Health Center for telephone consultation and on-site crisis intervention for encounters involving the mentally ill. Written protocols in the Sheriff's Policy and Procedures Manual describe each participating agency's responsibilities. Deputies carry wallet cards that list the steps for dealing with a suspected mentally ill person.

If a subject needs only outpatient mental health services, the deputy calls the mental health center for appropriate referrals. If the center's clinician believes the person may need hospitalization, the clinician telephones the psychiatric facility nearest the scene to arrange an evaluation. The sheriff's deputy transports the person to the facility. If the client's condition is volatile, however, the center dispatches a two-person team to the scene to provide crisis intervention and accompany the

deputy sheriff in taking the person to the hospital. In extreme cases, deputies may transport the individual directly to the center for assistance.

Deputies participate in the patient's evaluation at the facility, and they receive a letter within 72 hours informing them of the assistance the client received. By diverting a modest amount of staff members' time from their responsibilities to network tasks, agencies participating in the arrangement have not had to come up with any extra funds for the arrangement.

Discussion Questions

1. What are the challenges presented to police departments by the mentally ill, the public inebriate, and the homeless?

2. How can police departments develop networks with social service agencies, and what are the advantages of networking?

3. What techniques have police departments used to improve their communications with social service agencies?

4. How have changes in state civil codes played a role in facilitating (or hampering) police involvement with special needs populations?

Notes

1.   Wayne B. Hanewicz et al., "Improving the linkages between community mental health and the police," *Journal of Police Science and Administration,* 1982, 10: 218–223.

2.   Linda A. Teplin, *Keeping the Peace: The Parameters of Police Discretion in Relation to the Mentally Disordered,* Washington, D.C., National Institute of Justice, 1986.

3.   Peter Finn, "The health care system's response to the decriminalization of public drunkenness," *Journal of Alcohol Studies,* 1985, 46: 7–23.

National Institute of Justice / *Research in Action*

AIDS and the Law Enforcement Officer

Theodore M. Hammett, Ph.D., Abt Associates, Inc.

November/December 1987

AIDS (acquired immune deficiency syndrome) is both an increasingly serious public health problem and an extremely emotional issue that has engendered a great deal of fear and misinformation.

AIDS affects criminal justice professionals in two important ways. First, suspects and offenders are frequently people who engage in behavior that puts them at high risk for AIDS. As a result, many law enforcement officers and corrections workers are concerned that they are at increased risk of acquiring the AIDS virus through contact with these suspects and offenders. Second, law enforcement officers can serve a vital educational function in the community because they come into contact with many people who exhibit high-risk behavior—specifically intravenous drug abusers and prostitutes.

This article summarizes the latest medical information on AIDS, presents the concerns expressed by 35 police departments contacted for the National Institute of Justice by the Police Executive Research Forum (PERF), responds to those concerns, and offers suggestions on how law enforcement agencies can educate and protect their staff.

What is AIDS?

AIDS is caused by a virus known as Human Immunodeficiency Virus (HIV). It infects and destroys certain white blood cells, thereby undermining the body's ability to combat infection. One can be infected with HIV for years without ever developing symptoms of AIDS.

However, infected persons can transmit the virus even though they may not have symptoms.

The National Academy of Sciences estimates that 25 to 50 percent of HIV-infected persons will develop AIDS within 5 to 10 years of infection.

AIDS is not a single disease—there is a spectrum of reactions to the AIDS virus. An individual who has the AIDS virus may have no symptoms of illness whatsoever for an extended period following infection. To be diagnosed with AIDS, according to the definition established by the Centers for Disease Control (CDC), a patient must have one or more "opportunistic infections" or cancers in the absence of all other known underlying causes of immune deficiency.

Opportunistic diseases include a particular type of pneumonia, malignancies, and a type of skin cancer. Persons who die from AIDS die from such opportunistic diseases, not from AIDS itself.

Other symptoms include fever, weight loss, diarrhea, and persistingly swollen lymph nodes. Patients with such symptoms, but not meeting the CDC definition of AIDS, are generally considered to have "AIDS-related complex" (ARC). Although the symptoms of ARC may be debilitating, they are generally not life threatening. To date, not all persons who have ARC have developed AIDS.

Most patients who develop end-stage AIDS die within 2 years of diagnosis and very few live more than 3 years. Prospects for a vaccine or cure for the immediate future are not promising.

Testing for Antibodies to the AIDS Virus

Infection is identified through a blood test (called an ELISA test) that detects antibodies to the AIDS virus.

Originally developed to screen donations to blood banks, it is now the first step in testing individuals for infection. The presence of antibodies indicates that the immune system has attempted to fight off an AIDS-related infection. If the initial ELISA test is positive, a second ELISA test is performed; if that test is also positive, the results should be confirmed using the more accurate "Western Blot" test.

A confirmed positive result means that the individual has been infected, but the test cannot pinpoint the date of infection. Nor can the test predict if the person will develop ARC or AIDS. However, the Centers for Disease Control recommends that persons with positive tests be considered infected and infectious.

How is the AIDS Virus Transmitted?

The AIDS virus is difficult to transmit and is quite fragile when outside the body. It can be destroyed by heat, many common household disinfectants and bleaches, and by washing with soap and hot water.

As with hepatitis-B, the AIDS virus is transmitted through exposure to contaminated blood, semen, and vaginal secretions. This occurs primarily through sexual intercourse and needle-sharing by intravenous drug abusers. Transmission from infected mother to fetus or infant has also occurred.

Transmission of the AIDS virus has also been traced to blood transfusions and to blood products given to hemophiliacs. However, the Nation's blood supply is now considered safe as a result of universal screening of donated blood and heat treatment of blood products. CDC estimates that only about 100 transfusion-associated infections will occur annually out of a total of 16 million units of blood transfused.

The AIDS virus is not transmitted through casual contact. A number of studies have confirmed that the AIDS virus is not spread, for example, by sneezing, coughing, breathing, hugging, handshaking, sharing eating and drinking utensils, using the same toilet facilities, or other forms of nonsexual contact or activity.

There is no evidence of AIDS virus transmission in schools, offices, churches, or other social settings. There are no documented cases of police officers, paramedics, correctional officers, or firefighters becoming infected with the AIDS virus through performance of their duties.

Except for a very small number of cases of infection in health care workers attributed to accidental needle sticks or other exposure to blood, there are no reports of AIDS infection as a result of occupational contact.

Law Enforcement Concerns

AIDS is currently an important issue in the law enforcement community. Nearly all (33 of 35) of the police departments surveyed for this report stated that staff had "expressed some concern related to AIDS." Patrol officers—those most likely to have the greatest direct contact with the public—in almost all (94 percent) of the departments reported anxiety about exposure to the virus. However, other law enforcement personnel, including lockup staff, evidence technicians, laboratory staff, and detectives, also are concerned about AIDS.

The level of concern tended to be highest in departments serving jurisdictions with few AIDS cases. This indicates that apprehension—and especially misinformed fear—about AIDS may be inversely related to actual experience with those who have the disease. Knowledge and experience tend to calm unrealistic fears about AIDS.

Assaultive Behavior

Law enforcement officers express anxiety about a range of assaultive and disruptive behavior—particularly biting, spitting, and throwing of urine or feces. The fact is that one cannot be infected through biting unless the person who bites has blood in his mouth and that blood comes into contact with the victim's blood. The AIDS virus has been isolated in only very small concentrations in saliva and urine and not at all in feces. There are no known cases associated with transmission through saliva or urine.

Police Lockups

Officers working in lockup tend to be concerned about the same issues as officers on the street. However, lockup introduces two additional dimensions—the risk of infection to other prisoners and the threat of violence or intimidation toward infected individuals. The key to an effective lockup policy is careful supervision. Despite difficult logistical problems and limitations of time, staff, and facilities, departments must carefully assess the risks in not providing adequate supervision.

Casual Contact

Despite all the evidence that the AIDS virus is not transmitted through casual contact, fully two-thirds of the law enforcement agencies surveyed report that staff have expressed concern about becoming infected through casual contact in the performance of their duties.

Only regular and accurate education can counteract irrational fears. The plain fact is that no known cases of AIDS are attributable to casual contact. This is confirmed by studies of families, schools, and workplaces. Departments should keep informed of the latest research on the transmission of the AIDS virus, develop contacts with local medical experts, establish formal programs to monitor AIDS research, and disseminate key findings to staff as they become available.

Teaching the Facts

AIDS is a disease of high-risk behavior, not high-risk groups. Far too many people take the potentially dangerous position that the AIDS virus may be transmitted by contact with members of "high-risk groups." In fact, everyone must be concerned with a few well-defined types of activities—specifically unprotected sexual intercourse, sharing of needles, and other activities where blood, semen, or vaginal secretions are exchanged.

If the AIDS training does not convey this information, and if the tone is not properly balanced between caution and reassurance, it may encourage misinformed beliefs that in turn can severely affect the operational effectiveness and service delivery of a law enforcement agency.

It is counterproductive to train staff to wear gloves, gowns, and masks for all contact with persons known or suspected to be infected with AIDS or persons who engage in AIDS high-risk behavior. Such precautions are not normally necessary and may encourage the incorrect view that the AIDS virus can be transmitted by casual contact.

On the other hand, statements that complacently suggest that risk is limited to certain groups may seriously undermine the critical educational message that everyone must be careful about certain behavior and exposures.

Law enforcement officers, as well as other people, should be careful about sexual relationships and blood-to-blood contact with *all* persons—whether or not they have AIDS, appear to be ill, or exhibit high-risk behavior.

AIDS training should be keyed to specific law enforcement issues and situations. It is not enough to distribute generic informational materials. Training topics should include arrest procedures, searches, CPR, first aid, evidence handling, transportation of prisoners, crime scene processing, disposal of contaminated materials, lockup supervision, and body removal procedures.

The most effective training programs are those developed jointly by management, staff members, unions, medical experts, and health professionals. If possible, training on AIDS should be provided before staff develop irrational fears of the disease. It should be included in both recruit and regular inservice training.

Training should be conducted by a knowledgeable educator so staff can ask questions and receive accurate answers. Videotapes or slide presentations should be supplemented with question-and-answer sessions.

Law Enforcement Officers as Educators in the Community

Once they become knowledgeable about AIDS, law enforcement staff can exert a positive educational influence on their communities. Police officers can tell prostitutes, drug abusers, and those who have no way of hearing media messages about the risk involved in needle sharing and in unprotected sexual intercourse. Moreover, they can convey these important messages in clear, frank language understandable to people on the street.

Suggestions for Law Enforcement Agencies

In addition to conducting regular, authoritative training sessions about AIDS for both new and seasoned personnel, law enforcement agencies are advised to:

■ Develop and enforce consistent, rational AIDS policies regarding precautionary measures and protective equipment. Before proposing any precautionary measures, departments should weigh carefully their possible effects on operations and educational programs. (Figure 1 presents actions to take for specific incidents.)

- Ensure careful supervision of lockup areas to prevent sexual contact or needle sharing.
- Keep the department continuously abreast of AIDS research developments and pass all new information on to staff.
- Coordinate the department's AIDS training and policies with local public health departments, hospitals, emergency medical services, fire departments, and community-based AIDS action groups.

AIDS poses a range of complicated and potentially serious problems for law enforcement agencies. However, timely and rational policy choices, regular staff training keyed to specific law enforcement concerns, and careful consideration of possible legal liabilities can go far toward minimizing the effects of these problems on the delivery of police services to the public.

Police officers can also refer people to appropriate organizations for voluntary testing, diagnosis, medical care, and support services.

A law enforcement agency that invests in high-quality training for its staff invests in the welfare not

Who has AIDS?

The Centers for Disease Control's *AIDS Weekly Surveillance Report* recorded more than 40,000 cases of AIDS in adults and children in the United States through August 1987. More than 20,000 persons have died from AIDS.*

Of all persons with AIDS, 90 percent have a history of either homosexual/bisexual activities or intravenous drug abuse.

Homosexual/bisexual males constitute 66 percent of victims; 16 percent are intravenous drug abusers; and 8 percent are both homosexual and IV drug abusers. Table 1 provides a detailed breakdown of AIDS cases by category.

More than one-half (53 percent) of the cases have been

located in New York and California. New Jersey, Florida, and Texas collectively account for another 19 percent. AIDS cases are heavily concentrated in cities and major metropolitan areas.

Many public health officials believe that the portion of cases attributed to intravenous drug abuse is likely to grow dramatically in the next few years. Moreover, they believe the greatest potential for significant spread of infection to the heterosexual population is through infection of the sexual partners of intravenous drug abusers.

---

* Effective September 1, 1987, CDC revised the definition of AIDS. The revision broadens the scope of the definition and will result in significantly increased numbers of reported AIDS cases during the next publishing period.

Table 1   Confirmed AIDS cases by category

Transmission category	Percent of all cases
Homosexual/bisexual males	66
Intravenous drug abusers	16
Homosexual males and IV drug abusers	8
Transfusion recipients	2
Hemophiliacs	1
Heterosexuals	4
Undetermined[1]	3
Total	100%

[1]Includes patients with incomplete risk information (due to death, refusal to be interviewed, or inability to follow up on initial information), patients still under investigation, men reported only to have had heterosexual contact with a prostitute, and interviewed patients for whom no specific risk was identified. CDC believes that if full information were available it would be possible to assign these cases to other transmission categories.

Source, CDC, *AIDS Weekly Surveillance Report*, August 31, 1987.

Testing for Antibodies to the AIDS Virus

The antibody tests represent the best current means of tracking the infection status of individuals who may have been infected with the AIDS virus. It usually takes 6 to 12 weeks for antibodies to appear. If an officer tests negative immediately following an incident in which infection may have occurred and tests positive 2 months later, and there is no other known source of infection, this would be strong—although not incontrovertible—evidence that infection occurred as a result of that incident.

Because of potential legal liabilities, departments may wish to require, recommend, or make available testing for officers and other individuals involved in incidents. It is probably beneficial to the officer and his or her family to know whether infection has occurred, yet the officer must weigh the potential negative effects in terms of access to insurance, employment, and housing should positive test results become known. Counseling from a qualified health professional must be part of any testing procedure.

More than 70 percent of the departments surveyed for this study have policies for antibody testing after incidents in which infection may have occurred. However, few are clear and consistent. In 84 percent of the agencies, the policies apply only to testing of the staff members involved in the incident. Three departments reported policies that cover testing of both the staff member and the individual suspected of being infected with the AIDS virus.

Department policies on antibody testing should specify the rationale for the policy position and the procedures to be used in any testing program. All policies and procedures must, of course, take into account applicable State and local laws on confidentiality and reporting of results. At a minimum, written policies should address the following questions:

- **Who is to be tested?**
- **What is the purpose of testing?**
- **Is testing voluntary or mandatory?**
- **When and where are tests performed?**
- **What confirmatory tests are to be used?**
- **Who can and should be notified of the results?**
- **What are the requirements for pre-and post-test counseling?**

---

only of its own people but of the larger community as well.

Legal and Labor Relations Issues

More than one-half of the departments surveyed consider AIDS a potentially serious legal issue for law enforcement. Particular questions include the following:

- What are the department's responsibilities to report incidents in which the AIDS virus may have been transmitted?
- What policies should the department establish regarding HIV antibody testing in such cases?
- What would be the department's liability if an officer contracts the AIDS virus in the line of duty?
- What legal or labor relations issues are involved when an officer refuses to perform duties out of fear of AIDS?

- What are the department's responsibilities for protecting the public from infection when dealing with potential carriers of the virus?
- What are the department's responsibilities to prevent AIDS virus transmission in a police lockup?

Officers' Obligation to Perform Their Duty

Individuals assume a certain amount of risk when they become law enforcement officers. Their departments cannot be held liable for damages if, for example, they are killed or wounded by a gunshot from a suspect, unless established procedures were violated or the department was negligent. It is reasonable to assume that if an officer contracted the AIDS virus from a suspect or other individual, the situation would be treated in a similar fashion.

Any claim of the department's liability would be further weakened if the officer had been provided accurate, thorough, and regular training on AIDS. For example, consider a case in which an officer had *not*

Figure 1   Responses to AIDS-related law enforcement concerns

Issue/concern	Educational and action messages
Human bites	Person who bites usually receives the victim's blood; viral transmission through saliva is highly unlikely. If bitten by anyone, milk wound to make it bleed, wash the area thoroughly, and seek medical attention.
Spitting	Viral transmission through saliva is highly unlikely.
Urine/feces	Virus isolated in only very low concentrations in urine; not at all in feces; no cases of AIDS or AIDS virus infection associated with either urine or feces.
Cuts/puncture wounds	Use caution in handling sharp objects and searching areas hidden from view; needle stick studies show risk of infection is very low.
CPR/first aid	To eliminate the already minimal risk associated with CPR, use masks/airways; avoid blood-to-blood contact by keeping open wounds covered and wearing gloves when in contact with bleeding wounds.
Body removal	Observe crime scene rule: Do not touch anything. Those who must come into contact with blood or other body fluids should wear gloves.
Casual contact	No cases of AIDS or AIDS virus infection attributed to casual contact.
Any contact with blood or body fluids	Wear gloves if contact with blood or body fluids is considered likely. If contact occurs, wash thoroughly with soap and water; clean up spills with one part household bleach to nine parts water.
Contact with dried blood	No cases of infection have been traced to exposure to dried blood. The drying process itself appears to inactivate the virus. Despite low risk, however, caution dictates wearing gloves, a mask, and protective shoe coverings if exposure to dried blood particles is likely (e.g., crime scene investigation).

been told to cover open wounds, wear gloves when contact with blood was likely, and wash thoroughly after any contact with blood. If that officer were to develop an infection as a result of *not* taking these precautions, then the department might be held liable. This example underscores the importance not only of training but of documentation of training as well.

Agencies should make it clear that anxiety about AIDS does not free officers from the obligation to perform their duties. Four of the surveyed departments reported incidents in which officers refused to perform duties out of such fear. These incidents involved transportation of prisoners, searches, and handling of evidence. In almost every incident, the departments took swift and strong action against the officers involved, such as suspension without pay.

It appears that any legal claim supporting an officer's refusal to perform duties based on fear of AIDS would be difficult to sustain on two grounds: first, because the research is so clear on the unlikelihood of viral transmission through the types of contacts likely to be experienced by police officers, assuming standard precautions are taken; and second, because the officer assumes certain risks in accepting the job.

Agency Responsibility to Prevent Transmission

Because legislation and case law are still evolving, it is highly speculative to attempt to assess the legal implication of an agency's potential responsibilities to protect the public from AIDS. Should law enforcement agencies, for example, detain intravenous drug abusers or prostitutes who might spread the virus?

To sustain a legal claim against a department on the basis that the department has responsibility to prevent transmission, a plaintiff would first need to establish that law enforcement agencies legitimately bear such responsibilities and can legitimately be expected to carry them out.

A plaintiff would also need to prove that the infection was not contracted as a result of consensual conduct widely known to pose high risks of transmission. Based on these factors, it would appear very difficult to prove that a law enforcement agency violated its responsibility to protect the public.

However, more is involved in such situations than potential legal liability. In the next few years, more and more departments are likely to face the question of how to deal with prostitutes and others in police custody who may be infected with the AIDS virus. Law enforcement agencies should work with public health officials to develop clearly defined policies on how to handle such situations both to prevent continued transmission of the virus and to protect constitutional rights. Policies should be developed promptly so that they are in place before an incident occurs.

Responsibility to Prevent Transmission in Police Lockups

Claims of law enforcement agencies' responsibilities appear to be much more supportable when the conduct resulting in transmission of the AIDS virus was coerced rather than consensual and occurred in a place under the agency's supervision.

While lockups and other correctional facilities differ in significant ways, the experiences of prisons and jails may be instructive. Cases brought by inmates asking for protection from infected inmates are pending in several States. No cases have been filed yet by inmates seeking damages for allegedly contracting the AIDS virus while in a correctional facility.

Correctional systems (and presumably police lockups) have been required by courts to adhere to a standard of reasonable care in protecting inmates. In several cases, correctional systems and their officials have been held liable for damages resulting from homosexual rape and other assaults, on the ground of inadequate supervision.

However, correctional systems have not been held responsible for ensuring the *absolute* safety of persons in their custody. In several cases, for example, courts have held that a correctional system could be liable for damages resulting from assault only if its officials knew—or should have known—of the risk to the particular inmate.

Law enforcement agencies should be aware that they may face more difficulties than correctional facilities do in protecting prisoners from rape and other incidents because of the communal nature of lockups, the rapid population turnover, and the lack of formal prisoner classification. Therefore, adequate supervision becomes essential.

Discussion Questions

1. What exactly is AIDS, and what are its most common symptoms?

2. How is the AIDS virus transmitted, and who are the most likely carriers of the AIDS virus? Why do the characteristics of this disease present a special danger for law enforcement officers?

3. Should the danger of contracting the AIDS virus limit the activities of officers who fail potentially high-risk situations?

4. What are the responsibilities of law enforcement agencies in limiting the spread of AIDS?

The Judicatory System: Court Process and Sentencing Alternatives

Introduction

The court system that administers the criminal process includes lower criminal courts, superior courts, and appellate courts. Each state and the federal government has its own independent court structure unique to that particular jurisdiction. Where a crime is a violation of state law, it is ordinarily prosecuted in the state court, while offenses against federal laws are generally handled by the federal court system.

The lower criminal courts of any state, variously called police courts, district courts, or recorder's courts, deal with the largest number of criminal offenses. They are scattered throughout the state by county, town, or geographic district. They daily handle a large volume of criminal offenses, including such crimes as assault and battery, disorderly conduct, breaking and entering, possession of drugs, petty larceny, traffic violations, and juvenile offenses. Many cases are disposed of without trial, either because the defendant pleads guilty or because the circumstances of the offense do not warrant further court action. Where a trial is required in the lower courts, it often occurs before a judge rather than a jury, because the defendant often waives the constitutional right to a jury trial. Lower criminal courts, although primarily responsible for misdemeanor offenses, also process the first stage of felony offenses by holding preliminary hearings, making bail decisions,

and conducting trials of certain felonies where they have jurisdiction as defined by statute. The lower criminal courts often dispense routine and repetitious justice and are burdened with a heavy responsibility they are not generally equipped to fulfill. Characterized by cramped courtrooms and limited personnel, they remain a critical problem area in criminal justice administration.

The superior courts, or major trial courts, have general jurisdiction over all criminal offenses but ordinarily concentrate on felony offenses. They conduct jury trials with much formality and with strict adherence to the defendant's constitutional rights. In addition to conducting trials, these courts accept guilty pleas, generally give offenders longer sentences because of the more serious nature of their crimes, and in certain instances review sentences originally imposed by lower courts.

The highest state court is a supreme, or appeals, court, whose functions are similar to those of the United States Supreme Court in the federal judicial system. State supreme courts are appellate courts that do not conduct criminal trials. Appellate courts deal with procedural errors arising in the lower courts that are considered violations of rights guaranteed by state and/ or the United States Constitution, such as the use of illegal evidence. Questions of fact that were decided in the original trial are not ordinarily reviewed in the appellate process. The appellate court has the authority to affirm, modify, or reverse decisions of the lower criminal court.

In every criminal case, the state acts against the defendant before an impartial judge or jury, with each side trying to bring evidence and arguments forward to advance its case. Theoretically, the ultimate objective of the adversary system is to seek the truth, in this way determining the guilt or innocence of the defendant from the formal evidence presented at the trial. The adversary system ensures that the defendant is given a fair trial, that the relevant facts of a given case emerge, and that an impartial decision is reached.

The judicatory process is considered by many to be the core element in the administration of criminal justice. It is the part of the system that is the most formally organized and elaborately delimited by law and tradition. The criminal court outdates most other justice agencies and is the institution around which the others developed and to which they are by and large responsible. The judicatory process is what we as a nation depend on to control the excess of government; it regulates both the behavior of those who make the law as well as those who break the law. It is inherent to the American system that the court system be impartial, fair, and dispense equal justice under the law. While Americans are used to charges of "police corruption" or "prison brutality," they still expect the court system by its very nature to be beyond reproach.

Ideally, the judicatory process is expected to convict and sentence those found guilty of crimes while ensuring that the innocent are freed without any consequence or burden. The court system is formally required to seek the truth and to obtain justice for the individual brought before its tribunals and also to maintain the integrity of the government's rule of law. While on an ideal level the criminal court should hand out fair and evenhanded justice in a forum of strict impartiality and fairness, this standard of justice cannot be maintained in the nation's overcrowded court system. If all traffic, civil, and criminal cases are considered, American courts are forced to routinely process more than eighty million cases a year. To meet this challenge the court system has been forced to adapt legal shortcuts to the trial process. A system of "bargain justice" has developed that encourages defendants to plead guilty in exchange for special considerations such as reducing the seriousness or number of charges. Critics have tried to limit plea bargaining in recent years but so far it remains a difficult practice to control. To help in this task alternatives to the formal legal process have been suggested that take some of the burden off the court system. For example, dispute resolution and alternative courts divert minor civil and criminal cases from the formal justice system.

Once the outcome of a case has been determined, and in the event that the defendant is found guilty, the sentencing decision becomes the major focus of court decision making. Sentences serve not only to rehabilitate the offender but also to deter others from crime, to incapacitate dangerous offenders, and to create a sense of fairness and equity in the judicial process. Sentencing has come under fire in recent years because of charges of disparity and disorganization. Consequently, there have been efforts to reform and create a more rational sentencing approach by using guidelines that control judicial decision making.

The articles in this section address some of the most critical issues facing the American court system. First, Hugh Nugent and J. Thomas McEwen present findings from a national survey measuring the needs of one of the key players in the criminal process, the prosecuting attorney. Then Gail A. Goolkasian addresses one of the most important problems facing criminal court judges: confronting domestic violence. The final two articles in this section focus on sentencing. Richard Singer provides an overview of this critical issue, while Michael K. Block and William M. Rhodes analyze the impact of federal sentencing guidelines on the criminal justice system.

National Institute of Justice

Research in Action

Prosecutors' National Assessment of Needs

Hugh Nugent, Institute for Law and Justice
and J. Thomas McEwen, Institute for Law and Justice

August 1988

Prosecutors report their caseloads are increasing in both volume and complexity, that more offenders are being prosecuted, and that there are more hearings and motions per case. Delays in processing continue to be problems. Increased emphasis on the victims of crime, particularly children, is prompting prosecutors across the United States to increase the number of victim-witness assistance programs in their offices.

This research provides further details on these results and many other findings from a survey conducted under the National Assessment Program (NAP), sponsored by the National Institute of Justice (NIJ).

The primary aim of the survey is to identify key needs and problems in local and State criminal justice systems. To accomplish this, the Institute contracted with the Institute for Law and Justice, Inc. to conduct a national survey of approximately 2,500 practitioners from a sample of 375 counties across the country.

Included were all 175 counties having populations greater than 250,000 and a sample of 200 counties having less than 250,000 population. Persons receiving surveys in each sampled county included the police chief of the largest city, sheriff, jail administrator, prosecutor, chief judge, trial court administrator (where applicable), and probation and parole agency heads.

A total of 225 completed surveys was received from local prosecutors, a return rate of 61 percent. The distributions of responses by county population and by region[1] are shown in Exhibit 1. The nationwide survey addressed five general areas: background data on the prosecutor's office, criminal justice system problems, caseloads, operations and procedures, and staffing.

Background Characteristics

The background questions asked for descriptive data on the size, resources, and responsibilities of the responding prosecutors.

The 1985 median felony caseload of these offices is 1,750 cases, and the median office budget is $1.2 million. In response to a question on the financial resources available to their offices, 46 percent rate their resources as adequate, 45 percent as inadequate, and 9 percent as very inadequate.

Criminal Justice System Problems

The prosecutors were asked to rank a series of criminal justice problems identified in 1983 in the first National Assessment survey.[2] The problems involved the system as a whole, not just problems associated with prosecution. Exhibit 2 shows the average rankings. Prosecutors rank staff shortages as the most significant problem in their local systems. Prison crowding ranks second, followed by jail crowding. These three top ranked problems reflect an unfortunate combination of too many criminals and too few staff members to handle them.

Lack of coordination among criminal justice agencies ranks close behind crowding, followed by the public's lack of understanding of criminal justice agencies. Only a few respondents consider agency management or lack of staff skills to be significant problems.

The remaining sections of the survey—on caseloads, operations, procedures, and staffing—provided lists of potential needs and problems in each area. The prosecu-

Exhibit 1 Prosecutor respondents by county population

County population	Number	Percent
Less than 100,000	72	32
100–250,000	40	18
250–500,000	58	26
500–750,000	25	11
More than 750,000	30	13
Total	225	100 %

By region

Region	Number	Percent
New England	12	5
Mid-Atlantic	45	20
Great Lakes	41	18
Plains-Mountain	24	11
Southeast	54	24
Southwest	21	9
Far West	28	12
Total	225	100 %

Prosecutor activities and attorney assignments

Activity	Percentage of offices with activity	Median number of attorneys assigned
Screening unit	80	3
General felony caseload	96	9
Victim-witness unit	77	1
Career criminal unit	50	3
Misdemeanor cases	80	6
Child support collection	64	1
Other	77	3

tors were asked to rate each item on a scale of 1 (not a problem or need) to 4 (major problem or need) according to degree of importance for their agencies. In the discussion that follows, the ratings of 3 and 4 have been combined as reflecting a general need or problem. The term "major problem" or "major need" indicates the highest rating of 4.

Caseload

Caseload contributors. As reflected in Exhibit 3, over 90 percent of the prosecutors agree that an increased number of child-victim cases contributes significantly to caseload problems. Although one may hope

this reflects increased public awareness rather than increased victimization, these labor-intensive cases contribute disproportionately to caseloads.

Fifty-eight percent of the respondents indicate that the number of prosecutors has not kept pace with caseloads. Several factors may be contributing. For example, increases in motion hearings per case and motions filed per case are indicated by over 60 percent of the respondents. In counties of 500,000 to 750,000 people, both these problems are cited as contributors by almost 80 percent of the respondents. An increase in the percentage of cases going to trial is also regarded as a significant contributor by 38 percent of the respondents.

Increased felony case complexity is rated as a caseload contributor by 61 percent of the prosecutors. A regional feature on case complexity is that slightly over 70 percent of the prosecutors from the Southeast rate increased complexity as a caseload contributor. In contrast, only 27 percent of the New England prosecutors believe increased complexity contributes to caseload increases.

The population data show a strong correlation with the problem of delays of cases in court. Overall, 52 percent designate delays as caseload contributors. However, 77 percent of the prosecutors from the largest counties consider court delay to be a contributor to caseload problems, in sharp contrast to 35 percent of the smallest counties.

In survey responses to open-ended questions, many prosecutors report establishing special units to cope with increased caseload. These units include screening units, victim-witness advocate programs, career criminal programs, and major case units. Specific special positions include welfare fraud specialist, criminal case administrator, investigative aide, subpoena server, and liaison attorneys to law enforcement.

Many survey comments stress the importance of good communications with law enforcement agencies and with the courts. Easy access to prosecutors by law enforcement before arrest and preinvestigation before warrants issue are both mentioned as good procedures. Several respondents advocate regular meetings with the court. As a specific example of communications, one prosecutor mentions a superior court review program in which felony cases are referred to a superior court judge for discussion prior to preliminary hearings.

Diversion programs and early decision procedures also help relieve caseload problems. Among those identified are misdemeanor pretrial, juvenile diversion, DWI-deferred prosecution, and neighborhood mediation programs. One prosecutor has a 24-hour-decision policy on whether a case will be filed. Several emphasize the importance of getting early pleas to keep caseloads under control.

Organizationally, prosecutors frequently refer to vertical prosecution (in which one prosecutor is assigned responsibility for a case from intake to appeal). More often, however, trial teams, rather than individual prosecutors, handle cases as they proceed through a vertical system. One respondent recommends vertical handling to reduce caseloads in career criminal, sexual assault, and major narcotic vendor prosecutions.

The computer is a major factor in effectively controlling caseloads and keeping cases moving. Respondents identify computerized case management systems, computer-automated docket preparation, and docket call as effective in managing caseloads. In spite of the respondents' numerous successful efforts to reduce caseload problems, one prosecutor has a blunt solution: "More jails and prisons will reduce caseload."

Court delay.   Prosecutors were also asked to indicate the degree to which each of seven factors contributes to court delay:

- Too many continuances.
- Poor case scheduling.
- Use of open courts for actions that could be completed in chambers.
- Delay in assignment of defense counsel.
- Poor procedures for notification of witnesses.
- Inadequacy of computer information system.
- Abuse of discovery.

Over 65 percent of the respondents believe that excessive continuances are primary reasons for court delay. Once again, there are clear differences in the answers by population, with the smallest counties having the least trouble and the largest counties the most. Regionally, prosecutors from New England, the Southwest, and the Far West cite continuances as a problem more often than the rest of the Nation.

Poor case scheduling is considered a court delay contributor by 44 percent of respondents and inadequacy of computer information systems by 41 percent. The Southwest prosecutors report scheduling as a contributor to court delay more frequently than other regions (71 percent with 48 percent calling it a major contributor). In contrast, only 26 percent of the Southeast respondents feel scheduling is a problem.

Exhibit 2   Criminal justice system problems

Most serious

1
.
.
.
.
2
.
.
. <Staff shortages (35%)
3
. <Prison crowding (24%)
. <Jail crowding (15%)
. <CJ agency coordination (14%)
.
4
. <Public's lack of understanding (9%)
.
.
.
5
. <Agency management (3%)
.
. <Lack of staff skills (2%)
.
6
Least serious

Note: The number in parenthesis is the percent of respondents who ranked the problem as the most significant.

The prosecutors' narrative answers indicate many frustrations with the problem of continuances, as illustrated below:

- "Allow no continuances in superior court."
- "My policy is to oppose continuances."
- "Conduct status conferences and allow only short continuances when granted."
- "Require written memos to supervisors when the state requests continuance."
- "At arraignment, defendants are given 10 days to hire attorney or be interviewed for appointed counsel; if they don't, they are arrested again."
- "Institute cutoffs for guilty pleas."

Many courts control the delay problem by having the court administrator schedule cases by strict docket control or by an individual calendaring system. One prosecutor takes the lead himself as outlined in the following sequence: (1) prosecutor provides prompt

Exhibit 3   Caseload contributors

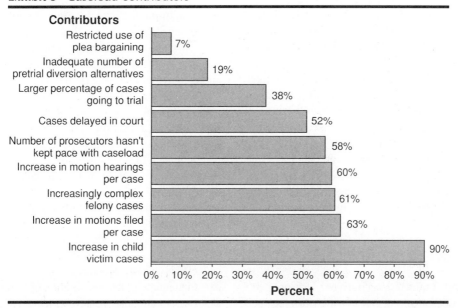

discovery, (2) court schedules prompt pretrial and trial, (3) prosecution refuses to plea bargain on trial day, and (4) same prosecutor handles from start to finish.

Some of the same answers regarding caseload management reappear in discussions of how court delay has been reduced. These include ongoing discussions with the judiciary to resolve problems, bimonthly meetings of all criminal justice agencies, and computerization.

Victim-witness programs.   Of the 225 surveyed, 174 prosecutors (77 percent) have victim assistance programs. The median number of employees assigned to such programs is three.

Most prosecutors (about 90 percent) indicate that their victim assistance programs usually involve child abuse, child sexual abuse, rape, and other sex offenses. Exhibit 4 shows the offenses most commonly involved in prosecutors' victim-witness programs.

The prosecutors most frequently cite notifying victims and witnesses of court dates as the main responsibility of their victim assistance programs. This service, which is provided by 91 percent of the programs, enhances the prosecution effort since case outcomes frequently depend on the evidence victims and witnesses provide.

Other key responsibilities include notification of case disposition (89 percent), providing printed materi-

als (87 percent), referring victims to counseling and social service agencies (86 percent), and notifying victims of the status of the investigation (83 percent). Exhibit 5 summarizes the primary responsibilities of the program.

In narrative answers about successful victim-witness programs, the respondents describe a variety of creative and effective approaches to program operation. Prosecutors frequently refer to assigning specific responsibilities within the office, using trained professionals from other agencies, and using volunteers. The need for victim-witness programs is evident in the following observation:

> Victims often feel left out or forgotten by the criminal justice process without practical advice or support. Our attorneys have heavy caseloads and can't always spend as much time with a person as that victim needs.

The following comments reveal the diverse services and activities that such programs perform:
- ■ "Coordinators perform the following functions: (1) notifying victims, (2) gathering and processing restitution information, (3) working with victims and witnesses on selected cases, and (4) coordinating with community groups."
- ■ "Witness notification; preparing witnesses for trial;

helping victims understand the system; providing crime compensation information, support, and guidance; making referrals to community resources; ensuring transportation, particularly for the elderly."

■ "The witness return program provides free hotel, airfare, and per diem, courtesy of local businesses."

■ "The child sexual abuse program includes an advocacy center, video taping in the prosecutor's office by a trained M.A. psychologist, expedited hearings, coordination with law enforcement, and direct grand jury presentations."

■ "We developed a coloring book for children who are victims/witnesses involved in the court process."

Operations and Procedures

Diversion and sentence alternatives. Respondents were asked to indicate the degree to which they feel their court systems need each of the following diversion and sentencing alternatives:

■ Drug diversion programs.
■ Alcohol diversion programs.
■ Other pretrial diversion programs.
■ Intensive probation.
■ Community service programs.
■ Work-release jail programs.
■ Restitution.

■ Short-term community incarceration.
■ Conditional dismissal (e.g., suspended proceedings).

Only two of the alternatives are cited as needs by a majority of respondents: restitution (59 percent of respondents) and intensive probation (55 percent).

At the other extreme, 62 percent of the respondents rate conditional dismissal as not needed at all. Only 27 percent report needs for drug diversion programs and other pretrial diversion programs. However, Southeast respondents cite a need for drug and alcohol diversion programs more than the rest of the country.

Pretrial and accusatory problems. Respondents were asked to rate the degree to which they face each of 13 different pretrial and accusatory problems:

■ Delay in receiving arrest information, preventing effective early screening.
■ Inadequate police preparation of crime reports.
■ Lack of adequate review with law enforcement on search warrants.
■ Inadequate details by police of proof supporting arrests.
■ Victim and other witness preparation.
■ Inaccurate name and address information for witness.
■ Early information on defendant background.
■ Inadequate police training related to obtaining confessions.

Exhibit 4   Offenses commonly involved in victim-witness programs

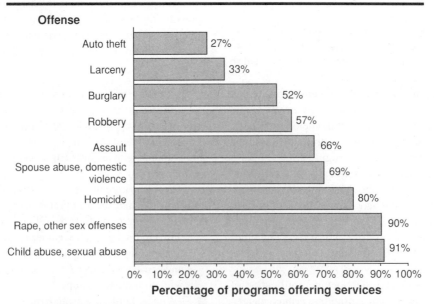

Percentage of programs offering services

Exhibit 5   Primary responsibility of victim-witness program

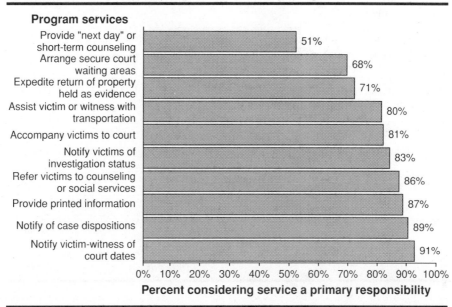

Program services

Provide "next day" or short-term counseling	51%
Arrange secure court waiting areas	68%
Expedite return of property held as evidence	71%
Assist victim or witness with transportation	80%
Accompany victims to court	81%
Notify victims of investigation status	83%
Refer victims to counseling or social services	86%
Provide printed information	87%
Notify of case dispositions	89%
Notify victim-witness of court dates	91%

0% 10% 20% 30% 40% 50% 60% 70% 80% 90% 100%

Percent considering service a primary responsibility

- Assignment of defense counsel.
- Motions procedures.
- Lack of formally accepted procedures for plea negotiations.
- Lack of pretrial conferences.
- Continuance policy.

The two most common problems (see Exhibit 6) cited are inadequate police preparation of crime reports (66 percent) and obtaining early information on defendant background (58 percent). The Southwest has the most difficulty obtaining early information on defendant backgrounds (75 percent). In contrast, only 29 percent in the Mid-Atlantic region cite this as a problem.

Inadequate details by police of proof supporting arrests is considered a problem by 50 percent of respondents. But the extent of the problem depends on where the prosecutor's office is located. Respondents in large counties report the problem half as frequently as those in smaller jurisdictions. Respondents in Plains-Mountain and Mid-Atlantic States have less problems receiving details from police than the rest of the country. Only 30 percent in these regions identify this as a problem, compared to 50 percent nationwide.

The least significant problems are lack of formally accepted procedures for plea negotiations and lack of pretrial conferences, rated as problems by less than 10 percent of respondents. Other problems deemed of little significance include lack of adequate review with law

enforcement on search warrants (a problem for 23 percent of the respondents) and assignment of defense counsel (a problem for only 14 percent).

Courtroom procedures. Prosecutors were asked to consider which of these six specific court procedures are problems in their systems:

- Trial continuance procedures.
- Calendaring system.
- System of voir dire.
- Management of victim-witness appearances.
- Procedures for victim impact sentencing.
- Courtroom security procedures.

Fifty-one percent of the respondents consider trial continuance procedures a problem, with 19 percent rating it a major concern. Consistent with the other data on court delay, continuance problems appear to be more serious in large counties. Next most frequently cited are calendaring systems, with 48 percent acknowledging a problem.

The four procedural areas least often cited as problems, in descending order of seriousness, are courtroom security procedures, procedures for victim-impact statements, the system of voir dire, and management of victim witness appearances. In an interesting regional variation, over half the prosecutors in the Far West state that the voir dire system is a problem, compared to 18 percent overall.

Exhibit 6   Pretrial and accusatory problems

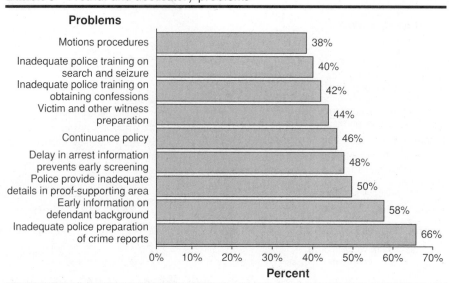

Management information systems.   A question about management information produced widely varied responses. The prosecutors were asked to consider 13 specific information areas and to state the degree to which their offices need improvements:

■ Original police charges.
■ Plea negotiations.
■ Dates of hearings.
■ Prior criminal history of defendant.
■ Victim-witness names.
■ Continuances.
■ Arresting officer names.
■ Defense counsel.
■ Attorney schedule conflict.
■ Bail-jail status.
■ Speedy trial status.
■ Pretrial diversion evaluation.
■ Information on codefendants.

At the top of the prosecutors' list is the need for information on prior criminal histories of defendants. Two-thirds of the respondents cite a need for improved information on criminal histories, and one-third consider it a major need. Only in the Mid-Atlantic States do less than half the prosecutors (37 percent) report a need for this information. Information on codefendants, essentially a variation on prior history of defendants, is needed by 45 percent.

Needs to improve management information are cited to a lesser extent in the following areas: attorney schedule conflicts (48 percent), continuances (40 per-

cent), speedy trial status (34 percent), and bail-jail status (37 percent). Regional differences emerge in the topic of information about continuances, with 75 percent of the prosecutors in the Southwest citing this as a need compared to only 23 percent in the Mid-Atlantic.

Most narrative answers on management information refer to computer applications of one kind or another. Among the successful projects reported by the respondents are prosecutor management information systems, court calendaring systems, and online systems serving all agencies of the criminal justice system from arrest through sentencing and probation.

Staffing and Training

Staffing.   As noted earlier, prosecutors view staff shortages as their most critical problem. Shortages are noted in the positions of attorneys (61 percent), investigators (57 percent), and clerical personnel (63 percent). To a lesser extent, they cite shortages for paralegals (42 percent) and administrative staff (26 percent).

The survey asked for ratings on five recruitment problems:

■ Low salaries.
■ Poor image of prosecution.
■ Shortage of qualified minority applicants.
■ Court location.
■ Civil service procedures.

The most frequently cited obstacle to successful staff recruitment is low salary, with 64 percent designating it a problem. A shortage of qualified minority applicants is considered a problem by 36 percent of the respondents. However, further analysis of the responses to questions show a strong correlation with county size. Only 16 percent of the respondents from counties under 100,000 people report shortages of qualified minority applicants, in contrast to 60 percent of counties over 750,000 people.

The two most significant retention problems are low salary increases and attorneys moving into private practice. Each problem is cited by about 66 percent of the respondents. Two other problems mentioned by about half the respondents are burnout and the lack of promotional opportunities.

Responses to staffing needs. The prosecutors were asked to describe specific projects or activities to solve staffing problems. Money answers appear in all categories—staff shortages, recruitment, retention, and training. One prosecutor puts it succinctly: "The whole issue is $." Because money comes from State and local legislative bodies, many emphasize the need for good relations with those bodies, although one describes it as "fighting with the Board of Supervisors."

Two answers more specifically identify what information needs to be presented to funding bodies to receive positive responses to staffing problems:

■ "Maintain accurate caseload data to support the proposed increase in personnel."
■ "Develop hard data to justify the pay increase."

Although still constrained by fiscal realities, some respondents suggest that better tracking and reporting procedures might contribute to achieving more satisfactory staffing levels.

Recruiting ideas include the following:

■ "Recruit third-year law students at major law schools."
■ "Establish and use summer intern check programs."
■ "Increase the focus on minority recruitment."
■ "Hire attorneys before they pass bar examination."

Other approaches to augmenting staff include summer law clerks and law student interns as allowed by a change in local rules.

Competitive salaries, better benefits, and regular rotation to other assignments repeatedly emerge as necessary to retain staff. Creative ideas for incentive programs include:

■ "Eight-week sabbatical after 4 years service, and 6-week sabbatical every 3 years thereafter; all in addition to regular vacation."
■ "Pride awards semiannually with wide recognition; regular evaluation; and promotion evaluation committee."
■ "Pay incentive for complaint screening on weekends."
■ "State law allowing use of funds from hot check fees to supplement prosecutor salaries."

The following comment aptly describes the staff retention challenge as extending beyond salary concerns:

> We have determined that regardless of salary scales, better morale, and officewide spirit of cooperation, and concern for each and every lawyer create an environment which has motivated lawyers to remain with the office.

Training. The most frequently cited training needs (see Exhibit 7) are trial practice skills (60 percent), new prosecutor training (54 percent), and stress management (50 percent). Other needs cited are for training in dealing with the public (44 percent), computer training for access to legal resources (42 percent), and training in general management skills (40 percent). The least critical training needs include statutory updates (cited by 25 percent), laws (23 percent), and appellate decision updates in criminal law (35 percent).

The suggestions on training identify a wide variety of well-known techniques including in-house training; manuals; newsletters; and participation in local, State, and national training programs. However, one unexpected answer reflects an innovative response to training needs:

> Legislature established a training fund to provide 50 cents as court costs in each criminal and traffic case for district attorney to use as a training fund for attorneys.

Summary

The majority of prosecutors believe the number of staff attorneys has not kept pace with caseloads, that a higher percentage of cases are going to trial, and that there are more motions filed per case. Some of the responses that prosecutors use in these problems include the establishment of special units (e.g., screening units, career criminal programs, and major case units), special

Exhibit 7 Staff training needs

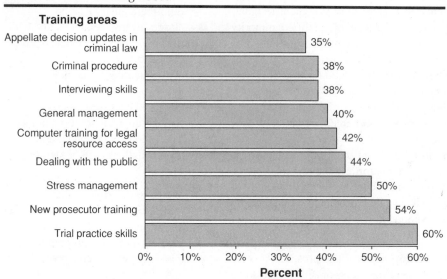

positions (e.g., welfare fraud specialist and investigative aides), more early-decision procedures, and use of computers for case control and movement.

Excessive continuances and poor case scheduling are mentioned as two main reasons for court delays in processing cases. Both problems are much more likely in large counties than in small counties. Further, both problems are more frequent in the Southwest than in other parts of the country.

The number of victim-witness assistance programs has increased in the last few years; 77 percent of the prosecutors have such a program. The cases handled usually include child abuse, sex offenses, homicide, domestic violence, and assault. Services usually offered are court date notifications, case disposition notifications, printed information, referrals, notification of investigation status, accompaniment to court, and transportation.

Notes

1. New England: Connecticut, Maine, Massachusetts, New Hampshire, Rhode Island, Vermont. Mid-Atlantic: District of Columbia, Delaware, Maryland, New Jersey, New York, Pennsylvania. Great Lakes: Illinois, Indiana, Michigan, Ohio, Wisconsin. Plains-Mountain: Iowa, Kansas, Minnesota, Missouri, Nebraska, North Dakota, South Dakota, Colorado, Idaho, Montana, Utah, Wyoming. Southeast: Alabama, Arkansas, Florida, Georgia, Kentucky, Louisiana, Mississippi, North Carolina, South Carolina, Tennessee, Virginia, West Virginia. Southwest: Arizona, New Mexico, Oklahoma, Texas. Far West: Alaska, California, Hawaii, Nevada, Oregon, Washington.

2. The 1983 National Assessment Program Survey was conducted for the National Institute of Justice by Abt Associates, Inc., Cambridge, Massachusetts

Discussion Questions

1. What do prosecutors consider their most significant criminal justice-related problems?
2. How do prosecutors try to reduce court delay?
3. How can training and recruiting strategies improve the role of the prosecutor in the criminal court?

National Institute of Justice

Research in Brief

Confronting Domestic Violence:
The Role of Criminal Court Judges

Gail A. Goolkasian

November 1986

The judge told him, in no uncertain terms, that the law doesn't allow him to assault me just because I'm his wife. He said that he'll send him to jail if he's brought back for another offense. Right there in the courtroom … you should have seen the look on his face. I think he knew the judge wasn't kidding, and that's when he decided to do something about it.

—a former battered woman

The Facts

"Domestic violence," also called "battering" and "spouse abuse," refers to assaultive behavior involving adults who are married, cohabitating, or have an ongoing or prior intimate relationship. In the overwhelming majority of cases, domestic violence is perpetrated by men against women.[1]

The facts about domestic violence are alarming. It was not until the mid-1970's that activists first succeeded in sparking public attention to the problem.[2] A well-known survey conducted in 1975 shattered the common perception that battering is a rare and inconsequential occurrence in our society.[3] Based on a national probability sample of more than 2,000 families, the researchers estimated that in the previous year over 1.7 million Americans had faced a spouse wielding a knife or gun, and well over 2 million had experienced a severe beating at the hands of their spouse.

These figures, which are based on self-reports, are believed to underestimate substantially the true scope of the problem. Ten years later, a 1985 replication of that survey found similarly high rates of spousal violence.[4]

Crime statistics bear out the lethal consequences of domestic violence: In 1985, for example, the FBI re-

ported that 30 percent of all female murder victims were killed by their husbands or boyfriends.[5]

Other facts are equally troubling. Rarely is domestic violence a single isolated event. Data from the National Crime Survey, conducted by the Bureau of Justice Statistics, shows that once a woman is victimized by domestic violence, she faces a high risk of being victimized again.[6]

It represents a pattern of behavior that tends to escalate both in frequency and severity over time, and is often carried from one generation to the next. Even if they are not the targets of violence themselves, children who witness domestic violence in their homes learn graphically that "this is how families behave."

Those who study and work with groups of abusers and battered women have found that many grew up in homes where domestic violence occurred.[7] Furthermore, there is a substantial body of evidence which indicates that children who are exposed to domestic violence suffer immediate and serious psychological harm.[8]

The Dynamics

For people whose lives have never been touched by domestic violence, it can be difficult to comprehend. To understand domestic violence, one must consider its context and its history.

For centuries men were legally and socially permitted to chastise their wives; "modest" battering or "modest" force was considered a legitimate way for men to maintain their ultimate control in the family.[9] But as wives and children ceased to be viewed as a husband's legal property, that rationale became obsolete.

Why Does He Do It?

Are batterers sick? Are they ignorant or poverty-stricken? Are they violent because they are addicted to alcohol or drugs? Do they batter because there is too much stress in their lives? Or do the women simply drive them to it?

The answer to all these questions is an emphatic no. Research has shown that domestic violence occurs within all social, economic, ethnic, and religious groups, although battering among disadvantaged socioeconomic groups is more likely to come to the attention of public agencies.

While many batterers abuse drugs or alcohol, many others do not. Countless numbers of people experience extreme stress without resorting to violence. And, while most batterers find a way to blame the victim for their own violent behavior, this is just an excuse.

There are two basic reasons why battering continues to exist today. First, violence is a highly effective means of control; often the victim of a domestic assault will spend a great deal of energy on trying to avoid subsequent assaults, including attempts to anticipate the needs, wishes, and whims of the abuser. Men who batter often explain their violence by saying that their victims will not do what they want them to, and they feel that as men they have a right to control "their" women. Second, men batter because they can; that is, because in most cases no one has told batterers that they must stop.

Recent research suggests that violence is less likely to recur once a clear message is given that battering is inappropriate behavior which will not be tolerated. Sherman and Berk found that domestic violence offenders who were arrested had almost half as much repeat violence during the following 6 months as offenders who were not arrested.[10] Langan and Innes' analysis of data from the National Crime Survey indicates that simply bringing a domestic violence incident to the attention of police seems to help prevent recurrences.[11]

In recent years, the battered women's movement has made tremendous strides in broadening awareness about domestic violence issues in public institutions as well as the community at large. There has been a great deal of legislative reform at the State level aimed at protecting battered women, treating domestic violence as a crime, and holding abusers accountable for their violent acts.[12]

Why Does She Stay?

For many people, this is perhaps the biggest puzzle about domestic violence. There is no simple answer.

The experience of battered women can be likened to that of a hostage or a prisoner of war; she is subjected to random violence and often forced into isolation from her relatives and friends. She frequently is threatened with increased violence if she tries to take any action against her abuser. Never knowing if the reality of violence might lead to death, battered women can be immobilized by fear.

Economic dependence is another factor that can prevent battered women from leaving. A woman without financial resources or a job outside the home may have to rely on the abuser to support herself and her children.

Furthermore, many experts point to the cyclical nature of domestic violence. Battered women are not constantly being abused, and batterers frequently become loving, kind, and contrite for a period of time following an attack.[13] Often the batterer knows he has gone too far and tries to convince the victim that it will never happen again. The victim wants to believe that this is true, that the violence has ended, and may succeed in believing it until the pattern is repeated time and again.

Despite these dynamics, many battered women do try to end the abuse by seeking outside help. Communities that have opened shelters for battered women and improved the institutional response to domestic violence report a huge influx of victims seeking an end to abuse. But pleas for help from battered women often go unanswered.

Public institutions and professionals in the community often fail to provide needed support and assistance. They may see the batterer when he is calm and articulate, and fail to believe that he is capable of such violence.

Physicians, hospital staff, welfare officials, mental health professionals, and the clergy have typically overlooked, ignored, or failed to act appropriately in domestic violence cases. Traditional training in these fields reflects a bias toward keeping the family together at all costs.

Barriers to action are even greater for women from certain racial, ethnic, religious, or cultural groups. For example, some women feel compelled to remain in abusive relationships because of their religious views on divorce, or because separation carries a tremendous social stigma in their community.

They may also feel that officials in public institutions hold racial and cultural stereotypes which will affect the amount of help they receive. Some women of color are more hesitant to press charges against their partners due to the common belief that minority men are sentenced more severely than white men for similar crimes. Therefore, a woman of color who chooses the court system may do so at the expense of terminating the support systems, including family and friends, within her own community.[14]

Finally, given the nature of domestic violence, the question "Why doesn't she leave?" seems misdirected. To say that the victim should leave does not address the conduct of the person responsible for the violence.[15] One former abuser put it simply: "If you don't deal with us, you're going to have the problem for the rest of eternity."[16]

Overview of the Criminal Justice Response

Although violence against the person is usually handled through criminal law, until recently most domestic violence cases entering the justice system were either screened out entirely or automatically routed to family courts. This practice reflected the view of society at large that domestic violence was a private family matter rather than a crime.

In the United States, most legal reform efforts have been aimed at the criminal justice process, instituting policies that reflect the serious criminal nature of domestic violence. The goal of criminal justice reforms is to eliminate the system's traditional avoidance and disdain for domestic violence cases, and to ensure that the law is enforced as vigorously as it would be if the parties were strangers.

It is also important to remember that domestic violence often involves a long history of abuse. Furthermore, because of the parties' relationship, a domestic violence offender typically has more access to the victim and is better able to intimidate and manipulate her.

Agencies within the justice system have begun to recognize their duty to provide legal remedies in domestic violence cases. Assault, battery, homicide, weapon use, kidnapping, and unlawful imprisonment are some of the most frequent crimes of domestic violence. More and more justice officials are realizing that a domestic violence incident constitutes a crime and, as with other crimes, the responsibility for taking legal action against an offender should rest with the justice system rather than the victim.

When justice agencies deliver a clear message that domestic violence is unacceptable behavior that will not be tolerated, this view is encouraged throughout society.

In many States, legislative reform aimed at improving the entire community response to domestic violence has forced justice agencies to modify past policies. For example, these laws can define the boundaries of proper police arrest practices, mandate data collection and reporting, require domestic violence training programs, provide for various forms of victim assistance, authorize the use of civil orders for protection, and increase the penalties for repeat offenders. These and other provisions may be embodied in a single domestic violence statute, or may be included in two or more separate pieces of legislation.

Police

Most attention concerning the role of the justice system has focused on police and, in particular, on whether or not police officers should favor arrest when they respond to calls involving domestic violence. In the past, most police departments discouraged officers from making arrests in "family disputes," advising officers to try to calm down the parties and make referrals to social service agencies in the community.[17]

Nonarrest strategies were harshly criticized for treating domestic assaults less seriously than assaults involving strangers, and for failing to provide adequate protection to battered women. Recent empirical research evidence from Sherman and Berk supports the growing consensus that arrest, consistent with State law, should be presumed the most appropriate police response to these incidents.[18]

Police departments throughout the country are beginning to educate officers about the dynamics of domestic violence, and are adopting official policies encouraging or requiring officers to arrest suspects in domestic violence incidents. State laws are expanding officers' legal authority to arrest in these cases; in most States, officers are now permitted—or, in some States, required—to arrest suspects in misdemeanor domestic violence incidents without obtaining a warrant even if they did not witness the crime, provided that they have probable cause to believe that a crime has been committed by the person being arrested.[19]

Prosecutors

The result of proarrest policies is often a large increase in the number of domestic violence cases entering the justice system. In recent years, several prosecutors' offices throughout the country have proposed and adopted policy improvements for these cases.

The prosecutorial policies reviewed by Lerman include: establishing domestic violence units in large offices to permit vertical prosecution and the development of prosecutor expertise on domestic violence cases; reviewing police reports on a regular basis to identify domestic violence incidents and conduct outreach to victims; developing objective filing and charging policies; and working with victim advocates, who can offer support and protection to victims and maximize the likelihood that victims will cooperate with prosecutors.[20]

Judges

Judges play a crucial role in shaping a community's overall response to domestic violence. Members of the judiciary can wield tremendous power as system advocates, by proposing changes in legislation and helping to educate the public about the criminal nature of domestic violence. They can also encourage improvements in police and prosecutor policy and court data collection and recordkeeping.

Judges have the power to demand information from law enforcement agencies if a paltry number of domestic violence cases are showing up in the courtroom, and can communicate with city or State government officials about the need to devote more resources to the problem (e.g., for victim advocates, shelters, or counseling programs).

Within their own courtrooms, judges determine the kind of attention domestic violence cases will receive from probation agencies. Judges can give a strong signal to probation officers that court orders and probation agreements must be monitored closely in these cases. In some States there are also statutory provisions that give judges special tools to handle domestic violence cases, such as formal orders for protection.

Furthermore, judges can have a positive impact by simply talking to the parties in domestic violence cases. Smith's study of the criminal court response to nonstranger violence found two ways that judges are critical in deterring future violence:

First, judicial warnings and/or lectures to defendants concerning the inappropriateness and seriousness of their violent behavior apparently improved the future conduct of some defendants. Second, judges occasionally counseled victims by telling them that they should not tolerate violent abuse, by suggesting counseling

programs, or both. For some victims, this official affirmation that they did not deserve to be hit helped them to realize that the abuse was not something which they simply had to tolerate. It seems likely that the judges' conduct would be especially critical to those individuals, both victims and defendants, appearing in court for the first time.[21]

In this vein, the Attorney General's Task Force on Family Violence urged judges not to underestimate their ability to influence a defendant's behavior, noting that "Even a stern admonition from the bench can help to deter the defendant from future violence."[22] As one judge told a defendant, "I don't care if she's your wife or not. A marriage license is not a hitting license. If you think the courts can't punish you for assaulting your wife, you are sadly mistaken."

Not surprisingly, the nonstranger violence study also found that the way a judge talks to the victim and defendant in court affects the victim's level of satisfaction with the justice system. Victims were more satisfied when judges were well-informed about domestic violence, provided referrals to shelters and other community organizations, and lectured defendants about the seriousness of their assaultive behavior.[23]

Restrictions on Pretrial Release

The vast majority of defendants in domestic violence cases are released prior to trial, usually on their own recognizance. The victim is especially vulnerable during the pretrial period, when the defendant may try to retaliate for her role in having him arrested, or threaten her with more violence if she cooperates with prosecution.

The court can protect the victim during this period by restricting the defendant's access to her as a condition of pretrial release. Practitioners feel that this kind of protection is needed in most domestic violence cases. State laws commonly authorize the issuance of protection orders (also called restraining or stay-away orders) in civil court. In most States, civil and criminal relief can be sought simultaneously, and a civil protection order can help the victim to get the protection she needs during prosecution.

Some State statutes which provide for civil protection orders also authorize criminal court judges to issue protection orders as a condition of pretrial release in domestic violence cases. This is preferable in criminal cases because victims are not required to go through a whole separate process and bureaucracy in order to get the necessary protection while charges are pending.

Lerman notes that criminal court judges can issue protection orders even without specific statutory authority, since they have wide discretion to impose conditions on the release of any defendant.[24] When there is no enabling legislation for issuance of protection orders in criminal cases, judges may find it useful to consult civil protection order statutes for guidance on what to include in such orders.

In most jurisdictions, a probation agency is responsible for investigating the defendant's eligibility for ROR (release on recognizance) and the need to attach specific conditions to pretrial release. As part of this investigation, probation officers should contact the victim for information about her particular safety needs. The probation officer and victim should explore release conditions available to the court and conditions that the victim feels she needs to protect her safety, such as limited or no contact by the defendant, allowing the defendant only supervised child visitation, or the temporary removal of weapons from the household.

Some judges are reluctant to issue an order of protection that excludes a man from his own home, fearing that this may violate his constitutional rights. However, State supreme courts that addressed this issue have found that such conditions do not violate due process, even if the order is administered on an ex parte basis.[25]

The importance of enforcing protection orders cannot be overemphasized. In some jurisdictions, critics have charged that the orders "aren't worth the paper they're written on." Indeed, an unenforceable order is worse than none at all, because it gives the victim the illusion that she has protection. Orders are most effective where violation constitutes a separate criminal offense, and police officers in the field can verify the existence, validity, and terms of an order when a violation is alleged. But even if violation is not a criminal offense in and of itself, charges such as trespassing or disturbing the peace can often be applied in addition to civil contempt.

Protection orders, or restrictions on the defendant's contact with the victim, can be imposed as a condition of bail as well as ROR. In certain cases, the circumstances may warrant a high cash bail to make pretrial release unlikely. This action is appropriate in especially serious cases, cases where the defendant has continually threatened the victim with more violence upon his release, and cases where the defendant has reassaulted the victim in the past even though a protection order was issued.

Pretrial Court Appearances

If possible, defendants in all domestic violence cases should be required to appear in court at the first opportunity following arrest, preferably before pretrial release. This demonstrates to the defendant that domestic violence is considered serious criminal conduct. If the defendant will be released prior to trial, holding him until a court appearance gives the victim time to seek safe housing. This requirement is embodied in some State domestic violence statutes.

In States without legislation mandating appearance at arraignment, a change in court rules may be necessary to impose this requirement. The initial court appearance is the best time to issue an order of protection, because it eliminates the need to locate the defendant to serve him with the order, and to verify that service took place. The defendant should be informed about the specific terms of the order, and should be required to sign a statement indicating that he understands these conditions before he is released from custody. A copy of the order should be given to the defendant, the victim, and the local law enforcement agency.

Victim Reluctance

Judges, along with police and prosecutors, frequently express frustration at the unwillingness of some battered women to "follow through" with prosecution. Victim reluctance raises some difficult issues.

To the extent that it results from intimidation by the defendant, reluctance is best addressed by protecting victims during the pretrial period. Reluctance may also stem from confusion, inadequate emotional or financial support, or lack of understanding about the process and end results of prosecution. In several courts, judges report that battered women are more willing to cooperate and testify when they receive information, emotional support, community referrals, and trial preparation from victim advocates who are assigned to each case.

There is considerable disagreement among experts regarding what action should be taken when victims are given protection and support, yet still refuse to testify. In some jurisdictions, victims are subpoenaed to give the justice system more control over prosecution and to demonstrate to the parties that the prosecutor is responsible for the case, thereby relieving pressure on the victim not to appear in court.[26] In other jurisdictions, subpoenas are issued to shield victims from pressure not to testify, but only if the victim so desires.

If a battered woman refuses to testify and is found in contempt, the judge can impose a disposition that addresses her needs, such as participation in a battered women's support group. Some experts argue that it is unfair to force all victims to testify, and that subpoenas are sometimes used to invoke inappropriate punitive measures against battered women.[27]

Ford asserts that at least some battered women use the threat of prosecution and punishment as leverage on the defendant to secure an acceptable arrangement, such as separation or participation in batterer counseling.[28] For these women, a refusal to testify may not be placing them in greater jeopardy or wasting the system resources that were already expended on their cases, but may in fact signify that the criminal justice system has enabled them to end the abuse.

While followup data on one small sample of cases support this view,[29] further research on the long-term impacts of prosecution is needed to guide policies in this area. If subpoenas are issued in battering cases, they should be used to protect battered women, not to punish them.

Even when prosecution is clearly in the best interest of the victim and the community, cases can sometimes be tried successfully without forcing victim testimony. Corroborating evidence may be available in some cases. For example, testimony may be available from a police officer or family member who was an eyewitness to the event or its consequences.

Judges can also permit expert testimony from qualified authorities, who can speak generally about the nature of battering. An expert witness who has interviewed the victim can confirm that she is a battered woman and identify some of the reasons why she is not present to testify herself. Expert testimony has the added benefit of educating the judge and jury about some of the dynamics and complexities of domestic violence.[30]

Sentencing

In the past courts often imposed lesser sanctions for domestic violence compared with violent crimes involving strangers. As one attorney observed:

> Sentences in this area are very much lighter than comparable situations of stranger violence. It's very discouraging when ... the sentence is so light that it's, in a sense, a final way of condoning the violence.[31]

Sentencing options and practices cover a wide range in domestic violence cases. In general, sentences should be aimed at holding offenders accountable, ending abusive behavior, and meeting the needs of victims and other family members. Multiple interventions are often appropriate. What "works" with one offender might fail completely with another, even in cases that are similar in many respects.

For example, some offenders comply with no-contact orders and court-ordered counseling because they are frightened by the prospect of serving time in jail, while others readily violate these orders, especially if they have gotten away with it before.

Fines can be imposed in accordance with State statutes. The amount of the fine, and the way fines are used, may be strictly defined by law. Sentences involving probation with a suspended jail or prison term are very common in domestic violence cases. Incarceration is both appropriate and necessary in cases involving more serious violence, a long pattern of abuse, significant threat of continued harm if the offender were released, or failure at previous alternatives to incarceration.

Restitution should be considered in communities where restitution programs are available for crime victims. Offenders should be ordered to reimburse the victim for expenses resulting from the crime, such as lost wages; shelter costs; medical, counseling, and other treatment fees; and replacement costs of any destroyed property.[32]

In an increasing number of jurisdictions, victim needs and preferences regarding sentencing are being communicated to the judge—sometimes as part of a probation agency's presentence investigation, a prosecutor's sentencing recommendation, or a formal victim impact statement.

Many battered women seek help in stopping the violence without incarcerating the abuser, particularly if they want to continue their relationship with the offender or must depend on the offender for financial support. Weekend or evening incarceration may be appropriate in cases involving less serious violence when the victim wants the offender to continue to work and support the family. Lerman notes that sentences should reflect victim wishes when this will not result in overly lenient penalties.[33]

Special Issues for Sentences Involving Probation

Probation sentences can be extremely useful in domestic violence cases, particularly in communities with batterer intervention programs that accept referrals from the courts. Judges usually have considerable flexibility in establishing the specific conditions of probation. It is essential to place restrictions on the offender that will protect the victim and other family members. Protection orders that were issued as a condition of pretrial release can often be extended through the probationary period. The specific terms of an order should be determined based on the victim's particular safety needs.

Participation in counseling or other intervention programs can also be ordered as a condition of probation. Specially-designed programs for batterers, aimed at ending their violent behavior, are available in a growing number of communities. Many batterer programs accept clients on probation who are referred by criminal courts.[34] Judges have found that these programs offer a useful dispositional alternative for many domestic violence cases, particularly in light of crowded prisons and jails. Some batterers need other kinds of intervention in addition to that which focuses on stopping violent behavior.

Treatment for alcohol or drug abuse is needed in many cases. When alcohol or drug problems exist, they usually must be addressed before the offender enters a specialized program for batterers, although there are some programs that can address both kinds of problems concurrently.

Although judges have found mediation to be an excellent forum for resolving some types of disputes, mediation is not an appropriate sentence for domestic violence offenders. Mediation requires the victim to participate in the offender's sentence and relies on the mutual goodwill and fairness of both parties in a situation where one party has consistently controlled and manipulated the other. Mediation or couples' counseling is appropriate in domestic violence cases only if both

parties seek it voluntarily, and the batterer has already succeeded in ending his violent behavior. Court-ordered intervention should focus solely on the offender.

Court-Ordered Counseling and Education for Batterers

Specially designed programs for batterers are a recent and promising dispositional alternative for offenders in some domestic violence cases. The number of programs is growing rapidly; they were virtually nonexistent a decade ago, and now there are over 100 across the country.[35]

The programs are working more and more with local courts. One recent nationwide survey of batterer programs by Pirog-Good and Stets-Kealey found that roughly one-third of all clients are sent by the court system.[36]

Many people are skeptical about court-ordered counseling for batterers, believing that counseling can only be useful if an individual participates voluntarily and truly wants to change his behavior at the outset. However, there is compelling evidence that court-ordered counseling is appropriate and, in many cases, effective in ending violent behavior.

Experts agree that batterers tend to deny or minimize the seriousness of their violent behavior and are unwilling to accept responsibility for the battering. As a result, batterers typically refuse voluntary treatment. By ordering an offender to counseling in lieu of incarceration, the courts give him a powerful incentive to enter and participate in the program.

While there is a dearth of research on batterer programs in general, there is some evidence that criminal justice referrals are effective. Pirog-Good and Stets-Kealey found that judges are the most likely referral source for programs with the highest completion rates.[37] The survey also indicated that clients referred by the criminal justice system may be more likely to stop further violence than clients who are referred by other sources, such as physicians and clergy.

Types of Programs

The primary goal of batterer programs is virtually universal: to stop the violent behavior. There are a variety of program affiliations among batterer programs that work with the courts.

Programs for court-ordered batterers are constantly being refined as we learn more about the complexities of domestic violence and as professionals gain more experience in working with this difficult and challenging group of clients. Group counseling and educational programs are the two major alternatives designed specifically for batterers that are currently available to the criminal justice system.

Effectiveness

Because the field is still new, there have been no formal evaluations of the long-term effectiveness of batterer intervention programs. Fortunately, some promising research efforts in this area are currently underway.

There is some evidence of success. A study commissioned by the Texas State Senate examined the clientele and effectiveness of three different programs that counsel batterers. The study found that the programs were effective in eliminating or reducing physical violence compared with precounseling levels in most cases, by the accounts of both the men and women involved.[38] Shepard found evidence that batterer counseling and education in Duluth, Minnesota, reduces abusive behavior and increases knowledge about the use of abuse as a means of controlling victims.[39]

While these programs do have great potential in many cases, their limitations must also be recognized. It is important to note that, for many offenders, battering represents a complex, long-term behavior pattern that is not easily changed. The kinds of programs currently available to the courts are simply insufficient to change these patterns in some cases. As Ganley observed, "It is very likely that, as in the field of alcoholism, different approaches will be successful with different individuals."[40]

Because of this reality, some courts now refer domestic violence offenders to professional counselors for an assessment session before ordering participation in a particular intervention program. When individual offenders are found to be inappropriate for available programs, the criminal justice system must impose other suitable sanctions.

Putting Teeth in Court Orders: Monitoring and Enforcement

Probation gives offenders a chance to avoid incarceration by meeting certain specified conditions, such as participation in a counseling program, compliance with

a protection order, and no further use of violence. If an offender's compliance with these conditions is not monitored and he is able to violate them without facing any negative sanctions, the court order—indeed, the entire criminal justice process—has failed in its mission. Probation should be revoked when the offender fails to adhere to the conditions that were established by the courts. In short, the court order must have "teeth."

Monitoring Compliance

In most jurisdictions, probation officers are responsible for monitoring compliance with the conditions of probation. The probation department must work with intervention programs in the community to: (1) establish ground rules for offender participation in court-ordered programs, such as the fees required and number of absences permitted; and (2) permit a two-way flow of information between counselors and probation officers, so that both parties can be informed about program attendance, reincidence of violence, and changes in probationary status.

Probation policies should require that a revocation hearing before the judge is requested according to court rules when an offender continues his violent behavior, exceeds the maximum number of absences from court-ordered sessions, violates the terms of a protection order, or otherwise fails to comply with probation conditions.

In courts without probation agencies, some judges have been able to establish special procedures to monitor compliance in domestic violence cases. For example, a judge in one rural Washington State area requires probationers to return to court at regular intervals with evidence of attendance at counseling sessions.

Revoking Probation

When a judge determines that an offender has violated the established conditions of probation, it is essential that the offender face some additional sanctions or requirements as a result. When probation is revoked, judges' sentencing practices vary a great deal based on the reason that the offender was brought back to court and the number of times the offender has failed in the past to comply with probation conditions.

In most cases, revocation should result in a period of incarceration, however brief, to let the offender know that the courts mean business. For example, a first-time offender who exceeded the maximum number of absences from counseling might be placed in jail for a short period of time—even a few days—and then placed on probation again and mandated back to counseling.

When there is a meaningful threat of revocation, many offenders do take the court orders seriously. A recent sample of over 400 cases referred to the House of Ruth batterer counseling program in Baltimore revealed that 70 percent of offenders ordered through supervised probation had completed the full program. It was well-known in this jurisdiction that judges had jailed some domestic violence offenders for refusing to cooperate.

Conclusion

Changes in the criminal justice treatment of domestic violence have created a range of alternatives to respond to and control this particular form of violence. As new methods evolve, judges play a critical role in shaping the community response to domestic violence and responding to cases that enter the criminal justice system.

There are some basic ways that judges can be more effective in these cases, even under a variety of legislative frameworks. These include: restricting the defendant's access to the victim during the pretrial period; communicating judicial concern about domestic violence to both the victim and defendant; considering a range of dispositional alternatives in an effort to impose sentences that reflect both the seriousness of the crime and the needs of victims and other family members; and strictly enforcing court orders and conditions of probation.

In most criminal courts, judges have the tools available to establish these kinds of procedures. Judges in many communities have taken a strong stand against domestic violence. In Baltimore, Maryland, for example, the Chief Administrative Judge of the District Court sends all new judges to a local domestic violence project to receive a 1-day orientation and training session on domestic violence issues and procedures to be followed in domestic violence cases.

Judge William R. Sweeney, who was instrumental in establishing domestic violence reforms in St. Louis County (Duluth), Minnesota, summed it up this way: "Being a judge, you make a lot of important decisions on a case-by-case basis. Unless you're an appellate judge, you can't have that much impact on the community as a whole. This is one thing that I feel good about, like I've really done something for my community."

Discussion Questions

1. To what does the term *domestic violence* refer?

2. Why do men become batterers? Why do women stay with an abusive mate?

3. What is the normal response of police and prosecutors to the problem of domestic abuse?

4. How can the criminal court effectively deal with domestic abuse? Can court-ordered counseling and education programs make a difference?

Notes

1. Data from the National Crime Survey found that 95 percent of all assaults on spouses or ex-spouses during 1973–77 were committed by men. U.S. Department of Justice, *Report to the Nation on Crime and Justice: The Data* (Washington, D.C.: Bureau of Justice Statistics, 1983), p. 21.

2. Erin Pizzey, *Scream Quietly or the Neighbors Will Hear* (Short Hills, New Jersey: Ridley Enslow, 1977), published in England in 1974.

3. Murray A. Straus, Richard J. Gelles, and Suzanne K. Steinmetz, *Behind Closed Doors: Violence in the American Family* (Garden City, New York: Anchor Press, 1980), pp. 26–26, 32–36.

4. Murray A. Straus and Richard J. Gelles, "Societal Change and Change in Family Violence from 1975 to 1985 as Revealed by Two National Surveys," *Journal of Marriage and the Family* 48 (August 1986): 465–479.

5. U.S. Department of Justice, *Uniform Crime Reports—1985* (Washington, D.C.: Federal Bureau of Investigation, 1986), p. 11.

6. U.S. Department of Justice, *Special Report: Preventing Domestic Violence Against Women,* by Patrick A. Langan and Christopher A. Innes (Washington, D.C.: Bureau of Justice Statistics, 1986), p. 1.

7. Jeffrey A. Fagan, Douglas K. Stewart, and Karen V. Hansen, "Violent Men or Violent Husbands? Background Factors and Situational Correlates," in *The Dark Side of Families: Current Family Violence Research*, ed. David Finkelhor, Richard J. Gelles, Gerald T. Hotaling, and Murray A. Straus (Beverly Hills: Sage Publications, 1983), pp. 49–67.

8. Honorable Marjory D. Fields, "Spouse Abuse as a Factor in Custody and Visitation Decisions," unpublished monograph, New York, 1986.

9. Nan Oppenlander, "The Evolution of Law and Wife Abuse," *Law and Policy Quarterly* 3, 4 (October 1981): 382–405.

10. Lawrence W. Sherman and Richard A. Berk, "The Specific Deterrent Effects of Arrest for Domestic Assault," *American Sociological Review* 49 (April 1984): 261–272.

11. U.S. Department of Justice, *Special Report: Preventing Domestic Violence Against Women.* Bureau of Justice Statistics.

12. Lisa G. Lerman and Franci Livingston, "State Legislation on Domestic Violence," *Response* 6 (September/October 1983).

13. Lenore E. Walker, *The Battered Woman* (New York: Harper and Row, 1979), pp. 55–70.

14. Catherine Avina et al., "The Response of the Judicial System," in Minnesota Department of Corrections, *Battered Women: An Effective Response.*

15. Honorable Marjorie D. Fields, Family Court, New York City, Personal Communication, July 10, 1986.

16. *Attorney General's Task Force on Family Violence, Final Report* (Washington, D.C.: U.S. Department of Justice, 1984), p. 22.

17. Morton Bard, *Training Police as Specialists in Family Crisis Intervention* (Washington, D.C.: Government Printing Office, 1970).

18. Sherman and Berk, "The Specific Deterrent Effects of Arrest for Domestic Assault."

19. Lerman and Livingston, "State Legislation on Domestic Violence."

20. Lisa G. Lerman, *Prosecution of Spouse Abuse: Innovations in Criminal Justice Response (*Washington, D.C.: Center for Women Policy Studies, 1981).

21. Barbara E. Smith, *Non-Stranger Violence: The Criminal Court's Response* (Washington, D.C.: National Institute of Justice, 1983), p. 96.

22. *Attorney General's Task Force on Family Violence, Final Report,* p. 36.

23. Smith, *Non-Stranger Violence,* pp. 90–92.

24. Lisa G. Lerman, "Placing Conditions on Pretrial Release of Batterers," *Response* (January/February 1981): 10; Nadine Taub, "Adult Domestic Violence."

25. Lisa G. Lerman, "Court Decisions on Wife Abuse Laws: Recent Developments," *Response* (May/June 1982): 3–4.

26. Lisa G. Lerman, *Prosecution of Spouse Abuse: Innovations in Criminal Justice Response* (Washington, D.C.: Center for Women Policy Studies, 1981), pp. 46–47.

27. Barbara J. Hart, "Testify or Prison!" Reading, Pennsylvania, 1983.

28. David A. Ford, "Prosecution as a Victim Power Resource for Managing Conjugal Violence," paper presented at Annual Meeting of the Society of Social Problems, San Antonio, Texas, August 1984.

29. David A. Ford, "Long-Term Impacts of Prosecution Outcomes for Incidents of Conjugal Violence: Evidence from Victim Case Studies," paper presented at Annual Meeting of Law and Society Association, San Diego, California, June 1985.

30. *Attorney General's Task Force on Family Violence, Final Report,* pp. 41–42.

31. Ruth Gundle, Esq., Oregon Legal Services, Portland, Oregon, in *Attorney General's Task Force on Family Violence, Final Report,* p. 12.

32. Ibid, p. 35.

33. Lerman, *Prosecution of Spouse Abuse,* pp. 47–50.

34. Some programs also accept clients referred by prosecutors' offices as a requirement of pretrial diversion, or referred by civil courts as a condition of a civil order for protection.

35. Maureen Pirog-Good and Jan Stets-Kealey, "Male Batterers and Battering Prevention Programs: A National Survey," *Response* (Summer 1985): 8–12.

36. Ibid.

37. Pirog-Good and Stets-Kealey, "Male Batterers and Battering Prevention Programs."

38. Texas Department of Human Resources, "An Evaluation of Three Programs for Abusive Men in Texas," by William A. Stacey and Anson Shupe, Arlington, Texas, 1984.

39. Melanie Shepard, "Summary: Evaluation of Domestic Abuse Intervention Project Counseling and Educational Program," Duluth, Minnesota, 1985.

40. Ganley, *Court-Mandated Counseling for Men Who Batter,* p. 5.

National Institute of Justice // *Crime File*

Sentencing

Richard Singer, Yeshiva University

1986

Historical Background

Sentencing is the process by which judges impose
punishment on persons convicted of crimes. The punishments imposed may range from probation without
conditions to the death penalty and also include fines,
community service, probation with conditions, and
incarceration in jail or prison.

For most of the 20th century, all American
jurisdictions had "indeterminate" sentencing systems.
Criminal statutes generally authorized judges to impose
a sentence from within a wide range. Probation to 5
years was a common range; probation to 25 years was
not unknown. The judge's decision was usually final;
appellate courts seldom considered appeals from sentencing decisions.

For defendants sentenced to prison, the judge's
sentence set the outer limits, but a parole board would
decide when the offender was released. The judge might
have imposed a "3-to-10-year sentence," but the parole
boards often had authority to release after 1 year, or after
the offender had served a designated fraction (often
one-third) of the sentence. Thus, whether the offender
served 1 year in prison, or 3, or 5, was generally up to the
parole board.

This system was called indeterminate because the
prisoner's actual time in prison would not be known, or
determined, until final release by the parole board. The
system of indeterminate sentencing could be justified
on a number of bases, but its primary theoretical rationale was that it permitted sentencing and parole release
decisions to be individualized, often on the basis of the
offender's rehabilitative progress or prospects.

Criminologists long accepted the view that an
offender's criminal misbehavior could be analogized to
a disease, which could be cured if properly treated in a
proper institution. Cure became a major goal of both
sentencing and incarceration; when released, the offender would enjoy a more satisfying, productive, and
lawful life; he would not commit additional crimes and
everyone's interests would be served. This medical
model of disease and cure required that offenders be
returned to the free world when professionals judged
that they were "cured."

Treatment programs were seen as essential, and
both vocational and psychological training programs
were introduced into prisons. This rehabilitative out-
look shaped even the vocabulary of criminal punishment. Prisons were often called "correctional" institutions; those for young adults were often called "refor-
matories." Indeterminate sentencing survived for so
long because it could be many things to different people.
For those not enamored of rehabilitation, its capacity for
individualizing punishment meant that offenders seen
as dangerous could be held for lengthy periods and
thereby be *incapacitated*. For those concerned with
retribution, indeterminate sentencing allowed sentences
to be individualized on the basis of an assessment of
each offender's unique circumstances and degree of
moral guilt. Finally, the threat and possibilities of severe sentences could be seen as a deterrent to crime.

The discretions of judges and parole boards were
exercised without legislative direction as to which
sentencing goals were primary, or which factors should
be considered in setting sentences or determining parole
release. Different judges in the same courthouse could
consider the same factor as either mitigating or
aggravating the defendant's culpability. Thus, for example, while one judge might consider drug addiction as a mitigating factor that justified reducing the

offender's sentence, another judge or parole board member might consider such information an indicator of future criminality, and a reason to increase the sentence.

Recent Changes in Sentencing

By 1970, indeterminate sentencing had come under attack. Some critics claimed that the wide, unreviewable discretions of judges and parole boards resulted in discrimination against minorities and the poor. Some were concerned about unwarranted sentencing disparities. Because sentences could not be appealed, there was nothing a prisoner could do about a disparately severe sentence. A considerable body of research demonstrated the existence of unwarranted sentencing disparities and many believed them to be inherent in indeterminate sentencing. In addition, highly publicized reviews of research on treatment programs concluded that their effectiveness could not be demonstrated; the resulting skepticism about rehabilitative programs undermined one of indeterminate sentencing's foundations.

None of these critiques of indeterminate sentencing was uncontroverted. Supporters of treatment programs argued that such programs could and do succeed, or that the evaluation research was flawed, or that programs failed because they were poorly managed, or underfunded, or targeted on the wrong categories of offenders. Judges, but not only judges, argued that sentencing disparities were not as great a problem as critics contended. First, because judges were able to consider all factors characterizing the offender, the offense, and the offender's prior criminal record, many judges argued that most sentences were soundly based and only appeared disparate. Second, because individual judges inevitably hold different opinions and values, and have different beliefs about the purpose of punishment, their sentences properly might reflect those differences.

The critics of indeterminate sentencing have successfully attacked it in many jurisdictions. Changes in sentencing laws have swept the country. Many new systems are "determinate" in that parole release has been eliminated and the duration of a prison sentence can be determined at the time of sentencing. States as different and dispersed as Maine and California, or Florida and Washington, have instituted major changes. These include the abolition of parole, the establishment of detailed statutory sentencing standards, and the

establishment of various systems of "presumptive" sentencing. A number of jurisdictions have established new administrative agencies called "sentencing commissions" and delegated authority to them to develop guidelines for sentencing.

Parole Reforms—Abolition and Guidelines

The attacks upon indeterminate sentencing moved several States to limit or eliminate the discretion of parole boards. A dozen States, including Pennsylvania, Connecticut, Maine, California, and Washington, have recently abolished their parole boards. While this has effectively eliminated the indeterminate aspect of sentencing, it has not necessarily affected the wide discretion held by judges. In the early 1970's, Maine eliminated the parole board but allowed judges to impose any sentence from within a very wide range authorized by law (e.g., probation to 15 years). The legislature provided no guidance as to the "appropriate" sentence within that range. At the other extreme, States like California abolished parole releases, but adopted detailed standards for judges' sentencing decisions. Some jurisdictions retained parole release but adopted parole guidelines. The Oregon parole board and the United States Parole Commission, among others, voluntarily adopted strict guidelines to standardize their release decisions. This reduced both the unpredictability of sentences and the *ad hoc* discretionary aspect of parole release that had bothered many critics.

Sentencing Commissions

In several States, including Minnesota, Pennsylvania, and Washington, sentencing commissions have developed comprehensive "sentencing guidelines" which attempt to standardize sentences, primarily on the basis of the offender's crime and his past criminal record. Of course, even where the legislature delegates the task of setting sentencing guidelines to a commission, it retains the right to ratify or reject the commission's proposals. The details of the guidelines systems vary substantially, as have their impacts. In Minnesota, it appears that judges have generally followed the guidelines and that sentencing disparities have been reduced. In 1984, Congress established a Federal sentencing commission to develop sentencing guidelines for the Federal system.

Presumptive Sentencing

Some of the new determinate sentencing systems provide a range within which the judge should impose sentences in ordinary cases. Others, such as North Carolina, New Jersey, and California, have established a single presumptive sentence. In California the "presumptive" sentence for a number of crimes is 3 years, but a judge may sentence an offender for either 2 or 4 years and still remain within the range authorized by the statute. For example in Minnesota the presumptive sentence is 49 months, but the judge may impose sentences between 45 and 53 months without leaving the range. In other States, however, that range may be much wider—20 to 50 years in Indiana for Class A felonies. If the range is too wide, one of the main reasons for removing indeterminacy—the effort to reduce disparities—may not have been achieved at all.

Not even the most restrictive of these schemes totally precludes the judge from imposing any sentence, so long as it is within the statutory minimum or maximum sentence. Even under sentencing guidelines, a judge may sentence outside the guidelines if a written statement of reasons is provided. Some States provide lists of aggravating and mitigating circumstances that may be considered in departing from the guideline sentence or range.

If the sentencing rules restrict discretion only for sentences of imprisonment but do not affect the judge's decision to imprison or not (the "in-out" decision), one purpose of the reform may be substantially frustrated. In California, for example, while the percentage of persons convicted of burglary who were sentenced to prison rose after new sentencing legislation was enacted, from 27 percent to 35 percent, nearly two-thirds of persons convicted of burglary received no prison sentence, while one-third received a prison term within relatively strict guidelines. In Minnesota, judges follow the in-out guideline in 91 to 94 percent of the cases, thereby establishing some consistency in these decisions. It could be argued that the decision whether to imprison is more important, at least in terms of disparity, than the decision of how long to imprison.

Voluntary Guidelines

Finally, many jurisdictions, such as Michigan and Denver, have experimented with "voluntary" sentencing guidelines, which provide judges with information on the "usual" sentence for the offense and the offender;

the judge is not obligated to follow these guidelines. Voluntary guidelines have generally been developed by judges or by advisory committees appointed by the State's chief justice. Some judges favor voluntary guidelines, even though they believe judges should retain full discretion over each individual sentence.

Arguments and Counter-Arguments

Recent changes in sentencing laws and practices have not gone unchallenged. Some, as noted above, question the premises for change and the critiques of indeterminate sentencing.

Other critics argue that retribution or "just deserts," the primary purpose of many modern sentencing laws, is philosophically unacceptable in the late 20th century, and that sentencing grids which substantially constrain judicial discretion are unfair because they forbid judges to consider mitigating factors and to act mercifully. Some also argue that the endorsement of retribution (albeit "equal" retribution) as a proper goal of sentencing has led to severely increased sentences, which these critics see as undesirable.

Another concern about the new sentencing laws is that the perceived rigidity of the statutes or guidelines enhances the discretion of the prosecutor, particularly during plea bargain negotiations. Judicial discretion at least is exercised in the open, while prosecutorial discretion is generally exercised behind closed doors.

There is another concern: If determinate sentencing systems retain "good time" (time off for good behavior) to reduce sentences, prison guards and other prison personnel may effectively become sentencers. Minnesota and most other States that have adopted determinate sentencing still provide for substantial good time; California recently enlarged the amount of good time a prisoner can earn off his determinate sentence and has therefore enlarged the discretionary power of prison officials to affect the actual duration of confinement.

Yet another criticism of sentencing reform is that it has contributed to recent increases in prison crowding, first by causing the sentencing to prison of many offenders who previously would have received probation, and second by removing the "safety valve" of early release on parole in the event of overcrowding. This problem was avoided in Minnesota, where the legislature specifically instructed the sentencing commission to take prison capacity into account when it developed the guidelines. Minnesota has entrusted to the commission the job of realigning the guidelines to avoid overcrowding if it arises. A similar provision is contained in newly enacted Federal legislation. The provision should be emulated by any State considering changes in the sentencing system unless, of course, the State's citizens are willing to bear the financial burden of building more prisons.

The controversy over indeterminate and determinate sentencing reflects deeper arguments over the purposes of the criminal law. For the past century, those who argued for uncertainty and indeterminancy sought to use the criminal sentence as a means of crime control. They sought to frighten the potential offender, to rehabilitate the "treatable" offender, and to incapacitate the incorrigible in order to reduce victimization in society. Recent sentencing changes, while partly based on empirical disillusionment with these goals, also draw upon the retributive notion of a fair, certain, and equal punishment for all those who inflict the same harm upon society. The dispute over the purposes of criminal sanctions has persisted for centuries, and the recent changes are unlikely to resolve that dispute.

Discussion Questions

1. What should be the purpose of sentencing—rehabilitation, deterrence, incapacitation, or retribution?

2. Is it more important that sentences be consistent, which probably means that judges will be deprived of much of their discretion, or that sentences be "individualized," which probably means that there will be significant unwarranted disparities?

3. Should sentencing decisions be influenced by the size of the prison population?

4. Do you believe judges and parole board members can assess when or whether offenders are rehabilitated?

5. If you were a legislator, which would you favor—determinate sentencing or indeterminate sentencing?

References

American Friends Service Committee. 1971. *Struggle for Justice: A Report on Crime and Punishment in America.* New York: Hill and Wang.

Blumstein, Alfred, Jacqueline Cohen, Susan E. Martin, and Michael H. Tonry, eds. 1983. *Research on Sentencing: The Search for Reform.* Washington, D.C.: National Academy Press.

Frankel, Marvin. 1973. *Criminal Sentences: Law Without Order.* New York: Hill and Wang.

Rothman, David. 1980. *Conscience and Convenience: The Asylum and Its Alternatives in Progressive America.* Boston: Little, Brown.

Singer, Richard G. 1979. *Just Deserts: Sentencing Based on Equality and Desert.* Cambridge, Massachusetts: Ballinger.

Tonry, Michael H., and Franklin E. Zimring, eds. 1983. *Reform and Punishment: Essays on Criminal Sentencing.* Chicago: The University of Chicago Press.

von Hirsch, Andrew. 1976. *Doing Justice: The Choice of Punishments.* New York: Hill and Wang.

National Institute of Justice / *Research in Action*

The Impact of the Federal Sentencing Guidelines

Michael K. Block and William M. Rhodes

September/October 1987

As part of the Crime Control Act of 1984, Congress created the U.S. Sentencing Commission as an independent body in the judicial branch of government. The seven voting and two non-voting members were appointed by the President and confirmed by the Senate.

The Commission was charged with establishing sentencing policies and practices for the Federal criminal justice system that fulfill the purposes of sentencing—punishment, deterrence, incapacitation, and rehabilitation. Specifically, the Commission was directed to produce guidelines that would avoid unwarranted sentencing disparities while retaining enough flexibility to permit individualized sentencing when called for by mitigating or aggravating factors.

The Commission began its work in 1985 and submitted guidelines to Congress April 13, 1987. The guidelines will automatically take effect November 1, 1987 unless Congress rejects them.

Part of Congress' charge to the Commission was to project the impact of the guidelines on the prison population. This is a new and possibly unique step in legislation of this kind. It represents an attempt to forecast policy implications—how changing sentencing practices will affect other parts of the system. This article summarizes the Commission's effort.

The guidelines will dramatically alter sentencing practices in the Federal criminal justice system. To determine the effect on actual sentences and prison population, we developed a sophisticated prison impact model. Sentencing information was collected on more than 10,000 recent cases so that the impact of the guidelines could be more accurately forecast.

Straight Probation Sentences Will Decrease

One of the effects of the guidelines will be to reduce straight probation—probation without any conditions of confinement. Under current practice, probation terms that require some confinement include probation with jail as a condition of probation, split sentences, and mixed sentences.

The guidelines create two new types of sentences similar in form to a split sentence. For minimum sentences of no more than 6 months, the defendant may receive a probation term that includes a period of intermittent or community confinement. For minimum sentences of no more than 10 months, the defendant's sentence may be "split" between incarceration and community confinement.

As Figure 1 indicates, 41.4 percent of all convicted defendants currently receive straight probation. After the guidelines are implemented, only 18.5 percent are projected to receive this sentence. Drug law violators offer a dramatic example. Straight probation sentences for convicted drug offenders are projected to fall to 5.1 percent.

For some especially serious crimes, probationary sentences in any form will decline greatly. Currently 41.4 percent of those convicted of crimes against persons receive some form of probation. This proportion is projected to decline to 25.4 percent after the guidelines are implemented. Probation and split sentences for robbery will decline from 26 percent to 5 percent (not specifically shown in Figure 1) and for drug offenses from 33.8 percent to 13.3 percent.

Summary of Projected Impact

■ "Straight" probationary sentences (i.e., sentences that require no form of confinement) will be reduced significantly.

■ For especially serious crimes, such as drug offenses and crimes against persons, probationary sentences will decline dramatically.

■ For other crimes, like property offenses, the proportion of sentences involving some form of probation will not change appreciably, although probation with a condition of confinement may be substituted for straight probation.

■ Average time served for violent offenses will increase substantially. For most property crimes, average time served will remain largely unchanged. Exceptions: burglary and income tax fraud, where average time served will go up.

■ Federal prison populations will grow markedly by the end of this century, more as a result of the Anti-Drug Abuse Act of 1986 and the career offender provision of the Comprehensive Crime Control Act of 1984 than as a result of the guidelines.

Average Time Served Will Increase Somewhat

Time served will increase on average from 15.8 months to 29.3 months under the guidelines, with most of this increase concentrated in a few crimes. For most crimes time served will remain essentially unchanged (see Figure 2).

In estimating the impact of the guidelines on the average length of sentences, we attempted to isolate the effects of the Anti-Drug Abuse Act of 1986 and the career offender provision of the Comprehensive Crime Control Act of 1984. The 1986 drug law significantly increases the minimum and maximum prison terms for most drug offenses. Additionally, the 1984 Act required the Commission to adopt guidelines that would assure that certain repeat offenders—those 18 or older who are convicted of a violent crime or drug offense and who had been convicted of two or more such crimes previously—receive sentences at or near the maximum term authorized. In accordance with this provision, the Commission established for these offenders guideline sentences close to the statutory maximums.

In most cases where neither the drug law nor the career offender provision are applicable, average sentence lengths are not altered radically. For these crimes (firearms, fraud, property, and immigration), the projected reduction in straight probation will be the major impact of the guidelines. More defendants will be confined, but for shorter terms than at present. Their confinement will frequently be in community-based or other minimum-security facilities.

Income tax evasion is the one crime not subject to either the drug law or the career offender provision where the guidelines themselves are projected to have a major impact on average sentence length. The average sentence is projected to more than double from a current level of less than 6 months to approximately 1 year. Not only will probation be reduced and hence the probability of confinement be increased, but the overall amount of confinement will also be increased. This increase in sentencing severity follows from treating income tax evasion like other frauds resulting in comparable dollar losses.

The Guidelines Alone Will Not Have a Major Impact on Prison Population

The precise effect of these changes on overall prison demand is not obvious. For example, a significant increase in the sentence for a crime rarely prosecuted will have little effect on prison demand. By contrast, a small increase or decrease in the average sentence for a frequently prosecuted crime may have a substantial impact.

The Commission has projected prison demand for the years 1992, 1997, and 2002. The projections for 1992 are believed to be the most accurate because prosecution policies are unlikely to change significantly over this time period. This is especially true over the next 3 years, during which the present administration will continue to influence prosecution policies.

Figure 1 Percentage of defendants receiving probation and split sentences under current practices and as projected under the guidelines

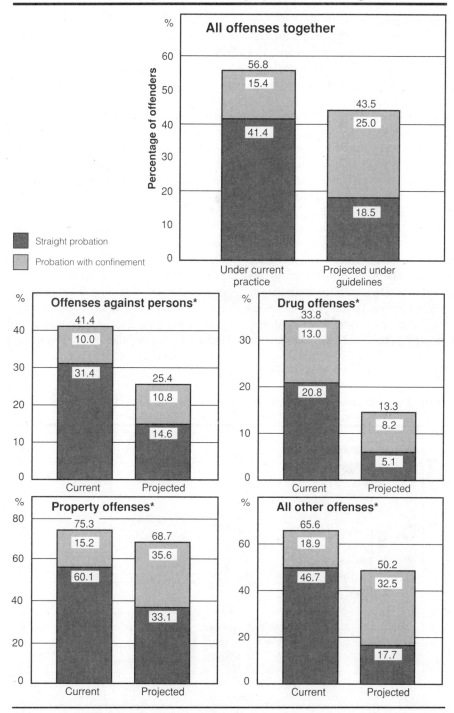

Note: In these charts, straight probation refers to probation without any period of confinement. Probation with confinement refers under current practice to probation with any form of incarceration (with jail as a condition, split sentences, and mixed sentences). Under the guidelines, probation with confinement also includes intermittent confinement or residence in a community treatment center.

*"Offenses against persons" includes homicide, assault, rape, and kidnapping. "Property offenses" includes embezzlement, forgery, property destruction, counterfeiting, and auto theft. "All other offenses" includes robbery, burglary/trespass, fraud, and income tax, firearms, and immigration offenses.

The 10-year projections merit somewhat less confidence. Nevertheless, they provide a general impression about prison demand over a longer time period. The 15-year projections are necessarily very speculative and are presented only so the long-term relative effects of the Anti-Drug Abuse Act, career offender provision of the Comprehensive Crime Control Act of 1984, and guidelines can be considered.

To estimate the impact on the Federal prison system of the guidelines, the Anti-Drug Abuse Act, and the career offender provision, we first had to establish as a "baseline" a projection of future prison demand in the absence of any change in current sentencing practices. Some assumptions necessarily had to be made about the future growth or decline in criminal prosecutions. This is difficult because criminal caseloads are determined by the crime rate, by expenditures on investigative and prosecutorial resources, and by administration policy as carried out by U.S. attorneys. To deal with these unknowns, two different scenarios were considered; one presumed "low growth" in the prosecution rate and the other presumed "high growth."

Figure 3 depicts 15-year prison population projections under low-growth and high-growth assumptions. Projections are given for both existing and future sentencing practices.

Even before considering the effect of these new statutes, prison population under the low-growth scenario is projected to increase 50 percent in the absence of any new statutes or change in sentencing practices.

The new drug law will cause a substantial increase in future prison populations—from 42,000 in 1987 to 85,000 in 1997. The number of inmates will double over the next decade *even under a low-growth assumption and even if the Commission did not exist.*

If we also take into account the career offender provision, *the incremental effect of the guidelines is relatively modest, only about 6 percent in 1992, 3 percent in 1997, and 2 percent in 2002.*

Under the high-growth projections, if prosecutions actually grow at this high rate over the 15-year period, we could expect more than a doubling of the present prison population without any change in sentencing practices.

Figure 2 Time served under current practice and projected impact of recent drug law, career offender provision, and guidelines

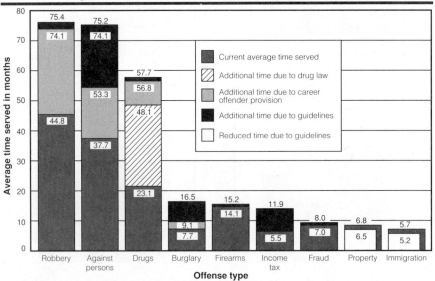

The average time served is reported for all offenders, including those not sentenced to prison, who are counted as having 0 months of imprisonment. Imprisonment includes prison, jail, and community corrections confinement.

Note: The impact of the guidelines on two other offenses is expected to be negative. The average time served for property offenses is expected to go down to 6.5 months from the existing 6.8 months. For immigration offenses, the time served is likely to go down to 5.2 months from the current 5.7.

History of Sentencing Guidelines

The idea of sentencing guidelines is relatively new— dating back a mere 15 years or so in the United States. But the problems guidelines seek to address are not. They result from sentencing practices that have evolved over many decades.

During most of this century, sentencing decisions were based on the idea that each case is unique and requires an individualized sentence, determined primarily by offenders' rehabilitative needs but influenced also be the traditional goals of deterrence, punishment, and incapacitation. Indeterminate sentencing laws were enacted that gave judges the authority to choose from a wide range of sentencing alternatives.

As judges exercised their discretion, very different sentences often were imposed for the same offense or for the same or similar kind of offender. Some disparity seemed to result from race, sex, or economic discrimination. Some plea bargaining decisions and the possibility of early parole also contributed to public perception that sentences were neither predictable nor fair.

Sentencing guidelines emerged as one of a number of solutions proposed by critics of indeterminate sentencing, offering guidance to judges without constraining them with absolute rules.

Guidelines were pioneered in the area of parole, through a 1972 pilot project for the U.S. Parole Commission, sponsored in part by a grant from the National Institute of Justice. To achieve the project's goal—more predictability in Federal parole decisions—researchers drew up "empirical" guidelines based on an analysis of the concerns underlying past parole decisions.

They developed a matrix that contained scales of offense severity and "parole prognosis" (probability of recidivism) on one axis and on the other a range of prison terms from which the prisoner's release date could be chosen. The project was so successful that guidelines were suggested for criminal sentencing decisions as well.

Voluntary Guidelines

In 1974, the National Institute of Justice initiated a series of feasibility studies of voluntary sentencing guidelines. These took place first in the Vermont District Courts and in the District Court in Denver, Colorado. Vermont dropped out, but Chicago, Phoenix, and Newark joined in. Results of the studies were encouraging, and in November 1976 Denver judges adopted voluntary sentencing guidelines—the first local jurisdiction to do so.

In 1979, the National Institute of Justice decided to test the feasibility of voluntary guidelines on a statewide basis in Maryland and Florida. If the same guidelines could be adopted by demographically and culturally diverse counties in these two States, then statewide guidelines were viable, it was reasoned.

Since the statewide guidelines had been devised by judges and were based on judges' previous decisions, it was assumed they would be easily accepted and widely used. Followup evaluations funded by the National Institute of Justice indicated, however, that voluntary guidelines did not have much impact on sentencing outcomes. Pockets of resistance were observed in both States.

Evaluators faulted the voluntary nature of the guidelines and the failure to enlist participation of defense and prose-

---

High-growth projections suggest that, given current trends in prosecutions, future demands on the Federal prisons will exceed present prison capacity by significant proportions. While we treat these projections as the upper limit of future prison demand, they are not beyond the range of experience. Over the last 15 years, the Federal prison population has more than doubled, from more than 20,000 to more than 40,000.

Under this high-growth scenario, the drug law is projected to have a substantial effect on future prison population. Because of the drug law, the prison population is projected to increase by over 17

percent in 1992, 39 percent in 1997, and 46 percent in 2002.

The effects of the guidelines are modest in comparison. Specifically, the additional effect attributable to the guidelines is 7 percent in 1992, 4 percent in 1997, and 4 percent in 2002. Although the impact of the guidelines is somewhat larger under this scenario than under the low-growth scenario, it is still modest. Even the upper bound of the impact of the guidelines on prison population is not likely to be significant. The same cannot be said for the impact of the new drug law, or for that matter, the career offender provision of the Comprehensive Crime Control Act of 1984.

History of Sentencing Guidelines   Continued

cution in guidelines development. Nonetheless, the voluntary guidelines were an important stage in the development of another model, the "sentencing commission" model, first tried by Minnesota.

The Minnesota Experience

Minnesota tackled the disparity issue head on by adopting a system that departed from exclusive reliance on previous sentencing practices, reflected a broad consensus, and encouraged compliance. The State adopted a model which has as its essential features a sentencing commission, presumptive sentencing guidelines, and appellate sentence review.

The sentencing commission is made up of judges, prosecutors, defenders, law enforcement officers, probation/parole agents, and citizens. Both prosecution and defense have a right to appeal a sentence they consider inappropriate. To further maintain consistency and judicial control over sentence implementation, Minnesota abolished parole.

The guidelines the commission submitted to the State Legislature in 1980 were not empirical but reflected instead the commission's own sentencing priorities. It adopted retribution as the dominant sentencing goal, and established very narrow felony sentencing ranges based on the seriousness of the offense and the offender's prior criminal history. The commission further adopted an explicit policy that the guidelines would not result in an increase in prison population.

The commission sought to eliminate race, sex, and economic discrimination by eliminating from sentencing decisions consideration of such personal factors as the of-

fender's education, employment, marital status, or living arrangements.

Use of the Commission Model Elsewhere

Other States have pursued somewhat different courses. For instance, Pennsylvania rejected its commission's narrow guidelines and instead adopted guidelines in 1982 that specify three sentencing ranges—a normal range, an aggravated range, and a mitigated range. Although compliance rates are high, the ranges are so broad that there is still room for considerable disparity. Other States—Maine, New York, and South Carolina—have explored the sentencing commission model but have not successfully implemented it. Connecticut abandoned it in favor of a statutory determinate sentencing system.

Washington State passed guidelines in 1984 that resemble Minnesota's but are slightly broader. The Washington guidelines apply to both felonies and misdemeanors and include statewide prosecutorial charging and bargaining guidelines as well. Compliance with the guidelines has been high in Washington.

The Middle Ground

In many jurisdictions, the development of sentencing guidelines is taking place amid a debate regarding the adoption of more drastic, legislatively mandated determinate sentencing on the one hand, and continuance of indeterminate sentencing on the other. Sentencing guidelines are viewed by many as offering a constructive "middle ground" between these two extremes. The current debate is largely over their substance and their implementation.

Problems in Projecting the Guidelines' Impact

One obvious factor that substantially influences any prison population forecast is the future level of crime. Except for short-term projections, however, no reliable method exists for predicting future crime rates. Moreover, changes in the sentencing structure can be expected to affect crime through deterrence and incapacitation.

Even if future crime rates could be predicted with an acceptable degree of accuracy, historical data indicate a weak relationship between changes in the number of offenses of a given type and changes in the contem-

poraneous level of Federal prosecutions. Such discrepancies result partially from the exercise of discretion by Federal prosecutors and partially from changing enforcement priorities. To the extent that priorities are set by the administration in office, predicting future priorities involves predicting the outcome of future elections and the policies successive administrations will pursue. These highly speculative factors make the forecasting problem especially difficult.

There is also the question of how closely Federal judges will follow the guidelines. Judges may depart from guideline sentences for factors not adequately considered in the guidelines, provided they explain in writing their reasons for departure. While the Commission does not expect departures from the guidelines to

Figure 3   Prison population projections

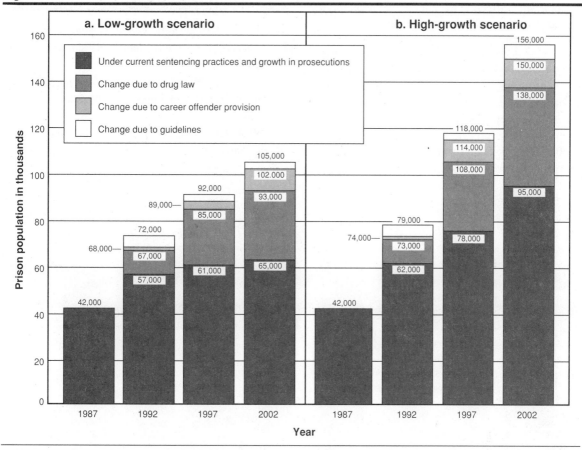

a. Low-growth scenario. The baseline projections for 1987–1989 are based on the average annual growth for the years 1982–1986. Thereafter, criminal cases were assumed to grow at a rate of 1 percent per year.

b. High-growth scenario. The baseline projections for 1987–1991 are based on the average annual growth for 1982–1986. Projections for 1992–2002 are based on the average annual growth that reproduces the same 15-year percentage growth for 1987–2002 that was observed for 1971–1986.

a. Low-growth scenario. The baseline projections for 1987–1989 are based on the average annual growth for the years 1982–1986. Thereafter, criminal cases were assumed to grow at a rate of 1 percent per year.

b. High-growth scenario. The baseline projections for 1987–1991 are based on the average annual growth for 1982–1986. Projections for 1992–2002 are based on the average annual growth that reproduces the same 15-year percentage growth for 1987–2002 that was observed for 1971–1986.

occur with great frequency, it is not known how often they will occur, which direction they will take, and how large they will be. Thus, the discretion to depart from the guidelines, which is integral to the legislation that established the Commission, creates uncertainty about the ultimate impact of the guidelines on actual sentences.

Future plea negotiations are another problem that clouds prison projections. Plea negotiations are an integral part of Federal criminal justice administration.

Recognizing the functional role of plea bargaining, the guidelines attempt to structure the bargaining process, not eliminate its practice. The plea bargaining environment must change under the guidelines, but the nature and extent of the changes are unknowable, creating additional uncertainty for projecting future sentencing practices.

Using sensitivity analysis, we adjusted impact projections to account for the uncertainty inherent in projecting future prison demands in the face of major policy innovations. All the results reported in this article are somewhat affected by alternative assumptions adopted for the sensitivity tests, but the major conclusions are substantively unaffected.

Against the backdrop of these various problems, one might nevertheless fear that any impact projections will be far too speculative to be trusted. But decisionmakers do not have the luxury of adopting this view. Failure to project the impact of the guidelines on sentences and on prison capacity as realistically as possible could convert an imprecise decisionmaking process into a wholly arbitrary one.

Discussion Questions

1. To what does the term *sentencing guidelines* refer?
2. What is the projected influence of guidelines on the federal prison population?
3. Discuss the five most important ways the adoption of guidelines will impact on the federal justice process?
4. What factors cloud projections of the effect guidelines may have on sentencing?

Probation and Alternative Sanctions

Introduction

The origins of probation can be found in English common law, where such devices as benefit of clergy, judicial reprieve, and recognizance were used to mitigate harsh sentences and avoid capital punishment. Subsequently, probation practices were established in the state of Massachusetts in 1841 by John Augustus, who voluntarily supervised and cared for young offenders considered deserving of a second chance. His efforts resulted in the enactment of the first statutory probation program in Massachusetts in 1878. Since that time, probation as a court action and a method of social service has been introduced in all the states and the federal government.

Today, probation is a legal disposition that enables the offender to remain in the community subject to conditions imposed by court order under the supervision of a probation officer. It allows the offender to continue working and providing for his or her family while avoiding the debilitating effects of incarceration. Social services are provided to help the offender adjust in the community; counseling, assistance from social workers, and group treatment, as well as the use of community resources to obtain employment, welfare, and housing, are offered to the offender while on probation. In providing these services, probation officers perform the dual functions of preparing presentencing reports for the court and supervising probationers in the community.

Alternative sanctions have been developed over the past decade to supplement probation because of (1) the failure of the prison system to reduce offender recidivism, (2) prison overcrowding, which has reached a crisis level, and (3) the need to provide some offenders with a correctional experience that is more secure than traditional probation but less confining than prison or jail. There are a variety of alternative sanctions under experimentation in jurisdictions around the United States. The most traditional and commonplace are fines, which have been used as a sole and supplemental sanction since the early origins of the common law. In the 1970s, community service and monetary restitution programs were developed with federal funding and have become institutionalized in a number of local jurisdictions.

In the 1980s, alternative sanctioning became the centerpiece of correctional innovation with the development of house arrest, electronic monitoring, and intensive probation supervision (IPS). While still in the developmental stages, these programs hold tremendous promise as reasonable alternatives to high-security institutions. And while some critics have questioned the legal and ethical implications of monitoring offenders with computers, the personal costs of alternative sanctions must be weighed against the system they are designed to replace: prisons and jails that are highly dangerous, overcrowded, and costly.

This section contains a number of papers analyzing the use of alternative sanctions. First, James M. Byrne provides an overview of traditional probation services. Then Sally T. Hillsman, Barry Mahoney, George F. Cole, and Bernard Auchter review the use of fines—one of the oldest forms of criminal sanctions. Then three papers highlight some of the current methods of alternative sanctioning: Joan Petersilia on house arrest and electronic monitoring; Billie S. Erwin and Lawrence A. Bennett on intensive probation supervision; Douglas C. McDonald on restitution and community service; and Annesley K. Schmidt on electronic monitoring.

National Institute of Justice / CRIME FILE

Probation

James M. Byrne, University of Lowell
1986

In 1985, 1.65 percent of male residents in the United States aged 18 and over were under some form of correctional supervision. Between 1983 and the end of 1985, the overall correctional population increased by nearly 600,000 offenders. Although prison crowding draws both national attention and increased resources, "probation crowding" poses a more immediate threat to the criminal justice process and to community protection.

Probation is the most commonly used sanction in the United States. Nearly three times as many convicted offenders are placed on probation each year as are sentenced to prison and jail combined. In 1985, 64.4 percent of the 2,904,979 adult offenders under correctional supervision were on probation. Both the probation and prison populations have been rising—10.7 and 6 percent, respectively, in 1983 and 7.4 and 8.4 percent, respectively, between 1984 and 1985.

Despite the "get tough" image of recent legislative initiatives, the United States relies primarily on a community-based system of sentencing. The Commissioner of Probation in Massachusetts, Donald Cochran, notes, "It is misleading and perhaps a disservice to talk about probation as an alternative to prison; in fact, our prison system currently functions as a last gasp alternative to the court's primary sanction—probation."

What Is Probation?

"Probation" is generally defined as a sentence served while under supervision in the community. It may include a prison or jail term which has been suspended, although there has been much recent discussion of the merits of defining probation as a sentence in its own right. One recent trend is for judges to use probation as a supplement to a period of incarceration. Combinations of prison and probation usually take one of four forms:

- **Split sentence.** The court specifies a period of incarceration to be followed by a period of probation.
- **Modification of sentence.** The original sentencing court may reconsider an offender's prison sentence within a limited time and modify it to probation.
- **Shock probation.** An offender sentenced to incarceration is released after a period of time in confinement (the shock) and resentenced to probation.
- **Intermittent incarceration.** An offender on probation may spend weekends or nights in a local jail.

The trend toward increased use of "mixed" sentences indicates a shift in both the perception and the purpose of probation. Punishment and community protection now take precedence over rehabilitation as a purpose of sentencing. Concerns of judges and other policymakers for community protection have resulted in dramatic changes in the supervision styles and strategies of probation officers. Many jurisdictions have developed specialized programs for "high risk" offenders, including house arrest, electronic monitoring, and other forms of intensive supervision. Probation officers are now directed to be less concerned with the provision of services for offenders (e.g., counseling, employment assistance) and more concerned with drug testing, curfew violations, employment verifications, arrest checks, surveillance, and revocation procedures. Probation is slowly and necessarily changing.

The Problem of Recidivism

A critical issue concerning probation policy is the extent to which probation can "control" offenders in the community. If probation officers cannot control the illegal behavior of probationers, then increased use of probation to reduce prison crowding seems ill-advised. To address the control issue, a number of related questions must be considered:

■ *What* level of recidivism is acceptable—20 percent, 30 percent, 50 percent?

■ *Who* should be placed on probation—felons (violent, property), misdemeanants, drunk drivers, delinquents?

■ *How long* should the probation department supervise offenders—6 months, 1 year, 5 years?

■ *How much* time, energy, and money should be spent on probation services to achieve an "acceptable" level of control?

Nationwide, roughly equal numbers of felony and misdemeanor probationers are supervised each year in the community, although the mix of offenders on probation varies from State to State. Thus, any comparison of overall failure (or recidivism) rates between States is difficult and often misleading.

Most offenders who are placed on probation succeed in the sense that they complete their probation without incarceration or revocation. Data for 1983 from 20 States reveal that the percentage of adult probationers who successfully completed their terms ranged from 66 percent in Mississippi to 95 percent in Vermont. The percentage of probationers incarcerated for a new offense (or, following revocation, for the original offense) varied from 5 percent in Vermont to 23 percent in Mississippi.

If "success" for probation is gauged by the percentage of probationers who are rearrested or rearraigned—rather than the much smaller percentage who are incarcerated—success rates are more modest. In addition, if administrative cases (such as drunk driving) are deleted from the analysis, even higher failure rates would be identified.

States that use a case classification system usually identify success and failure rates for offenders receiving minimum, moderate, and maximum (and in a number of States, intensive) supervision. In these States, failure rates (e.g., rearrest within 1 year) often are as low as 10 to 15 percent for "minimum" supervision cases and as high as 50 to 60 percent (or more) for maximum or intensive supervision cases.

Recent research reveals that felony probationers often pose significantly higher risks to the community than misdemeanor probationers. A recently completed evaluation of felony probation in California offers a graphic portrait of a probation system without adequate control over certain offenders. The researchers' conclusions deserve careful consideration:

> In our opinion, felons granted probation present a serious threat to public safety. During the 40-month follow-up period of our study, 65 percent of the probationers in our subsample were rearrested, 51 percent reconvicted, 18 percent were reconvicted of serious violent crimes (homicide, rape, weapons offenses, assault, and robbery), and 34 percent were reincarcerated. Moreover, 75 percent of the official charges filed against our subsample involved burglary/theft, robbery, and other violent crimes—the crimes most threatening to public safety. (Joan Petersilia et al. 1984, vii)

If the figures cited above are similar for other States, it is easy to wonder why we continue to put felons on probation.

According to Petersilia, the answer is an amalgam of history, expediency, and sentencing philosophy. First, historically, our prisons have been used for repeat offenders; probation has been the usual sanction for first-time felons.

Second, in many States placing more felons in prison rather than on probation is not a viable alternative. A majority of States are under Federal court order to build new prisons or to limit prison populations.

Third, many judges do not like to impose a prison sentence early in an offender's criminal career. Partly this is because of continued belief in rehabilitation. And partly it is because of the pessimistic view that no matter how great a threat to the community offenders may present at the time of sentencing to probation, the threat will be greater upon their release from prison.

Do prisons make offenders worse? In California, a recent study which examined the comparative failure rates of matched groups of convicted felons in prison and felons on probation supported the notion that imprisonment may increase the likelihood of future offending. Petersilia and Turner (1986) reported that prisoners had a significantly higher recidivism rate (72 percent) than a similar group of felons (including assaulters, robbers, burglars, drug offenders, and individuals convicted of theft) on probation (63 percent). They found no significant differences between groups in the seriousness of crimes committed or in the time before failure (6 months for both).

Restructuring Probation as an Intermediate Sanction

Limited prison and jail resources make it impossible to incarcerate all convicted offenders. One solution is to restructure probation to include a range of increasingly incapacitating community-based "control" programs for offenders who pose a significant threat to public safety.

A wide range of "intensive" community-based sentencing alternatives has been developed by legislators, judges, and correctional administrators. The main impetus has been prison crowding. In many States, probation departments have designed and implemented community-based programs for offenders who would otherwise be sentenced to prison or jail. Almost every State has developed one or more programs with names such as intensive probation supervision, house arrest, day reporting centers, and electronic monitoring. Federal probation agencies have embraced intensive supervision for specific categories of offenders (such as drug and white collar offenders).

Intensive Probation Supervision Programs

Intensive supervision programs are being considered or are in place in almost every State. The best known program is in Georgia. The attraction of the Georgia program is that it seems to accomplish two goals that are often viewed as antithetical:

> (1) restraining the growth of prison populations and associated costs by controlling selected offenders in the community, and (2) at the same time, satisfying to some extent the demand that criminals be punished for their crimes. The pivotal question is whether or not prison-bound offenders can be shifted into Intensive Probation Supervision without threatening the public safety. (Erwin and Bennett 1987, p. 1)

Judges in Georgia sentence an offender directly to intensive supervision. Key features of the Georgia program include a team approach to case management that has separate roles for probation officers and surveillance officers; small caseloads (25 per two-person team in most areas); mandatory curfews, employment, and community service; drug and alcohol monitoring on a regular basis; and five face-to-face contacts per week.

Does the Georgia program successfully control offenders in the community? Erwin and Bennett found that "of the 2,322 people in the program between 1982 and 1985, 370 (or 16 percent) absconded or had their probation revoked" (1987, p. 2). Very few of the "failures" were arrested for committing serious felonies.

Does the Georgia IPS program divert offenders from prison? The Georgia study indicates that there was a 10-percent decrease in the percentage of felons sentenced to incarceration during the study period, along with a corresponding 10-percent increase in probation caseloads statewide (not all the additional probation sentences called for intensive supervision). While these findings are impressive, the target population for the Georgia program was "prison-bound" nonviolent offenders, of whom 43 percent had committed property offenses, 41 percent drug or alcohol offenses, and 9 percent violent crimes. Other States that use IPS for offenders convicted of more violent crimes may not achieve similar results.

Preliminary figures suggest that Georgia's program has been cost effective. The average annual cost of incarcerating an offender in Georgia is $7,760, compared with an annual IPS cost of $985 per offender. Georgia requires probationers to pay probation fees (ranging from $10 to $50 per month), and these fees have been used to pay for the Georgia program.

Other IPS program models have been developed. In New Jersey's program, the offender is sentenced, incarcerated, and then allowed to "apply" to a resentencing panel for placement into the IPS program. The rationale is that a reduction of prison or jail populations can be assured if offenders are taken directly out of prison. Otherwise judges may sentence offenders to intensive supervision who would not have been incarcerated, thereby frustrating the goal of reducing prison crowding by diverting prison-bound offenders to IPS.

According to a preliminary evaluation of New Jersey's program by Pearson (1987), there are 31 contacts per month between probation officers, and probationers (including 12 face-to-face, 7 curfew, and 4 urinalysis checks). Other features of this model include:

■ Development of plans for life in the community (work, study, community services, etc.).

■ A requirement of full-time employment or vocational training and community service.

■ The use of a community sponsor and other support persons who will provide extensive assistance and direction to each participant.

Preliminary findings were revealing. Approximately 600 offenders have entered the program since it began. About one-third were returned to prison for technical violations before they completed their 18 months in the program. Overall, about 1 in 10 offenders committed a new crime, and 1 in 20 committed a new felony while under intensive supervision. The cost estimates for the New Jersey program are much higher than the cost associated with Georgia's program— $13,693 per year for an intensive supervision case, compared with $19,958 to $20,851 for an incarcerated offender (Pearson 1987, table 1).

Massachusetts offers a third approach to intensive supervision. The key features are that assignment to IPS occurs *after* the offender is placed on probation. The target population includes property offenders, drug offenders, and violent offenders (35 percent). Contact levels include four face-to-face and six collateral contacts per month.

Electronic Monitoring and House Arrest Programs

Electronic monitoring and house arrest programs exist in many States as separate programs, distinct from intensive probation supervision. These programs are more a demonstration of the fragmented nature of program development in the courts and corrections than a comprehensive effort to develop a range of new intermediate sanctions. A recent nationwide review of intensive probation supervision programs revealed a continuing trend by program developers to add both of these features to existing IPS programs.

Nationwide, only a small percentage of the probation population is being monitored, either by a person or by an electronic device. However, it is possible to envision both kinds of programs, along with intensive supervision, as successive steps in an increasingly intrusive community control program. In such a system, offenders' initial placement in a particular level of institutional or community control might be determined by a judge, with subsequent movement from the community to prison or from the prison back to the community determined by the offender's behavior. This procedure would continue the attempt to balance offender risk with appropriate punishment.

Taken together, the foregoing programs provide an intermediate set of punishments that offer the monitoring and incapacitation features of prison and the offender rehabilitation prospects of probation.

Discussion Questions

1. By subjecting offenders to intrusive conditions— unannounced drug testing, frequent contacts with probation officers, curfews—some intensive probation supervision programs are designed to be intermediate punishments that can be imposed instead of prison sentences. Can intrusive conditions like these make a probation sentence equivalent to a prison sentence?

2. What kinds of offenders should be sentenced to IPS and other intermediate punishments?

3. Because of the need to address prison crowding, some IPS programs are designed for offenders who would otherwise be sent to prison. Critics of such programs argue that they are often used instead for offenders who would otherwise receive *less* punitive sentences. This practice is sometimes said to "widen the net of social control." Is net widening necessarily bad?

4. Would you want your State to establish an IPS program?

5. What, in your view, should the purpose of probation be?

References

Bureau of Justice Statistics. 1984. "Probation and Parole 1983." U.S. Department of Justice, Bureau of Justice Statistics *Bulletin* (September). Washington, D.C.: U.S. Government Printing Office.

_____. 1987. "Probation and Parole 1985." U.S. Department of Justice, Bureau of Justice Statistics *Bulletin* (January). Washington, D.C.: U.S. Government Printing Office.

Byrne, James M. 1986. "The Control Controversy: A Preliminary Examination of Intensive Probation Supervision Programs in the United States." *Federal Probation* June: 1–16.

Clear, Todd R., and George F. Cole. 1986. *American Corrections*. Monterey, California: Brooks/Cole Publishing Company.

Cochran, Donald, Ronald Corbett, and James Byrne. 1986. "Intensive Probation Supervision in Massachusetts: A Case Study in Change." *Federal Probation* June: 32–41.

Corbett, Ronald J. 1985. "Punishment Without Prison: The Use of House Arrest." *Federal Probation* March: 13–17.

Erwin, Billie S., and Lawrence A. Bennett. 1987. "New Dimensions in Probation: Georgia's Experience with Intensive Probation Supervision (IPS)." U.S. Department of Justice, National Institute of Justice *Research in Brief* (January). Washington, D.C.: U.S. Government Printing Office.

McCarthy, Belinda R., editor. 1987. *Intermediate Punishments: Intensive Supervision, Home Confinement and Electronic Surveillance*. Monsey, New York: Willow Tree Press.

O'Leary, Vincent, and Todd Clear. 1984. Directions for Community Corrections in the 1990's. U.S. Department of Justice, National Institute of Corrections. Washington, D.C.: U.S. Government Printing Office.

Pearson, Frank S. 1987. "Preliminary Findings of Research on New Jersey's Intensive Supervision Program." M.S. on file.

Brunswick, N.J.: Rutgers University, Institute of Criminological Research.

Pearson, Frank S., and Daniel B. Bibel. 1986. "New Jersey's Intensive Supervision Program: What is it like? How is it Working?" *Federal Probation* June: 25–31.

Petersilia, Joan, and Susan Turner (with Joyce Peterson). 1986. *Prison versus Probation in California: Implications for Crime and Offender Recidivism*. Santa Monica, California: Rand Corporation.

Petersilia, Joan, Susan Turner, and James Kahan. 1985. *Granting Felons Probation: Public Risk and Alternatives*. Santa Monica, California: Rand Corporation.

National Institute of Justice

Research in Brief

Fines as Criminal Sanctions

Sally T. Hillsman, Vera Institute of Justice, Barry Mahoney, Institute for Court Management,
George F. Cole, University of Connecticut and Bernard Auchter, National Institute of Justice
September 1987

The fine is one of the oldest forms of punishment, its history predating Hammurabi. In 1973 the Task Force on Corrections of the National Advisory Commission on Criminal Justice Standards and Goals found that "properly employed, the fine is less drastic, far less costly to the public, and perhaps more effective than imprisonment or community service."

Until very recently, this recommendation has gone largely unheeded because too little was known of what constitutes proper administration of fines. Today, however, with record jail and prison populations and probation caseloads steadily rising, the fine is gaining renewed attention—especially since Western Europe increasingly uses fines even in nontrivial cases.

In the United States, fines are more widely used than many recognize: Well over a billion dollars in fines are collected in criminal courts each year. This form of punishment is used in some form by virtually all American courts, ranging from its rare use as the sole sanction for a felony in general jurisdiction courts to its regular use either alone or combined with other, often noncustodial sanctions in courts of limited jurisdiction.

How can fines be used more effectively in criminal cases? In the studies summarized in this *Research in Brief*, researchers describe and analyze court experience with imposition and enforcement of fines, concluding that judges and prosecutors need to consider more innovative uses of fines, particularly when offenders pose no serious threat to community safety.

An effective fine program requires that judges have adequate information about offenders' economic circumstances and use it in setting fine amounts. It also requires improved collection methods. The result can relieve pressure on probation services and jails while promoting confidence that sentences are fair and punishment is certain.

Pros and Cons

Proponents of the wider use of fines argue that—

■ It can be an effective punishment and deterrent for crimes of varying levels of severity. It can deprive offenders of their ill-gotten gains and, for some, contribute to rehabilitation.

■ It can combine with other noncustodial sanctions to meet multiple sentencing goals.

■ It can be adjusted to a level appropriate to an offender's individual circumstances and the seriousness of the offense.

■ It is relatively inexpensive to administer, usually relying on existing agencies and procedures.

■ It is financially self-sustaining; unlike incarceration and probation, fines produce revenue.

However, critics argue that—

■ Because fines cannot achieve the sentencing goal of incapacitation, they are inappropriate for offenders who pose a risk to the community.

■ Even when incapacitation is not the goal, fines tend to be low, thus limiting their degree of punishment.

■ Fines are easier for more affluent offenders to pay than for poorer offenders.

■ If a fine is high enough to avoid those problems, it is difficult to collect and adds to the administrative burdens of the court.

■ It is impossible to fine indigent offenders because the fine cannot be collected and may result in imprisonment for default.

These conflicting views reflect different perceptions of how fines actually work and their potential utility. Recent research on the use of fines, here and abroad, provides a base for improving policy and practice in this area.

Current Uses of Fines

A survey of 126 different types of courts around the country shows fines being used extensively (see Table 1), including use for a broad range of criminal offenses some of which are not trivial (see Table 2).

Judges in courts of limited jurisdiction report they impose fines, either alone (36 percent) or in combination with another penalty, in an average of 86 percent of their sentences. General jurisdiction judges report imposing fines about half as often (42 percent); fines as a sole penalty in less than 10 percent on average.

Fines are most often imposed on first offenders with known ability to pay. A third or more judges overall report imposing a fine in more than half the cases in which an adult first offender is sentenced for offenses such as these:

- Sale of an ounce of cocaine.
- Fraud in a land deal.
- Embezzlement of $10,000.
- Assault with minor injury.
- Auto theft of $5,000 value.
- Harassment.
- Bad check.

However, fines are not now being used in American courts as an alternative to incarceration or probation. If fines are used at all in cases at risk of imprisonment or community supervision, they tend to be add-ons to other sanctions. Few judges seem to use the fine alone if the offender has a prior record and the offense is moderately serious.

This contrasts sharply with practices in some Western European criminal courts where the fine is often a sole penalty and is widely used for repeat offenders.

As a policy matter, fines are viewed as an alternative to short-term imprisonment. In West Germany, when new legislation encouraged judges to avoid sentences to imprisonment of 6 months or less, such sentences dropped from 113,000 a year (20 percent of the total) to under 11,000 (1.8 percent) without any increase in longer term imprisonment.

Instead, fine-alone sentences increased from 63 percent of the total to more than 80 percent.[1]

Amounts of Fines

Most State penal codes set maximum amounts of fines for particular classes of offenses. Within that maximum, judges have wide discretion in setting the amounts of fines. Maximums tend to be low, although legislatures in many States are increasing them in anticipation that judges will need higher amounts to fine better-off offenders.

Fines actually imposed by judges tend to be well below statutory limits, partially reflecting the frequent judicial practice of imposing other monetary penalties as part of the sentence. These include restitution, victim compensation, court costs, directed contributions to governmental or private social agencies, probation supervision fees, and payment for alcohol or drug treatment.

---

1. Robert W. Gillespie, "Fines as an alternative to incarceration: The Gernman experience," *Federal Probation* 44,4 (December 1980): 20-26.

Table 1 Frequency of fine utilization for cases other than parking and routine traffic matters, by type of court

Type of court	All or virtually all cases	Most cases	About half	Seldom	Never	Total
Limited Jurisdiction	19	38	10	7	0	74
General jurisdiction (felony, misdemeanor, ordinance violation)	1	15	7	5	0	28
General jurisdiction (felony only)		0	5	4	13	2 24
Total	20	58	21	25	2	126

Source: Hillsman, Sichel, and Mahoney, telephone survey

Table 2   Types of offenses for which fines are commonly imposed, by type of court

	Limited juris. N = 74	Gen. juris. (felony, misd., and ordinance) N = 28	Gen. juris. (felony only) N = 24	Total N = 126
Driving while intoxicated/DUI	54	22	2	78
Reckless driving	30	9	0	39
Violation of fish and game laws and other regulatory ordinances	24	3	0	27
Disturbing the peace/breach of the peace/disorderly conduct	32	8	1*	41
Loitering/soliciting prostitution	15	4	0	19
Drinking in public/public drunkenness/ carrying an open container	14	5	0	19
Criminal trespass	10	2	1	13
Vandalism/criminal mischief/malicious mischief/property damage	9	3	3	15
Drug-related offenses (including sale and possession)	23	10	11	44
Weapons (illegal possession, carrying concealed, etc.)	6	2	1	9
Shoplifting	17	3	0	20
Bad checks	14	2	0	16
Other theft	19	9	8	36
Forgery/embezzlement	2	3	2	7
Fraud	1	4	1	6
Assault	29	14	5	48
Burglary/breaking and entering	2	6	6	14
Robbery	0	1	3	4

*Superior Court, Cobb County—1 percent of caseload includes misdemeanors
Source: Hillsman, Sichel, and Mahoney, telephone survey

At least 31 States authorize imposition of court costs; 11 States authorize surcharges on fines; 7 States permit "penalty assessments" on offenders. One Texas judge explained why he used fines infrequently: "After paying $56 court costs, $10 fee to the Crime Victim Compensation Fund, $200 public defender fee, and $100 to $500 in probation supervision fee, the defendant will be sufficiently punished."

"Tariff systems," however, appear to account more than other factors both for the low amounts imposed as fines in the United States and the limited use of fines as sanctions.

Tariff systems are informal understandings that fixed fine amounts will be imposed on all defendants convicted of a particular offense. These amounts are generally based on what can be paid by the poorest offenders. But the retributive trend in sentencing tends to focus judges' attention on the severity of a crime.

Lacking models of other ways to set fine amounts and also often lacking adequate financial information on defendants, judges apparently limit their use of the fine because tariff systems restrict their ability to reflect the seriousness of a crime.

Information for Sentencing

Judges were asked to indicate how often they were provided information on an offender's background and economic status and how useful they found this information.

In all courts, judges were more likely to have information about criminal records and the instant offense than about the offender's family and economic status. In fact, although courts of limited jurisdiction are more likely to assess fines, general jurisdiction judges have more economic information (Table 3).

In both kinds of courts, judges said the criminal record and circumstance of the offense are the most helpful information in determining the sentence and that the assets and income of the offender are the *least useful* information.

In view of the tariff system, this opinion is less anomalous than it might seem. If the variation in amounts of fines is limited and is related primarily to the seriousness of offenses, judges would have relatively little use at sentencing for information on offenders' economic status.

This in turn may explain the lack of consideration judges give to fines as sole sanctions for repeat offenders convicted of nontrivial crimes. If we are to explore policies emphasizing fines as a primary sanction and as an alternative to incarceration and probation, we must help judges routinely obtain information on offenders' economic circumstances and to increase the weight such information is given.

Obtaining financial information is relatively simple. Many European courts have been accomplishing these tasks smoothly for years, often in order to use a system of fine-setting known as "day fines."

Under day-fine systems, the number of fine *units* (or severity of punishment) is determined by the seriousness of the offense but *without regard to the offender's means*. The *monetary* value of each unit is then set explicitly in relation to what the offender can afford.

In Europe, this second stage relies primarily on self-reported information. These courts, which use fines extensively and in high amounts, find that reliance on

defendants to provide information on their economic status is not a barrier to the wider imposition of fines.

Judges' Attitudes on Fines

Judges across this country acknowledge many of the supposed advantages of fines as sentences. Furthermore, they disagree with many of the arguments against them. However, there seems to be little relationship between judges' attitudes toward fines and their use of them.

Judges tend to agree that fines are relatively easy to administer, that they help prevent crowding in correctional facilities, that they can be adjusted to fit the severity of the offense and the offender's income, and that fines help reimburse the costs of maintaining the criminal justice system.

The majority of judges also *disagreed* that statutes prevented them from imposing high fines, that decisions of the U.S. Supreme Court prevented their fining poor people, and that fines have no rehabilitative effect.

The survey revealed, however, that two views about fines commonly held among judges are a major impediment to the wider use of fines: That fines allow more affluent offenders to "buy their way out," and that poor offenders cannot pay fines.

Over half the judges agreed that "fines ordinarily have little impact on the affluent offender"—61 percent in courts of general jurisdiction and 53 percent in limited jurisdiction. While 61 percent of general jurisdiction judges agreed that "there is no effective way to enforce fines against poor people," half the limited jurisdiction judges—who do most of the fining in American courts—disagreed.

Upper-court judges are charged with sentencing offenders who are convicted of the more serious range of offenses. They would tend to hold the traditional assumption that high fine amounts are required to reflect offense severity and to regard it as unreasonable to assess such amounts on the poor. Equity considerations would also suggest to these judges that they cannot sentence more affluent offenders to significantly higher fine amounts.

While these same issues arise in the lower courts, they are probably less of an impediment because of the more limited range of seriousness of offenses dealt with in these jurisdictions. The low fine amounts in these courts reflect less serious offenses; they are viewed as

Table 3 Judges' information on offenders' economic status, by jurisdiction

	General (%)	Limited (%)
Employment	88	64
Income	74	41
Assets	57	25

Source: Cole, Mahoney, Thornton, and Hanson, mail survey

collectable from poorer offenders and, as tariffs, may be applied to the more affluent as well.

The survey revealed, finally, that judges' attitudes about fines, whether positive or negative, are not held very intensely. Until very recently, there has been little systematic examination of fine use and administration and virtually no attention to the potential advantages, disadvantages, or operational implications of expanded use of fines.

Collection and Enforcement

Among criminal sanctions, monetary penalties are typically the only ones implemented primarily by the court. For most other sanctions, the sentencing judge relies on another agency of government, usually in the executive branch, to see that the sentence is carried out.

The effectiveness of fine administration has important implications for the fine as a penal sanction and for the court as an institution. A fine is a court order. If it is not paid, the integrity and credibility of the court is called into question.

If fines *are* collected and enforcement regarded seriously, on the other hand, the resulting punishment may have rehabilitative value and deterrent consequences. If fines are known to be collected, judges and prosecutors may be more likely to see them as a useful alternative to incarceration or probation.

Finally, the payment of fines may be seen by the community as an important means of rendering deserved punishment while reimbursing the public treasury.

Many judges perceive problems in fine collection and enforcement procedures, but they are generally unaware what practices are effective. Research in the United States and in England emphasizes, for example, that aspects of the sentencing process itself are associated with the subsequent effectiveness of fine collection. These include setting the amount at a level the offender is able to pay, making only limited use of installment payment plans, and allowing relatively short periods of time for payment. However, such practices are not commonly followed by American courts.

Effective Enforcement

What can be done if the offender fails to pay a fine? Research in England and West Germany indicates that simple procedures, such as prompt notification to an offender that payments are in arrears, have positive results. Full payment occurs in many cases without further, more coercive and costly action.

In American courts, however, routine notification letters are not common. Instead courts tend to move immediately to issuance of an arrest warrant for the offender who has not paid. Sixty-eight percent of upper court judges and 85 percent of lower court judges said this was their procedure.

Reliance on warrants raises several important policy issues, including relationships within the justice system. Although enforcement of a warrant is important to the court, evidence abounds that serving a warrant for nonpayment of a fine has low priority for law enforcement agencies. And American courts generally give little professional administrative attention to enforcing fines.

A major reason for this is that many professional court administrators dislike taking the role of bill collector when the administrative costs may be greater than the amount of the fine. As a result, courts rarely designate one person or position as having ultimate responsibility for overseeing the outcome of a sentence to a fine and for seeing to it that the process is properly carried out.

Thus, no one is responsible or accountable if enforcement breaks down. There are few incentives to make fining a success, but rather incentives to pass the enforcement task on to someone else—to the police via an arrest warrant, for example.

Judges tend to view the actions of offenders as the major fine-collection problem rather than inadequacies in the court's administrative mechanisms. Sentencing judges tend not to be familiar with the administrative tasks involved in enforcing fines except when defendants in default are brought before their bench.

However, research both in England and in the United States indicates that sound administrative procedures must be set for fines to be collected routinely. It should be possible to do this without overly burdensome costs or undesirable levels of coercion.

Assuming fines are set properly in the first place with respect to the offense and to the offender's means, the court must make plain at sentencing that it views the fine as a serious obligation for which it unequivocally expects payment. Otherwise, specific coercive means will be employed.

The offender's payments must be closely monitored by people who take the collection responsibility seriously and who are held accountable for it. When an offender does not meet the terms set by the court, enforcement actions would be immediate and personal, with a steady progression of responses creating mounting pressure and increased threats of greater coercion.

Careful tracking of payments, swift notification by letter and telephone that payments are due, and credible threats of greater coercion (including the seizure of property) are effective. Research suggests that most nonpayment cases result from improperly set fines, administrative ineptitude, and failure to credibly threaten at the proper time.

Fines and Fairness

Many persons convicted of criminal offenses are poor. To what extent is it feasible to impose a fine and enforce it as a punishment for criminal behavior by such persons?

Being poor does not necessarily mean being entirely without financial resources. There are varying degrees of poverty, somewhat obscured by uniform application of the label "indigent."

Some poor people have income for comforts as well as necessities. Others have few comforts, but manage on small budgets. Still others are destitute, people who have no home and receive no social services. At the low end of the poverty spectrum—where we find a group of offenders who are in extreme need—fines are probably inappropriate, unless the offense is trivial and a nominal fine can be suspended.

Fines are meaningful elsewhere along the spectrum, however, even for persons with income well below the poverty line—including welfare recipients, the working poor, the temporarily or seasonally unemployed.

A fine imposed on a member of these groups may require substantial economy—and it should do so if it is to be truly a punishment. But paying a fine need not require grave hardship if it is tailored not only to the offense but also to the offender's resources.

At the other end of the spectrum are those offenders who are not by any conventional definition poor. Significant amounts of fines may be required to ensure an appropriate sanction in these cases, even if the offense is not major.

Many judges recognize these realities and tend to focus on a defendant's ability to pay a particular fine

rather than whether he or she is too poor to be fined at all. Indeed, poor people *are* being fined both in this country and in Europe, although both practices and views vary considerably.

Most judges surveyed indicated that they would be less likely to impose a fine if the defendant was unemployed or on public assistance—but 38 percent of the limited jurisdiction court judges said that this would make no difference in their sentencing decision. Another 6 percent said it would increase the likelihood they would impose a fine.

In order to develop an effective fine policy, we must think of offenders as ranging along a spectrum of economic circumstances as well as along a spectrum of offense severity and culpability. Only thus can prosecutors and judges think of fines not as a penalty for less serious crimes or an addition to other penalties, but as an integral part of their sentencing repertoire.

Table 4 shows how judges tend to think now. However, there would seem to be some potential for reducing the use of incarceration in cases such as this in which the criminal behavior carried a low risk of danger yet the offense seems to require punishment and not merely an admonition.

Experiences of courts in several Western European countries provide tested sentencing methods—particularly the use of the day fine—that could enable American judges to tailor fine amounts more precisely to variations in both severity of offenses and means of offenders.

The Day Fine

The day-fine system is a Scandinavian sentencing practice that has been adapted for use in West Germany. It enables sentencing judges to impose monetary punishments commensurate with the seriousness of the offenses and the culpability of the offender, while at the same time taking account of offenders' differing economic circumstances.

The basic notion is that the punishment should be proportionate to the severity of the offense but equal across individuals with differing financial resources.

Consider two offenders with similar criminal histories convicted of similar offenses but with different incomes and assets. Both would be "fined" the same number of units of punishment; however, the one who is more affluent would be fined a total dollar amount that is greater than the poorer offender is fined.

Table 4   Judges' choice of sanctions in hypothetical larceny case, by type of court

The hypothetical case: A 24-year-old male defendant is charged with larceny and criminal possession of stolen property. He is alleged to have removed a $40 pair of slacks from a department store, concealing them in a box that had a forged store receipt and leaving without paying. He was arrested outside the store. The defendant pleaded guilty to the criminal possession charge and the larceny charge was dropped.

Custody status: On $1,000 bail.

Family status: Single with no dependents.

Employment status: Janitor earning $160 per week.

Offender's record:	1979	Bad check	Convicted—restitution.
	1980	Bad check	Dismissed.
	1981	Larceny	Convicted—6 months probation.
	1982	Larceny	Convicted—1 year probation.

The instruction: On the basis of this information we would like your estimate of the sanction you would likely impose.

Sanction	General juris. N = 631 judges		Limited juris. N = 478 judges	
	%	N	%	N
Jail/prison only	40	252	27	130
Jail/prison plus fine	15	92	27	130
Jail/prison plus fine plus other	18	112	23	111
Jail/prison plus sanctions other than fine	17	109	11	54
Fine only	2	15	4	20
Fine plus sanctions other than jail	5	34	6	28
Other sanctions, alone or in combination, not including jail, prison, or fine	3	17	1	5
Total	100	631	100	478

Source: Cole, Mahoney, Thornton, and Hanson, mail survey

In the event of default, however, the sanctions imposed (e.g., jail time) would be the same for both because they would be based on the number of units of punishment, not the dollar amount.

Could European day-fine systems be adapted to American courts? About four out of five judges agreed that one of the advantages to fines is that they can be adjusted to fit the income of offenders as well as the severity of offenses. We can observe individual judges around the country attempting to do just this by modifying tariff systems to approximate the more formal day-fine systems of Europe.

U.S. judges cannot always accomplish this in a systematic fashion, partly because of the lack of routine information on offenders' means. But many judges (and prosecutors) around the country appear to be open to the idea; over half the judges felt a day fine could work in their own courts, and many said they were willing to try it.

The day-fine concept is attracting increased attention among American criminal justice planners and practitioners as they struggle with the problems of crowding in jails and prisons and as they become more dissatisfied with present sentencing alternatives.

A first effort to test the concept scientifically in American courts is underway in Staten Island, New York, with support from the National Institute of Justice, where a day-fine experiment is being planned by the Vera Institute of Justice in collaboration with the Richmond County District Attorney and the Richmond County Criminal Court.

Recommendations for Judges

■ Fines and other monetary sanctions are punishments and should be imposed high enough to reflect the seriousness of the offense and the prior record of the offender. At the same time, the amount must be within the offender's ability to pay.

■ In setting the fine, accurate information on the offender's economic status should be sought and the total of all monetary sanctions taken into account.

■ The defendant should be informed that prompt payment is expected, be told where to pay it, and advised of the consequences of nonpayment. The time allowed for payment should be relatively short, although unusual circumstances may suggest some flexibility.

Incentives should be used to encourage prompt payment. They may include reductions for early payment, penalties for lateness, and imposition of a suspended sentence to jail or community service.

■ Judges should use data on sentencing practices to periodically reexamine the ways they use fines, both alone and combined with other sentences.

Recommendations for Court Administrators and Clerks

■ Courts should ascertain what offender-related information is regularly provided to sentencing judges. Where there are gaps such as lack of information on offender income and assets, procedures should be devised to ensure that such information is consistently provided. For example, a probation department, pretrial services agency, or defense counsel could provide the information on a simple one-page form.

■ Judges should be regularly given data on the types of sanctions imposed on offenders convicted of specific types of crimes.

■ Using individual case records, fines-management information systems should be developed, containing six basic types of data: sentence imposed, inventory information, input-output informa-

tion, effectiveness in collecting fines, processing times and procedures, and identification of problem cases. Courts should improve collection methods, and sentencing judges should be aware of the methods used.

■ Administrative responsibility for enforcing monetary sanctions should be clearly fixed, with a senior member of administrative staff held accountable for the court's performance.

■ Goals for effective fine administration (e.g., percentage of cases in which fines are fully collected within 30 or 60 days) should be set, and the court's enforced performance monitored against these goals.

■ Procedures should be established to identify defaulters promptly and institute action against them.

■ Courts should make direct contact with offenders who fail to pay within the time period set. Prompt, noncoercive reminder letters and phone calls should be tried before a warrant issues. Judges should be fully aware of the procedures and their effectiveness.

Recommendations for Legislation

■ Where statutory ceilings on fine amounts are low, these should be raised.

■ Judges should be required to take account of offenders' economic circumstances in imposing fines and other monetary sanctions.

■ Statutory restrictions on the use of the fine as a sole sanction for specific offenses should be removed.

■ Statutes that provide for flat "dollars-to-days" equivalencies when fine balances are unpaid should be revised to ensure that offenders convicted of similar offenses and with similar prior records should serve essentially similar jail terms in the event of default.

■ Courts should undergo a periodic outside audit at least every 2 years to ensure that records are adequately maintained and that appropriate procedures are followed in enforcing fines and handling the money paid.

■ State court administrators should be explicitly authorized to establish basic minimum standards or requirements for recordkeeping and statistical reporting.

Discussion Questions

1. Discuss the pros and cons of using fines as a criminal sanction.

2. What are the current uses of fines? Could fines ever be an appropriate sanction for violent crimes?

3. What steps can be taken to make the collection of fines more effective?

4. What is a day fine and how can it improve the sanctioning options of the criminal courts?

National Institute of Justice / CRIME FILE

House Arrest

Joan Petersilia, The Rand Corporation
1988

What Is House Arrest and Why Is It So Popular?

As prison crowding worsens, the pressure to divert nondangerous offenders to community-based alternatives has increased. Since it is generally agreed that the public is in no mood to coddle criminals, such alternatives must be tough and punitive and not compromise public safety. House arrest sentencing is seen by many as meeting these criteria.

House arrest is a sentence imposed by the court in which offenders are legally ordered to remain confined in their own residences. They are usually allowed to leave their residences only for medical reasons and employment. They may also be required to perform community service or to pay victim restitution or probation supervision fees. In at least 20 States, "electronic bracelets" are being used to detect violations of house arrest.

While the goal of "house arrest" is easily understood—to restrict freedom—the mechanisms used to confine an offender to his home vary considerably. Typically, offenders participating in Intensive Probation Supervision programs are required to be in their residences during evening hours and on weekends. House arrest programs of this type now exist in Georgia, New Jersey, and Illinois.

In some instances, curfews are added to the offender's court-ordered parole or probation conditions. While curfews permit individual freedom in the community except for particular hours, more intrusive home incarceration programs restrict the offender's freedom in all but court-approved limited activities. These more intrusive programs now exist in Kentucky, Utah, Michigan, Oregon, and California. Several have been modeled on the house arrest program operated by the State of Florida.

Florida's Community Control Program

Florida's house arrest program, known as "Community Control," was established in 1983 to help alleviate prison crowding in the State. It is the most ambitious program of its type in the country, with about 5,000 offenders "locked up" in their homes on any one day. Leonard Flynn oversees the program's operations for the Florida Department of Corrections.

Florida's program targets "incarceration-bound" offenders, including misdemeanants and felons. Each offender is supervised by a community control officer, whose primary function is to ensure that the offender is adhering to court-ordered house arrest restrictions. The community control officer works nights and weekends to monitor compliance. For the more serious offenders, an electronic monitoring system is used. This system operates by having a central computer randomly telephone the offender during designated hours. The offender responds to the telephone call by placing a receiving module (contained in a watch-like wristband) into a modem. The computer verifies the action via a remote printer.

Offenders are permitted to leave their residences only for court-approved employment, rehabilitation, or community service activities. Participants must pay monthly supervision fees of $30 to $50 to offset the costs of supervision, pay restitution to victims, and provide for their own and their family's support.

Officials in Florida consider the house arrest program to be a resounding success. Since 70 percent of those 10,000 persons were believed likely to have been sent to prison otherwise, real cost savings have been realized. In Florida, it costs about $3 per day to supervise a house arrest offender, compared with $28 per day for imprisonment.

Florida's success, coupled with the intense pressure that nearly every State is feeling to reduce prison commitments, ensures that interest in house arrest will continue to grow. An additional impetus is provided by manufacturers of electronic monitoring equipment, who promote their products as a means to achieve public safety without incurring exorbitant costs. Consequently, it is important to consider the major advantages and disadvantages of house arrest programs as well as the larger conceptual issues that such sentencing practices raise.

Advantages of House Arrest

Cost Effectiveness.   The surge of interest in house arrest programs has come primarily from their financial appeal. House arrest (particularly without electronic monitoring) is thought to be highly cost effective. If the offender was truly prison bound, then the State saves not only the yearly cost of housing the offender (on average about $10,000 to $15,000 per year) but also reduces the pressure to build new prisons (at about $50,000 per bed).

If electronic monitoring equipment is used, house arrest is not as cost effective. The equipment is currently quite expensive. For instance, Kentucky spent $32,000 for 20 electronic devices, and Albuquerque, New Mexico, paid $100,000 for its first 25 monitor/bracelet sets.

However, manufacturers argue that such figures are misleading, since they reflect high "startup" costs that will decline as usage increases. Manufacturers also say that it is misleading to look only at the system's direct costs. Most house arrest programs require the offender to be employed. Such offenders continue to pay taxes and may be required to make restitution payments and pay probation supervision fees. Moreover, offenders can continue to support their families, saving the State possible welfare expenditures.

We do not now have sufficient information to compute the actual costs of house arrest programs. Nationwide figures show that house arrest programs without electronic monitoring cost anywhere from $1,500 to $7,000 per offender per year. House arrest with electronic monitoring costs $2,500 to $8,000. But these operational costs do not include the cost of processing any recidivists. According to recent estimates, the cost averages $2,500 for each recidivist rearrested and processed.

At this point we know that administering house arrest costs less than confinement in either State or local facilities, but the indirect costs that such programs entail have not been quantified.

Social benefits.   Most advocates believe that house arrest programs are "socially cost effective." A defendant who had a job before he was convicted can keep it during and after house arrest. By preventing the breakup of the family and family networks, house arrest can also prevent psychological and physical disruptions that may have lasting effects on the offender, the spouse, the children, and even the next generation.

Furthermore, house arrest has none of the corrupting or stigmatizing effects associated with prison. This is a particular advantage for first offenders who may not yet be committed to a life of crime. They will not come under the influence of career criminals or be exposed to the physical or sexual assaults of prison inmates. Keeping offenders from the criminogenic effects of prison was one of the major reasons Oregon and Kentucky officials devised house arrest programs for drunken drivers.

Most of those operating house arrest programs view the foregoing as an important advantage. While prisons are not designed to scar inmates psychologically, many believe this happens. If it does, avoiding this psychological damage is a desirable social goal, especially for young, inexperienced, or first-time offenders. If we could devise a sentence that would make such emotional scars less likely or less common without compromising public safety, surely it would be preferred.

Responsiveness to local and offender needs.   House arrest is flexible. It can be used as a sole sanction or as part of a package of sentencing conditions. It can be used at almost any point in the criminal justice process—as a diversion before an offender experiences any jail time, after a short term in jail, after a prison term (usually joined with work release), or as a condition for probation or parole.

House arrest can also be used to cover particular times of the day, or particular types of offenders. This is an attractive option for controlling offenders who are situationally dangerous. The drunk driver, the alcoholic who becomes assaultive in a bar, and the addict may all be likely candidates for house arrest.

House arrest also has potential applications for offenders with special needs—such as the terminally ill and the mentally retarded. For example, Connecticut is exploring use of house arrest for pregnant offenders. Another program includes an AIDS victim whose needs cannot be met in jail. Several States are developing programs for elderly offenders.

Implementation ease and timeliness.   Pressure to reduce prison crowding is immediate, and jurisdictions are looking for alternatives that can be developed quickly. Because house arrest sentencing requires no new facilities and can use existing probation personnel, it is one of the easier programs to implement (particularly if no electronic monitoring devices are used). House arrest programs, for the most part, do not require legislative changes and can be set up by administrative decisions. The conditions of house arrest are usually easy to communicate, facilitating implementation.

Policymakers also like the notion that the offender can be removed from the community quickly, at the first sign of misbehavior. House arrestees are usually on some type of suspended jail or prison sentence; the suspension can be revoked quickly and the offenders incarcerated if they fail to meet house arrest requirements. The "suspended sentence" status makes the process of revocation much simpler and faster than if the offender were simply on probation or parole.

Advocates of house arrest believe that the sentence is worth trying because it is less intrusive and less expensive than prison. But house arrest is not without critics.

Disadvantages of House Arrest

House arrest may widen the net of social control. Non-violent and low-risk offenders are prime candidates for house arrest; these offenders are least likely to have been sentenced to prison in the first place. As judges become more familiar with house arrest, they may well use it for defendants who would normally have been sentenced to routine probation with nominal supervision. Hence, a sentence originally intended to reduce crowding might instead "widen the net" of social

control without reducing prison and jail populations significantly. Alternatively, house arrest may be used as an "add on" to the sentence the judge would normally have imposed, thus lengthening the total time the offender is under criminal sanction.

In the long run, "widening of the net" with house arrest programs is a realistic possibility. If we begin to regard homes as potential prisons, capacity is, for all practical purposes, unlimited. Such possibilities have widespread social implications.

Alvin Bronstein, head of the American Civil Liberties Union's National Prison Project says: "We should be looking for ways to place fewer controls on minor offenders, not more. If these devices are used as alternatives to jail, then maybe there's no problem with them. If you're sending the same people to jail and putting people who otherwise would be on probation on them, it's a misuse. We're cautiously concerned."

If house arrest does widen the net of social control, it will have increased, rather than decreased, the total cost of criminal sanctions. However, some net-widening may be appropriate in some jurisdictions. One cannot assume that all offenders—particularly felons being supervised by overworked probation staff—are receiving supervision commensurate with the risk they pose to the community.

House arrest may narrow the net of social control. Some critics of house arrest are concerned that a sentence of house arrest is not sufficiently severe to constitute an appropriate punishment for many crimes. In many States, house arrest programs are intended for use as punishment in lieu of prison. If that intention is realized, some critics argue that the result will be, in effect, to depreciate the seriousness with which crimes are treated. Mothers Against Drunk Driving (MADD) has been particularly critical of house arrest for drunk drivers and sees such sentencing as a step backward for efforts to stiffen penalties. *Drunk drivers are frequent house arrest participants.* The lessened severity of punishment, in theory, may reduce the criminal law's deterrent effects. In addition, critics could argue, because some offenders will commit new offenses while on house arrest, the crime preventive effects that prison sentences achieve by incapacitation will not take place.

House arrest focuses primarily on offender surveillance.   Some worry that house arrest, particularly if implemented with electronic devices, will strike the final blow to the rehabilitative ideal. As probation officers focus more heavily on surveillance of offenders, human contact is reduced and the potential for helping offenders is diminished. Most probation officers monitoring house arrest participants admit they have little time for counseling.

Although the research evidence does not urge optimism about the rehabilitative effects of probation officers' efforts, many believe that it is important that humane efforts be made, and be seen to be made, to reform offenders.

While it is true that counseling is reduced in most house arrest programs, employment or enrollment in school is often required. It could be argued that having a job or a high school diploma may do more than counseling to reduce the long-term prospects of recidivism.

House arrest is intrusive and possibly illegal. Some critics object to the state's presence in individuals' homes, long regarded as the one place where privacy is guaranteed and government intrusion is severely restricted by law. The use of electronic devices raises the fear that we may be headed toward the type of society described in George Orwell's book, *1984*. In *1984*, citizens' language and movement are strictly monitored and used as tools of government oppression.

But house arrest, with or without electronics, is quite different from the *1984* scenario. House arrest is used as a criminal sentence and is imposed on offenders only after they have been legally convicted. It is imposed with full consent of the participant. And, indeed, its intent is to be used as an *alternative* to incarceration. Surely a prison cell is more intrusive than any house arrest program can be.

There have been no formal challenges to date concerning the legality of house arrest. But legal analyses prepared by officials in Utah and Florida conclude that house arrest, with or without electronic monitoring, will withstand constitutional challenges as long as it is imposed to protect society or rehabilitate the offender, and the conditions set forth are clear, reasonable, and constitutional.

Race and class bias may enter into participant selection. Because house arrest programs are in the experimental stage, administrators are extremely cautious in selecting participants. Most programs limit participation to offenders convicted of property crimes, who have minor criminal records and no history of drug abuse. Such strict screening makes it difficult to identify eligible offenders, and those who are eligible tend disproportionately to be white-collar offenders.

American Civil Liberties Union officials say the programs also discriminate against the young and the poor because, to qualify for most house arrest programs, a person generally needs to be able to pay a supervision fee, typically $15 to $50 a month. If electronic monitors are used, the fee is higher, and the offender needs to have a home and a telephone. Persons without these resources may have no alternative but prison.

This situation raises possible "equal protection" concerns and concerns about overall fairness. Some programs have instituted sliding scale fee schedules, and a few others provide telephones for offenders who do not have them.

House arrest compromises public safety. Some critics seriously question whether house arrest programs can adequately protect the public. Regardless of stringency, most advocates admit that house arrest cannot guarantee crime-free living, since the sanction relies for the most part on the offender's willingness to comply. Can a criminal really be trusted to refrain from further crime if allowed to remain in his home?

To date, both recidivism and escape rates for house arrest participants are quite low. Generally less than 25 percent of participants fail to complete the programs successfully. But the low rates result, in part, from such programs' selection of good risks. Eligibility requirements often exclude drug addicts and violent offenders. Profiles of house arrestees show that most have been convicted of relatively minor offenses. Such offenders have lower than normal recidivism rates, with or without the house arrest program. Without a controlled scientific experiment, it is impossible to know whether house arrest programs themselves or the characteristics of participants account for initial success. As house arrest sentencing becomes more widespread and is extended to other types of offenders, the public safety question will undoubtedly resurface.

On the need to proceed cautiously. The evolution and performance of house arrest sentencing invite close scrutiny. Such sentencing represents a critical and potentially far-reaching experiment in U.S. sentencing policy. If successful, house arrest could provide a much needed "intermediate" form of punishment. If unsuccessful, house arrest could lead to more punitive and expensive sanctions for a wider spectrum of offenders. Which scenario proves true in the long run will depend on whether policymakers take the time to develop programs that reflect the needs and resources of local communities.

Discussion Questions

1. What is house arrest sentencing, and why is it attracting the attention of criminal justice policymakers?
2. What are the principal advantages and disadvantages of sentencing convicted offenders to house arrest?
3. What is "net widening," and what are its possible effects on our criminal justice system?
4. Are neighborhoods being placed at risk when they serve as "community prisons?" What would your reaction be if house arrest programs were implemented in your neighborhood?
5. Most house arrest programs require that participants pay a "supervision fee" in order to offset some of the program costs. What are the pros and cons of this practice?

References

Berry, B. 1985. "Electronic Jails: A New Criminal Justice Concern." *Justice Quarterly* 2:1–22.

Corbett, Jr., Ronald P., and Ellsworth A. Fersch. 1985. "Home as Prison: The Use of House Arrest." *Federal Probation* March: 13–17.

del Carmen, Roland V., and Joseph B. Vaughn. 1986. "Legal Issues in the Use of Electronic Surveillance in Probation." *Federal Probation* June: 60–69.

Flynn, Leonard E. 1986. "Florida's House Arrest." *Corrections Today* July: 64–68.

Garcia, Eugene D. 1987. "Palm Beach County's In-House Arrest Work Release Program." In *Intermediate Punishments: Intensive Supervision, Home Confinement, and Electronic Surveillance*, edited by Belinda McCarthy. Monsey, N.Y.: Willow Tree Press.

McCarthy, Belinda, ed. 1987. *Intermediate Punishments: Intensive Supervision, Home Confinement, and Electronic Surveillance*. Monsey, N.Y.: Willow Tree Press.

National Institute of Justice. 1985. "Electronically Monitored Home Confinement." *NIJ Reports* SNI 194: 2–6.

Petersilia, Joan. 1986. "Exploring the Option of House Arrest." *Federal Probation* June: 50–55.

National Institute of Justice / *Research in Brief*

New Dimensions in Probation: Georgia's Experience With Intensive Probation Supervision (IPS)

Billie S. Erwin, Georgia Department of Corrections
and Lawrence A. Bennett, National Institute of Justice

January 1987

Georgia's Intensive Probation Supervision (IPS) program, implemented in 1982, has stirred nationwide interest among criminal justice professionals because it seems to satisfy two goals that have long appeared mutually contradictory: (1) restraining the growth of prison populations and associated costs by controlling selected offenders in the community and (2) at the same time, satisfying to some extent the demand that criminals be punished for their crimes. The pivotal question is whether or not prison-bound offenders can be shifted into Intensive Probation Supervision without threatening the public safety.

A new research study, partially funded by the National Institute of Justice, suggests that intensive supervision provides greater controls than regular probation and costs far less than incarceration. The study was conducted by the Georgia Department of Corrections, Office of Evaluation and Statistics, and was assisted by an Advisory Board funded by the National Institute of Justice. This Research in Brief summarizes the findings.

The Georgia Program

The IPS program began in 1982 as a pilot in 13 of Georgia's 45 judicial sentencing circuits. By the end of 1985, it had expanded to 33 circuits and had supervised 2,322 probationers.

While probation programs with varying degrees of supervision have been implemented throughout the country, Georgia's IPS is widely regarded as one of the most stringent in the Nation. Standards include:

- ■ Five face-to-face contacts per week;
- ■ 132 hours of mandatory community service;
- ■ Mandatory curfew;
- ■ Mandatory employment;
- ■ Weekly check of local arrest records;
- ■ Automatic notification of arrest elsewhere via the State Crime Information Network listing;
- ■ Routine and unannounced alcohol and drug testing.

The supervision standards are enforced by a team consisting of a Probation Officer and a Surveillance Officer. The team supervises 25 probationers. In some jurisdictions, a team of one Probation Officer and two Surveillance Officers supervises 40 probationers.

The standards are designed to provide sufficient surveillance to control risk to the community and give a framework to treatment-oriented counseling. The counseling is designed to help the offender direct his energies toward productive activities, to assume responsibilities, and to become a law-abiding citizen.

Most offenders chosen for the IPS pilot program were already sentenced to prison, presented an acceptable risk to the community, and had not committed a violent offense. A risk assessment instrument was used to screen offenders. While the majority of those selected fell into the category of nonviolent property offenders, a large number of individuals convicted of drug-and alcohol-related offenses also were included as the program developed. Some of these offenses also involved personal violence.

Of the 2,322 people in the program between 1982 and 1985, 370 (or 16 percent) absconded or had their probation revoked. The remaining 1,952 were successfully diverted from prison; many are still under some form of probationary supervision. Some have successfully completed their sentence.

The Evaluation Findings

The evaluation evidence strongly suggests that the IPS program has played a significant role in reducing the flow of offenders to prison. The percentage of offenders sentenced to prison decreased and the number of probationers increased. The kinds of offenders diverted were more similar to prison inmates than to regular probationers, suggesting that the program selected the most suitable offenders. IPS probationers committed less serious crimes during their probation than comparable groups of regular probationers or probationers released from prison. The extensive supervision required seems to exert significant control and thus gives better results.

The cost of IPS, while much greater than regular probation, is considerably less than the cost of a prison stay, even when construction costs are not considered. In addition, society receives thousands of hours of community service from IPS offenders. Criminal justice practitioners seem to accept the program as suitable intermediate punishment. Judges particularly like it because it increases local control.

The evaluation addressed seven major issues:

1. Did the program divert offenders from prison to an alternative operation?
The evidence indicates that intensive probation supervision diverted a substantial number of offenders from prison.

Georgia sentencing statistics from 1982 through 1985 show a 10 percent reduction in the percentage of felons sentenced to incarceration. At the same time, the percentage of offenders placed on probation increased 10 percent (from 63 percent in 1982 to 73 percent in 1985). Jurisdictions with intensive supervision teams showed an increase of 15 to 27 percent in the percentage of offenders on probation, markedly higher than the statewide average increase of 10 percent.

A 10 percent reduction in the percent of felons who were incarcerated represents major progress in easing prison crowding. The precise extent of the impact of intensive probation supervision cannot be determined, however, because many factors influenced judges' decisions to consider alternative sentences. Nevertheless, in view of the shift toward increased use of probation, the influence of intensive supervision must be considered substantial.

2. Would the felons who were placed in the IPS program have gone to prison if the program had not existed?
Because Georgia does not have determinate or presumptive sentencing guidelines, the judicial circuits historically have exhibited a great deal of sentencing disparity. In general, sentences in the rural circuits are more severe than in urban circuits. For this reason, selecting offenders for the program according to crime type or risk measure may not have achieved equal impact among the various circuits in diverting offenders from prison.

Hence, IPS administrators targeted a particular type of offender—specifically serious but nonviolent offenders who, without the intensive supervision option, would have gone to prison in the jurisdiction where they were sentenced. This carefully reasoned decision reflected the administrators' desire to achieve maximum support from the judiciary.

The evaluation results indicate that 59.4 percent of the IPS cases were more similar to those incarcerated than to those placed on probation. The results also suggest that 24.6 percent of those actually incarcerated were very similar to those probated. The evidence seems clear: the offenders actually sentenced to IPS resembled those incarcerated more than those who received probation.

3. Was risk to the community reduced?
The experience suggests that IPS sufficiently controls offenders so that risk to the community is markedly limited. The recidivism rates are considerably better for IPS offenders than for groups under regular probation and for those released from prison. IPS offenders commit fewer and less serious crimes.

Of the 2,322 offenders sentenced to the IPS program:
- 68 percent are still on probation under IPS or regular probation caseloads;
- 15 percent have successfully completed their sentences;
- 1 percent were transferred to other jurisdictions;
- 16 percent have been terminated from the program and returned to prison for technical violations or new crimes.

Only 0.8 percent of the IPS probationers have been convicted of any violent personal crimes (including simple battery, terroristic threat, etc.). Most new crimes have been drug and alcohol related offenses. To date, no IPS probationer has committed a subsequent crime that resulted in serious bodily injury to a victim. Of the 2,322 cases admitted to the program, the following serious crime convictions have resulted: 1 armed robbery, 6 simple assaults, 4 simple battery offenses, 1 terrorist threat, 18 burglaries, 19 thefts, and 3 motor vehicle thefts.

Table 1 shows the number and percent of rearrests, reconvictions, and reincarcerations for selected samples of offenders sentenced during 1983. Prison releasees had the highest rate of rearrest in all risk categories. IPS probationers had a higher rate of rearrest than regular probationers, which is not surprising considering the higher level of surveillance.

The recidivism pattern that begins to emerge from Table 1 involves greater intervention (e.g., more incarceration, tighter supervision) paired with more negative outcomes. This pattern tends to hold for most risk groups except offenders with high risk classifications. Offenders with high risk classifications who had been incarcerated showed the lowest percentage of reincarcerations in State prison; however, this same subgroup

had the highest rate of rearrest, reconviction, and reincarceration in jail.

The apparent variation in the go-to-prison rate may be attributed to some unknown factor rather than differences in offenders' behavior. For example, it is not unusual for a Georgia judge to decide that an offender may have been released from prison too soon. When that individual appears before the judge on a subsequent offense, the judge will often use jail, county work camps, or some other method of detention and supervision to ensure more direct control over the offender and the period of incarceration.

Recidivism patterns also may be affected by the selection process for the incarcerated sample. This group included only those who had been released for 18 months at the time of the study. Because screening for this group was done in December 1983, only those offenders who were released before July 1984 could be tracked. Thus, those tracked had experienced a short

Table 1 Outcomes for offender groups after 18-month tracking by risk classification[a]

Offender classification	No. of Cases	Rearrested		Reconvicted		Sentenced to jail or prison		Incarcerated in State prison	
		No.	%	No.	%	No.	%	No.	%
Low risk									
IPS probationers	12	5	41.6%	3	25.0%	3	25.0%	2	16.7%
Regular probationers	11	3	27.0%	0	0.0%	1	9.1%	1	9.1%
Prison releasees	13	6	46.2%	5	38.5%	4	30.8%	3	23.1%
Medium risk									
IPS probationers	62	21	33.9%	10	16.1%	10	16.1%	9	14.5%
Regular probationers	58	20	34.5%	14	24.1%	9	15.5%	6	10.3%
Prison releasees	12	7	58.3%	6	50.0%	4	33.3%	2	16.7%
High risk									
IPS probationers	69	24	34.5%	19	27.5%	14	20.3%	11	15.9%
Regular probationers	73	22	30.1%	18	24.7%	13	17.8%	10	13.7%
Prison releasees	47	27	57.4%	21	44.7%	10	21.3%	6	12.8%
Maximum risk									
IPS probationers	57	25	43.6%	15	26.3%	12	21.1%	11	19.3%
Regular probationers	58	26	44.8%	16	27.6%	11	19.0%	8	13.8%
Prison releasees	25	16	64.0%	9	36.0%	7	28.0%	6	24.0%
Total for all risk groups									
IPS probationers	200	80	40.0%	37	18.5%	39	19.5%	33	16.5%
Regular probationers	200	71	33.5%	48	24.0%	34	17.0%	25	12.5%
Prison releasees	97	56	57.8%	41	42.3%	25	25.8%	17	17.5%

[a]Numbers and percentages do not add across the columns because the categories are separate but not mutually exclusive. A percentage of those offenders arrested are convicted. Some of those convicted are placed in jail while others are returned to prison.

Risk scores are based on a Wisconsin instrument: scores are (0–7) Low Risk, (8–14) Medium Risk, (15–24) High Risk, and (25 and over) Maximum Risk.

period of incarceration—2 to 6 months. The early release means they were apparently deemed less serious offenders. This suggests that comparisons with more serious offenders released from prison would reflect an even more favorable view of the IPS group.

Table 2 shows the number of convictions for various crimes for the three groups of offenders. The IPS group was convicted of fewer serious new crimes against persons than either of the other two groups. Although not shown in Table 2, minor repeat offenses, primarily marijuana possession, were numerous. Judges reacted strongly in such cases since they felt the offender had already been given his last chance. Serious offenses were, however, remarkably infrequent.

While many IPS probationers were convicted for possession of marijuana and habitual alcohol-related offenses, the most serious new offenses were 4 burglaries and 1 armed robbery in which no one was injured. The regular probationers had more serious offenses; they committed 8 burglaries, 1 rape, and 2 aggravated assaults in addition to other less serious new crimes. The prison releasees were convicted of the most new crimes: 13 burglaries, 3 aggravated assaults, 2 rapes, and 2 armed robberies. This comparison suggests that IPS surveillance provided early detection of uncooperative behavior or substance abuse and effectively reduced danger before citizens were harmed.

Although more IPS probationers violated the conditions of probation than regular probationers (7 percent compared to 4.5 percent), this might be anticipated because IPS probationers were so closely supervised. What might not be expected is the very low number who absconded. Only one of the sample of 200 IPS probationers absconded compared to four of the 200 regular probationers.

4. How much did the program cost? Preliminary estimates suggest a savings of $6,775 for each case diverted from prison (see Table 3). If all 2,322 offenders placed in IPS through the end of 1985 were diverted, considerable savings were realized—more than $13 million.

It should be noted that these estimates are based on incarceration costs ($30.43 per day) and supervision costs only. The estimates do not include any capital outlay, which could quite legitimately be included because the prisons in Georgia are full. If the 1,000 offenders under the IPS program at any given time had been incarcerated, they would have filled two moderate-sized prisons which, if constructed, would have cost many millions of dollars.

Another benefit of IPS is the thousands of hours of public service IPS offenders provide. If these hours are valued at even minimum wage, the contribution to society would be considerable.

Probation supervision fees were critical to financing IPS. In 1982, the Georgia Department of Corrections instituted a policy that allowed judges to order probationers to pay supervision fees. The fees currently range from $10 to $50 per month. The policy followed an Attorney General's ruling that existing statutes permitted court-ordered fee collection if the fees were used to improve probation supervision. IPS was implemented at the same time the probation fee

Table 2   New serious crimes committed during 18-month followup period

Type of Crime	IPS probationers (No. = 200)		Regular probationers (No. = 200)		Prison releasees (No. = 97)	
	No.	%	No.	%	No.	%
Sale of Marijuana	0	0.0%	1	0.5%	0	0.0%
Sale of Cocaine	0	0.0%	1	0.5%	0	0.0%
Theft by Taking	4	2.0%	4	2.0%	3	3.2%
Auto Theft	0	0.0%	1	0.5%	0	0.0%
Burglary	4	2.0%	8	4.0%	13	14.0%
Aggravated Assault	0	0.0%	2	1.0%	3	3.2%
Robbery	0	0.0%	2	1.0%	0	0.0%
Armed Robbery	1	0.5%	0	0.0%	2	2.2%
Rape	0	0.0%	1	0.5%	2	2.2%

Table 3   Comparison of costs per offender (average days incarcerated or under supervision)

Incarcerated Offenders	Cost
255 days @ $30.43 = $7,759.65	$7,759.65
(Excludes capital outlay)	
IPS Probationers	$984.66
196 days @ $4.37 under IPS = $856.22	
169 days @ $.76 under regular probation = $128.44	
Cost avoidance per IPS probationer = $6,774.69	

collection system was initiated. No funds were requested from the legislature.

Judges, who had been vocal in requesting stricter supervision standards, were advised that intensive supervision would be phased in using resources made available through fee collection. The amount of money collected from fees exceeded expectations. Over the 4 years of operation, the money collected for probation fees exceeded IPS costs and was used for numerous additional special probation needs. This does not mean that IPS probation fees alone have supported the program—regular probation fees also were included. Georgia judges impose probation fees on a case-by-case basis. (The issue of probation supervision fees is of considerable interest—what level of fees should be levied on which offenders; what is the most effective collection process; and what kinds of penalties are imposed for nonpayment—but represents an entire study outside the scope of this *Brief*.)

5. What kinds of cases have been assigned to the IPS program?   Looking at the 2,322 offenders sentenced to the program through 1985, the following profile emerges: 68 percent were white, 89 percent were male, 46 percent were 25 years old or younger, and another 24 percent were between 26 and 30 years old. Forty-three percent were convicted of property offenses, 41 percent of drug- and alcohol-related offenses, and 9 percent were convicted of violent personal crimes.

6. What kinds of cases were most successful in the IPS program?   Drug offenders responded better to the IPS program than they did to regular probation (90 percent success rates during the 18-month followup study). Frequent contact during the evening and on weekends and the urinalysis monitoring may be particularly effective in supervising drug offenders.

The finding that offenders convicted of drug-and alcohol-related offenses had the highest success rates raises interesting questions because the program initially considered discouraging substance abuse offenders from being accepted in the program. But judges were obviously looking for constructive alternatives for substance abuse cases; hence staff training and urinalysis capabilities were increased.

Females succeeded at a slightly higher rate than males, as they did under regular supervision. There was no significant difference in outcome by race.

The evaluators used discriminant analysis techniques to predict which offenders might be most effectively supervised under an intensive program. These techniques enabled the evaluators to predict 64 to 68 percent of the variation in outcome. The analysis identified risk score as the most important variable in predicting that a probationer is likely to fail in the IPS program. Being a property offender was the next most important predictor. Sex of the offender, need score (a scale depicting the social service needs of the probationer), race, and drug possession each made small additional contributions to the predictions.

7. How well has the program been accepted? Judges are now among the strongest supporters of the program in part because the program has a high degree of accountability. A judge can contact an IPS officer about a case knowing that the officer has had direct, recent contact with the offender. The officer knows what the offender is doing and how he is adjusting.

IPS staff have maintained high morale throughout the life of the program despite long, irregular work hours and heavy paperwork. Few have abandoned the program; most who leave the program have been promoted to other jobs. Probation Officers who are interested in joining the program must add their names to a waiting list.

The Staff

Conflicts between the treatment and enforcement functions of a Probation Officer are well documented. One of the most interesting findings of the IPS evaluation is the near impossibility of separating treatment from enforcement. The Georgia design places the Probation Officer in charge of case management, treatment and counseling services, and court-related activities. Surveillance Officers, who usually have law enforcement or correctional backgrounds, have primary responsibility for frequently visiting the home unannounced, checking curfews, performing drug and alcohol screening tests using portable equipment, and checking arrest records weekly. The Surveillance Officer becomes well acquainted with the family and the home situation and is often present in critical situations. Both the Probation and Surveillance Officers report a great deal of overlap of functions and even a reversal of their roles.

Because the Surveillance Officer is in frequent contact with the probationer, a close supportive relationship often develops. The Probation Officer spends a great deal of time with court matters and screening potential cases and is thus sometimes viewed as the representative of the repressive aspects of probation. Such divergent roles could lead to conflict and general dysfunction. However, the small caseloads contribute to close, often daily communication among the staff. Thus the probationer's needs—whether for control or support—are clearly identified and the team develops a coordinated plan and follows it closely.

The evaluators report that one major benefit of the team approach may be the support that officers give one another. This enables them to maintain high morale in very demanding jobs. During the evaluation period, each officer became absorbed in attaining the goals of the cases rather than simply performing according to the job description. Roles overlapped and officers exhibited an impressive, cooperative team spirit. Some officers interchanged roles whenever circumstances required scheduling adjustments. Staff seemed to function with mutual respect and concern for each other and for the continuity of supervision.

Smooth staff functioning, however, was not achieved by accident. The program's Probation Offi-

cers were selected from among the most experienced and best available. The Surveillance Officers were hired by the Probation Division specifically for the new program. In addition, true teams might not have emerged without careful attention to training. A National Institute of Corrections grant supported concentrated staff training coordinated through the Criminal Justice Department of Georgia State University. The freshly trained and invigorated staff were seen as emissaries of the new intensive supervision, and their energetic and dedicated response to the program may well have contributed significantly to the program's success.

IPS is a Successful Option in Georgia

IPS has proven itself to Georgia officials and has become an integral part of the corrections system. Intensive Probation Supervision is a highly visible probation option that satisfies public demand for a tough response to crime while avoiding the costs of prison construction.

The cost of IPS, while much greater than regular probation, is considerably less than the cost of a prison stay, even when construction costs are not considered. In addition, society receives thousands of hours of community service from those in the IPS program. Criminal justice practitioners seem to accept the program as a suitable intermediate punishment. Judges particularly like it because it increases local control.

In Georgia, IPS is seen as one option on a continuum of increasing levels of control. Probation administrators, mindful of the public's increasing demand that probation clearly demonstrate appropriate punishment, have responded with a creative range of options. The options have varying degrees of severity and intrusiveness.

One rapidly growing alternative is the Community Service Program in which probationers perform court-ordered community service under the conditions of regular probation. The Community Service Program is far less intensive and less costly than most and is therefore able to manage a large volume of cases. Other alternative sanctions include placement in a community diversion center and Special Alternative Incarceration, which is a 90-day "shock" incarceration program.

By providing a series of graduated options, Georgia's Department of Corrections has responded seriously to repeat violators but also has shown a commitment to try alternatives to prison whenever possible. Instead of a stark prison-versus-probation decision, judges have a wider choice of sanctions. A highly innovative staff has taken the initiative to use the full range of options.

The attention focused on approaches developed in Georgia for identifying and diverting offenders from prison is well deserved. Georgia has exhibited ingenuity and commitment to try new ways to address a nationwide problem. The lessons gained through Georgia's experience are applicable in other locations that are experiencing similar problems with prison costs and crowding, although the population of offenders who could be diverted may vary a great deal. Jurisdictions that are considering implementing programs such as IPS should not only study Georgia's program; they should also define the target group in terms of their own

needs. There is no magic formula, but Georgia's experience demonstrates that enough people can be diverted to achieve significant cost savings without serious threat to the community.

Discussion Questions

1. What are advantages of intensive probation supervision over traditional sentencing practices?

2. Should the victim's needs be considered in the decision to grant an offender IPS in lieu of incarceration?

3. What kind of cases seem most successful in an IPS program?

4. How should IPS be evaluated: in terms of cost? in terms of recidivism?

National Institute of Justice // CRIME FILE

Restitution and Community Service

Douglas C. McDonald, Vera Institute of Justice

1986

Restitution's Ancient Roots

Court orders to pay restitution or perform community service as a penalty for crimes are being touted as new and innovative sentencing options, but these practices are rooted in practices that are far from new. Requiring offenders to compensate victims for their losses was customary in both ancient civilizations and in the less developed societies we often call "primitive." Victims, or their kin, typically took the lead in organizing the communal reaction to lawbreaking, and the desire for compensation was probably at least as common as the urge to retaliate.

Victim restitution fell into disuse when victims lost their central role in the penal process, a development that occurred when formally organized governments emerged and asserted their authority. Kings and their ministers defined a crime against an individual as a crime against the state, and the machinery of the state assumed the responsibility for administering criminal penalties. Victims desiring compensation were referred to the civil courts. Although judges here and there may have continued to order restitution payments as an adjunct to a criminal sanction, it is fair to say that restitution had effectively vanished from criminal law and procedure in Western societies by the 19th century.

Contemporary Restitution and Community Service

The idea resurfaced in the mid-1960's. Penal reformers advocated the use of two different types of restitution-oriented sanctions: direct compensation of the victim by the offender, usually with money although sometimes

with services ("victim restitution"), and unpaid service given not to the victim but to the larger community ("community service").

Community service sentences were formalized in the United States when judges in California's Alameda County Court devised, in 1966, a community service sentencing program to punish indigent women who violated traffic and parking laws. Too poor to pay a fine, these women were likely to be sentenced to jail. But putting them behind bars imposed a hardship on their families. By imposing community service orders, the courts broadened their store of available penalties, extracted punishment from the offenders, lightened the suffering visited upon their innocent families, avoided the cost to the public of imprisonment, and produced valuable services to the community at large. As Alameda County's judges gained experience with the new sentencing option, they broadened the program to include male offenders, juveniles, and persons convicted of crimes more serious than traffic or parking violations.

Community service sentences were given a big boost when the British Government instituted a nation-wide program in 1973. Within a few years, tens of thousands of offenders throughout the United Kingdom were placed on probation to work off community service obligations. The program demonstrated the feasibility of using the sentence on a large scale, and similar programs sprang up in the United States and other countries, including Australia, New Zealand, and Canada.

Victim restitution programs soon came onto the U.S. scene. In 1972, the Minnesota Restitution Program—probably the first such effort—gave prisoners convicted of property offenses the opportunity to shorten their jail stay, or avoid it altogether, if they went to work and turned over part of their pay as restitution to their victims. Courts throughout the country adopted the idea, modifying it in various ways, and began to incorporate restitution agreements into their sentencing orders.

Today, the most common practice is for the courts to determine the nature and extent of the restitution to be ordered and to impose it as a condition of probation. In perhaps a third of the programs, the scenario resembles that shown in the Crime File program. Prior to sentencing, judges refer to willing offenders and victims to court-appointed mediators to negotiate agreements specifying how offenders will compensate victims for their losses or injuries. These agreements are imposed as a condition of the sentence.

In many jurisdictions, victim restitution and community service result from an understanding among all parties—judge, prosecutor, offender, and victim—that criminal charges will be dropped once restitution is made or community service is performed. This practice is consequently not a sentencing alternative at all but a procedure for diverting the defendant from further prosecution.

Many critics are troubled by these pretrial diversion practices because courts or prosecutors sometimes obtain what amounts to a sentence from persons who, in many instances, might not have been found guilty had they exercised their right to full-blown adjudication. The preferred procedure, in the eyes of these critics, is to limit restitution or community service obligations to sentences imposed after guilt has been formally established.

Supporters, however, argue that diversion is beneficial precisely because persons not yet wedded to a life outside the law can avoid the stigma associated with a conviction and, consequently, may more readily become law abiding once again. Ultimately, whether one values or disapproves these diversion procedures depends in large part on how they are used and for what types of defendants.

Since the end of the 1970's, the number of community service and restitution programs has increased dramatically. To cope with a growing victims movement, toughened sentiments toward drunk drivers, and jail and prison crowding, State and local governments across the country are rapidly expanding the availability of both types of programs.

A recent survey estimates that there are at least 500 to 800 programs of different sizes for juvenile offenders in this country. No surveys have been done of adult programs in the past decade, but it is probably safe to guess that 250 to 500 programs serve the criminal courts. With increasing frequency, judges in jurisdictions lacking formally organized programs are also fashioning restitution and community service sentences of their own.

Even though community service and restitution have become more popular in recent years, it is important to recognize that they have still established little more than a beachhead in the American courts. Only a small minority of the courts in this country order either of these sentences with any regularity, and the proportion of offenders receiving them is even smaller. Most judges continue to rely primarily on the few sentencing options that have long been available—imprisonment, fines, probation, and in some States, suspended sentences or their equivalent.

Why Use the Sentences?

One barrier to broader acceptance of victim restitution and community service as criminal sentences has been the lack of agreement as to why the courts should impose them in the first place. What penal objectives should judges try to achieve with them? Should the courts punish offenders, rehabilitate them, or restrain them from committing more crimes? Should a sentence be imposed to serve primarily as a deterrent, a message aimed at would-be lawbreakers? Should victim restitution be supported because it has a beneficial effect on offenders or because it serves victims' needs? Or should the courts embrace these sentences as substitutes for imprisonment in the hope that they are more constructive and less costly to the taxpayer?

The answers to the preceding questions affect the choice of offender to be given the sentence, the nasty or rewarding nature of the work to be demanded, the burdensomeness of the financial restitution demands, and the strictness with which these sentences are enforced.

Many argue that these sentences can be all things to all people and thereby serve several penal purposes simultaneously. The missions of many programs are formulated in vague, abstract, and often idealistic terms. State laws usually provide little guidance because they are typically written to authorize use of the sentences for broad categories of offenses (for example, "all misdemeanors") without indicating *why* they are to be imposed. This results in considerable diversity of practice from one courthouse to another, and not infrequently, confusion within a single courthouse regarding the proper and acceptable place of these sentences.

However, this multiplicity and imprecision of goals is often a great advantage when the sentences are introduced into courts, because different judges may impose them for different reasons. Whether this will lead to the permanent establishment of these sentences is an open question.

One impulse animating restitution and community service sentencing has been the hope and belief that both may contribute to the rehabilitation of offenders. Disciplined work has long been considered reformative. In addition, offenders performing community service may acquire some employable skills, improved work habits, and a record of quasi-employment that may be longer than any job they've held before. Victim restitution, when it brings offenders and victims face to face, also forces offenders to see firsthand the consequences of their deeds and thus may encourage the development of greater social responsibility and maturity. Some theorists have also argued that offenders' psychic balance and self-esteem are restored when they compensate their victims directly or serve the community more generally.

But Do They Rehabilitate?

Unfortunately, very few studies have been done on the effect of restitution and community service on offenders. One study evaluated experiments in four different American juvenile courts. Youths were given at random either traditional sanctions or restitution orders, some of which included a community service obligation. In two of the four courts studied, juvenile offenders who were ordered to pay financial restitution or to perform community service had lower recidivism rates than those given other types of sentences. In the third court, the number of cases was too small to draw strong conclusions, but the findings suggested a similar effect. In the fourth court, there was no difference in subsequent criminality.

The effects of ordering adult offenders to make financial restitution have not been examined with any rigor, but the few existing studies of community service show less promising results than did the juvenile court study described above. British offenders ordered to perform community service were reconvicted at a relatively high rate (35 to 45 percent, depending on the study) within a year of sentence, a rate that was found to be roughly the same for comparable offenders who received either prison sentences or other nonincarcerative sentences.

Similarly, offenders ordered to perform community service in New York City were rearrested no less

often (and no more) than offenders of similar backgrounds who were sent instead to jail and subsequently released. One study of community service in Tasmania claims to have found more positive effects, but weaknesses in that study's research design make it hard to accept this conclusion with confidence.

Given the paucity of systematic attention to the effects of restitution and community service sentences, it is difficult to draw any strong conclusions about their effects except to say that we have no evidence that using them makes much difference in the subsequent criminality of adult offenders. For juveniles, the sentences may have some positive effect, for reasons not understood. We do not know much about whether serving these sentences has positive effects on other aspects of offenders' lives, such as their employment.

Substitutes for Imprisonment?

Both sentences are often advocated as sensible alternatives to incarcerative sentences. It is commonly believed that jails and prisons are schools for crime and that the ability to live in the free community deteriorates as one adjusts to life in the abnormal society of prisoners. As noted above, however, we have no evidence that these nonincarcerative sentences do any better or worse than imprisonment for adults with respect to later criminality. However, the studies tell us if prison or other sentences have greater deterrent or incapacitative effects than community service or restitution; these issues are addressed briefly below.

Is there consequently not a case for preferring use of restitution or community service to imprisonment, if only because imprisonment costs anywhere from $15,000 to $40,000 per prisoner per year and because it can cost as much as $80,000 to $100,000 to build a single cell? Many State and local governments, laboring under the burden of rising prison and jail populations, have been persuaded by this argument and have for this reason created community service and restitution programs for the courts to use.

Encouraging judges to substitute one of these sanctions for jail or prison terms has produced mixed and often disappointing results. Reducing the use of imprisonment is one of the explicit goals of the British policy, but research suggests that British judges use the community service sentence more often than not in instances when another nonincarcerative penalty would have been imposed. Very few of the American programs have been studied systematically, but the preponderance of young persons, white-collar offenders, and first offenders in these programs suggests that the likelihood of a jail sentence would have been very small for many of them.

Judges are reluctant to impose restitution or community service—or any other relatively unconventional sanction—if they believe that doing so does not serve their particular sentencing goals. To the extent that judges sentence persons to jail to incapacitate them temporarily—to take them out of circulation for awhile—community service or restitution will probably not be seen as an acceptable alternative. If judges are primarily motivated to rehabilitate offenders, these sanctions may appear to be attractive options, even though their effectiveness is not well supported by extensive research. But judges, in many instances, do not send offenders to jail to rehabilitate them. More often than not, they seek some mix of sanctions for the sake of punishment (because offenders deserve it), for the sake of deterring offenders or others from future criminality (to scare them straight), and for incapacitation.

Having to pay restitution or to perform unpaid labor can be seen as punitive, and *is* punitive. Both sentences create obligations that require some effort and that need to be backed up by coercive authority. If judges are to substitute these sentences for prison terms, they want to know that the conditions are enforced strictly. They also want to be sure that somebody has clear responsibility for seeing that the orders are carried out and that noncompliance is reported to the court. And judges may want these sentences to send this message to offenders: "You are being punished for your deeds. You must take responsibility for your actions and you must not break the law again, upon pain of further punishment." One attempt to "market" a punitive community service sentencing alternative to the courts may be found in a project conducted by the Vera Institute of Justice in New York City. The project demonstrated that judges will accept a nonincarcerative sentence as a substitute for jail if work obligations are enforced and are in essence punitive.

Which Way the Future?

Community service and victim restitution are important additions to the American courts' list of sentencing options. But their future will depend in part on how—and whether—we resolve the larger debate about the way we should respond to criminals. Beliefs about our ability to control crime were shaken badly by rising lawlessness during the 1960's and 1970's. Legislatures, courts, and the public have lurched from one proposed solution to another. In this unstable world, it is impossible to predict if these new sentences will find an enduring place in the courts or will pass out of existence as yet another fad. If we want to increase the odds that these sentences will become "institutionalized," probably the surest course is to clarify why judges should impose them, under what conditions, and within what limits. Reaching agreement on these questions will not be easy.

Discussion Questions

1. To what objectives (deterrence, incapacitation, rehabilitation, retribution) should criminal court judges give priority when determining the sentence to impose on adults convicted of property crimes? On property offenders with long records? On juvenile offenders charged with serious lawbreaking? For crimes involving threatened or actual violence against persons?

2. For what kinds of crimes and for what kinds of offenders should the courts order victim restitution? Community service?

3. What type of labor should offenders given community service perform and why? How many hours, days, or weeks should be required, and what rationale should be used in determining this?

4. Under what circumstances would victim restitution be preferable to a jail sentence? Why? And community service?

References

Hudson, Joe, and Burt Gagaway, eds. 1980. *Victims, Offenders, and Alternative Sanctions.* Lexington, Mass.: D.C. Heath.

Hudson, Joe, Burt Galaway, and Steve Novack. 1980. *National Assessment of Adult Restitution Programs: Final Report.* Duluth: School of Social Development, University of Minnesota.

McDonald, Douglas C. 1986. *Punishment Without Walls: Community Service Sentences in New York City.* New Brunswick, N.J.: Rutgers University Press.

Pease, Ken. 1985. "Community Service Orders." In *Crime and Justice: An Annual Review of Research,* Vol. 6, edited by Michael Tonry and Norval Morris. Chicago: University of Chicago Press.

Pease, Ken, and William McWilliams, eds. 1980. *Community Service by Order*. Edinburgh: Scottish Academic Press.

Schneider, Anne L., ed. 1985. *Guide to Juvenile Restitution*. Washington, D.C.: U.S. Government Printing Office.

Schneider, Anne L. 1986. "Restitution and Recidivism Rates of Juvenile Offenders: Results from Four Experimental Studies." *Criminology* 24: 533–52.

Young, Warren. 1979. *Community Service Orders*. London: Heinemann.

National Institute of Justice   /   *Research in Action*

Electronic Monitoring of Offenders Increases

Annesley K. Schmidt, U.S. Bureau of Prisons

January/February 1989

Officials in 33 States were using electronic monitoring devices to supervise nearly 2,300 offenders in 1988—about three times the number using this new approach a year earlier, according to a National Institute of Justice survey.

In 1988, most of those monitored were sentenced offenders on probation or parole, participating in a program of intensive supervision in the community. A small portion of those being monitored had been released either pretrial or while their cases were on appeal.

The first electronic monitoring program was in Palm Beach, Florida, in December 1984. Since then an increasing number of jurisdictions have adopted electronic monitoring to better control probationers, parolees, and others under the supervision of the criminal justice system.

To inform agencies considering monitoring programs, and to track the growing use of electronic monitoring, the National Institute has surveyed monitoring programs for the last 2 years. This article reports on the 1988 survey, compares the responses with those of the previous year, and sketches a contemporary picture of the use of electronic monitoring.

Where are the Programs?

As shown in Exhibit 1, 33 States in all regions had monitoring programs, a substantial increase over the 21 States with programs in 1987.

The level of monitoring activities varies widely. Florida and Michigan, with 667 and 461 electronically monitored offenders, respectively, account for a large proportion of the offenders—49.5 percent.

Many monitoring programs involve limited numbers of offenders. Responses were received from more than one locality in almost every State with such programs. Yet as Exhibit 1 shows, 7 States were monitoring between 25 and 49 offenders, and 12 were monitoring fewer than 25. Two States had established programs but were not monitoring any offenders on the date information was gathered. One State's program had not quite begun by February 14, 1988.

Monitoring programs have been developed by a broad range of State and local criminal justice agencies, from departments of corrections, probation, and parole, to court systems, sheriff's offices, and police departments. Some began a few days or weeks before the survey response date. About a quarter of the programs had been operating 4 months or less. Others, like the one in Palm Beach County, were more than 3 years old. Regardless of the length of time in operation, most programs were monitoring fewer than 30 offenders.

The two States with the largest number of electronically monitored offenders structure their programs differently. In Michigan, the State Department of Corrections monitors most offenders, and local courts, sheriffs, or private agencies monitor the rest.

In contrast, the Florida Department of Corrections monitors only a little over half the participating offenders. Another quarter are monitored by city or county agencies, including sheriff's offices, local departments of corrections, and police departments. Most of the rest are monitored by one of several private agencies that offer monitoring services, and a very small number are monitored by a Federal demonstration project.

Florida is a microcosm of the country as a whole in that monitoring activities take place in all areas—large metropolitan areas, medium-sized cities, small towns, and rural areas—by all levels of government. The government may provide the service with its own staff or contract for it. These public agencies represent all

Exhibit 1 Number of offenders being electronically monitored on February 14, 1988

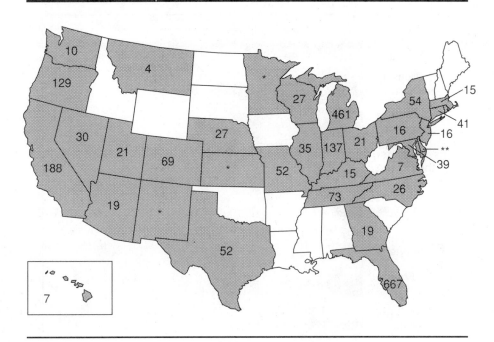

* Programs exist, but no offenders were being monitored on this date.

** No response.

Note: There are no programs in Alaska.

Who is Being Monitored and What Kinds of Offenses Did They Commit?

The characteristics of the 2,277 offenders monitored in 1988 do not differ much from those of the 826 who were monitored in 1987. Both years, the programs monitored mostly men, with women constituting 12.7 percent of monitored offenders in 1988 and only 10.2 percent in 1987.

Survey results show that offenders monitored in 1988 were convicted of a wide range of criminal violations (see Exhibit 2).

A quarter (25.6 percent) of offenders were charged with major traffic offenses. Most of the offenders in this group (71 percent) were charged with driving under the influence or while intoxicated. The other offenses in this category reflect primarily current or previous drunk driving convictions such as driving on a revoked or suspended permit.

In 1988, however, a smaller proportion of major traffic offenders were monitored than in 1987. This change reflects the expanding number of programs run by State departments of corrections, such as Michigan and Florida. Offenders monitored by these two States generally had committed more serious offenses. These State programs included prison-bound offenders or parolees and releasees from State institutions.

Property offenders were strongly represented. They committed a few closely related offenses—burglary (28 percent), thefts or larcenies (39.6 percent), and breaking and entering (16.6 percent).

Drug law violators constituted 15.3 percent of monitored offenders, with slightly over half of these charged with possession of drugs and the rest charged with distribution.

Exhibit 2 Electronically monitored offenders categorized by offense

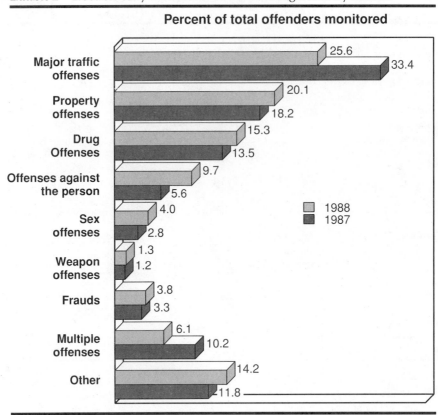

Percent of total offenders monitored

Major traffic offenses: 25.6 (1988), 33.4 (1987)
Property offenses: 20.1 (1988), 18.2 (1987)
Drug Offenses: 15.3 (1988), 13.5 (1987)
Offenses against the person: 9.7 (1988), 5.6 (1987)
Sex offenses: 4.0 (1988), 2.8 (1987)
Weapon offenses: 1.3 (1988), 1.2 (1987)
Frauds: 3.8 (1988), 3.3 (1987)
Multiple offenses: 6.1 (1988), 10.2 (1987)
Other: 14.2 (1988), 11.8 (1987)

1988
1987

How are the Offenders Monitored?

The monitoring equipment used can be roughly divided into two kinds: continuously signaling devices that constantly monitor the presence of an offender at a particular location, and programmed contact devices that contact the offender periodically to verify his or her presence (see box).

Survey results show that the continuously signaling equipment was used for 56 percent of offenders nationwide. Another 42 percent were monitored by programmed contact devices that mechanically verified that the telephone was being answered by the offender, and 2 percent were monitored by programmed contact devices without mechanical verification. Continuously signaling devices were used with roughly the same proportion of offenders in 1988 as 1987.

In 1988, however, many offenders had been monitored only a short time—54.1 percent for 6 weeks or less. Only 4.1 percent had been monitored for

between 6 months and a year and 1.4 percent for more than a year.

Offenders belonged to all age groups, in proportions roughly corresponding to the general population. In 1988 they ranged in age from 10 to 79, with 54.9 percent under age 30.

Program Features ...

Programs surveyed in 1988 varied in the way they paid for the sanction, the intensity of supervision, and failure rates.

Who pays? The survey answers show that in most programs the offenders do, with the exception of the Florida Department of Corrections. Charges are based on a sliding scale, with a maximum fee of $15 a day.

How often is the computer output reviewed? Some programs review it only during normal business hours (e.g., 9 to 5, Monday through Friday). Others provide continuous computer coverage and respond to the re-

How Electronic Monitoring Equipment Works

Electronic monitoring equipment receives information about monitored offenders and transmits the information over the telephone lines to a computer at the monitoring agency. There are two basic types: continuously signaling devices that constantly monitor the presence of an offender at a particular location, and programmed contact devices that contact the offender periodically to verify his or her presence.

Continuously Signaling Devices

A continuously signaling device has three major parts: a transmitter, a receiver-dialer, and a central computer.

The transmitter, which is attached to the offender, sends out a continuous signal. The receiver-dialer, which is located in the offender's home and is attached to the telephone, detects the signals sent by the transmitter. It reports to the central computer when it stops receiving the signal and again when the signal begins.

A central computer at the monitoring agency accepts reports from the receiver-dialer over the telephone lines, compares them with the offender's curfew schedule, and alerts correctional officials about any unauthorized absences. The computer also stores information about each offender's routine entries and exits so that a report can be prepared.

Programmed Contact Devices

These devices use a computer programmed to telephone the offender during the monitored hours, either randomly or at specified times. The computer prepares a report on the results of the call.

Most but not all programs attempt to verify that the offender is indeed the person responding to the computer's call. Programmed contact devices can do this in several ways. One is to use voice verification technology. Another is to require the offender to wear a wristwatch device programmed to provide a unique number that appears when a special button on the watch device is pressed into a touchtone telephone in response to the computer's call.

A third system requires a black plastic module to be strapped to the offender's arm. When the computer calls, the module is inserted into a verifier box connected to the telephone. A fourth system uses visual verification at the telephone site.

Note: Since the survey, several manufacturers have introduced a "hybrid" form of equipment. It functions like the continuously signaling devices, but when the central computer notes that the offender may have left at an unauthorized time, it telephones the offender and verifies that the person responding is the offender. If verification does not occur, notification is made of the violation.

---

port of a violation at any time of the day or night, weekday or weekend.

How do offenders fare in these programs? Some programs reported that few participants had failed to complete the program successfully while others reported that almost half had not completed the program. Most of the failures resulted from infractions of program rules such as not abiding by curfew hours or using alcohol or drugs.

The precise reasons for the variations in program completion rates are unclear, but one factor seems to be the control of intake. Some programs can refuse to accept offenders that they deem inappropriate for the program but others cannot.

... and Some Problems

Survey respondents noted a variety of problems that they had for the most part resolved. Some programs, for instance, initially had difficulty gaining acceptance within their agencies for either the program or the equipment that would be used. After proper training and successful tests of the program, however, confidence grew.

Offenders had to learn to handle the equipment properly and understand what was expected of them. Their families also had to adapt to limiting their use of the telephone so the computer calls could be received.

Other problems were related to the equipment itself. In several jurisdictions, there was a "shakedown" period when operators learned to use the equipment correctly, interpret the printout, and deal with power surges and computer downtimes.

Poor telephone lines, poor wiring, and "call-waiting" features on the telephones caused other technical problems. Occasionally, an offender's home was located too close to an FM radio station or other strong radio wave broadcaster. Some difficulties were overcome by repairing lines or wires or by using radio-frequency filters.

A few program managers said they had encountered unanticipated costs—for extra telephone lines, special interconnections, underestimated long-distance charges, and supplies. Most of those surveyed, however, thought equipment manufacturers were responsive to their concerns.

The Future of Electronic Monitoring

Electronic monitors have been available commercially for only a short time, but their use has grown rapidly. Recent discussions with manufacturers suggest the growth continues. Some existing monitoring programs have expanded, and more programs have been launched since the 1988 survey was completed.

The National Institute of Justice is following use of the sanction and supporting ongoing research that will

help policymakers decide if, when, and for whom the sanction is appropriate in their own jurisdictions. Institute research is assessing how well electronic monitoring of offenders protects the community.

Discussion Questions

1. What are the legal and ethical dilemmas presented by hooking up a probationer to a computer?
2. If a computer check determines that an offender is not home at his or her alloted time, should probation be revoked?
3. Are there some crimes for which electronic monitoring would never be appropriate?
4. Does electronic monitoring weaken the deterrent effect of the law?
5. Should electronic devices be used with probationers? parolees? community correctional center residents? Are they appropriate for juvenile offenders?

Correctional Institutions and Practices

Introduction

There is a vast correctional system in the United States. There are about 3,300 county jails, which house about 250,000 detainees and sentenced inmates. There are also about 700 state prison facilities, with a population of approximately 600,000 sentenced felons. More than thirty states are under court order to reduce prison crowding.

Despite its tremendous size and cost, the correctional system suffers from an extremely poor performance record. It has not been able to offer public protection, nor does it effectively rehabilitate criminal offenders. It is often plagued with high recidivism rates (many offenders return to crime shortly after incarceration). High recidivism rates are believed to result from the lack of effective treatment and training programs within incarceration facilities, poor physical environments and health conditions, and the fact that offender populations in many institutions are subjected to violence from other inmates.

Despite these problems, corrections plays a critical role in the criminal justice system. By exercising control over those sentenced by the courts to incarceration the system acts as the major sanctioning force of the criminal law. As a result, the system of corrections has many responsibilities, among them protecting society,

deterring crime, and—equally important—rehabilitating offenders. Both proper restraint and effective reform of the offender are the system's most frustrating yet awesome goals.

In the narrow sense, the system of corrections represents the institutional care of offenders brought into the criminal justice system. A person given a sentence involving incarceration ordinarily is confined to a correctional institution for a specified period of time. Different types of institutions are used to hold offenders. First, the jail holds offenders convicted of minor offenses or misdemeanors and "detainees"—people awaiting trial or those involved in other proceedings such as grand jury deliberations, arraignments, or preliminary hearings. In some jurisdictions, the jail is used only to house pretrial detainees, while a second type of institution, known as a house of correction, holds sentenced prisoners who commit less serious offenses and are incarcerated for less than a year.

Jails are often considered the worst of all penal institutions because of their poor physical conditions, lack of adequate staff, and archaic custodial philosophy. Many of these short-term institutions are administered by local county governments who are not equipped to adequately fund correctional facilities. Little is done in the way of inmate treatment, principally because the personnel and institutions lack the qualifications, services, and resources.

Prisons or penitentiaries house inmates convicted of felonies who are in need of secure confinement. They are often divided into minimum-, medium-, and maximum-security institutions. Maximum-security facilities hold the most dangerous hard-core felons who may have committed serious drug-or violence-related offenses. They have high walls, cells, close security, and large inmate populations. Medium-security prisons might be physically similar to more high-security institutions but have inmate populations considered more amenable to treatment. In contrast a minimum-security prison might house inmates transferred shortly before their release because of their adjustment while in the correctional system and/or new arrivals who have committed white collar or other nonviolent crimes; they offer inmates much freedom, they have good correctional programs, and they have small, homogeneous populations.

Most new inmates are first sent to a reception and classification center, where each is given a diagnostic evaluation and assigned to an institution that meets individual needs as much as possible within the system's resources. The diagnostic process in the reception center may range from a physical examination and a single interview to an extensive series of psychiatric tests, orientation sessions, and numerous personal interviews. Classification is a way of evaluating inmates and assigning them to appropriate placements and activities within the state institutional system.

When entering the assigned institution, the offender is placed in available programs in accordance with the diagnostic evaluation. Most institutions offer varying degrees of programs and services that include health and medical care, counseling, academic education, recreation, vocational training, religious study, visiting privileges, and many other special interest activities. These programs and services combine to form the treatment component of institutional confine-

ment. Although most programs look good on paper, they generally serve only a small proportion of inmates; other programs are ineffective, and some do not exist at all. Thus the philosophy and process of rehabilitation and treatment on which these programs are based are often more rhetoric than reality.

The corrections system is undergoing a period of crisis. Administrators at both the state and local levels are now facing the problem of AIDS in the offender population. Since so many inmates have had experience with IV drug use the fear of AIDS in the correctional population is a real one. There is also significant overcrowding in many state jurisdictions (California alone holds 50,000 inmates). The construction of costly new facilities is a current and future necessity. Administrators must come up with reasonable strategies to overcome correctional crowding. It has been suggested that efficiency can be gained through the privatization of corrections: allowing private companies to build and run correctional facilities under state contract. Experimental private prison programs are being operated today on the federal, state, and local levels around the country.

The papers in this section were chosen because they highlight important issues in traditional correctional administration. The first two papers focus on the administration of local jails: Andy Hall discusses efforts to alleviate jail overcrowding and W. Raymond Nelson describes how jail administration can be made more efficient. The next two articles deal with the prison system and focus on an exceedingly important innovation in corrections: privatization. John J. DiIulio, Jr., presents practical advice on the private sector management of prisons and jails and Barbara J. Auerbach, George E. Sexton, Franklin C. Farrow, and Robert H. Lawson review the role of private industry in prisons. Finally, Harry K. Wexler, Douglas S. Lipton, and Bruce D. Johnson discuss a criminal justice system strategy for treating cocaine-heroin abusing offenders in custody.

National Institute of Justice

Research in Brief

Systemwide Strategies To Alleviate Jail Crowding

Andy Hall, Pretrial Services Resource Center

January 1987

The words "jail" and "crowding" seem inseparable these days. A 1983 National Institute of Justice survey of more than 1,400 criminal justice officials from all parts of the country identified jail and prison crowding as the most serious problem facing criminal justice systems.[1]

The reality of more prisoners than available beds creates a dilemma for local justice officials. Crowded jails may compromise public safety through a lack of space to confine those who pose serious threats to the community. Lawsuits challenging crowded conditions may constrain a community's ability to incarcerate.

A recent Bureau of Justice Statistics *Bulletin* notes that 22 percent (134) of the Nation's 621 largest jails (those with a capacity of more than 100) were under court order in 1984 to expand capacity or reduce the number of inmates housed, and 24 percent (150) were under court order to improve one or more conditions of confinement.[2]

Building or expanding facilities is often necessary to house those who must be incarcerated. The time and costs of construction and operation of new institutions, however, argue that other options should not be overlooked.[3]

For the local sheriff or jail administrator, jail crowding creates increased prisoner and staff tensions, increased wear and tear of facility and equipment, budgetary problems from over-time staffing, and an inability to meet program and service standards. Less frequently recognized are the problems crowding creates for other justice system officials:

- Judges, prosecutors, probation and parole, and other officials often find crowding a severe constraint in cases where jailing offenders appears necessary but space is unavailable.
- Prosecutors, public defenders, and pretrial services officers find their functions impaired by delayed access to inmates caused by difficulty in processing large numbers of offenders.
- Court functions overall may suffer when crowding affects the movement of inmates to and from scheduled appearances.

Too often, however, agencies outside jail management are not fully involved in efforts to cope with the problem.

Many jurisdictions address the symptoms of jail crowding but leave the underlying causes unaddressed. Other jurisdictions, however, view jail crowding as a problem that demands the cooperative involvement of all key figures in the local justice system.

Given the success of this *systemwide* approach in a number of locations, the National Institute of Justice sponsored development of *Alleviating Jail Crowding: A Systems Perspective* (NCJ 99462, 1985), based on a survey of justice system officials and programs throughout the United States. The report stresses that while construction of new facilities may be part of a community's solution to crowding, emphasis must also be placed on ensuring that existing bed space is used effectively. Accordingly, the report highlights the role of each local criminal justice agency in ensuring the effective use of jail bed space to prevent crime and maintain public safety. This *Research in Brief* summarizes the full report.

Looking at the Local Justice System

Virtually every decisionmaker in the local justice system exercises discretion that can affect the jail population. Jurisdictions using a systemwide approach to jail crowding see the local justice system as a screening mechanism that can be modified to enhance the use of scarce jail space.

These jurisdictions develop case-processing flow-charts to understand the details of their case-handling process from the initial contact to final disposition. Flowcharts illustrate the stages of the legal process, specify the points at which decisionmaker actions affect the jail population, and identify opportunities to alleviate crowding.

Understanding the local flow of cases can help policymakers identify program and process changes to reduce crowding. Program changes frequently involve eliminating the jailing of persons whom a community deems inappropriate for criminal justice processing, such as the mentally ill.

Process changes improve system efficiency, eliminating case-handling "catch points" that unnecessarily prolong the confinement of persons who might eventually be released through bail, probation, or transfer to the State prison.

Reducing length of confinement often becomes the first focus of population reduction, because efficiency measures are generally less costly and more readily implemented than new programs. Local analysis often reveals that the primary underlying cause of crowding is excessive length of confinement due to inefficient case processing.

How System Decisionmakers Can Affect Jail Crowding

System studies in a number of jurisdictions have suggested, as one judge said, "a lot of little ways" to halt or reverse jail population increases without releasing serious offenders. The following discussion highlights just a few of the "little ways" available at different parts of the system.

Law Enforcement

Decisions surrounding local arrest practices—whether to arrest, transport to jail or stationhouse, book or detain for bail setting—are critical determinants of jail population size. Law enforcement practices both before and after arrest can be modified to reduce jail admissions. Jurisdictions such as San Diego County, California, and Frederick County (Winchester), Virginia, use perhaps the most common form of prearrest diversion through short-term "sobering up" facilities for public inebriates.

San Diego has been successful in reducing crowding through the use of a privately operated detoxification reception program where inebriates must remain for a minimum 4-hour period. Though in a largely rural area, the Winchester, Virginia, detoxification program, operated by the Division of Court Services, has also diverted a large number of persons from jail.

Similar prearrest diversion programs are in effect for persons involved in family disputes[4] and for homeless persons in a number of jurisdictions throughout the United States.

Law enforcement officials in Galveston County, Texas, have instituted practices to divert the mentally ill—a population that frequently makes up 10 to 20 percent of a jail's population. A team of deputies receives special training to assist in meeting the emergency needs of the mentally ill, thereby allowing the agency to take them directly to a mental health facility.

Many agencies also use a number of postarrest practices such as stationhouse release before booking, field citations, and court-delegated authority to release suspects according to a bail schedule to eliminate unnecessary confinement.

Jail Administrators

Elected sheriffs or appointed jail executives are often viewed as the managers most affected but least powerful in dealing with jail crowding. While having little direct control over admissions and length of confinement, jail administrators nevertheless can help reduce crowding by assuring ready access for pretrial release screening and bail review.

Quick access to detainees tends to be a common characteristic of successful programs to reduce jail crowding. For example, the sheriff in Mecklenburg County (Charlotte), North Carolina, allows pretrial services staff to be present during the jail admissions process, which gives them access to defendants and speeds decisionmaking.

Individual judges often lack feedback regarding prisoners in jail awaiting or following adjudication. Yet such information is of interest to the court and critical to jail population reduction. The Bexar County (San Antonio), Texas, administrator provides data to help judges monitor the court status of prisoners and prevent length of confinement from being extended through oversight or inattention.

In some other jurisdictions, jail administrators are delegated authority to release defendants pretrial or divert drunk drivers to treatment centers. Other administrators help develop nonjail pretrial-release and sentencing options or cooperate with other jurisdictions to alleviate crowding on a multicounty basis.

Prosecutors

Prosecutors act at more case-handling decision points than any other officials. This gives them an especially important role in containing jail population growth.

Early case screening by prosecutors reduces unnecessary length of confinement by eliminating or downgrading weak cases as soon as possible. Assistant prosecutors in Milwaukee County, Wisconsin, review arrests around the clock by examining police records and conducting meetings between complainants and suspects. This practice enables Milwaukee prosecutors to decide on the appropriate charge within 24 to 36 hours after arrest.

Prosecutors in Milwaukee also use "vertical case processing"—assigning the same attorney or team of attorneys to prosecute a case from start to finish. Though not necessarily the case in all jurisdictions, reassigning cases from one assistant prosecutor to another while the matter is before the court—"horizontal case processing"—may cause stagnation in caseflow, increased requests for continuances, and lengthened time to trial.

Prosecutor cooperation is essential for alternatives in arrest, pretrial confinement, and sentencing. Prosecutor participation and leadership are essential to the effectiveness of task forces dealing with jail crowding. Since the prosecutor "owns" cases on behalf of the State, others are rarely willing to propose case-handling changes without the prosecutor's support.

Recognizing that a lack of space to confine dangerous persons is a threat to public safety, prosecutors in a number of jurisdictions have taken an active role in reducing jail crowding by serving on "key court officials" groups or chairing jail population reduction boards.

Pretrial Services

Providing background information on defendants, release recommendations, and other pretrial assistance can be an important component of solutions to crowding. Pretrial services can often help merely by adjusting staff schedules to ensure timely screening and interviews for a maximum number of defendants.

In Mecklenburg County, North Carolina, for example, pretrial services and magistrate bail setting are available 24 hours, 7 days a week. In Kentucky, pretrial staff are on call 24 hours a day to interview persons arrested, notify judges by phone of the prisoner's qualifications for release, and supervise the release process if nonfinancial bail is authorized.

Limited release authority is delegated to pretrial services staff in an increasing number of jurisdictions. In San Mateo County (Redwood City), California, pretrial staff are authorized to release misdemeanor suspects prior to their first court appearance. Seattle, Washington, is experimenting with delegated release on certain felony charges.

Many pretrial programs respond to jail population pressures by expanding the range of release options (conditional and supervised release, third-party custody, unsecured bail, deposit bail) and by conducting regular bail reviews for those detained for trial.

A National Institute of Justice study found that supervised release programs in Miami, Florida; Portland, Oregon; and Milwaukee, Wisconsin, significantly reduced the bail-held population without significantly increasing the risk to public safety.[5]

Judiciary

Judges make more decisions affecting jail population than anyone else; this often makes them leaders in seeking jail-crowding solutions. Judges can issue summonses instead of arrest warrants; provide guidelines authorizing direct release by police, jail, and pretrial staff; and provide bail setting outside normal court hours. Evaluators of the 4-year Jail Overcrowding Reduction Project of the former Law Enforcement Assistance Administration found that the project's most successful sites were those with strong judicial leadership.

Many courts provide 24-hour bail-setting magistrates. The King County (Seattle), Washington, District Court has a "three-tier" release policy that reduces court time, jail admissions, and length of confinement. The court-established guidelines specify the charges for which pretrial services staff may (1) release without consulting the court, (2) release after phoning a duty judge, or (3) make recommendations to the court in the most serious felony cases.

Reducing court delay is crucial to effective use of jail space. Bexar County, Texas, seeks to eliminate "dead time" by having the court administrator work with a jail case coordinator to identify cases in need of special attention and processing steps that can be shortened. Each judge receives weekly a list of prisoners awaiting indictment, trial, sentencing, or revocation in his or her court.

One result is a 50-percent time saving in disposing of misdemeanor charges and thus a significant cut in overall length of confinement.

Many judges have worked to extend the range of nonjail sentencing options, using probation supervision, suspended sentences, fines, community service and restitution, halfway house placements, and specialized treatment facilities as true alternatives to incarceration.

A growing number of courts now defer service of jail sentences, when the jail is at capacity, in cases in which jail is believed an appropriate sentence but immediate jailing is not essential for the community's safety.

Defense

The National Institute's field test on Early Representation by Defense Counsel found that early screening for indigency, defender appointment, and defendant contact can decrease length of confinement and thus yield substantial savings of jail space.[6] Vertical case processing in defense offices also helps cut length of confinement.

In Mecklenburg County, pretrial conferences between defense and prosecution help identify, eliminate, or downgrade marginal cases and facilitate plea negotiation. Both offices can thus budget staff time efficiently and lessen pretrial confinement.

In St. Louis, Missouri, efforts to reduce staggering defender caseloads by appointing private attorneys in felony cases have also reduced case disposition time, stimulated bail review, and resulted in shorter pretrial confinement.

Probation and Parole

Not only do probation and parole agencies provide nonjail alternatives for sentencing, they can enhance case-processing efficiency by streamlining presentence

investigation (PSI) procedures and expediting revocation decisions. All this helps cut length of confinement.

In Brevard County, Florida, the jail population oversight committee spotlighted PSI delays and worked with probation and parole officers to cut PSI preparation time from 90 days to 30 or 35 days for jail cases. The county also cut to 24 hours the time required for decisions on probation revocation, thus decreasing the use of jail beds for persons on probation "hold" orders.

Outside the Local Level

State legislation, court rules, executive orders, and other "external factors" can affect jail populations. Guidelines on diversion, bail policy, appointment of legal counsel, sentencing practices, and jail operation all can affect the range of solutions available.

Other outside factors that need to be considered in local planning for jail use include local demographics, availability of State and Federal resources, public opinion and media coverage of criminal justice issues, activities of local civic groups and community organizations, and political campaigns and referendums.

Outside the System

Organizations outside the justice system can be instrumental in alleviating shortages of jail space by providing emergency shelter, detoxification, and treatment facilities for the mentally disturbed, public inebriates, and drunk drivers. Many jurisdictions use local mental health centers to provide prompt mental health assessments, diversion, and outpatient treatment. Private agencies in several jurisdictions provide temporary shelter for juveniles, pretrial supervision, and community-service placements.

Formulating Solutions

While individual parts of the system can help through such practices as those highlighted above, one or two agencies in the local justice system are not enough to bring about comprehensive solutions to crowding. Jail crowding results from the actions of many, with their decisions interacting to determine jail admissions and length of confinement. Effectively combating crowding requires taking into account the interactive nature of the problem.

Jurisdictions that successfully implemented a systemwide approach to jail crowding have identified as critical needs (1) the participation of key decisionmakers in formulating solutions and (2) detailed information on case processing and on the actual characteristics of the jail population.

Key Decisionmaker Participation

Whether it is a "jail population management board" or some other body, experience in many jurisdictions argues for a forum that encourages communication and participation by judges, prosecutors, sheriffs, police, probation officials, and other policymakers in developing solutions to crowding.

Collective involvement provides increased awareness of the impact of one agency's actions on another and of the other agency's procedures. Also, recommendations of a broadly constituted planning group are more likely to gain systemwide support. Finally, the political pragmatism that may accompany committee action may permit some participants to support more imaginative policies.

Information

A systemwide approach to jail crowding requires improved information about jail use. In addition to the detailed flowcharts that help assess the timeliness of case-processing decisions and the availability of nonjail options, planners need information on precisely who or what type of person is in jail and why and how long they stay. This permits administrators to learn the frequency of admissions and the size and variation of distinct segments of the jail population, as well as indicating sluggish case processing.

Statistical analysis of the population identifies symptoms of jail crowding, greatly enhancing the ability to identify and treat the causes. But while jail population data are valuable, they should not overshadow case-processing information.

Analysis of data on the jail population might show, for example, that persons detained before trial are released only after 7 to 10 days. Alone, this finding could indicate the need for a special pretrial services program to expedite screening and bail review. Infor-

mation on caseflow, however, might reveal the actual cause to be inefficient case processing.

Evaluation information is also critical to developing effective strategies. Evaluation data should be collected and analyzed to determine if planned modifications in decisionmaking are being made and the resulting positive or negative implications for crowding and public safety.

Implementing Strategies and Conclusions

Localities that take a systemwide approach to jail crowding generally follow some important steps:

Involve all key system decisionmakers;

Collect all necessary data on jail population and case processing;

Identify, implement, and evaluate appropriate changes in programs or processes; and

Inform the public of system changes when initiated and successful strategies when confirmed.

While many communities have taken great steps, experience has also confirmed the complexity of the jail crowding problem and the futility of seeking a panacea through one or two changes. Long-term success requires a variety of solutions and, most important, the time, patience, and attention of the entire criminal justice community.

Discussion Questions

1. What role can pretrial intervention play in relieving jail overcrowding?

2. If existing jails are overcrowded, should more be built or alternatives found?

3. What role can prosecutors and defense attorneys play in relieving overcrowded jails?

Notes

1. Stephen Gettinger, "Assessing Criminal Justice Needs," National Institute of Justice *Research in Brief*, June 1984, NCJ 94072.

2.   *Jail Inmates* 1984.

3.   Those jurisdictions that must build or expand jails can learn from the experiences of others through the National Institute of Justice Corrections Construction Initiative. For information, call 800-851-3420 or 301-251-5500 and ask to speak with a corrections specialist.

4.   In violent family disputes, however, research now indicates that arrest is the preferred police response. This research, now being replicated under NIJ sponsorship, was reported in Lawrence W. Sherman and Richard A. Berk, *Minneapolis Domestic Violence Experiment*, Washington, D.C., Police Foundation, 1984, NCJ 98905.

5.   James Austin, Barry Krisberg, and Paul Litsky, *Evaluation of the Field Test of Supervised Release—Final Report*, 1984, NCJ 95220.

6.   An executive summary of the *Early Representation by Defense Counsel* evaluation, by E.J. Fazio, Jr., et al., is available in microfiche as NCJ 97595.

National Institute of Justice // Construction Bulletin

Cost Savings in New Generation Jails: The Direct Supervision Approach

W. Raymond Nelson, Criminal Justice Consultant

July 1988

With many American communities facing the financial burden of jail construction, a new inmate-management concept offers a timely possibility of reducing costs. Many local governments are now considering "new generation" jails with an innovative management method known as direct supervision. This *Construction Bulletin* presents evidence suggesting how this new approach may save construction dollars and reduce operating costs.

Background

Local governments have earmarked approximately $3 billion for jail facilities currently being designed or under construction.[1] Further increases in the local jail are estimated at 21,000 each year—the equivalent of a new 400-bed jail every week.[2]

Agencies concerned about the rising cost of jail construction are considering an approach termed "new generation" because it departs from conventional concepts in both facility design and inmate management. The new approach offers opportunities for cost savings, as management is less reliant upon expensive construction, high security hardware, and advanced technology.

Inmate-Management Options

Most local jails do not use direct-supervision management. For several decades, the trend in jail management and architecture has been to reduce contact between staff and inmates as much as possible. Architectural barriers isolate inmates by dividing the institution into distinct staff and prisoner areas.

The design of a jail and its operating policies reflect each other. As shown in Figures A–C, there is a different architectural response for each management option. In this way, the "new generation" jail represents a style of design intended to facilitate direct contact between officers and inmates.

Most American jails fall into one of three architectural and inmate-management categories: (a) "intermittent surveillance," (b) "remote surveillance," or (c) "direct supervision." The most common architectural designs and management categories are "intermittent surveillance" and "remote surveillance."[3]

Intermittent Surveillance

Like a hospital, jails of linear design and intermittent surveillance management have rows of cells along surveillance corridors. As shown in Figure A, the staff is unable to observe all inmate housing areas from one location and has to patrol inmates' living areas to provide intermittent surveillance. Not surprisingly, most prisoner behavior problems occur during the intervals between the intermittent patrols.

Remote Surveillance

Jails using pod-type design and remote surveillance management have divided the inmate living areas into pods or modules. As shown in Figure B, approximately 50 cells are clustered around dayrooms that are under continual observation by staff in a central control room. The pod is frequently divided into three or four units.

Figure A   Intermittent surveillance

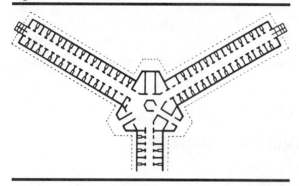

Figure B   Remote surveillance

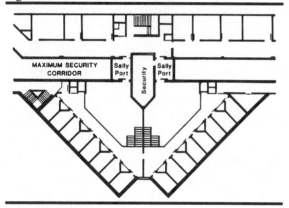

Figure C   Direct supervision

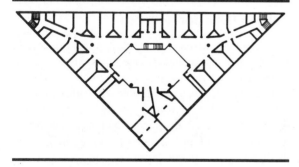

Since cell doors are electronically controlled from the officer's control room and communication with inmates is by intercom, officers do not have direct contact with inmates.

The main reason most new jails are designed in this fashion is to enhance inmate surveillance in comparison with traditional linear designs. However, these jails limit staff contact with inmates by isolating the officer in a secure control station.

In anticipation of destructive behavior, both "intermittent surveillance" and "remote surveillance" include high security fixtures, furnishings, and finishes. Despite these costly items, however, vandalism and graffiti are still prevalent in many of these jail environments.

Direct Supervision

Jails with "direct supervision" stand in sharp contrast. As shown in Figure C, a direct supervision jail differs from the conventional approach because the officer is stationed *inside* the housing unit. This concept encourages direct interaction between staff and inmates to prevent negative inmate behavior, and it groups inmates into living units of approximately 50 cells that can be efficiently managed by one officer. Rather than separating staff from inmates by security barriers, as is usual, the new approach places officers in direct contact with prisoners at all times. The new concept combines principles of human behavior and facility design to create detention environments that facilitate the officer's effectiveness.

While some aspects of the two pod designs are similar (cells clustered around a dayroom, for example) the differences are dramatic. The furnishings, fixtures, and finishes found in the direct-supervision housing pod are usually of normal, commercial grade. Staff assigned to the units work among inmates 24 hours a day. Approximately a dozen detention facilities in the United States currently use this form of inmate management, and as many as a hundred more are under design or construction.

To many people, direct supervision appears to fly in the face of conventional wisdom. They believe that lessons learned in operating traditional linear jails do not provide much support for this new concept. "What can be gained," they ask, "by exposing officers to continuous contact with prisoners and equipping the facilities with furnishings and fixtures that are not designed to resist abusive behavior?"

However, managers of direct-supervision jails respond that officers are placed in inmate housing units precisely in order to increase staff and inmate safety, and that it is unnecessary and perhaps counterproductive to pay a high price for secure, vandal-proof fixtures, furnishings, and finishes when officers are in a position to supervise inmate behavior continuously.

This response does not win many immediate converts. More and more jail managers, however, *are* convinced after seeing the direct-supervision concept in action. Although direct supervision inmate management concepts and principles will prove workable in almost any detention environment, they can be implemented more feasibly in a facility specifically designed for this purpose.

Following formal recognition by the National Institute of Corrections (NIC) in 1983, direct supervision has been endorsed by the American Jail Association, the Committee on Architecture for Justice of the American Institute of Architects, and the American Correctional Association. It has also been incorporated into the Standards for Adult Correctional Institutions and Standards for Adult Local Detention Facilities of the Commission on Accreditation for Corrections. With such support, it may be considered by many to be state of the art for inmate management and housing unit design.

To identify potential cost savings of "new generation" jails, NIJ sent a questionnaire to 12 local jurisdictions. Survey questions concerned operating and capital costs of each facility and requested specific data to substantiate respondents' observations.

Nine of the institutions surveyed were operating direct-supervision facilities and three were under construction. Of the nine jurisdictions currently operating direct-supervision institutions, four were designed for that purpose, three were originally designed for remote surveillance and then converted to direct supervision, and two were designed to accommodate either direct supervision or remote surveillance. At the time of the survey, the nine operating facilities had been practicing direct supervision from 1 month to 5 years.

The small number of institutions in the sample and the wide variations in operating conditions made accurate comparisons very difficult. Despite these obstacles to developing an objective cost evaluation, the questionnaire yielded many similar, if not identical, responses that may prove useful to decisionmakers exploring cost-effective alternatives to traditional jail management and design.

Personnel Issues

Personnel costs represent the greatest cost for local jails; managing personnel their most critical concern. Operating costs comprise approximately 90 percent of a jail's lifecycle costs, and personnel expenditures account for approximately 70 percent of a jail's annual operating cost.[4] In a 1982 survey of 2,500 local jails, the National Sheriffs' Association discovered that personnel was the number one management concern.[5] When cost savings are being considered, therefore, potential impact on personnel operations must receive the highest priority.

Effective Management

Administrators of the nine operating facilities agreed unanimously that direct-supervision inmate management is an effective technique for managing their institutions. However, several pointed out that increased management attention and staff training were required.

One administrator stated that it takes a great deal of management time to encourage teamwork and to remove the feeling of isolation that staff may have when assigned alone to a housing unit. Another manager reported that direct supervision contributed to the effectiveness of his management by reducing conflicts between staff and inmates and by allowing for closer inmate supervision. One went so far as to say, "It is the most positive trend in jail administration that I have encountered in my professional career."

Improved Staff Morale

While all respondents operating direct supervision jails reported that staff morale was improved, few were able to quantify this observation in terms of cost savings. When the respondents were asked to substantiate their claims that direct supervision had a positive impact on staff morale, they cited the following:
- Improvement in staff attitudes.
- Decrease in staff tension.
- Reduced use of sick leave.
- Improved treatment of inmates by staff.
- Decreased number of staff-inmate conflicts.
- Improved institutional cleanliness and orderliness.
- Reduction in employee misconduct and confrontations with management.

When compared to the conventional approach, direct supervision jails assign an officer much greater responsibility for inmate behavior. Rather than remain inside a locked work station, an officer actively supervises all inmates in the housing unit, rather than merely observing them. This assertion of authority has prompted many officers to note that the new approach takes control away from the inmates and places the officer in charge of activity in the housing unit.

Reduced Sick Leave

Sick leave is an indicator that offers quantifiable measurement. All but one of the responding direct supervision jail administrators indicated that use of sick leave had declined since the introduction of direct supervision. The only exception was a jurisdiction (Pima County) in which staff were obliged to work regularly scheduled overtime for 18 months with only one day off per week.

A study of the Manhattan House of Detention conducted by the National Institute of Corrections in 1985 revealed that sick leave usage for calendar 1984 was significantly less than the average for the city's other four houses of detention.[6] This difference amounted to an annual cost avoidance of 1,810 staff-days, equal to eight full-time positions, or approximately $250,000 in overtime expenditures if overtime were used to fill the vacancies.

Is it fair to conclude that the reduced sick-leave usage is entirely attributable to direct-supervision management techniques? There is no method for absolutely determining why these staff members did not use as much sick leave as staff in traditional detention environments. Nevertheless, improved working conditions and job enrichment are characteristic of "new generation jails," strongly implying that they may result in lower sick-leave usage.

Improved Working Conditions

As the work force continues to diminish, as is predicted for the remainder of this century, the importance of improved working conditions for staff will increase.[7]

The growing demand by the private sector for trainable employees indicates that jails will face increasing personnel problems before the end of the 20th century. A jail that can offer safe, clean, and orderly working conditions, as well as opportunities for fulfillment and career advancement, will be in a good position to compete for qualified employees.

Staffing Level

Perhaps the most important question is, do "new generation" jails require more staff than other jails, or can this approach result in staff savings? The answer of course varies to the degree that jail staffing patterns vary. The direct-supervision facility currently under construction in Dade County, for example, will house 1,000 inmates. It will require approximately half the staff needed to operate the County's older linear jail, which houses approximately 1,300 inmates.[8]

On the other hand, several facilities surveyed have relatively high staffing ratios, where there are fewer than 48 cells in a housing unit.

Housing unit staffing is the best area in which to identify the staffing benefits of direct supervision. A wide variety of settings over the past decade have consistently demonstrated that one officer can effectively supervise approximately 50 inmates, and several institutions have assigned more than 50 inmates to a housing unit with satisfactory results.

Texas is an example of a State where specific staffing ratios are contained in jail standards, requiring one housing area officer for every 48 inmates. In other jurisdictions, higher ratios are acceptable. Readers will have to determine if housing area staffing ratios of 1 officer to 48 or 64 inmates are suitable for the circumstances in their jurisdictions.

Managers of direct supervision jails often cite staff efficiency as an example of improvements over traditional designs. Since traditional jails separate staff from inmates, officers are virtually unable to supervise behavior. Addition of more staff positions has little positive impact since officers are simply *observing* inmate behavior.

For example, jails with management problems or crowding may elect to add more staff. All too often, however, this action fails to improve conditions. This cycle causes more and more staff to be added to traditional jails.

In contrast, the direct supervision jail may operate effectively under a variety of adverse conditions with a fixed number of personnel. The efficiency of fewer staff is possible because personnel are in constant contact with the inmate population, thereby allowing staff to *control* the situation at all times.

Safe Working Environment

Personal safety is an important determinant of the quality of a work environment. All "new generation" jails reported fewer incidents of violence. Pennsylvania's Bucks County, for example, reported that fights have dropped by at least 50 percent; the use of disciplinary segregation has diminished by 30 percent. New

Jersey's Middlesex County reported that in its 18 months of operation with direct supervision, it has had no incidents of inmate-officer or inmate-inmate violence. Colorado's Larimar County reported, "Much less violence; we are in charge for a change!"

Construction Costs

Several factors suggest that direct-supervision inmate management contributes to reduced construction costs. All the "new generation" jail administrators reported construction savings:

Commercial-grade *plumbing fixtures* can replace vandal-proof stainless steel fixtures in general population living areas. The degree of cost savings here obviously depends on the differences in the costs of fixtures and installation. The average cost of major brands of stainless steel combination toilet fixtures is approximately $600 per unit.[9] In contrast, a porcelain water-closet and lavatory, comparable to those used in Federal Prison System facilities, list at approximately $350.[10] When installation and accessory costs are considered, the difference is approximately $200 per cell.

Although some believe that the increased durability of steel fixtures will offset the extra cost, "new generation" jails have not reported a significant problem with breakage. Moreover, the cost difference would pay for many replacements.

Another new concept is elimination of lavatory and toilets in every cell. Cells with access to centralized plumbing areas might be considered for some inmate housing units. In a recent analysis of this option, it was determined that "dry" cells cost approximately $5,000 less per cell than "wet" cells.[11] For this reason, some counties are now reviewing this option as a cost-saving measure.

- *Lighting fixtures* in the general population living areas need not be vandal proof. A good quality commercial fixture designed for frequent use is sufficient. A security surface-mounted fluorescent fixture costs approximately $435 installed, compared with $120 for a commercial grade surface-mounted fluorescent fixture installed.[12]
- The cost of secure *control stations* on each living unit can be eliminated. When concrete, glazing, electronics and equipment are included, the cost of a control station may be $50,000 or higher for each housing unit, depending on the extent of the electronics.[13]

- The cost of *walls and glazing* to divide 48-cell living units into smaller 12-or 16-cell subunits, as is the custom in "remote surveillance" detention facilities, can be eliminated. Security glazing is very costly, and as much as $25,000 to $50,000 may be spent on each housing unit.
- *Furniture* for use by inmates in general population living areas can be of normal commercial quality rather than the more expensive vandal-proof line. For example, a four-person stainless steel table with attached seating costs $975 installed, compared to $320 for a comparable commercial pedestal table with four chairs.[14]
- *Cell doors, frames, and hardware* in the general population living areas can be commercial or institutional types rather than heavy steel doors and sliding gates. Hollow core metal doors of the type used in schools and hospitals are proving to be very effective in direct supervision jails.

The differences in cost are significant. An electronically-controlled maximum security door with frame costs approximately $2,300 installed, while a hollow metal door and frame costs approximately $300.[15]

Cost avoidance is another important consideration. If exterior walls are reinforced with concrete and steel, it may not be necessary to duplicate this expense for interior walls. Facilities now being built with direct supervision management have utilized hollow block for interior partitions, and rely upon exterior walls for the essential security "envelope."

Table A shows cost savings that may be realized for each 48-inmate housing unit. By selecting less costly materials and hardware, officials planning direct-supervision jails may save up to $203,580 per housing unit when compared to the traditional approach.

This is not to say that all direct supervision jails are less expensive to build than the conventional detention facilities being built today. Variations in cost among "new generation" jails may result from unique differences in basic architectural characteristics of each of these jails.

The Manhattan House of Detention, for example, was constructed within the shell of an old facility and incorporated all options for operating the facility as either podular-remote surveillance or direct-supervision. The Multnomah County Detention Center was built within a highrise multipurpose criminal justice center. The relatively high cost of these facilities is attributable to special circumstances governing their design.

Table A Potential savings* construction costs
(per housing unit)

Item	Amount saved
Plumbing fixtures	$200 x 48 = $ 9,600
Lighting fixtures	$315 x 48 = $ 15,120
Control stations	$50,000 x 1 = $ 50,000
Walls/glazing	$25,000 x 1 = $ 25,000
Tables	$655 x 12 = $ 7,860
Cell doors, frames, electronic controls	$2,000 x 48 = $ 96,000
	$203,580

*All costs factored for typical housing unit of 48 inmates.

Maintenance Issues

Reduced maintenance costs were consistently reported by the respondents as benefits of the direct-supervision approach.

Experience with direct supervision establishes that there may be substantially less vandalism in general population living areas, and perhaps certain interior areas could be built to school or hospital standards. Although the Chicago Metropolitan Correctional Center's interior cell walls were made of concrete block, 11 years of experience suggests that even gypsum board would have been satisfactory in the general population housing units.

Building Maintenance

Building maintenance is an important area in which respondents reported lower costs. Respondents indicated that there were fewer broken windows and lights and fewer fires, and that plumbing repairs and painting were needed less often. The Contra Costa County Detention Center administrator reported that the county's old facility needed to be painted each year, while the new facility is being painted for the first time since it was built 5 years ago.

The Manhattan House of Detention, New York City's only direct-supervision facility, has surprised local officials with an unprecedented absence of graffiti.

All respondents reported that they have had less graffiti, and several said they have encountered virtually no graffiti at all. Two respondents pointed out that while they saw much less graffiti on the living unit, they found just as much in the court holding tank, which is designed and supervised in the traditional manner.

Behavioral inconsistencies displayed by inmates exposed to two different kinds of management and design practices within the same institution are convincing evidence of the strong influence that a jail environment can have on inmate behavior.

Supplies and Equipment

Officials also reported less frequent damage to supplies and equipment. The responses uniformly indicated less need for repair and replacement of clothing, television sets, mattresses, and linen. Inmate vandalism rarely occurs in direct-supervision facilities.

Although few facilities have kept records, the Pima County Detention Center provided some cost comparisons that graphically illustrate this point. In the old Pima County Detention Center inmates ruined 150 mattresses each year. Every week approximately two television sets had to be repaired and 15 to 25 sets of inmate clothing were lost. During the first 2 years that Pima County has occupied its new detention center, it lost no mattresses, repaired only 2 television sets, and lost only about 15 sets of inmate clothing.

Several respondents reported an increased use of cleaning supplies in their new facilities, indicating, again, a sense of pride in maintaining them.

Summary

Specific staffing cost savings derived from direct supervision will depend, of course, on local circumstances. When considering this alternative, officials may also review indirect benefits such as reduced sick leave and increased staff safety. Reduced maintenance costs and less expensive construction components have been consistently reported and documented.

Not only can significant cost benefits be derived from the direct-supervision approach, but such vital objectives as reduced violence and improved working conditions will also be realized. As Naisbitt and Aburdene observed in their book, *Reinventing the Corporation,* "We are living in one of those rare times in history when the two crucial elements for social change are present—new values and economic necessity." Jurisdictions interested in reducing capital, operating, and human costs may find the direct-supervision concept worth further exploration.

Discussion Questions

1. What is the "direct supervision" approach to jail management?
2. How can jail administrators best deal with the personnel issues they confront in the management of local facilities?
3. What are the biggest jail construction costs, and how can the direct supervision technique save money?
4. Should inmates be required to repay the county for their stay in a jail, or would this encourage judges to overuse incarceration for minor crimes?

Notes

1. Based on a projection of data provided by a survey of 30 States conducted as of December 31, 1985, by Kimme Planning and Architecture under a grant from the National Institute of Corrections.

2. Bureau of Justice Statistics, *1983 Jail Census* (Washington, D.C.: Bureau of Justice Statistics), 1984.

3. Stephen H. Gettinger. "New Generation Jails: An Innovative Approach to an Age-Old Problem" (Washington, D.C.: National Institute of Corrections), 1984.

4. Dale Sechrest. *Correctional Facility Design and Construction Management* (Washington, D.C.: National Institute of Justice), 1985, pp. 96–99.

5. National Sheriffs' Association, *The State of Our Nation's Jails* (Washington, D.C.: National Sheriffs' Association), 1982.

6. Herbert R. Sigurdson, *The Manhattan House of Detention: A Study of Podular Direct Supervision* (Boulder, Colorado: National Institute of Corrections), June 1985.

7. In their recent book, *Re-inventing the Corporation*, futurists John Naisbitt and Patricia Aburdene contend that, "By 1987, there will be a negative net gain in the labor force: More people will be leaving than will be entering."

8. Harper & Buzinec Architects/Engineers, Inc., *Comparative Analysis of Design Schemes, Dade County Stockade Expansion* (Coral Gables, Florida), 1983.

9. Cost analysis prepared by the construction management firm of CRSS Constructors, November 1985.

10. List price quoted by American Standard for stock items AS-2529.014 watercloset and AS-0356.015 lavatory, March 1986.

11. Cost analysis conducted by Kimme Planning and Architecture, November 1985. It should be noted that the cost reduction includes redesign of all size and dayroom layout as well.

12. *Building Construction Cost Data 1985, 43rd Annual Edition* (Kingston, Massachusetts: Robert Snow Means Company, Inc.), 1984.

13. Kimme *Planning and Architecture*, estimates for planned facility.

14. Stephens Inc., catalog of institutional supplies, Spring-Summer, 1985.

15. Southern Steel Company, price list for detention and institutional hardware and furnishings, 1985.

National Institute of Justice   *CRIME FILE*

Private Prisons

John J. DiIulio, Jr., Princeton University

1988

Recent Developments

The quality of life inside America's prisons and jails continues to be a major public policy issue. By some definitions, most correctional facilities are crowded; by any definition, many of them are unpleasant, violent, and unproductive. In dozens of States, all or part of the correctional system is under court order to change and improve. Where new facilities are being built, often the aim is as much to improve conditions as to increase capacity. Meanwhile, the public has been paying more and more for corrections. In 1975, expenditures by State correctional agencies totaled around $2.2 billion. In 1987, spending will be about six times that amount.

Practitioners, activists, policymakers, and scholars have been searching for ways to relieve America's ailing correctional complex. In the 1960's and early 1970's, one popular answer was to stop building secure institutions and to deinstitutionalize offenders—"Tear down the walls!" In the 1980's, amid the ongoing search for meaningful alternatives to incarceration, proposals have been made to give the private sector a significant role in the administration, finance, and construction of correctional facilities and programs—"Sell the walls!"

By the beginning of 1987, three States had enacted laws authorizing privately operated State correctional facilities, while more than a dozen were actively considering the option. In 1985, Corrections Corporation of America (CCA), a leader among the 20 or so firms that have entered the "prison market," made a bid to take over the entire Tennessee prison system. Though this bid was unsuccessful, CCA now operates several correctional facilities, among them a Federal Bureau of Prisons halfway house, two Immigration and Naturalization Service facilities for the detention of illegal aliens, and a 370-bed maximum-security jail in Bay County, Florida. On January 6, 1986, U.S. Corrections Corporation opened what is currently the Nation's only private State prison, a 300-bed minimum-security facility in Marion, Kentucky, for inmates who are within 3 years of meeting the parole board.

More than three dozen States now contract with private firms for at least one correctional service or program. The most frequent contracts involve medical and mental health services, community treatment centers, construction, remedial education, drug treatment, college courses, staff training, vocational training, and counseling.

The paramount question in the debate over the privatization of corrections is not whether private firms can succeed where public agencies have ostensibly faltered, but whether the privatization movement can last.

Many observers believe that the movement, though only 6 or 7 years old, is already running out of steam. They point to such things as the failure of CCA to win control of the Tennessee system, Pennsylvania's 1-year statutory moratorium on privatization initiatives, enacted in 1986, and the fact that private prison operations have not advanced much beyond the proposal stage in most jurisdictions.

Other observers, however, see privatization as a response to three main factors—soaring inmate populations and correctional caseloads, escalating costs, and the widespread perception that public corrections bureaucracies have failed to handle convicted criminals in ways that achieve public protection, deterrence, just punishment, and humane, cost-effective rehabilitation.

Major Issues and Controversies

At least three sets of questions need to be considered about the privatization of corrections.

1. Can private corrections firms outperform public corrections agencies? Can they produce and deliver more and better for less? What present and potential costs and benefits, if any, are associated with the private administration, construction, and financing of correctional institutions and programs?

2. Should the authority to administer criminal justice programs and facilities be delegated to contractually deputized private individuals and groups, or ought it to remain fully in the hands of duly constituted public authorities? What, if any, moral dilemmas are posed by private-sector involvement in these areas?

3. Does privatization present a single "either-or" bundle of policy alternatives or does it pose multiple choices?

At this stage, it is impossible to answer empirical questions about the cost effectiveness and efficiency of private correctional programs. The necessary research simply has not been done, and relevant data remain scarce. Theoretical speculations, anecdotes, and raw statistics abound, but there is as yet little dependable information to tell us if or how privatization can work, or at what human and financial cost.

Much of the discussion of the morality of privatization has centered on the profit motive of the firms involved. It is not clear, however, that the moral dilemmas posed by privatization—if, indeed, any exist—are related primarily to the fact that CCA and its counterparts are out to make money. The philosophical waters surrounding the issue are deep and muddy.

Conceptually at least, privatization is not an "either-or" issue. Corrections includes prisons and jails, probation and parole, and various community programs ranging from compulsory drug abuse treatment to fines and restitution. Most correctional programs include administrative, financial, and construction components. Any of these correctional program components may be public or private. Thus there are numerous possible permutations of private involvement in corrections, only some of which provoke substantial controversy.

The Debate

Pro. Proponents of privatization claim that it can shave anywhere from 10 to 25 percent from the Nation's correctional budget. Unlike government bureaucracies, advocates argue, private firms are freed to a degree from politics, bureaucracy, and costly union contracts. Private companies must answer to their investors and satisfy the terms of their contract with the government or risk losing it.

As in any open market, the firms must compete with each other to maximize services while minimizing costs or go out of business. Thus, for example, the claim is made that private construction projects will be completed cheaply and on schedule, unlike public construction projects which often suffer costly overruns and meet with countless delays. While government agencies enjoy a virtual monopoly and need not strive to improve the quantity and quality of services, it is argued, private firms will have every incentive to economize and will be held accountable at every turn.

Further, privatization may engender a legislative climate more receptive to proposals to repeal laws that now limit or forbid production and sale of prison-made goods. Operators of private facilities have incentives to produce and sell inmate-made goods and might help persuade lawmakers to authorize prison industry as an effective cost-saving measure and thus to join the movement to transform prisons and jails into "factories within fences."

Finally, it is argued that private firms will be a source of technical and managerial innovations in a field in which most experts believe new methods are needed.

Con. Opponents of privatization claim that major cost cutting can be achieved only at the expense of humane treatment. Private firms, it is reasoned, have no incentive to reduce crowding (since they may be paid on a per-prisoner basis) or to foster less expensive (and to the private firm, less lucrative) alternatives to incarceration. Indeed, critics charge, since prisons have traditionally been financed through tax-exempt general obligation bonds, privatization encourages prison construction. Elected officials can pay for construction through lease arrangements that fall within government's regular appropriation process, thereby avoiding the political problems involved in raising debt ceilings or gaining voters' approval of bond issues. The firms' staffs, it is predicted, will be correctional versions of "rent-a-cops"—ill-trained, under-educated, poorly paid, and unprofessional.

In theory, concerns about staffing, compliance with correctional standards, use of force (lethal and nonlethal), strikes, fiscal accountability, and bankruptcy can be addressed through tightly drawn contracts. Opponents worry that, in practice, government regulation will prove inadequate and that the costs of regulation will more than consume any savings from privatization.

Finally, critics argue that privatization can neither minimize the liability of governmental units under Federal civil rights laws (under which most "conditions of confinement" litigation has been brought), nor relieve the government of its moral and constitutional duty to administer the criminal justice system.

The Context

Historical, political, budgetary, administrative, and philosophical dimensions of "private prisons" ought to be considered as background for the debate.

History.   State, Federal, and local governments in this country have long contracted for a wide range of goods and services, from solid waste disposal and moviemaking to weapons research and transportation. Indeed, for much of the 19th century and well into the 1960's, numerous States and localities contracted for penal services. In Texas, Michigan, California, Arkansas, and many other jurisdictions, all or part of the prison system has at one time or another been privately owned and operated.

The history of private-sector involvement in corrections is unrelievedly bleak, a well-documented tale of inmate abuse and political corruption. In many instances, private contractors worked inmates to death, beat or killed them for minor rule infractions, or failed to provide them with the quantity and quality of life's necessities (food, clothing, shelter) specified in often meticulously drafted contracts.

Is this history bound to repeat itself? Could such abuses occur today beneath the eyes of a watchful, activist judiciary and vigilant media? Has the corrections profession itself grown beyond the days when such situations were tolerated? To date, no private corrections firm has been found guilty of mistreating inmates or bribing officials, and most private facilities are accredited. What, if any, institutional "checks and balances" exist to ensure that this does not change as the industry matures and becomes more powerful politically?

Politics.   Much of domestic politics in this country involves competition and struggle among two or more groups which seek to influence public policy. Correctional policy, however, is often made in the context of what political scientists like to call "subgovernments"—small groups of elected officials and other individuals who make most of the decisions in a given policy area. As the late penologist and correctional practitioner Richard A. McGee observed, since the 1960's correctional policy has been affected by a larger than ever contingent of "coaches, customers, and critics," among them Federal judges. Still, the coaches are relatively few, the customers are virtually powerless, the critics are divided (liberals versus conservatives), and the institutions are normally hidden from public view (except in the immediate aftermath of a major disorder or scandal).

Will privatization perpetuate correctional subgovernments, or will it serve to break them up? If the former, is there a danger that private executives will enter into relationships with public officials that undermine the whole array of regulatory mechanisms, perhaps fostering a correctional version of the military-industrial complex? If the latter, will the quality of correctional activities necessarily improve (and the costs of these activities decrease) as a result?

Budget.   Correctional spending has been rising rapidly. Relative to other categories of public expenditure, however, corrections ranks close to last. Less than three-quarters of a penny of every dollar of total government spending goes into corrections. Even if CCA and the other firms were willing to run every single facet of America's correctional complex for free, it would not produce significant relief in public expenditures. In the context of public spending generally, corrections is an unpromising place to try to save money.

Nevertheless, corrections represents the fastest growing part of the budget in dozens of States and local jurisdictions. The belief that privatization can cut costs without reducing services might prove true if the "prison market" develops into something akin to what economists have called "perfect competition" (many firms, few barriers to entering the industry, prices set according to marginal costs). It might also prove true if the firms are driven to introduce money-saving technologies and managerial innovations.

Right now, however, it is not clear whether, or how, these goals will be met. Corrections, especially the administration of secure institutions, is a labor-intensive "business." Roughly three-quarters of the corrections budget goes to personnel costs. The most expensive (and difficult) correctional activity is the management of higher custody prisons, but the private firms have shown little eagerness to take a crack at running the Nation's "Atticas" and "San Quentins." Thus far, they have engaged in what critics call "creaming"—getting contracts for correctional facilities and services in which offenders are not hardcore, facilities are new or recently renovated, and profits are more predictable and easier to generate. To avoid political headaches, the firms have for the most part steered clear of jurisdictions with strong public employee unions, but it is precisely in such jurisdictions that costs are highest. There is as yet no evidence to suggest that privatization can lead to the adoption of new and better correctional programs and practices or cheaper financing arrangements.

Administration. The practices and performance of public correctional agencies vary widely. In administering prisons, some jurisdictions have relied on paramilitary structures while others have employed more complex management systems. Some field services units have adopted computer technologies; others have not. Some prisons are orderly; others are riotous. Some jails are clean; others are filthy. Some agencies offer a rich menu of work and educational opportunities; others offer few or offer them only on paper. And some departments spend much money per prisoner and perform badly while others spend less and seem to do much better.

Whatever else it may suggest, the existence of such concrete differences in correctional practices and outcomes makes it impossible to accept that public correctional bureaucracies have failed. What are the administrative and related factors associated with better public correctional facilities and programs? Only after we have studied the enormous variation in the public sector experience does it make good sense to ask whether private firms can do better (and more consistently) than government bureaucracies. From an administrative perspective, the issue is not public versus private management, but under what conditions competent, cost-effective management can be institutionalized. On this and related questions about privatization, the jury is still out.

Philosophy. In weighing the morality of private prisons, the profit motive of the privatizers may be less important than is commonly supposed. The real issue may be instead whether the authority to deprive fellow citizens of their liberty, and to coerce (even kill) them in the course of this legally mandated deprivation, ought to

be delegated to private, nongovernmental entities. Inescapably, corrections involves the discretionary exercise of coercive authority.

Even if the corporations were to offer their correctional services for free (as do a small number of foundations and other groups), and even if it were a certainty that the firms could reduce costs and improve services without realizing a single fear of their opponents, would privatization be justifiable? What is the proper scope of the government's authority? Where does its responsibility begin? Where does it end? Should the government's responsibility to govern end at the prison gates, or are not imprisonment (and other forms of correctional supervision) the most significant powers that the government must exercise, on a regular basis, over a large body of citizens?[1] All other things being equal, does it matter whether the patch on the correctional officer's sleeve reads "State of Tennessee" or "Corrections Corporation of America?"

Taken seriously, the moral issues surrounding private prisons are far and away the most interesting, challenging, and important problems the subject poses. In studying or debating this subject, we may be tempted to avoid philosophical questions entirely or (worse still!) to address them casually, to wrap them in polemics, or to "settle" them by making abrupt recourse to the name (or well-known maxim) of some famous, long-dead writers whose views appear to support our own. Let us resist.

Discussion Questions

1. What are prisons, jails, and other correctional activities for (e.g., retribution, deterrence, public protection, rehabilitation)? Do you believe that private companies can better achieve these goals, for less money, than government can?

2. Do private prisons represent an improper—or immoral—delegation of public authority? How, if at all, might this question apply to private financing and construction of correctional facilities?

3. Suppose CCA became CJCA—"Criminal Justice Corporation of America"—providing not only excellent private correctional services but excell-

---

[1] In 1986, about 1 out of every 33 adult males in America was under some form of correctional supervision.

ent private policing, prosecutorial, and judicial services as well; would that be going "too far"? Why? Why not?

4. Is it possible to conceive of recent privatization initiatives as the latest (albeit unfinished) chapter in the history of American penal reform?

5. Apart from privatization, or in addition to it, what other ways might there be to address America's correctional problems?

References

Babcock, William G., ed. 1985. "Corrections and Privatization: An Overview." *Prison Journal* LXV(2).

McGee, Richard A. 1981. *Prisons and Politics*. Lexington, Mass.: Lexington Books.

Mullen, Joan. 1985. "Corrections and the Private Sector." *NIJ Reports* SNI 191:1–8. Washington, D.C.: National Institute of Justice.

National Institute of Justice

Issues and Practices in Criminal Justice

Work in American Prisons
The Private Sector Gets Involved

Barbara J. Auerbach, George E. Sexton, Franklin C. Farrow, Ph.D., Robert H. Lawson
Criminal Justice Associates

May 1988

Introduction

During the last ten years correctional administrators and private business men and women in a number of states and counties have developed private-sector prison industries. These experiments, in which goods and services produced by prisoners are sold on the open market, are worthy of serious attention because of the rare opportunities they offer to generate positive change inside the prison while providing a valuable resource to the private sector and to society.

Private-sector jobs inside prison walls can produce benefits for prisoners and for society at large and meaningful work experience will help men and women leaving prison to adjust to the mainstream of American life. To be most effective, jobs held in prison must teach both the responsibilities and the benefits of the realworld workplace: a task made to order for the private sector.

Two important factors influence the potential for success of public-private initiatives: (1) private-sector prison industries are supported both by prisoners and by prison staff; and (2) unlike many reform attempts in the past, there is broad-based ideological support for private-sector involvement in prison work—liberals and conservatives alike endorse meaningful work for prisoners.

This appears to be the rare case in which everyone can benefit:

■ The department of corrections gains a program that provides meaningful work for a segment of its prison population, usually at little cost to the prison and generally at a quality level that is difficult to achieve under solely public auspices.

■ The prison gains access to private-sector expertise and also benefits from the presence of private-sector personnel, which helps to "normalize" prison life.

■ By earning a real-world wage during incarceration, prisoners are able to provide financial support to their families, and the training and experience gained through private-sector employment enhances the possibility of being hired upon release. As one prison administrator said: "We want the private sector in here because they are the state of the art. They know what it takes to hold a job out here."

■ The taxpayer benefits from private-sector prison industries in that funds generated through wage deductions for room and board contribute to state revenues. Funds contributed to victim compensation programs and family support create direct benefits for recipients. State and federal income taxes withheld from prisoner wages add to the general revenue.

■ Private-sector businesses, confronted in the mid-1980s with overseas competition and the need for workers who can meet fluctuating production and service needs, gain a valuable labor resource.

Opportunities for the Future

Opportunities that could lead to expansion in the size and number of private-sector prison industries over the next decade include: (1) flexibility on the part of labor and business interests; (2) governmental and political support; and (3) economic trends.

Flexibility of Labor and Business. Officials of organized labor and the Chamber of Commerce interviewed for this study indicated a willingness to be flexible in their positions on private-sector prison industries. Both groups acknowledge that they have some responsibility to help solve the prison crisis, and both recognize that the total number of jobs involved is relatively small.

The AFL-CIO in particular has had a long-standing interest in the rehabilitation of prisoners, as witnessed by the apprenticeship programs it has sponsored in prisons over the years. Leaders of that organization have made it clear that they do not oppose private-sector prison industries but wish to be involved in their development, both because of the knowledge they bring to the subject of work and because active involvement would help to ensure that projects avoid the displacement of organized labor's membership.

Leaders of the U.S. Chamber of Commerce have been similarly encouraging. Eighty percent of the Chamber's membership is made up of small businesses whose concerns lie more with Federal Prison Industries and traditional state prison industries than with private-sector prison industries (Federal Prison Industries and many state prison industries have priority in the procurement of government contracts, in many cases shutting out small businesses that wish to bid on such contracts). Chamber officials want to be consulted for the same reasons that organized labor officials do, and their expertise would be equally valuable in the development of private-sector prison industries.

Governmental and Political Support. The assistance and encouragement of the Justice Department have been remarkably consistent for more than a decade, and there are strong indications that the department will continue to be supportive. The National Institute of Justice and the Bureau of Justice Assistance currently are working to assist in the development of private-sector prison industries. On the political level, the idea that private-sector expertise can be brought to bear on the problem of prisoner idleness holds great appeal. During the last decade both conservative and liberal political leaders have found the concept promising, and there has been little opposition except in states experiencing extreme economic hardship. At a time in our history when political leaders are searching for positive approaches to crime and corrections, private-sector prison industries clearly provide one answer.

The National Association of Counties has worked to inform and assist its membership in the development

of private-sector prison industries, and there is evidence that the concept works well on the county level. The George Washington University's National Center for Innovation in Corrections[1] reports a significant number of inquiries from private-sector companies. The Correctional Industry Association, made up of state prison industry representatives, regularly discusses private-sector prison industries at its regional and national meetings.

Economic Trends. According to labor and economic experts consulted for this study, the aging of our population will lead to a shortage of younger workers, probably by the mid-1990s. Moreover, it is widely noted by such experts that attitudes toward some kinds of work are changing. Fewer workers are content with routine jobs, even though their training does not prepare them for work of a more complex nature. Workers increasingly are interested in flexibility in the workplace, shortened hours, and other quality-of-worklife issues, which are particularly important in labor-intensive jobs where negative attitudes can have drastic consequences for the quality of the product or service.

In addition, the impact of automation on the labor force has been, and will continue to be, the creation of distinctly separate types of work. There will be an increasing need for educated professionals to design and build manufacturing and service systems, for competent middle-level technicians to maintain those systems, and for less skilled workers to operate the systems at the entry level. Displacement is occurring at the middle level, but at the entry level there is an increasing need for workers. As the nation moves to a service economy, new opportunities at the entry level inevitably arise. Finally, American manufacturing and service operations moving overseas are largely labor-intensive operations whose managers claim they can no longer operate profitably in the U.S. labor market.

Most of these trends present opportunities to examine the potential of prison labor in helping to meet some of the nation's economic needs. Prisoner workers on the whole are young, and, for the foreseeable future, there will continue to be a large prison population. Experience with private-sector prison industries has shown that prisoners' attitudes toward meaningful work under fair conditions are extremely positive—during their incarceration most are eager for the opportunity to be engaged in private-sector jobs. Given the limited education and experience of most prisoners, coupled with the high turnover in the prison population, it is not realistic to train prisoners for highly skilled occupations. However, it is realistic to aim at entry-level positions that can translate into better jobs upon release.

The flight of labor-intensive businesses overseas, driven by the search for lower costs, may be partially offset by private-sector prison industries, which can offer incentives in terms of rent and utilities, may be geographically closer to the current plant site, and do not require that the business adjust to a new country with all of the political and social frustrations that such moves often entail.

There are negative aspects to these trends as well. Might not machines take over the kinds of work that are likely to be available to prisoners in the future? Why should the state subsidize the private sector by providing health care coverage to prisoner workers at no cost to the private sector? Perhaps most important, if labor-intensive American companies are moving overseas because of high labor costs, how can the prison compete, given the need to pay comparable wages to avoid unfair competition and exploitation?

Other negative trends may diminish opportunities for prison labor. It is now estimated, for example, that approximately seventeen million leased and part-time workers are in the labor force, and they will compete with prisoners for entry-level jobs. Many of the ten to fifteen million illegal aliens who now work at entry-level and other jobs are acquiring legal status under new immigration laws. Structural unemployment has resulted in an increase in the number of chronically unemployed; if discouraged workers and underemployed workers are added to the unemployment statistics, it might reveal a more dire labor picture than is now commonly accepted. Evidence of the creation of a permanent underclass in the United States, with a concomitant decrease in the middle class, will mean more competition for low-skill jobs.

These disquieting developments in the free-world economy are set forth here primarily because of the potential for competition between private-sector prison industry workers on the inside and entry-level workers in the free world. Private-sector prison industry workers, once released, face an uncertain reception in the job market. It is important to recognize that the employment of released prisoners is as much a function of community resources and attitudes as it is of the experience and skills of an individual worker. However, the chances of being hired upon release, as well as long-term employment prospects, clearly are enhanced for those inmates with private-sector work experience prior to release.

Many types of businesses can succeed financially in the prison setting if they have a clear-cut business reason for using prison labor, can tailor their production processes to the prison setting, and provide effective supervision. The use of inmate labor is not a solution for poorly managed operations, but, with adequate training and supervision and appropriate production processes, inmates can produce at quantity and quality levels equal to a free-world work force. Departments of corrections can meet a variety of goals if they are willing to respond to private-sector needs and to commit the necessary resources—generally space and staff diverted from other uses. Both private businesses and corrections departments must consider the costs and benefits of private-sector prison industries to make a realistic assessment of their value.

In order for the private sector to make the best possible use of the prison labor force, what is now needed is a coordinated effort by the states and the federal government. The simultaneous occurrence of the social and financial crises caused by prison overcrowding and the need for entry-level labor in the nation's industries opens a window of opportunity for growth in private-sector prison industries. If society can "win" by increasing prisoners' ability and desire to join the work force, and if each of the parties to the venture can "win" through the creation of prison jobs, then it is time to give serious consideration to the establishment of such ventures on a broad scale.

Scope of the Report

This report describes current developments in private-sector prison industries, analyzes costs and benefits for both the public and the private sectors, and suggests strategies for future growth. The information it contains is intended to help public- and private-sector managers take advantage of opportunities mentioned earlier and build on the costs and benefits of private-sector prison industries. The report informs policy makers about critical issues and problems that must be addressed if these ventures are to expand in the future.

The report is based on the findings of a nationwide survey of current private-sector prison industries. Project staff reviewed the literature, surveyed all fifty states by telephone or mailed questionnaire, and interviewed public and private participants in five jurisdictions: Arizona, California, Minnesota, Nevada, and Hennepin County, Minnesota. Arizona was selected because of the rich variety of its experiments with private-sector prison industries; California because of its planning process and because it hosts the only project involving youth; Minnesota because it has the most projects and the longest history of private-sector involvement; Nevada because it illustrates the powerful influence of local conditions on private-sector prison industries; and Hennepin County because it is the only local jurisdiction with significant experience over several years.

Information also was gathered from experts in labor, business, economics, and corrections who gave thoughtful consideration to the question of how private-sector prison industries could fit into shifting economic trends and become a mainstay in the nation's prisons. Finally, the report draws on a wealth of information collected by the authors in the course of providing technical assistance to prison industries over the last decade.

Experience with Private-Sector Prison Industries

The experiences of four states and one county—Arizona, California, Minnesota, Nevada, and Hennepin County, Minnesota—illustrate both the successes and the failures in private-sector prison industries and some of the relationships that may exist between corrections departments and private firms in operating these ventures. A number of other good programs might have been included: for example, in Kansas a single individual dedicated to change in the state's prisons operates two industries employing inmates outside the prison walls; in Utah state-run industries have had good results selling goods and services on the open market; and Washington hosts a number of successful private-sector prison industries located on prison grounds.

The projects highlighted here each offer lessons of their own, but some common threads are seen: the importance of planning and an overall strategy; the power of outside interest groups; the importance of economic profitability; the need for experienced management and for production tasks matched to skill levels of workers. The forces operating at state and local levels also appear to be more potent than those at the national level. The attitudes of state governors and legislators have had more direct bearing on the success of private-sector prison industries than those of Congress. State unemployment rates have meant more than the national employment picture. The problems of a state correctional system, or even a single prison, and the viewpoints of correctional administrators have been more significant determinants of action than the generalizations of writers and researchers. Finally, the best inter-

ests of a specific company in a particular location at a given time ultimately have determined the decisions and actions of that company's management.

Arizona

The Arizona Department of Corrections hosts one of the longest-running and most successful private-sector prison industries in existence today, and much can be learned from its successful operation. Several early projects failed, however, and from these there are lessons to be learned as well. Prison overcrowding and the lack of a clearly articulated strategy in the past may have contributed to failure, but outside forces played the major role.

In 1981 Governor Bruce Babbit signed into law S.B. 1191, which created Arizona Correctional Enterprises (ARCOR) as a division of the Arizona Department of Corrections. This legislation encouraged private-sector involvement not only by authorizing private-sector employment of prisoners and contracting with the private sector for the production of goods and services, but by establishing a policy board composed of representatives of the private sector.

In July 1981 Arizona received provisional certification from the Law Enforcement Assistance Administration for a project in which prison inmates would be hired to work in a Phoenix slaughterhouse that was being closed by its owners, Cudahy Food Co., in a move to cut costs. Since this was the only pork slaughterhouse remaining within the state, the Arizona Pork Producers Association proposed to purchase the plant and use prisoner labor to staff it. However, although the state labor union had accepted the proposal, the national union opposed it, largely because of its opposition to similar cost-cutting moves by the parent company throughout the country, and the project therefore was not initiated.

The ROBE Program. ARCOR subsequently activated the PIE certification for its Resident Operated Business Enterprises (ROBE) program. The ROBE program was an association of small businesses owned by prisoners and licensed by ARCOR to operate within the prisons. Association members paid rent and utilities and a monthly membership fee of 2 percent of sales, for which they received technical assistance from ARCOR in establishing and operating their small businesses.

By January 1983 there were fifty-two ROBEs operating inside Arizona's prisons. They employed a total of 103 inmates in thirteen categories of handicraft and service-oriented businesses. Most of the service businesses had prison staff as their principal clientele, while the handicraft enterprises sold the majority of their wares to dealers in the Phoenix area.

Eventually, primarily because of inmate gang activities, the ROBE program became too difficult to administer and ARCOR sharply reduced its scope in 1984. At the same time, the corrections agency voluntarily relinquished its PIE certification to the Department of Justice.

Projects at Perryville. In 1983 and 1984 two Phoenix-based firms established cooperative ventures with ARCOR inside the Arizona Correctional Training Facility at Perryville. Commercial Pallet Company contracted with ARCOR for the manufacture of wooden shipping pallets. Twenty-six inmates worked in the pallet project during 1983, producing $70,000 in sales. ARCOR terminated its contract with Commercial Pallet in 1985 because the company would not pay inmate workers at the minimum wage level as required by departmental policy for all such enterprises.

A second project, jointly operated by ARCOR and Wahlers Manufacturing Co., represented a unique relationship between corrections and the private sector in that the company's role in the latter part of the contract was limited to that of an investor. Wahlers, a subsidiary of Prestige Systems, Inc., is a Phoenix-based manufacturer of office furniture that had been hiring inmates on work release for some years. The company wanted to augment its civilian work force and decided to help capitalize a small plant inside Perryville. In 1983, with an average daily work force of fifteen inmates who earned $3.50 per hour, the shop generated over $700,000 in revenue through the sale of office partitions and computer tables in both the state-use and open markets. Wahlers eventually pulled out of the shop because of its failure, in the opinion of company management, to generate sufficient return on investment.

In January 1987 three cooperative ventures were operating inside Arizona's prisons. Barker Blinds, Inc., employs fifteen women in its plant near the Arizona Center for Women in the manufacture of a diverse line of window shades and blinds. Classic Coil, Inc., contracts with ARCOR for the assembly of wire products at Perryville, and Best Western International, Inc., operates a travel reservations center at the Arizona Center for Women.

Best Western's Reservations Center. In 1981 Best Western International, Inc., had a problem: its interna-

tional marketing and reservations center in Phoenix needed a readily available work force of trained telephone reservations agents to handle the overflow of phone calls for room reservations during peak call volume periods and on holidays and weekends. Best Western staff approached the Arizona Department of Corrections with the idea of hiring prisoners. About six months later ACW prisoners were booking Best Western rooms for guests calling from throughout the country on the chain's toll-free line.

The company has since installed additional computer terminals, and currently the ACW center has thirty work stations staffed by inmate employees. By November 1986 the center had processed more than 2.5 million calls representing more than $72 million in room reservation sales. On a given day the women at ACW process about 10 percent of Best Western's total domestic calls.

The ACW center operates from 5 a.m. to midnight or as needed according to call volume. Reservations agents work twenty to forty hours per week and are supervised by a Best Western operations manager and three Best Western supervisors. The institution screens all applicants and maintains a pool of eligible candidates who are interviewed by Best Western Human Resource Management staff for job openings. Selection criteria for the ACW reservations agents are the same as those for agents at the main reservations center. Starting salaries are the same as those for reservations agents at the main center: $4.50 per hour, with an increase of up to 12 percent after nine months. ACW agents also are eligible for Best Western employee incentive programs. Employees at ACW are subject to the same policies and procedures as all Best Western employees, including those governing disciplinary actions and job requirements. Each ACW employee, in addition to paying federal, state, and social security taxes, contributes 30 percent of her net wage to offset the costs of incarceration. Since 1981 ACW agents have had $182,000 withheld in taxes and have paid over $187,000 to the state for room and board. Over $112,000 has been paid in family support.

Since start-up in 1981 Best Western has hired more than 175 women at ACW. The company also has hired fifty of its ACW employees upon their release from prison. Policies have been adjusted to treat post-release employment as a lateral transfer rather than a new hire, thus preserving benefits earned prior to release. Twenty-four former ACW reservations agents currently are working at Best Western headquarters. Nine have been promoted to clerical positions in marketing, membership administration, and reservations.

Largely because of the manner in which Best Western has managed this operation, it represents one of the most positive illustrations of the potential of private-sector employment of inmates. The reservations center serves a demonstrable purpose for the company. Best Western staff have made a conscious commitment to treating inmate workers as employees in every sense of the word. Institution management has recognized the value of the program and has taken the necessary steps to ensure its success. The center serves as an incentive to the general inmate population, many of whom hope for a job here before release. In short, the institutional climate is positively affected by the presence of the center and the opportunities it offers.

California

The experience of California with private-sector prison industries is instructive because of the unusually thorough planning undertaken prior to start-up and because the inmate workers involved are juveniles. In 1981 the California legislature amended the Welfare and Institutions Code to allow the Department of the Youth Authority to establish industrial programs for its wards. Passage of this legislation was particularly interesting in light of the long-standing opposition of labor and business to similar legislation for adult offenders. The California Prison Industry Authority in the Department of Corrections is still restricted to the state-use market.

In 1982 the Youth Authority Department's Ward Employment Program Review recommended that youthful offenders by given the opportunity to develop employment skills in real work settings provided through partnerships with private industry. The following year the director of the department commissioned a fourteen-member task force composed of representatives of the private sector, organized labor, the public, and the Youth and Adult Corrections Agency to develop a plan for the implementation of Free Venture-Private Industry.[2]

The first two Free Venture industries were established in the Preston School of Industry in 1985. Preferred Assembly Services, a sheet metal prefabrication company, employed wards to assemble housings for electronics equipment. Vanson Trailers contracted with the department for the assembly of metal boat trailers and three-wheeled off-road vehicles. Preferred Assembly and Vanson operated for only a year, but the department nonetheless was encouraged by these initial experiments because the reasons for their short tenure were related to business conditions and not to shortcomings in the correctional agency itself. The department realized that the challenge it faced was to identify, recruit, and select the most appropriate private-sector firms to locate inside its facilities.[3]

TWA at Ventura. Trans World Airlines has proved to be an ideal example of a private-sector partner for the Youth Authority Department. Influenced by the success of Best Western's reservations center at the Arizona Center for Women, TWA began employing male and female youthful offenders at the Ventura Training School in January 1986. As does Best Western, TWA views its institution-based reservations center as a practical solution to a perplexing business problem—quickly rallying a work force to absorb surges in reservations calls. The Ventura reservations center, located about fifty miles from TWA's Los Angeles center, has been designed to handle 175,000 calls per year—all from marginal overflow traffic.

The Youth Authority Department constructed a building, which it is leasing to the airline, and the airline brought in telephones and computers. Sales at the Ventura center in 1986 were $934,000, and the cost of sales was about $1.00 per call cheaper than TWA's other reservation centers.

The ten to twenty wards employed by TWA at Ventura are paid the same wage as the airline's other reservations agents: $5.67 per hour. They are guaranteed a minimum of two hours work per day and, by virtue of their status as provisional employees, are limited by TWA to a maximum of 900 hours per year. Their provisional status also disqualifies them from receiving benefits to which full-time employees are entitled. Prior to employment as a reservations agent, each ward must complete an eighteen-week junior college accredited training course taught by Youth Authority Department education staff.

During its first year of operation the Ventura reservations center had a total payroll of nearly $90,000. From these wages the wards paid over $13,000 in taxes, $15,000 in room and board, and $11,000 in victim compensation. In 1986 two of the six reservations agents recommended by the airline for special achievement notice were from the Ventura center.

TWA is the only unionized private-sector participant in a private-sector prison industry directly employing inmate workers. In 1986 the airline flight attendants struck the company for several months and claimed that the Ventura reservations agents, who, like their counterparts in TWA's other reservations centers, were not unionized, were being used as strike breakers. As a result of this job action a California assemblyman held hearings on the issue and proposed legislation that would have severely restricted the Youth Authority's ability to develop future private-sector prison industries. However, when the hearings confirmed that the wards were not being used as strike breakers, the proposed bill was shelved by its sponsor and the union withdrew its protest.

Other Free Venture Projects. Also joining the Free Venture program in 1986 were Olga Manufacturing Co., Public/Private Partnerships, Inc., and North County Industries. During the year in which it operated at Ventura, Olga Manufacturing employed ten wards in a power sewing operation and paid them $3.35 to $5.91 per hour, the same rates as its free-world employees receive. The Ventura shop's gross payroll for 1986 was nearly $82,000. From their wages the wards paid FICA and state and federal income taxes in addition to the Youth Authority Department's mandated deductions of 15 percent of gross wages for victim compensation and 20 percent for room and board. However, Olga was not able to operate its Ventura plant profitably, and in the second quarter of 1987 it moved the operation to Mexico, where approximately half of the company's production is carried out. The Work-Rite Corp., a manufacturer of uniforms, has subsequently taken over Olga's space at the institution.

Public/Private Partnerships, Inc., is a private non-profit corporation that employs fifty youthful offenders at the Youth Training School at Chino in the microfilming of medical records. An unusual feature of this operation is its use of Job Training Partnership Act funds[4] by the employer, who provides a mandatory six-week training program. Wards in training are not paid, but at completion they receive a $500 stipend. Those who successfully complete the course are offered full-time employment in the microfilm unit.

Olympic Tools contracts with the department for the manufacture and assembly of metal tool boxes at Chino. North County Industries contracts with the Paso De Robles facility for the construction of wooden road markers and barriers. The wards in each of these shops work for the department and are paid the minimum wage.

The experience of the California Youth Authority demonstrates the value of a formal planning process,

not only as a means of anticipating potential problems and developing realistic goals, but also as a means of generating the necessary degree of support at all levels of the department. In a department with no experience with industrial programs and thus a need to adapt institutional programs, policies, and procedures to accommodate the requirements of private employers, the overwhelming staff acceptance of this new effort has been impressive. On the other hand, the California experience shows that even with extensive planning, not all problems can be avoided.

Minnesota

The Minnesota Department of Corrections has a long tradition of private-sector involvement in its industrial program. Unlike most state correctional industry programs, Minnesota Correctional Industries never lost the legal authorization to sell goods and services on the open market within the state.

As early as 1972 the Minnesota Department of Corrections was utilizing the assistance of the Governor's Loaned Executive Action Program Task Force to bring private-sector management techniques and practices to its industrial operations. In 1973 the legislature authorized private-sector operation of businesses on prison grounds, and at one time in the mid-1970s three small privately owned firms operated inside Minnesota's prisons. The only surviving member of this original trio of privately owned and operated businesses is Stillwater Data Processing, Co., which operates under certification by the Bureau of Justice Assistance.

Established in 1975 with a $55,000 grant from a consortium of foundations and corporations in the metropolitan area, Stillwater Data Processing is a private, non-profit corporation that provides custom computer programming, software development, and disk duplication services to the private sector in the Twin Cities area. The company is managed by two civilians and has a work force of thirteen inmates who earn between $3.35 and $9.35 per hour. During the twelve years in which the company has been operating it has employed hundreds of prisoners with a total gross payroll of almost $1.5 million of which over $450,000 has been withheld in taxes.[5]

A second non-profit corporation, Insight, Inc., employs eighteen prisoners in Stillwater and Lino Lakes correctional facilities. The primary mission of Insight is to provide post-secondary educational opportunities for Minnesota prisoners. The company performs telemarketing for the private sector and provides computer instruction to the long-term, homebound disabled to pay the costs of educating prisoners participating in its college programs.

Subcontracts with Private Firms. But the real story of Minnesota's involvement with the private sector lies in the various subcontracting relationships it has developed over the years with companies throughout the state and the sale of its own diversified line of goods and services on the open market. In the late 1970s Minnesota Correctional Industries performed a variety of light manufacturing, assembly, and finishing services for several large businesses. Prisoners at Lino Lakes refurbished telephones for Western Electric Co., assembled valves for Cornelius Co., and de-burred metal products and provided warranty service repairs for Toro, Inc. Certainly the largest and most visible of these subcontracting relationships, however, was the disk drive assembly plant sponsored by Control Data Corp. (CDC) at Stillwater.

In 1980 CDC was faced with a problem—how to deal with the employment impacts of technological breakthroughs. Magnetic Peripherals, Inc., a subsidiary of CDC, was manufacturing disk drives using a process technology that was changing significantly and rapidly. Given the uncertainties inherent in such a market, the company wanted to buffer its work force through the use of supplemental contractors whose workers would not be severely inconvenienced if production were interrupted from time to time. CDC decided to use inmate workers for its disk drive assembly process because of the flexibility inherent in such a labor force.

CDC provided technical assistance to MCI in setting up the plant, which was located in vacant industrial space inside the prison, and trained the MCI civilian supervisory crew and inmate work force in the assembly process. Initially the plant employed fifty workers producing disk drives. In later years of the contract the production of wire harnesses was added, employment levels rose to a high of 150, and the purchase order between MCI and the company called for sales of up to $2.5 million per year. The project was certified by BJA, and workers earned wages ranging from $3.35 to $5.96 per hour.

The MCI electronics assembly plant won both production and quality awards during its tenure, and CDC management was pleased with its performance. However, in late 1985 the company shifted the assembly process to western Europe to be closer to the primary market for its products.

Other MCI Shops. Each of the state's other adult correctional facilities also hosts MCI shops that either contract with the private sector or sell inmate-made goods and services directly on the open market. For example, at the newly opened women's facility in Shakopee up to twenty prisoners work in MCI's data entry program converting B. Dalton & Co.'s purchase orders into receivables files in a disk-to-tape system. Eleven women work in the facility's subcontract/assembly operation, which has performed a variety of light manufacturing and assembly services for hundreds of small and large companies in the state. Several female prisoners also have recently begun conducting telemarketing research surveys for the Safeway Food chain. This particular project appears to be working better than the telemarketing sales contract MCI had for a year with Transcontinental Telemarketing, Inc., because the degree of difficulty is not as great in conducting surveys as it was in successfully completing the sales called for in the Transcontinental project.

Prior to receiving PIE certification in 1981, the metal fabrication plant at Stillwater restricted the sale of its diverse line of farm machinery and support equipment to dealers within the state. Now the Minnesota Line is sold by five MCI sales staff and 330 dealers in seven Midwest states.[6] In addition to selling heavy equipment under its own brand name, MCI also manufactures and markets farm machinery under the Viking label through a system of thirty dealers affiliated with Associated Merchants, Inc. The shop employs ninety-three prisoners who perform a variety of metal fabrication processes, including design, foundry work, cutting, shearing, shaping, and welding, and also sells metal products other than farm machinery to numerous large and small businesses. In 1986 total sales for Stillwater's metal fabrication plant amounted to about $3 million. In the last four years the plant has had a total prisoner worker payroll of over $1.3 million, of which nearly $45,000 has been withheld in taxes. Over the same period inmate workers in the plant have contributed almost $41,000 from their wages to compensate crime victims. Minnesota is generally regarded as the foremost exponent of the involvement of the private sector in correctional industries. It has the longest unbroken tradition of serving private-sector markets. The Control Data shop represents a major success story. In contrast to most other correctional agencies, Minnesota's industrial program is highly decentralized, with each institution largely responsible for the success of its own industrial activities, including those involving the private sector. There has been limited departmental planning, and each institution has developed its own objectives and methods of implementation.

Minnesota has had experience with both the customer and the employer models and relies heavily on private-sector involvement in four institutions. It has therefore contributed significantly to the growing body of knowledge about private-sector prison industries.

Nevada

Nevada, a pioneer in the initiation of private-sector employment of incarcerated offenders, has had a great deal of recent experience with private industry. Nevada turned to the private sector for inmate employment out of expediency. The Department of Corrections has a very small prison industry program, and state corrections officials in the past relied heavily on work release for inmate work assignments. In the 1980s, as the number of prisoners ineligible for work release increased with the state's soaring prison population, correctional staff looked to the private sector as a means of combating inmate idleness.

In 1982 Key Data Processing, Inc., installed computer equipment inside the Nevada Women's Correctional Center in Carson City and employed twenty-five female offenders in data processing applications for a year before it ceased operation due to a lack of demand for its services.

In 1983 General Household Items, Inc., (GHI) was purchased by an entrepreneur who already owned and operated a plasma processing center in the Northern Nevada Correctional Center. After purchasing the broom and mop company, its new owner, who also hired the company's free-world plant manager, moved the operation from Oklahoma into the Southern Desert Correctional Center forty miles outside Las Vegas. By spring 1984, shortly before it shut down, GHI had a mixed work force of civilians and twenty prisoner employees.

GHI's management, which had no prior experience in the broom trade, and its plant manager, who had no prior experience in supervising a prisoner work force, failed to anticipate the difficulty of maintaining a pool of trained workers who could master the complex techniques of mass production of corn brooms in a prison with a high turnover rate. Because inmates routinely failed to meet production quotas on schedule, GHI hired experienced civilian broom makers to work alongside its prisoner employees. The majority of prisoner workers were unable to produce at even the company's base piece rate, which was tied to the federal minimum wage,

and the company instituted a "training" period of several months and a corresponding "training" wage of $1.00 per hour. Unfortunately, GHI sold the brooms produced by its prisoner-trainees in interstate commerce, a clear violation of the wage requirements of the Fair Labor Standards Act since the employees who produced the brooms were paid less than the federal minimum wage.

In 1984 a California-based competitor of GHI complained to Congress through the National Broom and Mop Manufacturers' Association about the sale of GHI's products in that state. This complaint eventually led to an investigation of the company's payroll practices by the Department of Labor's Wage and Hours Division, which subsequently levied a penalty of more than $90,000 against GHI for payment of back wages to its inmate employees. GHI ceased operations shortly after imposition of the fine.

GHI's experience exemplifies the lesson learned by many private companies and correctional agencies: private-sector involvement is not risk-free for either party. Industries that have critical production tasks requiring lengthy training periods—in GHI's case the winding and cutting of corn brooms—will require a stable, long-term labor pool that can be trained and retained long enough to become productive and efficient. Institutions with high turnover rates are not the best candidates to host industries with these kinds of labor requirements. GHI's experience in the industry to be located in a prison is critical to the success of the business. It is unrealistic to expect a manager to learn both a new industry and the problems of operating in a prison at the same time.

Las Vegas Foods, Inc., began employing up to thirty prisoners inside the Southern Desert Correctional Center in 1983 in the cleaning, mixing, and packaging of salads for sale to casinos. The company continued to operate inside the prison until the end of 1986 when the institution did not renew its lease because of a more critical need for the space the enterprise was occupying.

Vinyl Products, Inc. By 1985 the Northern Nevada Correctional Center (NNCC), on the outskirts of the state capital of Carson City, faced serious problems of overcrowding and idleness. Opportunities for productive work were scarce and program dollars to support the expansion of existing industries or the development of new ones were virtually non-existent.

Vinyl Products Manufacturing Co., a producer of waterbeds located in downtown Carson City, had a problem too. The company could not find enough workers to keep up with increasing demand. Many of Vinyl Products' competitors, facing similar problems, had located production facilities overseas but had experienced serious problems with product quality.

Vinyl Products had been hiring prerelease inmates from NNCC since 1978 to work its graveyard shift. When it asked for more workers in the mid-1980s the institution was able to provide only a few minimum-security inmates. At that point Vinyl's president directed his production staff to examine the feasibility of opening a feeder plant inside the prison.

Just thirty days after its initial proposal to establish a plant inside NNCC, Vinyl Products was employing twenty-five inmates inside the prison. Two years later the company had increased its prison-based work force to nearly 120 employees on three shifts. This increase was accomplished without a single layoff in the company's downtown plant.

Vinyl's prisoner employees perform the same manufacturing tasks as their co-workers outside: cutting, sealing, inspecting, and packaging a diverse line of mattresses. Originally the company restricted inmate workers to the production of its simplest product line; however, their satisfaction with both productivity and quality levels led them to add to the NNCC plant the manufacture not only of the full product line but of custom mattresses as well.

Vinyl's prisoner employees and downtown workers earn the same pay rates ($3.35 day shift, $4 night shift) and receive the same benefits, including paid holidays and vacations, although health care costs are paid by the state. Production at the NNCC plant is supervised on each of three shifts by Vinyl production managers, who evaluate prisoners' job performance every ninety days, just as they do with employees in their downtown plant.

Since the start of business inside the prison in 1985, Vinyl has hired nearly 200 prisoners. These inmate employees have paid over $167,000 to the state's general fund in the form of room and board charges, provided an estimated $127,000 in support to their families and over $34,000 in compensation to victims, and have had over $112,000 withheld in taxes.

Like Minnesota, the Nevada Department of Prisons has operated its industrial program under a management philosophy of decentralization, with each institution head largely responsible for the success of industrial activities. At the Northern Nevada Correctional Center, the warden has played an influential role in the development of private-sector prison industries.

His willingness to adapt institutional procedures to meet the needs of private employers has contributed significantly to the success of the Vinyl Products operation. The fact that NNCC had a stable institutional environment with no history of violence made it easier for the necessary adjustments to be made.

At Southern Desert, on the other hand, the problems of opening a new institution and the difficulties of training staff (both new hires and those transferred from other institutions) exacerbated the problems faced by an entrepreneur trying to start a new business without adequate management experience.

Hennepin County, Minnesota

Although private-sector prison industries have been of primary interest to state correctional agencies, counties have shown increasing interest as swelling jail populations and local funding problems make jail administration more difficult. The mixture of sentenced and unsentenced prisoners, the short stays even of sentenced prisoners, and the lack of suitable space for industrial activities complicate the development of successful private-sector prison industries in jails.

Hennepin County's Adult Correctional Facility in suburban Minneapolis established its industrial program in 1981 to meet the needs of local manufacturers for labor-intensive functions such as cleaning, sorting, assembling, and packaging that are typically contracted out to job shops. The county's ACF Industries provides work for a co-ed work force of twenty-five inmates who are paid the state minimum wage of $3.55 per hour. Customers are charged a burden rate of $6.00 per hour for finished work. The shop, which is managed by a former district sales manager for Allis-Chalmers, Inc., concentrates on securing work that is generally too difficult for sheltered workshops to complete successfully but not so complex that it cannot be mastered by a work force with built-in high turnover rates.

ACF Industries, with total sales of $30,000 a month in 1987, competes with other job shops on the basis of its competitive rates, quality work, and timely delivery. Over the years it has performed a variety of services for large and small firms in the area, including cleaning silverware for Northwest Orient Airlines, packaging records and tapes for Viking Records, and repairing damaged microwave ovens for Litton Industries. Since 1981 ACF's prisoner workers have contributed more than $133,600 toward the cost of their incarceration.

In 1986 Shingobee Enterprises entered into a cooperative arrangement with Hennepin County whereby the county provides space and labor and the company provides equipment, materials, management, and production supervision for the manufacture of cedar plant holders, bird feeders, and other garden ornaments. The twenty inmates working in the shop earn $3.55 per hour and work for the correctional facility, which bills the company for their labor.

Shingobee, originally located in a small town in northern Minnesota, moved its operation to the Minneapolis area after market expansion pushed its production demands beyond the capacity of the local labor force. The firm's owner was attracted to the county jail because of its willingness to provide space and to bear the cost of workers' compensation and liability insurance.

Discussion Questions

1. What are some of the different forms the prison industry takes?
2. What are the advantages and/or disadvantages of the private prison industry?
3. Is it fair to employ inmates in paying jobs while unemployment exists outside prison walls?
4. Should inmates be allowed to work in sensitive industries such as credit card data processing or electronics work for the Defense Department?

Notes

1. Due in part to the strong interest of Chief Justice Burger, the National Center for Innovation in Corrections was established at The George Washington University to provide a base for the furthering of cooperative ventures in prison industries. The Center was partially funded by the National Institute of Corrections and the National Institute of Justice.

2. The California Youth Authority operates under a legislative mandate different from that of the Adult Department of Corrections. The 1981 law enables the Youth Authority to "manufacture, repair, and assemble products ... for sale to or

pursuant to contract with the public..." However, Article X, Section 6, of the state constitution (adopted in 1879) says that "The labor of convicts shall not be let out by contract to any person, copartnership, company or corporation..."

There is no comprehensive definition of "convict" in the constitution, and when the Youth Authority was considering this issue some policy makers speculated that it could be argued that youthful offenders or wards are not "convicts" covered by the constitutional provision since the prohibition was adopted prior to the existence of the Department of the Youth Authority and, by extension, prior to the existence of "wards." However, a review of the remarks of the convention delegates revealed that their intent in passing the prohibition was to protect the community from unfair competition resulting from contracts for "cheap" institutional labor. Age would therefore seem to be irrelevant. With this in mind, the Youth Authority Department has adopted the position that its contracts with the private sector are for the supply of goods and services rather than the supply of youthful offender labor. Further, the Youth Authority has adopted a policy guaranteeing that wards employed in Free Venture Industries will be compensated at prevailing wages for their services.

3. In its approach to private-sector prison industries, the Youth Authority differs from the adult Corrections Department in two key respects: it has no prior experience with industrial work programs (either state-use or oriented to the free market); and its primary motivation in establishing such industries is not to combat idleness but to enhance its education programs by providing general employment skills to its wards. The latter partially explains why Free Venture Industries have been placed under the Youth Authority's education staff.

4. The Job Training Partnership Act provides federal funds through the state Office of Economic Development for vocational training for certain categories of disadvantaged citizens, including inmates.

5. Unlike most other states that have private-sector prison industries, Minnesota does not collect room and board fees from its inmate workers. The department found it cumbersome to collect the fees and difficult to determine a fair rate since its inmate workers live in widely varying types of housing. To avoid charges concerning equal protection under the law the department decided to abandon its room and board charge policy, even though a federal court had found, and the Eighth Circuit Court of Appeals confirmed, that such policies did not violate equal protection laws.

6. The Minnesota Line is sold in Illinois; Iowa, Minnesota, Montana, North Dakota, South Dakota, and Wisconsin.

National Institute of Justice

Issues and Practices

A Criminal Justice System Strategy for Treating Cocaine-Heroin Abusing Offenders in Custody

Harry K. Wexler, Narcotic and Drug Research, Inc.
Douglas S. Lipton, New York State Div. of Substance Abuse Services
and
Bruce D. Johnson, New York State Div. of Substance Abuse Services

March 1988

Research Findings

The Problem

Recent research provides ample evidence that offender populations are composed of large numbers of drug abusers—and that drug-involved offenders commit substantial numbers of undetected crimes.

Very recent cocaine and heroin abusers constitute a majority of the arrestees and inmates in jails and prisons in New York City and some other jurisdictions.

National surveys of jail and prison populations, smaller self-report studies, and urine testing results indicate that increasing proportions of offenders are users of drugs and that cocaine use is increasing the most rapidly. More than three-quarters of the nation's inmates and almost all inmates in New York City report illicit drug use.[1] Similarly, self-report studies among prison and jail inmates in California, Michigan, and Texas reveal that approximately half are heroin users and many are daily heroin users.[2] Recent urinalysis-based studies of arrestees in Washington, D.C. reveal that well over half test positive for at least one illicit drug and a quarter test positive for two or more illicit drugs.[3] In a recent Manhattan study the level of cocaine use had doubled since 1984. Eighty-

three percent of arrestees in September and October 1986 tested positive for cocaine, compared with 42 percent in 1984; the increase in cocaine was found at all age levels and for all offenses.[4] Comparable increases have also been reported in Washington, D.C.[5]

Frequent users of heroin and cocaine in the general population exhibit a multiproblem lifestyle that may include a pattern of persistent criminal behavior.

Drug addiction is a chronic relapsing condition that is part of a complex multiproblem lifestyle which is highly resistant to rehabilitation. Several studies show that daily or near daily heroin users—many of whom also use other illicit substances daily—are not in treatment, and do not seek treatment. Many also consume alcohol heavily. They average over 200 non-drug crimes and hundreds of drug distribution offenses annually, yet are unlikely to be arrested more than once a year, and then spend less than a month in incarceration. The majority commit many crimes for which they are not arrested or incarcerated, but because of sheer volume of activity, they still have many more arrests and incarceration periods than non-drug offenders. Over half their generally modest income comes from drug distribution activities. They usually spend most of that income on drugs. Daily heroin abusers also generally do not have a residence nor make their own meals, but rather stay and eat with a relative or friend. They do not receive or seek public assistance. They have no legal employment during a typical week nor do they seek any. Thus, they are typically an economic burden on the poorest members of their low-income communities. Many aspects of their lifestyle also put them at high risk for violence and many other social and health problems such as AIDS, alcoholism, and TB. Therefore, whatever treatment programming is applied to this population, it must contend with all or most of these problems if it is to achieve long-term changes in this lifestyle.[6]

Data about chronic cocaine users' crime rates are not as well developed. Recent evidence from street and treatment setting interviews with crack users indicate that about 60 percent admit paying for their cocaine with money derived from illicit sources—ranging from drug dealing and prostitution to theft and robbery. The persons using cocaine, however, generally come from more varied socioeconomic backgrounds than heroin users, their lifestyles vary accordingly, and many do not ever get arrested. Nevertheless, the lifestyles of cocaine abusers who do become involved with the criminal justice system appear to be very similar to those of heroin abusers, as cocaine users often also use heroin.[7]

The Criminal Justice Response

While much remains to be learned about the precise nature of the links between doing drugs and doing crime, the two behaviors are clearly associated. Yet criminal justice agencies have few strategies for routinely detecting and intervening in the drug use of arrested heroin and cocaine abusers. The justice system focuses almost exclusively on its criminal processing functions of arrest, adjudication, probation, incarceration, and parole. Even these interventions often represent a limited intrusion on the criminal activities of the drug abusing offender.

> **Criminal justice agencies, with rare exceptions, do not seek or use information about the drug use of persons who are arrested or convicted of crimes.**

Little effort is made to identify drug abusers, to record information about their drug use, to provide treatment (other than detoxification) while in jail or prison, to refer them to treatment programs in the

community, or to use such information in plea bargaining or case dispositions (where legally appropriate). Only a few jurisdictions maintain any information about the drug use of arrestees or convicted offenders, and there is a strong likelihood that the drug information in their records is both incomplete and inaccurate because it is most often based on self-report and not substantiated through urinalysis. Thus, information that could help inform criminal justice processing is not generally available.[8]

> **To the extent that criminal sanctions are applied, their ability to interrupt the life style of the vast majority of cocaine-heroin abusers is minimal.**

Nationally, only a low percentage (less than 10 percent) of all felony arrests lead to a felony conviction resulting in incarceration. Over half of all felony arrests (60 percent in Manhattan) lead to conviction, but there is much variation by jurisdiction. Typically, offenders plead guilty to lesser charges and are sentenced to time served, a fine, community service, probation, or a few months in jail. Consequently, the vast majority of offenders, mainly those arrested on less severe felony and misdemeanor charges, are at liberty within three months after arrest. In addition, many felony offenders (a significant portion of whom are involved with drugs) are at liberty on bail or on personal recognizance while awaiting trial. Active heroin-cocaine users have higher failure-to-appear rates and much higher rates of re-arrest while out on bail than offenders not involved with drugs.[9]

The Efficacy of Criminal Sanctions

Little evidence is available that criminal justice sanctions alone are as effective as drug treatment in reducing the drug use and criminality of cocaine-heroin abusers at liberty. The central value of the criminal process may lie in the leverage that can be exerted to bring hardcore drug abusers into treatment.

> **Existing evidence does not show that criminal justice sanctions (fine, probation, or parole, or length of time served) reduce criminality or drug use more effectively than drug treatment among cocaine-heroin abusers.**

It is not known whether or to what extent jail or prison time alone suppresses post-incarceration criminality or cocaine-heroin abuse among drug involved offenders. The limited evidence available suggests that two-thirds or more of arrested heroin abusers return to heroin-cocaine use and their diverse criminal patterns within three months after release from detention. In contrast, several studies of drug treatment outcomes with criminal justice clients (mainly probationers) show substantial post-treatment reductions in both drug use and criminality.[10] Outpatient clients in methadone treatment report less than half as much criminal activity as heroin abusers not in treatment. Compared with their pretreatment criminality, methadone clients report 50 to 80 percent less crime during treatment.[11] Even among those who continue criminal activity during treatment, methadone clients report reduced involvement in serious crimes such as robbery, burglary, or dealing of heroin or cocaine; they report mainly low-level property crimes, con games, and sale of marijuana or pills.[12]

Residential drug programs have sizable proportions (frequently over half) of clients who are on probation or parole or under related legal pressure, and whose criminality is near zero while in the residential program. This near-zero criminality of cocaine-heroin abusers while in residential programs is documented for therapeutic communities in several cities. A study of treatment facilities in New York found that about a third of residential clients were criminal justice referrals and had extensive criminal histories. These clients tended to stay longer and have as good or better outcomes than clients with similar pretreatment criminal and drug abuse histories who were not referred by the criminal justice system.[13]

The coercive power, surveillance potential, and time offered through criminal justice sanctions, open significant opportunities for effectively treating cocaine-heroin abusers.

Although criminal justice sanctions alone may have uncertain value in reducing the criminality of drug involved offenders, those sanctions can serve a powerful role by facilitating effective drug treatment. There are a variety of pressures that bring hardcore drug abusers into treatment: parents, employers, loved ones, and friends may all apply psychological and social pressures. The most powerful pressure, however, may be the threat of legal sanction—the threat of arrest and conviction, and most importantly, the threat of incarceration. The leverage created by this threat, and by the sanction itself, permits treatment to be considered as a viable option by serious abusers. Moreover, by reduc-

ing early program termination, it allows the treatment and aftercare to continue for the length of the permissible custody.

Cocaine-heroin abusers typically wish to avoid the "hassles" associated with changing their lives. When the alternative is lengthy incarceration, cocaine-heroin abusers may be more willing to be referred to drug treatment. If, however, the alternative is a short jail sentence, detainees and jail inmates may prefer the incarceration rather than diversion to long-term drug abuse treatment.

Unfortunately, relatively few arrested offenders voluntarily seek treatment.[14] Many offenders are referred by the criminal justice system to drug treatment as the result of negotiated plea bargains in which the offender agrees to enter treatment instead of receiving a substantial sentence. For many years, TASC (Treatment Alternatives to Street Crime) has operated in selected jurisdictions to recruit clients and negotiate with court staff for release of offenders to drug programs. TASC clients are more likely to select treatment because the alternative is considered more onerous.

Few cocaine-heroin abusers in custody volunteer for drug treatment unless the treatment program is seen as an attractive alternative. Prison inmates seek out in-house treatment programs because they often provide better living conditions, a safer environment, parole release considerations, and an opportunity to possibly change one's lifestyle. In-prison programs that offer such conditions are substantially better able to recruit participants than those which do not. Although these offenders may not be completely sincere at admission, there is an opportunity for the program to engage them in an effective treatment experience. In short, the threat of substantial sanctions (for arrestees) or the promise of better in-prison conditions (for those in custody) can operate as extremely useful incentives for treatment. Nevertheless, it must be understood that a significant proportion of offenders who have long chronic heroin or cocaine abuse patterns will not want treatment under any circumstances.

Some Dimensions of Effective Drug Abuse Treatment

As the preceding section has demonstrated, the criminality of heroin abusers is substantially reduced while they are receiving some form of treatment. The experiences of effective programs suggest that whatever treatment method is used must have a sound theoretical and empirical basis for its implementation. Additionally, the treatment method must emerge from a powerful social restoration tradition (discussed further below) that is capable of teaching offenders to interact with others in less deviant, more socially acceptable ways. Such an approach must be credible to participants and not be perceived to be coercive and authoritarian. The approach must have the capability to convince offenders that the demanding path to a socially acceptable lifestyle is worthwhile despite their deprived backgrounds, their experience with quick criminal profits, and their recognition that there is a low probability they will be caught for their crimes.

Despite the often cited conclusion that "nothing works", evidence from the research literature continues to accumulate that some programs have been successful in reducing recidivism.[15]

The majority of successful programs have been based on a social learning theory of criminal behavior.[16] According to this theory, criminal behavior is learned through a process of social interaction with others. Thus, pro-social behaviors must be learned to replace deviant behavior. Effective approaches include: therapeutic communities, self-help groups, family therapy, contingency contracting, role playing and modeling, vocational and social skills training, training in interpersonal cognitive problem-solving skills, and other programs involving ongoing peer monitoring of participants' behavior.[17]

Successful programs have several things in common: authority structures that clearly specify rules and sanctions, anti-criminal modeling and reinforcement of pro-social behavior, pragmatic personal and social problem-solving assistance, program staff knowledgeable about the use of community resources, and relationships between staff and clients which are empathic and characterized by open communication and trust. Ex-offender-addict counselors who serve as credible role-models of successful rehabilitation also are often utilized.[18] The "Stay 'N Out" program (see Appendix A) provides an example of a successful program that employs these treatment principles.

Conversely, unsuccessful programs are frequently based on a medical (disease) model of criminology which suggests that criminal behavior is a sickness.[19] Similarly, intervention programs based on deterrence models (e.g., "Scared Straight") have shown very limited effects and have even been associated with in-creased offending.[20] Other types of programs that have been unsuccessful include those that rely solely on open communication, "friendship" models, inmate-directed therapy groups, and those that are non-directive.[21]

While inmate-directed therapy groups have not had a record of success, behavioral programs that are simply imposed—without involving inmates in their development—do not appear to work either. Such programs are often focused on anti-social rather than pro-social behaviors and as a result give undue attention and reinforcement to negative behavior. Other features of unsuccessful programs include the failure to either neutralize or utilize the inmate's peer group and failure to sustain continuity of care after release from prison.[22]

A number of factors have been identified that degrade treatment integrity and impede treatment success.[23] Many are common to intervention programs in any setting. The absence of sound theoretical basis for treatment is a typical obstacle to the development of successful programs. Often, the quality and intensity of treatment interventions are inadequate. Sometimes programs propose treatment interventions that are based on sound principles which are not followed when the program is implemented. Another common problem is lack of staff training and treatment experience, and/or their inadequate commitment to both the clients' and program success.

Other impediments to the establishment and maintenance of successful treatment programs are related to a lack of correctional system support and the negative influence of inmate subcultures. Fundamental differences between custodial and treatment perspectives often contribute to the failure of the correctional environment to support program staff and goals. The lack of support from the custodial forces of an institution is exacerbated within prisons by the negative influence of the anti-authoritarian and anti-therapeutic "prisoners' code." Under this code, suspicion colors most interactions between staff and inmates. The result may be a program that receives neither staff support nor inmate cooperation.

Time in community drug treatment is inversely related to post-treatment cocaine-heroin abuse and criminality.

Turning to a more quantitative dimension of treatment programming, the available research clearly suggests the longer heroin and cocaine abusers remain in treatment, the greater the reduction in post-treatment criminality. Those who remain in community-based residential, methadone, or out-patient programs for more than three months have lower levels of both post-treatment heroin and cocaine abuse and criminality than those who drop out before three months and significantly lower rates than their own pre-treatment levels. Subsequent months of treatment in these programs yield even greater reductions in post-treatment criminality, especially after 12 months of treatment and after each subsequent treatment cycle.

Treatment personnel generally agree that it is hard even to stabilize the cocaine-heroin abuser's lifestyle in three months, much less begin to transform long-standing patterns of deviance. After three months, clients can begin to be comfortable with the treatment regime and start to make progress in changing disruptive patterns in their lives. However, due to the chronic relapsing pattern characteristic of the drug addict, several "cycles of treatment" are frequently necessary for hardcore drug abusers to achieve substantial improvement in their behavior and lifestyle.

Clients who leave treatment early against program advice are significantly more likely to recidivate than those who complete the recommended program. Early leavers who later return to treatment ultimately have less heroin use and criminality than those who fail to return.[24]

Outcome studies have shown that the first 12 months in treatment are critical to long-term reductions in criminality after leaving treatment. For cocaine and heroin abusers who are incarcerated and who participate in prison-based therapeutic community programs, the optimum period of treatment appears to be nine to twelve months followed by release into the community. Longer stays are associated with diminishing results. It is believed this occurs for two reasons: First, longer periods of program participation while in prison creates increased dependency on the program and less transference of the learned experiences to the community upon release. Secondly, some persons are transferred as rehabilitated back into the general prison population after completing more than a year of treatment, and the criminal subculture undermines some gains made during the treatment period. Thus, the timing of treatment and release for prison inmates with serious drug abuse problems needs to be coordinated to achieve the optimum outcome.[25]

Conclusion

Clearly, much has been learned about effective ways of reducing the drug involvement of heroin and cocaine abusing offenders. Given the chronic recurring nature of addiction, no program can realistically expect to eliminate severe heroin and cocaine abuse for all offenders. Yet even if a program succeeds only in reducing the frequency of use, substantial reductions in criminality may follow. The evidence is clear: cocaine-heroin abusers commit much less crime when they use once or twice a week or less often than when they use once a day or more often. If, for example, daily cocaine-heroin users were placed under court-directed intensive surveillance and frequent urine monitoring which curtailed their use of drugs by half or more, a very substantial drop in their criminality would be likely to occur, especially in crimes such as robbery and burglary.[26]

Policy Recommendations

What steps should be taken by the criminal justice system to deal more effectively with the drug-involved offender? Based on the research findings discussed in the preceding section and the experience and opinions of the authors, this section presents a series of policy recommendations. While it may not be possible to institute all or even most of these recommendations in many jurisdictions, they are offered as goals or guidelines for the practitioner. We argue that the interventions proposed will improve the system by leading to the effective integration and coordination of offender supervision and drug treatment approaches.

Beginning with the crucial need to identify heroin and cocaine abusers at arrest, the recommendations focus in turn on jail-based interventions, in-prison programs, and community treatment options. Also included are system-wide recommendations pertaining to the organization and staffing of drug abuse treatment programs. All of the recommendations presented in this section call for the criminal justice system to supervise cocaine-heroin users frequently and systematically:

■ Convicted cocaine-heroin abusers under community supervision should be intensively supervised and compelled to attend treatment for their maximum period of custody. Optimal supervision includes near daily validation of employment, time in residence, associations, and absence of drug use.
■ Convicted cocaine-heroin abusers sentenced to prison should be required to participate in drug treatment for nine months to one year prior to release *and* to continue in community treatment as a condition of parole. Their urine and behavior should be

carefully monitored while under field supervision to insure attendance and prevent relapses.[27]

■ Steps should be taken to ensure that drug-involved offenders in city and county detention facilities are placed in treatment after release. During their confinement, methadone maintenance should be continued for addicts previously assigned to this program or initiated for other heroin users. Naltrexone combined with urine surveillance should be used for those heroin users on work release who opt for drug-free treatment.

The Identification of Drug-Involved Offenders

In areas with a large number of heroin and cocaine users, urinalysis should be used to identify these users at arrest.

Most cocaine-heroin abusers who have contact with the criminal justice system are arrested about once per year. Results of the pretrial drug-testing program operating in Washington, D.C. suggest that recent users of cocaine or heroin can be identified accurately at arrest through urinalysis. By collecting urine samples from all arrestees, and analyzing the specimens for five types of drugs including opiates, the D.C. Pretrial Services Agency has been able to identify and increase supervision of drug users released pending trial. These procedures appear to have reduced the rates of rearrest and failure-to-appear. Moreover, by systematically retaining the results of the urine tests, the information has been made available to help determine appropriate criminal sanctions for those arrestees ultimately convicted.[28]

The costs of a urine testing program may be amply justified in any jurisdiction with a significant drug problem. As in D.C., the data collected should be systematically maintained and used for determining conditions of pre-trial release and sanctions for those convicted. In particular, the opportunity should be seized to present appropriate treatment options.

Jail-Based Interventions

Treatment orientation and referral to drug treatment programs should be instituted in metropolitan courts and jails.

A central intake staff and/or representatives of drug treatment programs should be present at court and in

jails. All offenders who test drug positive at arrest should be required to attend orientation and preliminary intake procedures while in detention. These preliminary treatment steps may help ensure that those who are released from custody are placed in appropriate treatment after returning to the community.[29]

Full treatment interventions, however, should not be initiated for cocaine-heroin offenders who will be free of custody in less than three months. It is neither cost effective nor therapeutically wise to implement full treatment programming when there is little expectation that treatment can be completed.

Methadone programs should be permitted to maintain clients in jails to facilitate resumption of treatment at the end of detention.

Methadone treatment has proven effective in reducing daily heroin use and substantially reducing criminality among heroin abusers. Enrolled methadone clients who are arrested can be maintained on methadone while detained. In this way, return to methadone treatment upon release after short-term jail custody would be facilitated. Those who are convicted and sentenced to incarceration should be given the option (when medically recommended) to remain on methadone or to detoxify from methadone and enter an in-prison therapeutic community. Consideration should also be given to initiating methadone treatment in jails for chronic heroin addicts. Heroin addicts serving short sentences who are introduced to methadone treatment while incarcerated are more likely to enter and remain in methadone maintenance treatment in the community when they are released from custody.

Daily naltrexone consumption should be used for some convicted heroin abusers in combination with drug-free treatment and intensive supervision.

For *heroin-abusing* offenders who receive jail or probation sentences and who opt for drug-free treatment, use of naltrexone (Trexan®), combined with urine surveillance, could be instituted. Its use with jail inmates on work release or school furlough appears particularly appropriate. Naltrexone is an easily administered narcotic antagonist drug which taken daily produces almost immediate withdrawal symptoms in addicts when they use an opiate, but is harmless to nonaddicts. It is most effective with heroin-addicted offenders who have a high level of community integration. It has no effect on cocaine, however; therefore, urine monitoring *must* be sustained.[30]

In-Prison Treatment

Therapeutic communities and other intensive milieu drug treatments should be made available to cocaine-heroin abusing state prisoners about one year prior to parole eligibility.

A successful therapeutic community, the "Stay 'N Out" program (see Appendix A), was developed at two correctional facilities in New York State—one for men and one for women. This model therapeutic community in prison holds the greatest promise for changing hard-core, drug-abusing inmates and reducing recidivism.[31]

Despite their proven effectiveness, few therapeutic communities such as "Stay 'N Out" are in place for criminally involved drug abusers. One of the factors that limits the creation of additional programs of this type is the concern that such programs might engage in activities that threaten security and encourage inmate resistance to the correctional system. Nonetheless, correctional administrators learn quickly as they become exposed to the operation of well-run programs that such undesirable variance can be avoided. In fact, in institutions where most of these programs have been established, the wardens and correctional officers frequently are their most vocal champions. To encourage their development, however, staff and administration need education and training. Further, a number of fiscal and practical issues have to be addressed prior to implementation.

The implementation of prison-based treatment programs requires isolation from the general prison population.

The inimical influence of the criminal inmate subculture ("prisoners' code") will inevitably undermine any attempts to establish viable programming if the program is not isolated from this anti-therapeutic force. Separate living quarters, recreation, food services, etc. should be maintained within the institution for this separation to be ideally effective. Total isolation is, however, neither necessary nor desirable; rather, some contact with the general inmate population is useful for the purpose of allowing the inmate in treatment to see where he has come from and how much he has changed. In addition, the contact experience provides the opportunity for the program resident to test both his new prosocial values against the inmate subculture and his

resistance to negative influences. This kind of isolation is most possible in medium security institutions with dormitory-type housing space where one dormitory or two are physically segregated or separable from the main institution.

Prisoners in therapeutic communities who make good treatment progress should be paroled to residential drug-free programs that sustain the therapeutic community model prior to completion of their sentence. They should be required to stay in treatment as a condition of parole until their date of maximum custody or until the program deems them recovered.

It is essential for the successful treatment of cocaine-heroin abuser offenders to maintain continuity-of-care from the outset of treatment to termination of custody. While there is benefit from prison treatment alone, these effects are augmented and sustained by continuing that specific treatment in the community.

Ideally, release to the community facility would be contingent on the progress made during in-prison treatment. Under this incentive system, specific behaviors would be rewarded with a specified number of restitution or release "points" that might be administered as a form of "good time" system. Alternatively, prisoners might earn more favorable conditions of confinement or higher status and associated program privileges. However it is administered, the basic notion is to reinforce the desirability of pro-social behaviors.

Community Treatment Programs

Drug-abusing misdemeanants should be considered for community-based sentencing alternatives.

In lieu of confining drug-involved offenders in jails and county penitentiaries, a range of intermediate sanctions should be considered for heroin and cocaine abusers convicted of misdemeanors. These might include house arrest with electronic monitoring, intermittent sentences (e.g., weekend or evening incarceration), TASC programs, or residence in a facility such as a "halfway in-halfway out" center (a "HiHo"). Again, in any of these alternatives offenders would ideally be able to achieve release status more quickly by providing drug-negative urine samples, routinely attending and participating positively in treatment sessions, paying back their victims, and providing evidence of prosocial activity.[32]

The community treatment resources available to support intermediate sanctioning policies range from self-help groups that meet once a week for a couple of hours to residential facilities that provide 24 hour supervision and programming. At a minimum, almost all communities have an Alcoholics Anonymous or Narcotics Anonymous group that provides a context for recovering substance abusers to meet, discuss day-to-day steps for maintaining a drug free life, and participate in many different types of social activities not involving alcohol or drugs.[33] Some communities provide drug treatment counseling through the Department of Mental Health. And in many cities, recovering substance-abusers operate group homes that use many of the same principles of Alcoholics Anonymous or therapeutic communities found in prison programs.

TASC programs run throughout the nation provide staff who are familiar with the particular resources available for drug-involved offenders in specific communities. And almost all states have an agency that periodically determines the availability of both private and public programs available for drug treatment. A list of these agencies is available from the National Association of State Drug and Alcohol Abuse Directors, in Washington, D.C.[34]

Even if no other treatment is provided, heroin-cocaine abusers who are on probation and parole should be required to have frequent urine tests.

Drug-abusing offenders on probation or parole who are in no special treatment programs, as a minimum should be routinely required to provide specimens for urinalysis over the entire length of their probation or parole. At the outset the frequency of urinalysis should be near daily, and decreased as positive progress warrants. The effective monitoring of urinalysis results will help to interrupt relapse to daily heroin or cocaine use, and, hence, high-rate criminality is likely to drop substantially.[35] When drug positive urines are detected, offenders should be immediately confronted, clearly warned after the first such incident, be required to enter treatment for diagnosis and assessment after the second positive urine, and be required to remain in treatment if relapse seems imminent or has occurred. Refusal to enter treatment upon an affirmative diagnosis should be considered a violation of release conditions.

Organization and Staffing Issues

The integrity of the treatment programs for convicted offenders must be maintained by developing structural safeguards of independence and autonomy from correctional management.

All too often well designed interventions operated by competent and motivated agency and institutional staffs do not succeed. Usually, the efforts are not trusted by the criminal justice clients, are overwhelmed by the difficulty of the clients' problems, are weakened by inadequate funding and institutional resistance, and are subject to high rates of staff burnout and turnover. For a treatment program to last long enough to make a substantial difference, it must maintain its own integrity, i.e., honesty and commitment to the treatment goals and program participants. The staff must also have sufficient independence and autonomy to deliver on their promises.

Treatment programs conducted by organizations independent of (but closely linked to) corrections agencies are more likely to maintain their integrity than programs operated by correctional staff within institutions or community corrections settings. This suggests that an outside agency working in cooperation with or under contract to the Department of Corrections may be the most appropriate treatment organization. Management responsibility for the rehabilitation program should be assigned to a team of committed treatment professionals, as well as ex-addict/ex-offender peer counselors. For this approach to work, the power and authority of the treatment team should be comparable to and complement the criminal justice authority. This management group should be associated with and monitored by respected professional self-help/therapeutic community organizations, for example, Therapeutic Communities of America.

Probation and parole officers should have their functions divided into Surveillance Officers and Community Treatment Team Leaders.

For many years, correctional observers have debated the wisdom of vesting probation and parole officers with the potentially conflicting responsibilities of surveillance and treatment. In the opinion of the authors, surveillance and treatment functions of field supervision officers should be separated to resolve the inherent conflicts and strengthen each function. Essential to the effectiveness of the treatment/counseling relationship is trust and confidentiality. Persons under field supervision are unlikely to freely admit criminal acts or drug use to someone in a position to return them to prison for such violations. Therefore, surveillance and rehabilitation responsibilities should be handled by staffs who work separately but cooperatively to avoid role confusion for both officer and offender. As the next recommendation suggests, both types of officers should be augmented by carefully selected ex-offender-addicts who would serve as Monitors for the Surveillance Officers and as Treatment Team staff for the Community Treatment Team Leader.

The Treatment Team staff should rotate between working in prison and the community to maintain continuity between the rehabilitation efforts in both environments. For in-prison programs, the objective of separating custodial and treatment functions is satisfied by the organization discussed in the preceding point.

Former addict-offenders who have shown clear evidence of prosocial change should have training and employment opportunities, for example, as Monitors and Treatment Team members.

Large numbers of offenders who have been chronic cocaine-heroin abusers are unable to gain and to keep legal employment. Their background is so limited and so stigmatized that legal employers are reluctant to employ them, and suspicious after they do. Thus, even after making good treatment progress, many offenders may still be unable to gain stable employment. First, systematic skill development and training programs should be provided. Second, providing employment to ex-addict-offenders within the treatment program itself is a valuable opportunity to deal with this unemployment issue as well as cope with shortages of field supervision personnel.

The employment of ex-addict-offenders in a variety of progressively more responsible paraprofessional and professional roles will help new monitoring and drug treatment systems function effectively. They also will serve as role models to offenders they supervise. The ex-addict offenders are the role models (as in "Stay 'N Out") whose presence demonstrates the realistic possibility of achieving successful rehabilitation. Graduation from a drug treatment program, evidence of successful integration into community life, and additional training are prerequisites for the employment of ex-

addict-offenders as Monitors and Treatment Team members.

Conclusion

By substantially reducing their cocaine-heroin abuse, the criminality of drug-involved offenders may be reduced by 20 to 50 percent or more. To do so, however, the criminal justice system must develop an alliance with the drug treatment system geared to achieve the goals of effective rehabilitation, enhanced prosocial behavior, and reduced recidivism.

The difficulties inherent in bringing about this alliance should not be minimized. Some reallocation of resources clearly will be required, with all the tensions attendant on any significant shift in funding and operational priorities. If custodial and treatment functions are to be effectively separated, recruitment, training, and retraining programs will have to be developed for community corrections personnel. Institutional corrections environments must be prepared to accept independent treatment organizations. Procedures must be developed to identify and train those therapeutic community graduates best qualified to become competent treatment team members and monitors. The problem of intensive community resistance to accepting community treatment facilities (HiHo's) that house felons and substance abusers must also be addressed. Within prisons, space will have to be reallocated to create therapeutic communities to house clients during treatment. If institutions are converted for total therapeutic community utilization, abandoned mental hospitals may be utilized, with significant capital expenditures necessary for conversion. Beginning at the point of arrest, screening procedures will have to be developed to monitor drug use and to identify cocaine-heroin users who can most benefit from the proposed interventions.

Perhaps most important, cooperation will be needed among stable drug abuse agencies and drug treatment programs and criminal justice organizations (courts, probation, corrections, and parole) that traditionally have had competing political and fiscal interests and often lack a history of successful joint ventures. Careful documentation of pilot results will also be needed to evaluate whether the system is moving in desired or unanticipated directions. For this, evaluation researchers will have to be in place from the outset. Since many problems will arise that have the potential for compromising the interventions, the evaluation design must provide decision makers with timely information to assist them in formulating corrective actions. At the same time, ongoing dissemination of outcome information through professional and media channels will help foster and maintain the support necessary to accomplish the changes proposed.

Appendix A—"Stay 'N Out": A model for prison-based drug treatment

"Stay 'N Out" is a therapeutic community (TC), in part based upon the Phoenix House model, that has been operating in the New York State prison system for the last ten years. Over time the program has been modified to operate more effectively within the prison environment. The program has been fortunate to be operated by many of the founding staff who have provided the vision, commitment, and determination necessary for a successful prison program.

An early evaluation of the "Stay 'N Out" program indicated that it was successfully implemented, maintained a positive TC environment, and produced positive psychological and behavioral changes in participants. In 1984, the National Institute on Drug Abuse funded an evaluation of "Stay 'N Out", comparing it to two other prison-based programs in New York State and a control group of inmates on program waiting lists, but receiving no treatment. A milieu program and a standard counseling program were the comparison groups. Although participants were not randomly assigned to these treatment conditions, preliminary results of the comparison are provocative. The data indicate the "Stay 'N Out" participants who remained in the program for nine to twelve months were less likely to have problems while on parole than either those who left "Stay 'N Out" earlier or those in other prison-based programs. For example, "Stay 'N Out" participants who remained in the program more than nine months were more likely to have a positive parole discharge (80 percent positive) than those who remained in the program less than three months (50 percent positive). Positive parole discharge is defined as no reported violations of parole during the parole custody period. Long-term (9–12 months) participants of the other programs studied also had fewer cases of positive parole discharge; the milieu program reported a 56 percent positive discharge rate and the counseling program a 47 percent positive rate.

Preliminary analysis indicates that long-term "Stay 'N Out" participants may also have a more encouraging pattern of re-arrest than those in the other programs. Continuing follow-up shows that only 27 percent of the TC participants were re-arrested compared to 35 percent of the milieu participants, 50 percent of the counseling participants, and 42 percent of the waiting list persons. In addition, TC participants averaged 18 months to re-arrest compared to 11 months for the milieu and nine months for the counseling group. These data should be interpreted with caution, however, as variation in the actual number of days at risk may vary greatly among samples.

Program overview

"Stay 'N Out" programs were begun as a joint effort among New York State Division of Substance Abuse Services (DSAS), New York Therapeutic Communities (NYTC), New York Department of Correctional Services (DOCS), and the New York State Division of Parole. Currently, NYTC operates the programs, DOCS supplies funding, and Parole provides increased opportunities for program residents. The DSAS Bureau of Research and Evaluation continues to evaluate the program.

The current program consists of two treatment units for male inmates in one facility with 35 beds per unit (a total capacity of 70 beds), and one treatment unit with 40 beds for women inmates in another facility. Each unit is staffed by a total of seven persons, including both professionals and para-professionals. Inmates selected for the programs are recruited at State correctional facilities. The criteria for selection are: history of drug abuse, at least 18 years of age, evidence of positive institutional participation, and no history of sex crimes or mental illness. "Stay 'N Out" clients are housed in units segregated from the general prison population. They eat in a common dining room, however, and attend morning activities with other prisoners. The optimum length of treatment is from nine to twelve months. Most program staff are ex-addict-offenders who are graduates of community TCs; they act as "role models" exemplifying successful rehabilitation. The course of treatment is a developmental growth process with the inmate becoming an increasingly responsible member of the program.

During the early phase of treatment, the clinical thrust involves assessment of client needs and problem areas. Orientation to the prison TC procedures occurs through individual counseling, encounter sessions, and seminars. Clients are given low-level jobs and granted little status. During the later phases of treatment, residents are provided opportunities to earn higher-level positions and increased status through sincere involvement in the program and hard work. Encounter groups and counseling sessions are more in-depth and focus on the areas of self-discipline, self-worth, self-awareness, respect for authority, and acceptance of guidance for problem areas. Seminars take on a more intellectual nature. Debate is encouraged to enhance self-expression and to increase self-confidence.

Upon release, participants are encouraged to seek further substance abuse treatment at cooperating community TCs. Extensive involvement with a network of community TCs is central to the program's operation. Staff and senior residents of community TCs visit "Stay 'N Out" on a regular basis to recruit resident inmates for their programs. These visitors provide inspiration since they are ex-addicts and ex-felon role models who are leading economically and socially productive lives.

"Stay 'N Out" Components

Program Elements

■ Isolated Unit
■ Utilization of Ex-Offender/Ex-Addict Staff
■ Establishment of Psychological and Physical Safety
■ Hierarchical Therapeutic Community
■ Confrontation and Support Groups
■ Individual Counseling
■ Community and Relationship Training
■ Program Rules with Opportunities to Learn from Misbehavior
■ Immediate Discharge for Drug Possession, Violence and Sexual Misbehavior
■ Developing Pro-Social Values: Honesty, Responsibility, and Accountability
■ Continuity-of-Care: Networking with Community TCs

Administrative Components

■ DOC Contract Arrangement with Private Agency
■ Administrative Offices Outside Prison
■ Membership in Local and National Professional Organizations
■ Maintain Political Relations with Alternative Funding Sources and Legislators

Institutional Relations

■ Earned Respect of Prison Administrators and Guards
■ Development of a Model Unit Impressive to Visitors
■ Placement of Program Residents in Important Prison Jobs

Relations With Inmate Culture

■ Earned Respect of General Population Inmates
■ Opportunities to Test TC Values

Notes

1. BJS 1983c,d,e,f; 1985a; 1986b,d, Sanchez and Johnson 1987.

2. Chaiken and Chaiken 1982; Chaiken 1986.

3. Toborg 1984; Toborg et al. 1986; Carver 1986; Wish, Brady, and Cuadrado 1984, 1986.

4. Wish 1987.

5. Wish 1987; John Carver 1987 (personal communication): DC Pretrial Services Agency; 400 F St., NW; Washington, DC 20001.

6. Anglin and McGlothlin 1984; Ball, Shaffer, and Nurco 1983; Collins, Hubbard, and Rachal 1985; Hanson et al. 1985; Johnson et al. 1985; Johnson and Wish 1987; Sanchez and Johnson 1987.

7. Hanson et al. 1985, Johnson et al. 1985; Johnson and Wish 1987; Sanchez and Johnson 1987; Hunt, et al. 1984.

8. Belenko 1981; Carver 1986; Chaiken and Chaiken 1984; Toborg et al. 1986; Wish 1986; Wish et al. 1980; Wish, Brady, and Cuadrado 1986; Chaiken and Chaiken 1987.

9. Belenko 1984; BJS 1983f; Lynott 1986; Petersilia et al. 1985; Wish, Brady, and Cuadrado 1986.

10. Anglin and McGlothlin 1984; BJS 1983f; DeLeon 1984a,b; 1985; Hubbard et al. 1984; Robins 1973; Sells 1974; Sells and Simpson 1976.

11. Anglin and McGlothlin 1984; Dole and Joseph 1979; DesJarlais et al. 1982; Hubbard et al. 1984; McGlothlin 1979; McGlothlin, Anglin, and Wilson 1977; McGlothlin and Anglin 1981a,b; Senay 1984, 1985; Simpson 1984.

12. Kleinman and Lukoff 1975; Hunt et al. 1984; Hunt 1985.

13. DeLeon et al. 1980; DeLeon, Wexler, and Jainchill 1982; DeLeon 1984a,b, 1985 Hubbard et al. 1984; Simpson and Sells 1982; Tims and Ludford 1984; Wexler and DeLeon 1977; Wexler and Williams 1986.

14. Carver 1986; Collins and Allison, 1983; Goldsmith et al. 1984; Hunt et al. 1984; Johnson et al. 1985; Wish, Brady, Cuadrado 1986; Wish 1986.

15. Alexander and Parsons 1973; Andrews 1980; Chandler 1973; Gendreau and Ross 1979; Peters 1981; Philips, Phillips, and Wolf 1973; Ross and McKay 1976; Walter and Mills 1979; Wexler, Lipton, and Foster 1985; Wexler and Williams 1986.

16. Bandura 1979; Nettler 1978; Niezel 1979.

17. Gendreau and Ross 1983–1984.

18. Andrews and Kiessling 1980; Lee and Haynes 1980; Platt, Perry, and Metzger 1980; Ross and McKay 1976; Wexler and Williams 1986.

19. Balch 1975; Ross and Gendreau 1980.

20. Blumstein, Cohen, and Nagin 1978; Critelli and Crawford 1980; Erickson, Gibbs, and Jensen 1977; Hart 1978.

21. Craft, Stephenson, and Granger 1964; Fenton 1960; Grant and Grant 1959; Kassebaum, Ward, and Wilner 1971.

22. Ross and McKay 1978.

23. Gendreau and Ross 1979; Quay 1977; Rappeport et al. 1979; Repucci et al. 1973; Sechrest et al. 1979a,b.

24. Des Jarlais et al. 1982.

25. Wexler, Lipton, and Foster 1985.

26. Ball et al. 1979, 1981; Collins, Hubbard, and Rachal 1985; Des Jarlais et al. 1982; Hunt, Lipton, and Spunt 1984; Johnson et al. 1985; Nurco et al. 1985; Sanchez and Johnson 1987; Speckart and Anglin 1986a,b.

27. Anglin and McGlothlin 1984; Carver 1986; McGlothlin, Anglin, and Wilson 1977.

28. Carver et al. 1986; Toborg et al. 1986; Wish et al. 1980, 1983; Wish, Brady, and Cuadrado 1984, 1986; Wish, Cuadrado, and Montorana 1986; Wish, Cuadrado, and Montorana 1986.

29. Collins, Hubbard, and Rachal 1985; National Association of State Drug Abuse Program Coordinators 1978; Toborg et al. 1975.

30. Brahen 1983; Brahen et al. 1979.

31. Wexler 1985; Wexler and Lipton 1985; Wexler, Lipton, and Foster 1985; Wexler and Sharron 1985; Wexler and Williams 1986.

32. Wish, Brady, and Cuadrado 1986.

33. Chaiken, Marcia 1979.

34. NASAD is located at 444 W Capitol St., NW, Suite 530; Washington, DC 20001.

35. Carver 1986; Chamlee 1986; Toborg et al. 1986.

References

Alexander, J.F. and Parsons, R.J. 1973. Short-term Behavioral Intervention with Delinquent Families: Impact on Family Process and Recidivism. *Journal of Abnormal Psychology*, 81, 219–225.

Andrews, D.A. and Kiessling, J.J. 1980. Program Structure and Effective Correctional Practices: A Summary of the CAVIC Research. In R.R. Ross and P. Gendreau (eds.) *Effective Correctional Treatment*. 1980. Toronto: Butterworths.

Andrews, D.A. 1980. Some Experimental Investigations of the Principles of Differential Association Through Deliberate Manipulation of the Structure of Service Systems, *American Sociological Review*, 45, 448–462.

Anglin, M.D. and McGlothlin, W.C. 1984. Outcome of narcotic addict treatment in California. Pp. 106–128 in Frank M. Tims and Jacqueline P. Ludford (eds.), *Drug Abuse Treatment Evaluation: Strategies, Progress, and Prospects.* Research Monograph Series 51. Rockville, Md.: National Institute on Drug Abuse.

Balch, R.W. 1975. The Medical Model of Delinquency: Theoretical, Practical, and Ethical Implications. *Crime and Delinquency*, 21, 116–129.

Ball, J.C., Shaffer, J.W. and Nurco, D.N. 1983. The day-to-day criminality of heroin addicts in Baltimore: A study in the continuity of offense rates. *Drug and Alcohol Dependence*, 12 (1): 19–142.

Ball, J.C., Rosen, L., Flueck, J.A. and Nurco, D.N. 1981. The criminality of heroin addicts when addicted and when off opiates. Pp. 39–65 in J.A. Inciardi, (ed.), *The Drugs-Crime Connection*. Beverly Hills, Calif.: Sage.

Ball, J.C., Rosen, L., Flueck, J.A. and Nurco, D.N. 1982. Lifetime criminality of heroin addicts in the United States. *Journal of Drug Issues*. 3: 225–239.

Ball, J.C., Rosen, L., Friedman, E.G. and Nurco, D.N. 1979. The impact of heroin addiction upon criminality. Pp. 163–169 in L. Harris (ed.), *Problems of Drug Dependence*, 1979. Research Monograph Series 27, Rockville, Md.: National Institute on Drug Abuse.

Bandura, A. 1979. The Social Learning Perspective: Mechanisms of Aggression. In H. Toch (ed.) *Psychology of Crime and Justice*. New York: Holt, Rinehart and Winston.

Belenko, S. 1981. Drugs and the criminal justice system: The processing and impact of drug cases in New York. Report prepared for Joseph A. Califano, New York State Heroin and Alcohol Study.

Belenko, S. 1984. Lower east side narcotics arrests, August 1982: Court outcomes and rearrests. Research Department. New York: New York City Criminal Justice Agency.

Blumstein, A., Cohen, J., and Nagin, D. (eds.) 1978. Deterrence and Incapacitation: Estimating the Effects of Criminal Sanctions on Crime Rates. Washington, D.C.: National Academy of Science.

Boyle, J.M. and Brunswick, A.F. 1980. What happened in Harlem? Analysis of a decline in heroin use among a generation unit of urban black youth. *Journal of Drug Issues*: 109–29.

Brahen, L.S., Capone, T., Bloom, S., Adams, H.E., Seniuk, M.P. and DeJulio, P. 1979. An alternative to methadone for probationer-addicts: Narcotic antagonist treatment. *Journal of Drug Education*, 9 (1): 117–132.

Bureau of Justice Statistics (BJS). 1981. *Expenditure and Employment Data for the Criminal Justice System, 1978*. Washington, D.C.: U.S. Department of Justice.

Bureau of Justice Statistics (BJS). *Jail Inmates 1982*. Bulletin. Washington, D.C.: U.S. Department of Justice.

Bureau of Justice Statistics (BJS). 1983b. *Justice Expenditure and Employment in the U.S. 1979*. Washington, D.C.: U.S. Department of Justice.

Bureau of Justice Statistics (BJS). 1983c. *Prisoners and Alcohol*. Bulletin. Washington, D.C.: U.S. Department of Justice.

Bureau of Justice Statistics (BJS). 1983d. *Prisoners and Drugs*. Bulletin. Washington, D.C.: U.S. Department of Justice.

Bureau of Justice Statistics (BJS). 1983e. *Prisoners in Prison*. Bulletin. Washington, D.C.: U.S. Department of Justice.

Bureau of Justice Statistics (BJS). 1983f. *Report to the Nation on Crime and Justice*. Washington, D.C.: U.S. Department of Justice.

Bureau of Justice Statistics (BJS). 1985a. *Jail Inmates 1983*. Bulletin. Washington, D.C.: U.S. Department of Justice.

Bureau of Justice Statistics (BJS). 1985b. *Justice Expenditure and Employment Extracts: 1980 and 1981*. Washington, D.C.: U.S. Department of Justice.

Bureau of Justice Statistics (BJS). 1985c. *Justice Expenditure and Employment, 1982*. Bulletin. Washington, D.C.: U.S. Department of Justice.

Bureau of Justice Statistics (BJS). 1986a. *Felony Case-Processing Time*. Bulletin. Washington, D.C.: U.S. Department of Justice.

Bureau of Justice Statistics (BJS). 1986b. *Jail Inmates 1984*. Bulletin. Washington, D.C.: U.S. Department of Justice.

Bureau of Justice Statistics (BJS). 1986c. *Justice Expenditure and Employment, 1983*. Bulletin. Washington, D.C.: U.S. Department of Justice.

Bureau of Justice Statistics (BJS). 1986d. *Prisoners in 1985*. Bulletin. Washington, D.C.: U.S. Department of Justice.

Carpenter, C., Glassner, B., Johnson, B.D., and Loughlin, J. 1987. *Kids, Drugs, Alcohol, and Crime*. Lexington, Mass.: Lexington Books, forthcoming.

Carver, J.A. 1986. *Drugs and crime: Controlling use and reducing risk through testing*. NIJ Reports. Washington, D.C.: National Institute of Justice.

Chaiken, J. and Chaiken, M. 1982. *Varieties of Criminal Behavior*. Santa Monica, Calif.: Rand Corporation.

Chaiken, M.R. 1979. *Alcoholics Anonymous: A Sociological Study*. University Microfilms.

Chaiken, M.R. 1986. Crime rates and substance abuse among types of offenders. Pp. 12–54 in Bruce D. Johnson and Eric Wish (eds.), *Crime Rates Among Drug-Abusing Offenders*. Final Report to National Institute of Justice. New York: Narcotic and Drug Research, Inc.

Chaiken, M. and Chaiken, J. 1983. Crime rates and the active offender. Pp. 11–29 in J.Q. Wilson (ed.), *Crime and Public Policy*. New Brunswick, N.J.: Transaction Books.

Chaiken, M. and Chaiken, J. 1984. Offender Types and Public Policy. *Crime and Delinquency*, 30: 2, 195–226.

Chaiken, M. and Chaiken, J. 1987. Selecting *'Career Criminals' for Priority Prosecution*. Submitted to National Institute of Justice, Washington, D.C.: U.S. Department of Justice.

Chaiken, M.R. and Johnson, B.D. 1988. *Characteristics of Different Types of Drug-involved Offenders*. Issues and Practices. Washington, D.C.: National Institute of Justice.

Chamlee, D.L. 1986. Personal communication. (Chief of Federal Probation.)

Chandler, M.J. 1973. Egocentrism and Antisocial Behavior: The Assessment and Training of Social Perspective-Taking Skills. *Developmental Psychology*, 9, 326–333.

Collins, J.J. and Allison, M. 1983. Legal coercion and retention in drug abuse treatment. *Hospital and Community Psychiatry*, 34 (12): 1145–49.

Collins, J.J., Hubbard, R.L. and Rachal, J.V. 1985. Expensive drug use and illegal income: A test of explanatory hypotheses. *Criminology*, 23 (4): 743–64.

Craft, M., Stephenson, G., and Granger, C.A. 1964. A controlled trial of authoritarian and self-governing regimes with adolescent psychopaths. *American Journal of Orthopsychiatry*, 34, 543–554.

Critelli, J.W. and Crawford, R.F. 1980. The effectiveness of court ordered punishment: fines versus punishment. *Criminal Justice and Behavior*, 7, 465–470.

DeLeon, G. 1984a. Program-based evaluation research in therapeutic communities. Pp. 69–87 in F.M. Tims and J.P. Ludford (eds.), *Drug Abuse Treatment Evaluation: Strategies, Progress, and Prospects*. Research Monograph Series 51. Rockville, Md.: National Institute on Drug Abuse.

DeLeon, G. 1984b. *The Therapeutic Community: Study of Effectiveness*. Rockville, Md.: National Institute on Drug Abuse.

DeLeon, G. 1985. The Therapeutic Community: Status and Evolution. *International Journal of the Addictions*, 20 (6–7): 823–845.

DeLeon, G., Wexler, H.K. and Jainchill, J. 1982. The therapeutic community: success and improvement rates 5 years after treatment. *International Journal of the Addictions*, 17 (4): 703–47.

DeLeon, G., Wexler, H.K., Schwartz, S., and Jainchill, N. 1980. *Therapeutic communities for drug abusers: studies of treatment environment*. Paper presented at a meeting of the American Psychological Association.

Des Jarlais, D.C., Joseph, H., Dole, V.P., and Schmeidler, J. 1982. Predicting post-treatment narcotics use among patients terminating from methadone treatment. *Advances in Alcohol and Substance Abuse*, 2 (1): 57–68.

Division of Criminal Justice Services. 1986. Criminal Justice Statistics for New York State. Albany.

DSAS (Division of Substance Abuse Services). 1985a. Estimates of Taxes Paid by Working Methadone Patients in 1981. Treatment Issues Report No. 30. New York.

Dole, V.P., and Joseph, H. 1979. The Long-term Consequences of Methadone Maintenance Treatment. Final Report to National Institute on Drug Abuse. New York: Rockefeller University.

Erickson, M.L., Gibbs, J.P., and Jensen, G.F. 1977. The deterrence doctrine and perceived certainty of legal punishment. *American Sociological Review*, 42, 305–317.

Fenton, N. 1960. Group counseling in correctional practice. *Canadian Journal of Corrections*, 2, 229–239.

Gendreau, P. and Ross, R.R. 1979. Effective correctional treatment: bibliography for cynics. *Crime and Delinquency*, 25, 463–489.

Gendreau, P. and Ross, R.R. 1983–1984. Correctional treatment: some recommendations for effective intervention. *Juvenile and Family Court Journal*, Winter: 31–39.

Goldsmith, D.S., Hunt, D.E., Lipton, D.S., and Strug, D.L. 1984. Methadone folklore beliefs about side effects and their impacts on treatment. *Human Organization*, 43 (4): 330–40.

Grant, J.D. and Grant, M.Q. 1959. A Group Dynamics Approach to the Treatment of Non-Conformists in the Navy. *Annals of the American Academy of Political and Social Science*, 322, 126–135.

Hanson, B., Beschner, G., Walters, J.M., and Bovelle, E. 1985. *Life with Heroin: Voices from the Inner City*. Lexington, Mass.: Lexington Books.

Hart, R.J. 1978. Crime and punishment in the Army. *Journal of Personality and Social Psychology*, 36: 1456–1471.

Hubbard, R.L., Rachal, J.V., Craddock, S.G., and Cavanaugh, E.R. 1984. Treatment outcome prospective study (TOPS): client characteristics and behaviors before, during, and after treatment. Pp. 42–68 in F.M. Tims and J.P. Ludford (eds.), *Drug Abuse Treatment Evaluation: Strategies, Progress, and Prospects*. Research Monograph Series 51. Rockville, Md.: National Institute on Drug Abuse.

Hunt, D. 1985. *The Violent Offender in Treatment*. Paper presented at meeting of Academy of Criminal Justice Science, Las Vegas, Nevada.

Hunt, D.E., Lipton, D.S., and Spunt, B. 1984. Patterns of criminal activity among methadone clients and current narcotics users not in treatment. *Journal of Drug Issues*. (Fall): 687–702.

Johnson, B.D., Goldstein, P., Preble, E., Schmeidler, J., Lipton, D.S., Spunt, B., and Miller, T. 1985. *Taking Care of Business: The Economics of Crime By Heroin Abusers*. Lexington, Mass.: Lexington Books.

Johnson, B.D. and Wish, E.D. 1987. *Criminal Events Among Seriously Criminal Drug Abusers*. New York: Narcotic and Drug Research, Inc.

Kassebaum, G., Ward, D. and Wilner, D. 1971. *Prison Treatment and Parole Survival: An Empirical Assessment*. New York: Wiley.

Kleinman, P.H. and Lukoff, I.F. 1975. *Methadone Maintenance—Modest Help for a Few: Final Report*. New York: Addiction Research and Treatment Corporation Evaluation Team, New York: Columbia University School of Social Work.

Lee, R. and Haynes, N.M. 1980. Project CREST and the Dual-Treatment Approach to Delinquency: Methods and Research Summarized. In R.R. Ross and P. Gendreau (eds.) *Effective Correctional Treatment*. 1980. Toronto: Butterworths.

Lynott, D. 1986. Operation Pressure Point. Presentation to NIDA Community Epidemiology Work Group. New York: New York City Police Department.

McDonald, D. 1980. *The Price of Punishment: Public Spending for Corrections in New York*. Boulder, Colo.: Westview Press.

McGarrell, E.F., and Flanagan, T.J. (eds.) 1985. *Sourcebook of Criminal Justice Statistics—1984*. U.S. Department of Justice, Bureau of Justice Statistics. Washington, D.C.: U.S. Government Printing Office.

McGlothlin, W.C. 1979. Criminal justice clients. Pp. 203–209 in Robert L. DuPont, Avram Goldstein and John O'Donnell (eds.), *Handbook on Drug Abuse*. Rockville, Md.: National Institute on Drug Abuse.

McGlothlin, W.C. and Anglin, M.D. 1981a. Long term follow-up of clients of high-and low-dose methadone programs. *Archives of General Psychiatry*, 38: 1055–63.

McGlothlin, W.C. and Anglin, M.D. 1981b. Shutting off methadone: costs and benefits. *Archives of General Psychiatry*, 38: 885–92.

McGlothlin, W.C., Anglin, M.D. and Wilson, B.D. 1977. *An Evaluation of the California Civil Addict Program*. Rockville, Md.: National Institute on Drug Abuse.

Miller, J.D., Cisin, I.H., Gardner-Keaton, H., Wirtz, P.W., Abelson, H.I., and Fishburne, P.M. 1982. *National Survey on Drug Abuse: Main Findings 1982*. Washington, D.C.: U.S. Government Printing Office.

National Association of State Drug Abuse Program Coordinators, Inc. 1978. TASC: *An Approach for Dealing with the Substance Abusing Offender: Guidelines for Development of a Treatment Alternative to Street Crime Project*. Washington, D.C.: U.S. Department of Justice.

Nettler, G. 1978. *Explaining Crime*. New York: McGraw-Hill.

Nietzel, M.T. 1979. *Crime and Its Modification: A Social Learning Perspective*. New York: Paragamon.

Nurco, D.N., Ball, J.C., Schaffer, J.W., and Hanlon, T.E. 1985. The criminality of narcotic addicts. *Journal of Nervous and Mental Disease*, 173 (2): 94–102.

Peters, R. 1981. Deviant Behavioral Contracting with Conduct Problem Youth: A Review and Critical Analysis. Department of Psychology, Queens University. Kingston, Ontario.

Petersilia, J., Turner, S., Kahan, J., and Peterson, J. 1985. *Granting Felons Probation*: *Public Risks and Alternatives*. Santa Monica, Calif.: Rand.

Philips, E.L., Phillips, R.A., and Wolf, M.W. 1973. Behavior shaping works for delinquents. *Psychology Today*, 6, 75–79.

Platt, J.J., Perry, G.M., and Metzger, D.S. 1980. The evaluation of a heroin addiction treatment program within a correctional environment. In R.R. Ross and P. Gendreau (eds.) *Effective Correctional Treatment*. 1980. Toronto: Butterworths.

Quay, H.C. 1977. The three faces of evaluation: what can be expected to work. *Criminal Justice and Behavior*, 4, 341–354.

Rappeport, J., Seidman, E., and Davidson II, W.S. 1979. Demonstration research and manifest versus true adoption: the natural history of a research project. In R.F. Munoz, L.R. Snowden, and J.G. Kelly (eds.) *Social and Psychological Research and Community Settings*, 1979. San Francisco: Jossey-Bass.

Repucci, N.D., Sarata, B.P., Saunders, J.T., McArthur, A.V., and Michlin, L.M. 1973. We bombed in Mountville: Lessons learned in consultation to a correctional facility for adolescent offenders. In I.I. Goldberg (ed.) *The Helping Professions in the World of Action*. 1973. Boston: D.C. Heath.

Robins, L.N. 1973. *A Follow-up of Vietnam Drug Users*. Washington, D.C.: U.S. Government Printing Office.

Ross, R.R. and Gendreau, P. 1980. *Effective Correctional Treatment*. Toronto: Butterworths.

Ross, R.R. and McKay, H.B. 1976. A study of institutional treatment programs. *International Journal of Offender Therapy and Comparative Criminology*, 20, 165–173.

Ross, R.R. and McKay, H.B. 1978. Treatment in corrections: requiem for a panacea. *Canadian Journal of Criminology*, 120: 279–295.

Sanchez, J.E., and Johnson, B.D. 1987. Women and the drug crime connection: crime rates among drug-abusing women at Rikers Island. *Journal of Psychoactive Drugs*, 19 (2): 205–216.

Sechrest, L., West, S.G., Philips, M.A., Redner, R., and Yeaton, W. 1979a. Some neglected problems in evaluation research: strength and integrity of treatments. In L. Sechrest, S.G. West, M.A. Philips, R. Redner, and W. Yeaton (eds.) *Evaluation Studies Annual Review* (Vol. 4), 1979a. Beverly Hills: Sage.

Sechrest, L., White, S.O., and Brown, G.D. (eds.) 1979b. *The Rehabilitation of Criminal Offenders*. Washington, D.C.: National Academy of Sciences.

Senay, E.C. 1984. Clinical implications of drug abuse treatment outcome research. Pp. 139–150 in Frank M. Tims and Jacqueline P. Ludford (eds.), *Drug Abuse Treatment Evaluation Strategies, Progress, and Prospects*. Research Monograph Series 51. Rockville, Md.: National Institute on Drug Abuse.

Senay, E.C. 1985. Methadone maintenance treatment. *International Journal of the Addictions*, 20 (6–7): 803–22.

Sells, S.B., and Simpson, D.D. 1976. *Effectiveness of Drug Abuse Treatment*. Vols. III, IV, and V. Cambridge, Mass.: Ballinger.

Simpson, D.D. 1984. National treatment system evaluation based on the drug abuse reporting program (DARP) followup research. Pp. 29–41 in Frank M. Tims and Jacqueline P. Ludford (eds.), *Drug Abuse Treatment Evaluation: Strategies, Progress, and Prospects*. Research Monograph Series 51. Rockville, Md.: National Institute on Drug Abuse.

Simpson, D.D. and Sells, S.B. 1982. Effectiveness of treatment for drug abuse: an overview of the DARP research program. *Advances in Alcohol and Substance Abuse*, 2 (1): 7–29.

Speckart, G. and Anglin, M.D. 1986a. Narcotics use and crime: a causal modeling approach. *Journal of Quantitative Criminology*, 2: 3–28.

Speckart, G. and Anglin, M.D. 1986b. Narcotics use and crime: an overview of recent research advances. Presentation to Drugs, Alcohol, and Crime Conference, sponsored by National Institute of Justice. San Francisco, California.

Time. 1986. Drugs: The enemy within. September 15: 58–73.

Tims, F.M. and Ludford, J.P. (eds.) 1984. *Drug Abuse Treatment Evaluation: Strategies, Progress, and Prospects*. Research Monograph Series 51. Rockville, Md.: National Institute on Drug Abuse.

Toborg, M. 1984. *Drug use and pretrial crime in the District of Columbia*. *Research in Brief*. Washington, D.C.: National Institute of Justice.

Toborg, M.A., Bellassai, J.B., Yezer, A.M.J., Carver, J., Clarke, J., and Pears, E. 1986. The Washington, D.C. *Urine*

Testing Program for arrestees and defendants awaiting trial: a summary of interim findings. Washington, D.C.: Toborg Associates.

Toborg, M.A., Levin, D.R., Milkman, R.H., and Center, L.J. 1975. *Treatment alternatives to street crime (TASC): an evaluative framework and state of the art review*. Washington, D.C.: Lazar Institute.

Walter, T.L., and Mills, C.M. 1979. A Behavioral-Employment Intervention Program for Reducing Juvenile Delinquency. In J.S. Stumphauzer (ed.), *Progress in Behavior Therapy with Delinquents*. 1979. Springfield, Illinois: Thomas.

Wexler, H.K. 1985. *Therapeutic communities' role in the privatization of corrections*. Paper presented at Ninth World Conference of Therapeutic Communities, San Francisco, California, September.

Wexler, H.K. and DeLeon, G. 1977. The therapeutic community: multivariate prediction of retention. *American Journal of Drug and Alcohol Abuse*, 4 (2): 145–51.

Wexler, H.K. and Lipton, Douglas S. 1985. *Prison drug treatment: the critical 90 days of re-entry*. Paper presented at meeting of the American Society of Criminology, San Diego, California.

Wexler, H.K. and Sharron, A. 1985. *Prison drug treatment: two year followup of successes and failures*. Paper presented at meeting of the American Society of Criminology, San Diego, California.

Wexler, H.K., and Williams, R. 1986. The "Stay 'N Out" therapeutic community: prison treatment for substance abusers. *Journal of Psychoactive Drugs*, 18 (3): 221–230.

Wexler, H.K., Lipton, D.S., and Foster, K. 1985. *Outcome evaluation of a prison therapeutic community for substance abuse treatment: preliminary results*. Paper presented at meeting of the American Society of Criminology, San Diego, California.

Wish, E.D. 1982. *Are heroin users really nonviolent?* Paper presented at meeting of the Academy of Criminal Justice Sciences, Louisville, Kentucky.

Wish, E.D. 1986. Personal Communication.

Wish, E.D. 1987. *Drug use forcasting: New York 1984 to 1986, NIJ Research in Action*. Washington, D.C.: National Institute of Justice, U.S. Department of Justice, February.

Wish, E.D., and Johnson, B.D. 1986. The impact of substance abuse on criminal careers. Pp. 52–88 in Alfred Blumstein, Jacqueline Cohen, Jeffrey A. Roth, and Christy A. Visher, *Criminal Careers and "Career Criminals."* Volume 2. Washington, D.C.: National Academy Press.

Wish, E.D., Brady, E., and Cuadrado, M. 1984. *Drug use and crime in arrestees in Manhattan*. Paper presented at the 47th Meeting of the Committee on Problems of Drug Dependence, New York, Narcotic and Drug Research, Inc.

Wish, E.D., Brady, E. and Cuadrado, M. 1986. *Urine testing of arrestees: findings from Manhattan*. New York: Narcotic and Drug Research, Inc.

Wish, E.D., Cuadrado, M., and Mortorana, J.A. 1986. *Estimates of drug use in intensive supervision probationers: results from a pilot test*. New York: Narcotic and Drug Research, Inc.

Wish, E.D., Klumpp, K.A., Moorer, A.H. and Brady, E. 1980. *An analysis of crime among arrestees in the District of Columbia*. Institute for Law and Social Research. Springfield, Va.: National Technical Information Services.

Wish, E.D., Johnson, B.D., Strug, D., Chedekel, M., and Lipton, D.S. 1983. *Are urine tests good indicators of the validity of self-reports of drug use?* Paper presented at meeting of the American Society of Criminology, Denver, Colorado.

Zedlewski, Edwin. 1987. *Making Confinement Decisions: Research in Brief*. Washington, D.C.: National Institute of Justice, U.S. Department of Justice, July.